# HISTORY OF OLD FRENCH LITERATURE

# A HISTORY *of*
# OLD FRENCH LITERATURE

## FROM THE ORIGINS TO 1300

By URBAN TIGNER HOLMES, JR.

*Professor of Romance Philology*
*University of North Carolina*

*NEW YORK*

RUSSELL & RUSSELL · INC

To *the Memory of*

EDWARD STEVENS SHELDON
1851-1925
Professor of French Philology
Harvard University

# PREFACE

The printed version of this History could be called a second edition as most of the material circulated first in mimeographed form. It has benefited from use in the Romance seminars at the University of North Carolina and at the Ohio State University where my good friend Professor A. H. Schutz tried it out with some success. The text has been read, either in whole or in part, by Professors J. J. Parry, George Coffman, F. A. G. Cowper, J. C. Russell, Ralph Boggs, and Raphael Levy, who were kind enough to offer suggestions in their special fields of interest.

In view of the fact that this book will find its way into the hands of European reviewers, we should like to state the need which it is expected to satisfy in America. It is only too true that many of our advanced students cannot read German satisfactorily and there is always a small number who do not feel at ease with French. For these we hope to offer in convenient form the results of the best research in France and Germany. But there is another need equally great. American learned journals do not circulate as freely abroad as they should and this means that theories and suggestions proposed by American scholars often receive no mention in histories published in Europe. This is a deficiency which I am sure European scholars would be glad to see remedied; the rates of exchange have not been favorable for the export of American books and periodicals to other countries. It is true also that this History to which we now introduce our readers lays emphasis upon facts and dates rather than upon critical study. Our graduate students do not have intensive preparation in medieval history and virtually all the monuments of medieval French literature are entirely new to them. One can only be truly critical when there is a basis of factual knowledge, such as the French student must be slowly acquiring from the early years of his *lycée* training. If this were a history of English literature we could take more of the hard descriptive facts for granted and indulge ourselves more freely in the charm and freshness of medieval literature.

The general reader who peruses our text must be reminded of something else. It can be conservatively stated that very few competent scholars think alike on all points covered in this volume. The specialist in medieval literature lacks the newspapers, diaries, and often the parish records, which make the study of modern literature a science. A large part of what is said about medieval literature is hypothesis, based upon internal evidence from the few literary works which have survived.

Imagine a critic some seven hundred years from now who has nothing but a mangled copy of *An American Tragedy,* with the title page gone, and two novels of Sinclair Lewis, in similar condition, trying to form some lucid idea of satire (?) in twentieth century American literature. Just so the historian of medieval literature must weave his way through the suggestions made by other scholars, discarding now one theory and now accepting another. It is unfair to accuse a medievalist of error because he does not say the same as some one else, unless there is positive proof present. In many cases, in the following pages, we have stated all the varying hypotheses and left the decision to the reader.

There can be no doubt that Old French literature has a certain unity and characteristics that disappear rapidly after 1300. The medieval period continues for another two hundred years but the conditions and the spirit of letters are not the same. It is also true that the literature of this Middle French period has not been investigated with the thoroughness that has been displayed towards the twelfth and thirteenth centuries; there remain an unusual number of problems to be solved. We may at some future date issue a companion volume which will close with the reign of Louis XII (1498-1515).

We wish to acknowledge aid received in special problems from the following post-graduate students at the University of North Carolina: Charles Neal, Alma Blount, Imogene Riddick, Louis B. Stabler, Elliott Healy, G. C. S. Adams, George R. Sulkin, G. W. Fenley, J. L. Smith, and Mrs. Lucy Estes Grimsley. Our debt to Robert W. Linker can be expressed only with difficulty. His initiative has made it possible for this book to be issued and sold at a price which is within the reach of every scholar and student. When the system of marketing scholarly books in America is given more attention there will be no occasion for the slow sale and high prices now considered a necessity.

U. T. H., Jr.

Chapel Hill, N. C.

# CONTENTS

[ ix ]

## COMMON ABBREVIATIONS

| | |
|---|---|
| AfrB | Altfranzösische Bibliothek |
| AJP | American Journal of Philology |
| ALMA | Archivum Latinitatis Medii Aevi *or* Bulletin du Cange (Paris: Champion) |
| APF | Anciens Poètes de la France (Paris: F. Vieweg) |
| ArchRom | Archivum Romanicum |
| BEcCh | Bibliothèque de l'Ecole des Chartes |
| BEcHE | Bibliothèque de l'Ecole des Hautes Etudes |
| BELz | Bibliothèque Elzévirienne |
| BN | Bibliotheca Normannica (Halle: Niemeyer) |
| Brom | Bibliotheca romanica (Strasbourg: Heitz) |
| CdiHF | Collection de documents inédits pour l'histoire de France |
| Cfmâ | Classiques français du moyen âge (Paris: Champion) |
| CHFmâ | Classiques de l'histoire de France au moyen âge (Paris: Champion; and Société d'Edition "Les Belles Lettres" since 1933) |
| EETS | Early English Text Society |
| EM | Elliott Monographs |
| EUM | Essays in Comparative Literature by Members of the English Department of the University of Michigan |
| FFC | Folklore Fellows' Communications (Helsingfors, Finland). The abbreviation Mt. should be read *Märchentypus.* |
| GrL | Gesellschaft für romanische Literatur (Halle: Niemeyer) |
| HLF | Histoire littéraire de la France |
| HSN | Harvard Studies and Notes in Philology and Literature |
| IFS | Publications of the Institute of French Studies (New York: Columbia University Press) |
| JEGP | Journal of English and Germanic Philology |
| JHS | The Johns Hopkins Studies in Romance Literatures and Languages |
| JS | Journal des Savants |
| LV | The series published by the Literarischer Verein of Stuttgart |
| MLN | Modern Language Notes |
| MLR | Modern Language Review |
| MPhil | Modern Philology |
| NeuphMitteil | Neuphilologische Mitteilungen |
| PhilQ | Philological Quarterly |
| PL | The *Patrologiae cursus completus* . . . Latin series (Paris: 1844-1861) |
| PMLA | Publications of the Modern Language Association of America |

| | |
|---|---|
| Rdp | Romans des douze pairs |
| RFor | Romanische Forschungen |
| Rlr | Revue des langues romanes |
| Rom | Romania |
| RomB | Romanische Bibliothek (Halle: Niemeyer) |
| RRev | The Romanic Review (New York: Columbia University Press) |
| RT | Romanische Texte (Berlin: Weidmannsche Buchhandlung) |
| SATF | Société des anciens textes français (Paris: E. Droz) |
| Shf | Société de l'histoire de France |
| SmlT | Sammlung mittellateinischer Texte (Heidelberg: Winter) |
| Spec | Speculum |
| SPhil | Studies in Philology |
| SrT | Sammlung romanischer Übungstexte. |
| TAPA | Transactions of the American Philological Association |
| UCp | The University of California publications |
| UIS | The University of Illinois Studies in Language and Literature |
| UPSR | The University of Pennsylvania Studies in Romanic Languages and Literatures. |
| UtexSE | University of Texas Studies in English |
| ZfcPh | Zeitschrift für celtische Philologie |
| ZfrPh | Zeitschrift für romanische Philologie |
| ZfrSL | Zeitschrift für französische Sprache und Literatur |

# HISTORY OF OLD FRENCH LITERATURE

# INTRODUCTION

The study of Old French literature began certainly with Claude Fauchet (1530-1601) and his *Recueil de l'origine de la langue et poesie françoise, ryme et romans* (Paris, 1581). He mentioned one hundred and twenty-seven poets living prior to 1300, with frequent quotations and all the information he could gather concerning their lives and works. The inspiration for this task, which few of his contemporaries could appreciate, came to Fauchet from his studies in legal history, as shown in his *Origines des dignitez et magistrats de France, etc.*, and in his *Antiquitez gauloises et françoises*. He searched out and read scores of old manuscripts which others were neglecting, and he ended by loving these musty tomes and folios for themselves. Centuries were to elapse before Fauchet had a worthy successor, though we must mention in passing his contemporary, Etienne Pasquier, in whose *Recherches de la France* (Paris, 1560-1621) there is some account of medieval literature; but Pasquier refers in his letters to Fauchet as more competent. During the seventeenth century nearly everyone was ready to agree that

> Villon sut le premier, dans ces siècles grossiers,
> Débrouiller l'art confus de nos vieux romanciers.
> (Boileau, *Art poétique*, I, 117-118)

The eighteenth century revived a weak interest in the Middle Ages, under the guidance of such men as Lebœuf and Barbazan. The *fabliaux* and satirical lyrics appealed to the *philosophes;* the churchmen, particularly the Benedictines of Saint-Maur, felt an urge to bolster faith with erudition. But the Pre-Romanticists and the Romanticists themselves gave early literature the prominence and attention which it has not lost at the present day. François Raynouard (1761-1836), Claude Fauriel (1772-1844), B. de Roquefort (1777-1834), Le Roux de Lincy (1806-1860), Paulin Paris (1800-1881), Francisque Michel (1809-1887), were some of the interested pioneers who studied and published for the first time many of our Old French texts. They were not exact or historical in their criticism. Medieval French literature they viewed as a type of primitive, spontaneous expression, which they compared with Homer, the Sanskrit epics, the Arabian Nights, the Norse sagas, and the modern Greek war songs—the *chansons des Klephtes*. Their viewpoint was that of Comparative Literature as yet uncontrolled in its flights of imagination.

In 1865 Gaston Paris (1839-1903), the son of Paulin Paris, published his *Histoire poétique de Charlemagne* (Paris: Franck). Here we find no mention of the Sanskrit *Mahabharata* nor of the Persian *Shahnameh*, only a sane presentation of facts limited to the investigation of Old French literature. This was the birth of our present day methodology. From then on studies multiplied, and students specialized, until today there is an active personnel of scholars at work on medieval French literature in all the countries of Europe and in North America.

With the opening of the twentieth century, and markedly since the Great War, a still newer point of view has come among us. Today we unite an interest in medieval literature, not with a vague study of Homer or of the Klephtes, as in the days before Gaston Paris, but with the other departments of medieval thought and life. If one would know literature one must have some concept of political, social, and economic history, as well as of art, daily life, science, and philosophy. There has been also a sober return to the ideas of Fauriel and the Romanticists, but this is now called Comparative or General Literature, and it forms a separate department.

Since 1904 there have been two well defined groups of opinion struggling for mastery in the field of medieval literature. They are the school of Joseph Bédier, and those who continue to believe in popular origin, oral tradition, and spontaneous development for the various genres. When we say the school of Bédier we are thinking of such intimates and pupils of his as Faral, Lucien Foulet, and Edgar Piguet; but Ph. A. Becker, Wendelin Foerster, and L. Clédat initiated prior to Bédier similar opinions on the aristocratic origins of medieval literature. The others, advocates of collective creation, oral transmission, and spontaneous development, are followers of Herder, Grimm, and Uhland; they believe that primitive man is brought by instinct to express in gesture, and then in language, the things that he perceives and wishes to communicate. Man without writing is apt to have a prodigious memory. He communicates as an act of solemn import to his children and successors the oral tradition and literature that he himself has been taught. As this literature passes from mouth to mouth, from generation to generation, it is unconsciously modified, and from its very origins it is of collective authorship. The idea of a narrative poem does not arise complete from the lips of a primitive man. The first one to conceive of the crude beginning imparts it to his neighbor who makes improvement and so on till the poem reaches the stage of writing. Poetry that has been created naturally, free from all rule and restraint, is, by nature, beautiful.

The Bédier school, including its few predecessors, says that such popular origin as we have just sketched *did* exist for folklore, for popular tales of no serious import intended for mere amusement. They passed from peasant to peasant subject to little control. But medieval man was not so primitive as an African savage. His historical or triumphal narratives, his poetry, his romances, were the work of individuals, of clerics, of poets inspired, and perhaps hired, for the purpose. There is a bit of genuine history drawn from a chronicle behind each epic: there is imitation of Vergil, Ovid, and other classics in the production of the lyrics and of the romances. A close scrutiny of the medieval period reveals, behind the silence of lost material, not a primitive Dark Age of savage Germans and Celts, but an enlightened aristocratic clergy who continued to be steeped in their Latin letters. The people are not very original; the lower classes come to the upper for their inspiration. This inspiration, distorted and popularized, is our medieval literature as it was eventually written.[1]

A solution to this controversy assuredly lies in a combination of the two schools of thought. This we shall emphasize throughout the present work. There are the three degrees of civilization; the savage, the peasant, and the cleric. The *sauvage pur* did not exist in early medieval France. The peasant was occasionally quite primitive and capable of spontaneous production of literature, but he was timid and sought his models from the familiar—from what he learned from the cleric. Only the savage has no models apart from nature. So we must take account of Bédier, Faral, and Foulet, first of all. In the kernel they are correct—but they are too absolute. Oral tradition cannot be denied entirely, and much of this oral tradition in France and England must have come, for instance, from the Celts of Britanny and of Wales. It is true that a people's poet who could read would know of Vergil and of Ovid; but people danced and sang even when they could not read. Whence came their inspiration?

We are drawing upon the admirable summary of the problem by Pierre Kohler in the *Mélanges Baldensperger* (Paris: Champion, 1930), II, 1-18.

### THE TRANSITION FROM ANCIENT LITERATURE

If it be true, then, that medieval literature at its best grew from the aristocratic learning of the cleric, combined with the creative talent of the more primitive peasant (and it must be remembered that most of the medieval clergy were drawn from peasant ranks), it is necessary to observe the state of aristocratic learning in the earlier Middle Ages before vernacular genres came into being. This learning doubtless contained the germs of what was to follow. Under the late Roman Empire all classical learning emanated from, and had its seat in, the public schools. These continued a determined, though weakening existence till 529 *A.D.* when Emperor Justinian closed all schools of pagan learning.

[1] For presentation of a similar view consult A. H. Krappe in *Spec* X, 270-6.

The place of these institutions was taken by the monastic and episcopal schools which grew up in the great monasteries and in the cathedrals. These were to endure as the sources of all instruction throughout the Middle Ages, until the revival of secular education in the fifteenth and sixteenth centuries.

The Church from its origin was publicly divided on the question of classical learning. The early fathers, Tertullian (160-240), Saint Jerome (331-420), and Saint Augustine (354-430), admitted its sinfulness but could not deny its charm. Beginning with the third century, the Church initiated a Latin literature of its own, mostly lyric hymns. Saint Ambrose (340-397), Bishop of Milan, attained a rare beauty in compositions of this sort. Hilary of Poitiers (310-366) is worthy of mention here because he was a native of Gaul. Only three of his hymns have survived in fragments and they do not inspire much praise. The Spaniard Prudentius (348-405) was the first great Christian poet, though not fully appreciated till the close of the fifth century; from then on he commanded an outstanding position throughout the Middle Ages. The lyrics in his *Cathemerinon* or "Hymns for the Christian's Day," and in his *Peristephanon* or "Book of Martyrs," can be read with those of Catullus and Horace without disparagement. His *Psychomachia* or "Battle of the Soul," is weaker as an aesthetic composition, but it represents the first Christian allegory—a type which fascinated the later centuries and culminated in more worldly allegory such as the *Roman de la rose*.

Ausonius of Bordeaux (310-394?), a lukewarm Christian, had the subjective, emotional outlook of the Christian poet, but he did not put it to the same use. He was a professor of rhetoric who served for a time as imperial tutor and received the consulship (379). There is a bit of charm which glimmers through his excess of form and rhetoric, particularly in descriptions of nature and of his journeys through parts of Gaul. Sidonius Apollinaris (430-      ?), later Bishop of Clermont, lived to see his beloved land invaded by the Visigoths in 485. He could not forget that he had been a Roman citizen, and although his poetry is not of a high order, he remained one of the many connecting links between the old Roman thought and the new order of the barbarians. It was because of men such as he that the Germans fostered Latin letters and that they adopted the artistic civilization of the conquered. After him must be mentioned another poet under barbarian régime, the Italian Venantius Fortunatus (540-600), who, towards the end of his life, was named Bishop of Poitiers. He wrote a mass of epigrams, epitaphs, etc., in which he was greatly influenced by pure classical tradition. He is rather lacking in the individualism of the typical Christian poet, if we may except certain of his hymns inspired by his patron, Queen Radegunde, which exhibit a rare inspiration indeed and could hardly be surpassed. Two of these are his *Vexilla regis prodeunt* and his *Pange lingua,* both of them Passion hymns. He has the Platonic tradition.

Poetry at its best passed to the East and to Ireland during the next few centuries. By this we mean that there were few productions of note from 600 to 780 save in these more exotic lands. With the revival of learning at the courts of Charlemagne and of his immediate successors, the Carolingian Renaissance (780-877), there are again some charming productions, among them those of Alcuin, Paul the Deacon, Paulinus of Aquileja, and others.

We have noted with Professor P. S. Allen the presence of two spirits during this transition period, the Classical and the Romanesque.[2] The first is the degenerated tradition of Catullus and Horace—also Vergil— while the second is subjective, emotional, and individualistic, a new departure that we first recognize in Petronius Arbiter (d. 66) but which is, of course, as old as man and perhaps even older. It enters into most of the Christian poetry and is continued by such as Hilary of Poitiers and Ausonius. Among the great classicists of the period we must list Venantius Fortunatus and the much later Rabanus Maurus (780-820), a pupil of Alcuin, Walafrid Strabo (809-876), and Lupus of Ferrières who, alas, was a great classicist but no poet. During the early Middle Ages all literature, and it is in Latin, may be said to have consisted of saints' lives and pious legends, panegyrics and obituaries, fables, proverbs, exempla, moralizing verse on continence, science, etc., catalogues of natural history, epigrams and letters, hymns, necrologies, eclogues, incantations, condemnations of heterodoxy, ecclesiastical chronicles, biographies, and epics. This appears to be an unpromising collection of ashes out of which the Twelfth-Century Renaissance of vernacular and Latin literature was to appear; but the reader would be surprised! In this conglomeration of material there is not only lyric beauty, as in the hymns and other lyric verse, but there is occasional humor, knack of story telling, grandeur of viewpoint, all of which show that the early medieval Frenchman could not have failed to develop his *chanson de geste* and his romance had later conditions not been so favorable as they were to be.

### VERSIFICATION

There are four types of verse accent which are possible:

1. Sentences balanced against each other, as in Hebrew.
2. Quantitative accent, as in Latin and in Greek.
3. Stress accent, in late Latin poetry as well as in Germanic verse. In Germanic verse this is frequently accompanied by alliteration.
4. Equal number of syllables to the line, with rhyme or assonance.

[2] *The Romanesque Lyric* (Chapel Hill, N. C., 1928).

The last is the only type of verse found in French and Provençal territory, so we are concerned with it alone. H. P. Thieme (*Essai sur
l'histoire du vers français,* Paris: Champion, 1916, Ch. V) has reviewed
in a thorough way the many theories that have been suggested for the
origins of this type of verse, and we cannot do better than refer the reader
to his study. It has been suggested that the eight-syllable verse in Old
French poetry is a descendant of the Latin iambic dimeter. Stengel asserted, with considerable reason, that the oldest type of the French
decasyllable line is that divided six-four by the caesura, and that this was
a continuation of the Latin saturnian (or of some other Latin verse having from twelve to fourteen syllables with an accent on the sixth, and
eleventh or twelfth syllables). The French alexandrine or twelve-syllable
meter may be derived from the Greek trimeter or from the iambic tetra-
meter, catalectic or acatalectic.

By the third century A. D. the vulgar, and consequently the military
population of Rome, had lost the sense of vowel quantity and they
began to make use of a stress rhythm in their verse. A noteworthy
example is to be seen in two poems by the Christian poet Commodianus
(*ca.* 249): his *Instructiones* and the *Carmen apologeticum.* In the days
of Cicero the public could not tolerate such barbarousness but rose up in
horror at the theatre when an actor misplaced a quantity. By the fourth
century educated writers such as Ambrose sought to make the ictus of
quantitative verse and the grammatical stress accent fall together. This
involved a careful choice of words. Here are two examples of the fourth
century hymn:

> Iam meta noctis transiit,
> Somni quies jam praeterit,
> Aurora surgit fulvida
> Et spargit coelum lux nova.
> Te lucis ante spiritus
> Et caritatis actibus
> Ad instar illud gloriae
> Nos innovatos effice (Hilary).

> O Lux beata, Trinitas,
> O principalis unitas,
> Iam sol recedit igneus,
> Infunde lumen cordibus!

> Te mane laudum carmine
> Te deprecamur vespere.
> Te nostra supplex gloria
> Per cuncta laudet saecula (Ambrose).

The next step in the history of versification was the complete aban-donment of quantity in favor of grammatical stress accent. This must have been accomplished by the year 600. An excellent reference on the transition from quantitative to stress verse is M. G. Nicolau, *L'origine du "cursus" rythmique et les débuts de l'accent d'intensité en Latin* (Paris, 1930). See also F. Lot in *ALMA*, VI, 97-159.

The ten-syllable verse became the standard for the *chansons de geste;* the eight-syllable remained most favorable for religious verse and it was also adopted for the romance. It is worthy of note that several of the monuments of Old French poetry are in the eight-syllable: the *Passion,* and the *Saint Leodegar.* The alexandrine or twelve-syllable meter replaced the eight in certain of the twelfth-century romances; occa-sionally it replaced the ten-syllable in later epics. Probably this twelve-syllable verse was best adapted to reading and not to oral presentation by singing or chanting. The reading public increased extensively after 1200.

Verses of four and six syllables were occasionally used in Old French didactic poems for simple folk. These were perhaps intended for easy memorizing, since psychologists tell us that the memory span for the average individual is not over six syllables.

Seven- and nine-syllable lines occur in lyric poetry, the seven notably in the lyrics of *Aucassin et Nicolette*. Verses of one, two, three, and four syllables are found in refrains. Lyric poetry in Old French is character-ized by a variety in verse length, save in the *chanson à toile,* which is a short narrative poem. Refrains are also found in the epics, viz., the famous *Aoi* in the *Chanson de Roland,* and the *Lunsdi al vespre* of the *Chanson de Guillaume*. The presence of such a refrain in a *chanson de geste* is supposed to argue great age. This theory has been opposed.

Old French and Provençal poetry prefer masculine rhymes to feminine. The opposite is true for Italian verse.[3]

The caesura is present in ten- and twelve-syllable lines only. In the ten there are three possible divisions: 4-6, 5-5, 6-4. The 4-6 division is nearly universal for the *chansons de geste;* the 5-5 sometimes occurs in lyrics; the 6-4 is found in a few epics, notably in the Franco-Provençal *Girart de Roussillon*. The twelve-syllable line is always divided 6-6. If the caesura is preceded by a feminine vowel it is called an epic caesura, and the vowel is not counted as a syllable. The term is due to the pop-ularity of this feminine caesura in the ten-syllable epics of the division 4-6.

Assonance, rhyme, and occasionally alliteration are found in Old French poetry. In assonance there is an agreement of the final vowels

---

[3] For discussion of the details of Old French versification the best reference is A. Tobler, *Vom französischen Versbau alter und neuer Zeit* (5th ed.; Leipzig: Hirzel, 1910).

only (feminine *e* does not count); in simple rhyme the preceding or following consonant also agrees. Rich rhymes and leonine rhymes are not intentional before the later thirteenth century, though rich rhymes are not a rarity. We believe rhyme is just as old, if not older, than assonance (see the Latin hymns quoted), but assonance was in favor in the earlier period of Old French literature. It gave way markedly to rhyme at the close of the twelfth century, but continued to be preferred for the *chansons de geste*. The romances were nearly always in rhymed couplets, of which the sense unity was not broken before Chrétien de Troyes. The saints' lives and didactic poems were often in the monorhymed stanza form. The stanza was, of course, used in lyric verse. The epics and romances were composed in *laisses*. The *laisse* is a division of undetermined length varying from five to eighty lines, and it may even exceed these limits. It marks a unit in the action or in the poet's thought. This variability aided the poet in avoiding tediousness of recital and made it easier to emphasize certain parts of the action. Each *laisse* was constructed on a separate rhyme or assonance. Frequently the desire for emphasis made a repetition of material necessary. Then the poet would repeat, almost in the same words, but using a different assonance or rhyme. These two *laisses* are then called *laisses similaires*.

A diphthong resulting from the breaking of a vowel was usually counted as one syllable. Otherwise hiatus in the interior of a word remained. Hiatus between the final vowel (usually feminine *e*) of one word and the initial vowel of a following could or could not remain. The usage in each of these cases sometimes varied.

In the interior of a verse we know there was an accent on the last syllable before the caesura and on the final syllable of the line (excluding the feminine *e* in both cases).

### DIALECTS

As we are now nearing the close of this introduction, some account must be taken of the thesis of Gertrud Wacker, *Dialekt und Schriftsprache im Altfranzösischen,* presented at the University of Berlin in 1916. Her conclusions are well worthy of note. She believes that there was some feeling for a standard, literary form of Old French beginning in the early twelfth century. At that time the *koiné* or generalized dialect of Normandy was quite similar to Francian, the speech used in Paris and the Ile-de-France. Poets tended to mix these two. But after the middle of the century the literary language admitted the passage of $\bar{e}$ to $\bar{a}$ and of *ei* to *oi* and Francian predominated. At the beginning of the thirteenth century the importance of the bourgeois literature of Picardy grew so great that many a minstrel writing in literary Francian allowed an occasional Picard form to creep into his lines.

According to Miss Wacker we have only two works written in pure Norman, without a Francian admixture, and they are the *Roman du Mont-Saint-Michel* of Guillaume de Saint Paier and *Livre des manieres* of Etienne de Fougères. There was, however, a great deal of literature composed in England in the Anglo-Norman dialect, and the *koiné* of Champagne was immortalized by Chrétien de Troyes. With the turn of the thirteenth century the minstrels of Picardy brought their native dialect to the fore.

The importance of this theory is that we can no longer be certain such a work as the *Chanson de Roland* was written by a Norman because of certain Norman dialect traits. In the early thirteenth century an occasional Picard form in the rhyme does not necessarily mean that the author was from Picardy. These Picardisms may have had a "quaint flavor" for a poet who was a resident of Anjou. It was before the dialect of Picardy had spread in courtly esteem that Conon de Béthune was blamed for his *patois artésien* by Philip Augustus and his mother, Queen Adèle de Champagne, in the presence of Countess Marie de Champagne (III, 5-14).[1]

I am quite ready to admit that a literary dialect was considered advisable very early, in order to flatter the ears of the powerful nobles of Normandy and France, but a poet's native vulgarisms must have continued to creep in. Miss Wacker's study forces us to use extreme care in utilizing dialect criteria, but it does not warrant our taking the sweeping view that the investigation of a poet's dialect is valueless.

[1] Ed. A. Wallensköld *(Cfmá)*.

# BIBLIOGRAPHY

In keeping with a more general approach to the pursuit of literature, we advise the student to become familiar with certain reference books for the study of medieval French civilization:

POLITICAL HISTORY:

E. Lavisse (general editor), *Histoire de France illustrée,* depuis les origines jusqu'à la révolution (Paris: Hachette, 1913), Vols. I, II, III.

More elementary is J. V. Duruy, *Histoire de France, etc.* (Paris: Hachette, 1892) which has been translated into English and published in the Everyman series as, *A Short History of France* (New York: Dutton).

Camille Jullian, *De la Gaule à la France* (Paris: Hachette, 1922) and his *Histoire de la Gaule* (Paris: Hachette, 1908-24, 6 vols.).

As references to the source material of French medieval history the student should acquire familiarity with, Auguste Molinier, *Les Sources de l'histoire de France* (Paris: Picard, 1901-6, 3 vols.).

Ulysse Chevalier, *Répertoire des sources historiques du moyen âge, bio-bibliographie* (Paris: Picard, 1905-1907, 2 vols.).

and, by the same author,
*Répertoire des sources historiques du moyen âge, topo-bibliographie* (Montbéliard, 1894-1903).

L. J. Paetow, *A Guide to the Study of Medieval History* (New York: Crofts, 1931).

SOCIAL HISTORY:

A. Luchaire, *Social France at the time of Philip Augustus,* tr. E. K. Krehbiel (New York: Holt, 1912).

P. Boissonnade, tr. Eileen Power, *Life and Work in Mediaeval Europe (Fifth to the Fifteenth Centuries).* (New York: Knopf, 1927).

Léon Gautier, *La Chevalerie* (Paris, 1885).

DAILY LIFE:

Alwin Schulz, *Das Höfische Leben zur Zeit der Minnesinger* (Leipzig, 1889, 2 vols.).

C. V. Langlois, *La vie en France au moyen âge, d'après des romans mondains du temps* (Paris: Hachette, 1926).

and, by the same author,
*La vie en France au moyen âge, d'après des moralistes du temps* (Paris: Hachette, 1926).

L. F. Salzman, *English Life in the Middle Ages* (Oxford, 1926).

J. Evans, tr. E. Droz, *La civilisation en France au moyen âge* (Paris: Payot, 1930); the English original is *Life in Mediaeval France* (Oxford, 1925).

SPIRITUAL LIFE:

C. V. Langlois, *La vie spirituelle, d'après des écrits en français à l'usage des laïcs* (Paris: Hachette, 1926).

COSTUME:

Camille Enlart, *Manuel d'archéologie française*, Vol. III, *Le costume* (Paris: Picard, 1916).

Jules E. J. Quicherat, *Histoire du costume en France, depuis les temps les plus reculés jusqu'à la fin du XVIIIᵉ siècle* (2nd ed., Paris: Hachette, 1877).

E. R. Goddard, *Women's Costume in French Texts of the Eleventh and Twelfth Centuries* (Baltimore, JHS, 1927).

ECONOMIC HISTORY:

L. F. Salzman, *English Industries of the Middle Ages* (2nd ed., Oxford, 1923),

and, by the same author,

*English Trade in the Middle Ages* (Oxford, 1931).

M. Poëte, *Une vie de cité, Paris* (Paris: Picard, 1924, 3 vols.).

H. Pirenne, *Medieval Cities* (Princeton, 1925).

CULTURAL BACKGROUND:

H. O. Taylor, *The Mediaeval Mind* (4th ed., London and New York, 1925). Reprinted in 1927 and 1930.

J. E. Sandys, *History of Classical Scholarship* (3rd ed., Cambridge, 1921), Vol. I.

C. V. Langlois, *La connaissance de la nature et du monde, d'après des écrits français à l'usage des laïcs* (Paris: Hachette, 1927).

C. H. Haskins, *Studies in the History of Mediaeval Science* (Cambridge, 1924),

and, by the same author,

*The Rise of Universities* (New York: Holt, 1923).

R. L. Poole, *Illustrations of the History of Mediaeval Thought and Learning* (2nd ed., London, 1920).

C. J. Singer, *Studies in the History and Method of Science* (Oxford, 1922-1924, 2 vols.).

L. Thorndike, *A History of Magic and Experimental Science* (New York, 1923-34).

J. K. Wright, *The Geographical Lore of the Time of the Crusades* (New York, 1925).

ARCHITECTURE:

Camille Enlart, *Manuel d'archéologie française*, Vol. I, *Architecture religieuse* (2nd ed., Paris: Picard, 1920-1927, 3 parts); Vol. II, *Architecture civile, navale, et militaire* (2nd ed., Paris: Picard, 1932).

E. E. Viollet-Le-Duc, *Dictionnaire raisonné de l'architecture française du XIᵉ au XVIᵉ siècle* (Paris, 1858-68, 10 vols.).

CHRONOLOGY AND GENEALOGY:

Le Comte de Mas Latrie, *Trésor de chronologie, d'histoire et de géographie* (Paris, 1889). A revision of this has been undertaken by John La Monte, but the task is such a huge one that it will necessarily be long before it can be completed.

*L'Art de vérifier les dates,* by the Benedictine congregation of Saint-Maur
(Paris: Desprez and Cavelier, 1750; and many later editions).
A. Capelli, *Cronologia e calendario perpetuo* (Milan: Hoepli, 1906).

PHILOSOPHY:

E. H. Gilson, *La philosophie au moyen âge* (Paris: Payot, 1922-1923, 2
vols.); tr. A. H. C. Downes, *The Spirit of Mediaeval Philosophy* (London, 1936).

M. De Wulf, *Histoire de la philosophie médiévale,* vol. I (6th ed., Louvain,
1934). The other volumes of this work will soon appear in revised
form.

GEOGRAPHY:

P. Amédée Jaubert, tr. *Géographie d'Edrisi* (Paris, 1836-1840, 2 vols.).

There is no bibliographical guide to French literature previous to 1500
similar to the *Manuel bibliographique de la littérature française moderne*
(4th ed.; Paris: Hachette, 1931, 2 vols.) of Gustave Lanson. It is possible
to fill out this lack with the aid of a number of standard references, with
which the student should hasten to familiarize himself. For books and
articles in the medieval field appearing between 1858 and 1874 he should
consult the *Jahrbuch für romanische und englische Sprache und Literatur.*
For the years 1875-1913, and 1924-1926, inclusive, the supplementary bibliography issued by the *Zeitschrift für romanische Philologie* is an uner-
ring guide. Eventually this bibliography will include all the years since
1875, but the preparation has been somewhat retarded. The *Literaturblatt
für germanische und romanische Philologie* is more difficult to use but it
will aid in filling in the gaps for the material not covered as yet by the
*Zeitschrift.* The Arthurian group of the Modern Language Association
of America has issued *A Bibliography of Arthurian Critical Literature*
(New York, 1931 and 1936, 2 numbers), supplementing the bibliography
in the *Evolution of Arthurian Romance* (Göttingen, 1923, 2 vols.) of the
late J. D. Bruce, covering the years 1922-1935. The compilers, Professors J. J. Parry and Margaret Schlauch, have been very liberal in their
interpretation of the term *Arthurian,* so that this comprises many titles
that are of interest for Old French literature in general. The catalogue
deposits of the Library of Congress, of the Widener Library at Harvard,
of the University of Michigan Library and of still other large libraries
are available in many institutions. Another valuable aid is W. J. En-
twistle's *The Year's Work in Modern Language Studies* (Oxford,
1931—). Some information on Old French editions will be found in
Pauline Taylor's "Bibliography of Romance Linguistics," *RRev,* XVII
(1926) and XXI (1930).

Also of interest for general bibliography is the *Catalogue général des
livres imprimés de la Bibliothèque Nationale* (Paris, 1897—). One hun-

dred and thirty-seven volumes have appeared to date: *A* to *Piossens*. The *Catalogue général de la librairie française* (Paris, 1897—) is invaluable. The thirty-four volumes carry lists from 1840 to 1925, inclusive, and are the work of Otto Lorenz, D. Jordell, and Henri Stein. This will be continued. In the meantime the student should use the *Catalogue Valdras* (Paris: V. Rasmussen, 1930—) which gives yearly lists of the French book trade, from 1929 to date.

The chief secondary histories of medieval French literature which are in use today are:

Gaston Paris, *La littérature française au moyen âge* (5th ed., Paris: Hachette, 1914).

Gaston Paris, *Esquisse historique de la littérature française au moyen âge* (Paris: Champion, 1922).

Carl Voretzsch, *Einführung in das Studium der altfranzösischen Literatur* (3rd ed., Halle, 1925), tr. F. Meyer du Mont (New York: Stechert, 1931).

Hermann Suchier and A. Birch-Hirschfeld, *Geschichte der französischen Literatur* (Leipzig and Vienna, 1913), Vol. I.

Joseph Bédier and Paul Hazard, *Histoire de la littérature française illustrée* (Paris: Larousse, 1923-24), Vol. I.

W. A. Nitze and E. Preston Dargan, *A History of French Literature from the Earliest Times to the Great War* (3rd ed., New York: Holt and Co., 1934).

Robert Bossuat, *Le moyen âge* (Paris: Gigord, 1931). This is the first volume of an extensive *Histoire de la littérature française* which is appearing under the direction of J. Calvet.

Gröber's account in the *Grundriss der rom. Phil.*, II, 1. Abt., 433-1247, is a remarkably full reference, though rather difficult for the beginner. The *Histoire littéraire de la France*, Vols. I-XII (Paris, 1735-1763); XIII-XXVI (Paris: F. Didot, 1814-1873); XXVII-XXXVI (Paris: Impr. Nat., 1877-1926), a colossal task begun by the Benedictines of Saint-Maur, and now as far as the middle of the fourteenth century, is of the utmost value to the research student. It must be used with control, however, as some of the material has been superseded. Vols. I-XXIII were reprinted 1865-95.

Gaston Paris, in the two works cited above, deals with the literature by types rather than by chronology. Since Gaston Paris' death, in 1903, many new theories have been advanced which are necessarily lacking in his books, but that these books are the foundation stone of much that has been written since goes without saying, and the student should be thoroughly familiar with them. As long as Old French literature is studied, homage must be rendered to Gaston Paris. Voretzsch's book is especially useful for its bibliography. The presentation is very concise. The earlier portion of the Bédier and Hazard history (contributed by E. Faral and

Bédier), as well as the first chapters of Nitze and Dargan, are excellent from many points of view. Due to the general nature of these works the treatment of the Middle Ages is somewhat brief. The illustrations in the Bédier and Hazard should be examined frequently. The volume by Bossuat is also undetailed; it is written more from the standpoint of appreciation. Bossuat follows Bédier and Faral in their more extreme view of clerical versus popular origins, and does not cite conflicting authorities in his otherwise excellent bibliographies.

The research student of Old French literature should make frequent use of the *Catalogue of Romances* (3 vols.; London, 1883-1910), by H. L. D. Ward and J. A. Herbert; also of the series of notices and extracts from important MSS which Paul Meyer published yearly in the *Bulletin de la Société des Anciens Textes,* in *Romania,* and on occasion in the *Notices et extraits des mss. de la Bibliothèque Nationale et autres bibliothèques* (Paris: Imprimerie Nationale).

The authoritative history of Latin literature in the Middle Ages is the *Geschichte der lateinischen Literatur des Mittelalters* (München: C. H. Beck, 1911-1931, 3 vols.) of Max Manitius. This covers in an unparalleled manner all Latin literature from the age of Justinian till the close of the twelfth century. These volumes form a part of the series known as *Handbuch der Klassischen Altertumswissenschaft.* Gröber's *Grundriss,* Vol. II, pt. I, is a good reference. For those who desire a briefer account in English there is *A History of the Later Latin Literature* (London: Routledge, 1931), by F. A. Wright and T. A. Sinclair.

It would not be amiss to close with a few remarks on the bibliographical material in the present book. As a heading for every chapter we cite a limited number of books and articles which have a general bearing upon the content. Any one conducting a course in Old French literature would do well to have these constantly on his seminar shelves, and the students should consult them frequently. At the close of the chapters one will find a list of the available editions of the works discussed. Seldom do we cite more than one edition of a given text; exceptions are made in the case of poems such as the *Roland* and the *Life of Saint Alexis,* where there is disagreement in the methods of preparing the text. In the body of our chapters we have included additional references which have bearing on specific points. It is quite possible that, in choosing between what should go at the head and what should be placed within, we have been inconsistent, but such inconsistency will not impede the student. Where no specific authority is cited, the reader should look for verification in the general references. Whenever the present writer attempts a decision of his own he makes use of the first singular pronoun, as distinguished from the editorial "we."

# CHAPTER I

## THE CAROLINGIAN PERIOD

CONSULT:

Eginhard, *Vie de Charlemagne* (Paris: CHFmâ, 1923).

Foerster and Koschwitz, *Altfranzösisches Uebungsbuch* (6th ed.; Leipzig, 1921).

Joseph Bédier, *Les légendes épiques* (3rd ed.; Paris, 1926-29), IV, 437 ff.

Inasmuch as many of the *chansons de geste,* or epics of the twelfth and thirteenth centuries, are centered around a legendary Charlemagne, it is only proper to begin our study with the historical figure of this great emperor of the West. His father was Pepin the Short, first king of the Carolingian dynasty (754-768), and his mother was Bertrada, or Bertha, daughter of the Count of Laon. Later tradition transformed this lady into Bertha *as grans piés,* daughter of the King of Hungary. Charles began to reign, jointly with his brother Carloman, in 768. Carloman was not loyal to Charles, but he caused him little trouble as he died in 771. The widow and children of Carloman fled to the court of Didier, King of Lombardy, under the care of a knight named Ogier. Thus began Charles's Lombard wars. He remained sole ruler of his empire and confined his brother's family in a cloister. The chief events of his reign were:

773-774. his conquest of the Lombards, in the upper half of Italy.

772-804. his wars in Saxony, during which some 4,500 pagan Saxons were slain, thousands were baptized, and many were moved to other provinces.

778-812. the seven expeditions which he sent into Spain, although he personally led only the first; the others were conducted by his sons.

787-796. wars against the Avars, who at that time inhabited Pannonia, the vast region to the east of Bavaria, between the Danube and Illyria.

789. war against the Wiltzes, between the Elbe and the Oder.

On Christmas day, 800 A. D., Charles was crowned emperor in the Church of Saint Peter's at Rome. He died in 814.

These deeds of conquest and the memory of his great personality lived on in the minds of men and found a vigorous, though blurred reflection in the later *chansons de geste.* After all, Charles was for them the baptizer of the Saxons—and other pagans—the traditional leader of Christianity. In point of fact no other ruler in France could match his deeds before the reign of Philip Augustus.

There should not be forgotten Charles's personal contribution to learning, the so-called Carolingian Renaissance. Gerward, the imperial librarian, was the first to designate him as *Carolus Magnus,* or Charlemagne. The great ruler saw the extreme decadence into which the study of Latin letters had fallen since the days of Sidonius (close of fifth century), and he determined to remedy it (780). At first his purpose was merely to instruct the clergy, to teach them to chant, read, and write correctly the Latin language. His utilitarian purpose soon included the instruction of the newly converted peoples, that they might read for themselves the precepts of Christianity. This movement towards the revival of culture, under the guidance of such scholars as Charlemagne drew to his court, spread into a love of letters for their own sake. Among these scholars were Alcuin the Englishman, Clement of Pisa, Paulinus of Aguileja, Paul the Deacon or Lombard, Theodulf of Orleans, Anghilbert, and others.

Alcuin was formerly an inmate of the Abbey at York and was thoroughly imbued with the same humanistic learning, brought from Ireland and Italy, which had inspired the great Bede (675-735). Alcuin came to Charlemagne in 782 and was the King's constant advisor on educational matters till 796 when he retired to the Abbey of Saint Martin at Tours. There he developed a school of manuscript copyists who refined, even if they did not originate, that marvellous Carolingian minuscule hand which survives today in small Roman type. Alcuin died in 804. Charlemagne issued decrees in 787-789, and as late as 804, requiring the village clergy to open elementary schools and refusing all high positions of trust to those who remained ignorant. It has been suggested that this *Renaissance* of letters by Charlemagne was the fork where Vulgar Latin ceased to exist, being supplanted among the educated by Middle Latin, an artificial, school cultivation of ancient Latin, and being continued among the uneducated by a further debased speech, a low Romance dialect, which was soon to drift into Old French. In other words it was the grammar of the schoolmen, such as they were, that kept late or Vulgar Latin to a semblance of Latin. Once this grammar control was transferred to a revived, artificial tongue, entirely foreign to average speakers, then their daily speech became rapidly corrupt in pronunciation and grammar. (Consult F. Lot in *ALMA,* VI, 145-152.) It was the revival of popular literature after 1000 A. D. which furnished a stabilizing influence once more on the speech of the people.

It must not be forgotten that Charles was a Frank, a German; but he spoke Latin as easily as his mother tongue, and understood Greek, if we are to believe implicitly his biographers. He was of medium height, thick-set, with a rather weak voice. He was extremely kind to strangers and his generosity was proverbial. If this picture is kept in mind it will be interesting to note its transformation in the course of legendary history.

Charlemagne was succeeded by his son, Louis the Pious, in 814. Louis was a weak king and was deposed twice by his turbulent sons (830, 833) and twice restored. He, too, was not forgotten by the later writers of *chansons de geste* when they sought an ungrateful or pusillanimous king around whom to center the action.

In 817, Louis the Pious made a division of his empire among his three sons, Pepin, Lothair, and Louis. But in 823 a fourth son was born to him by his second wife, Judith of Bavaria, and this son, who was christened Charles, became the father's favorite. In 832 Louis cancelled the division he had already made and gave Alemania to Charles, a boy of nine years. This grant was followed by Aquitaine in 833, and Burgundy, Provence, and Septimania in 837. It was in 838 that the brother Pepin died. In view of this, King Louis reassigned the whole empire in 839, giving all the provinces in the Jura and the valley of the Rhone, east of Meun, to Lothair; to Louis he gave Bavaria; the western territory, Romance speaking, was assigned to his youngest son, Charles. Aquitaine continued in the hands of Pepin's son, Pepin II, until 848. Louis the Pious died in 840.

For the first time in history (840) there was a France, speaking Romance, and a Germany, speaking German. Charles, now known as the Bald, was king of the Gallo-Franks, Louis was king of the Germans, and Lothair held Italy as well as "Lotharingia," or Lorraine. The obvious strategic policy which suggested itself to Charles and Louis was a coalition against their brother, in an effort to force him out. This resulted in a meeting between the two plotters at Strasbourg where each king and his men swore publicly. Charles made his oath in German and his men in Gallo-Romance, Louis reciprocated in Gallo-Romance and his people in German. These oaths have been preserved in Nithard's history of the sons of Louis the Pious. They are considered our earliest document in the Romance of Gaul. They contain the earliest known Old French. Unfortunately, the scribe who wrote them out intentionally latinized some of the spellings. Probably no one had yet attempted to put on parchment the rapidly changing Romance tongue. A phonetic system for representing its peculiar sounds was, as yet, unformed. The value of these *Oaths* is purely historical or linguistic, and they require no analysis here. Professor J. W. Thompson has sought unconvincingly to prove that the Romance oaths were a late tenth-century forgery, since German was the language of northern Gaul in the ninth century.[1] Charles the Bald was a forceful figure, the last that can be called worthy of the

[1] *Spec* I (1926), 410.

Carolingian line. He seized complete control of Aquitaine from his nephew, in 848; in 869 he secured Lorraine, which he soon had to divide with Louis. He made an unsuccessful attempt to seize Germany when Louis died in 876. He was crowned Emperor of the West by Pope John VIII on December 25, 875. In the *chansons de geste* which were to follow, this Charles is hopelessly confused with his grandfather, the great Charlemagne.

After 838 the Norsemen and Danes began to touch annually upon the shores of France. In that first year, Hasting, their leader, burned all the territory between the Loire and the Cher. He besieged Tours but was put to flight for the time being. As a means of defense, Charles the Bald proclaimed, in 843, the Edict of Mersen, which may be roughly called the beginning of feudalism. He forced every man who had not the means to protect himself to put his person and his property into the service of some one who could guarantee protection. But no vassal of this kind was obliged to follow his lord to war except against a foreign enemy. The Norsemen continued to give so much trouble that the populace was terrorized. In 886, Paris was besieged. In 912 Charles the Simple finally ceded a portion of Neustria to Rollo, a Norman chieftain. Rollo (or Rou as his name was spelled by the French) was accordingly baptized at Rouen and granted in marriage Gisela, Charles's daughter. This is the beginning of the great Duchy of Normandy which, after a hundred years, was to spread its influence much farther.

The personal influence of the Carolingian kings after Charles the Bald (d. 877) was very small. We list their names for completeness' sake, with the dates of their accessions to the throne:

Louis II, the Stammerer .......................... 877
Louis III and Carloman .......................... 879
Carloman alone ................................. 882
Charles the Fat ................................. 884
Eudes (Count of Paris, a non-Carolingian) ......... 887
Charles III, the Simple (d. 929) ................... 893
Robert (brother of Eudes) ........................ 922
Louis IV, d'Outre-mer ........................... 936
Lothair ......................................... 954
Louis V ........................................ 986

This historical sketch brings us close to the year 1000. Strange to say, we have no influential or characteristic work, either in history or letters, from the actual reign of Charlemagne. Nennius, who wrote after 800, was a Welshman living on the island of Britain. During Charles's lifetime the clerics were more occupied with teaching and interpretation than with creative writing. The great Emperor once dead, it was possible to view his career with the proper perspective, and so a number of biographies then came into being. The most important of these is the *Vita Karoli* of one Eginhard, or Einhard, written in 830 or shortly after and modelled closely in form and content after the lives of the Caesars of Suetonius. Eginhard was born in the valley of the Maine around 775; he was reared first in the monastery of Fulda and later at the court of the Emperor. Louis the Pious, who had been his schoolfellow, appointed Eginhard his secretary and eventually confided to him the supervision of Lothair, his eldest son. Eginhard withdrew from public life in 828 and died in 840. The Charlemagne whom he knew was not the active man of the early wars, but the great Emperor from 800 on. Unfortunately, Eginhard in his biography followed too closely his model, Suetonius. This often resulted in inaccuracy and wrong proportion, which force us to use this life with caution.

A *Vita Karoli Magni* was composed by an unknown Saxon cleric, presumably between 888 and 891. The author is always referred to by modern scholars as the *Poeta Saxo*. The first four books, written in Latin hexameters, are based upon annals both Frankish and Saxon. The fifth book, in distichs, is founded in part upon the above mentioned biography of Eginhard.

A certain cleric from Aquitaine, Ermoldus Nigellus (or the Black), who had been banished to Strasbourg by Louis the Pious, kept imploring the mercy of the King. He has left us a long poem in four divisions entitled *Carmina in honorem Hludovici*. There is but little originality in this lengthy eulogy which narrates the King's life from 781 to 826. Most of its style and terminology were pillaged outright from Vergil, Ovid, Sedulius, and others.

An anonymous writer from Limousin, known as the Astronomer because of his manifest interest in heavenly bodies, composed a *Vita Hludovici Pii* shortly after 840. He was a great admirer of Louis. Nithard, a grandson of Charlemagne—the illegitimate child of his daughter Bertha by Anghilbert—wrote the *Historiarum libri quatuor* (843), which is a history of the sons of Louis the Pious, especially of their civil wars from 840 to 843. It is in this account that we find incorporated the famous *Oaths of Strasbourg*. This work of Nithard, which has come down to us in a single manuscript of the tenth century (B. N., lat. 9768), was dedicated to Charles the Bald and written at his command. No account is to be taken of a second manuscript (B. N., lat. 14663) which is a fragmentary fifteenth-century copy of the other.

In a manuscript of the middle of the sixth century we meet for the first time a collection of lives of the early monks and saints in Egypt which was known throughout the Middle Ages as the *Vitae patrum*, or more correctly the *Vita patrum*. This heterogeneous collection, divided into ten books and an appendix, was not a single unit, but the gathering together of individual lives, originals, and translations from the Greek, by a number of authors. Many are by Saint Jerome, Rufinus (d. 410), Pelagius, a certain Joannes, and Paschasius. As we shall see, this collection was much appreciated in France in the thirteenth century. Of the many early individual lives, not forming a part of this collection, let us take account of the *Life of Saint Radegunda,* by Venantius Fortunatus, composed between 587 and 600, and of the *Life of Saint Caesarius, Bishop of Arles* (d. 542), by three other bishops, Cyprianus of Toulon, Firminius and Viventius. Still others are said to have had a hand in the composition of this second life. It is supposedly contemporary with its subject. The *Life of Sainte-Geneviève,* the patron of Paris (d. *ca.* 500), is often attributed to the sixth century, but there are some who believe it was composed in the Carolingian era. The *Life of Saint-Remi* (or Remigius) (d. 532), which is extant, is the composition of Hincmar in the year 878. He claimed to be using as his source an early sixth century version; this is doubted. Gregory of Tours, author of the celebrated *Historia Francorum* (576-593), also composed numerous pious works: a *Liber in gloria martyrum* (586-590), *Passio SS. Septem Dormientium* (translated from the Syriac), and the lives and miracles of Saint Martin of Tours, Saint Julian, Saint Andrew the Apostle, and a treatise in *Vita patrum* (596).

The real age of the Latin saint's life is the Carolingian era and the eleventh century. We refer the student to the list in Molinier and elsewhere and speak in passing of one life which has some bearing upon the origins of the epic. It is the life of Saint Faro, or Burgundofaro, Bishop of Meaux, who died in 672. This was composed by a successor to the See at Meaux two hundred years later, Bishop Hildegarius (d. 875).

Paulus Diaconus revised the *Breviarium,* or short history of Rome of Eutropius (composed in 369 A. D.). Paulus continued the recital down to the year 565 in the reign of Justinian. Towards the year 1000 the work was still further continued to include the year 806, by Landulphus Sagax. The whole passed in the Middle Ages under the title *Historia miscella* and it is important because it was the chief source of the medieval man's knowledge of ancient Rome.

So far we have noted only one work from the Carolingian age written in the vulgar tongue, the *Oaths of Strasbourg* (842). There were four others which have survived.

The first of these is the *Saint Eulalia,* a sequence intended to be sung in the office of the Mass on December 10, the feast day of Saint Eulalia. An explanation of the term *sequence* would not be out of place.

The order of the Mass begins with: Introit, Kyrie Eleison, Gloria in

Excelsis, Dominus Vobiscum, Collect, Epistle, Gradual, Gospel, etc. The Gradual, originally a psalm epitomizing the Epistle, ends in *alleluia*. Early in the history of the Church the last note of this *alleluia* was expanded into a *melisma,* or melodious succession of notes on the concluding vowel *a*. In the eighth century there was a further step—new words were substituted for the *a* in the form of a series of rhymed strophes of two lines each. The first line was called the strophe and the second, the antistrophe, which were frequently sung in relay by two separate choirs. A conclusion was still later added—an independent line of shorter or longer form. The hymn which was developed in this fashion was called a sequence, a prose, or a trope. It followed immediately after the Gradual, between the Gospel and the Epistle. It was usually in Latin, but, as we now observe, it could be in the vernacular. Some of the Latin sequences have become famous: the *Dies Irae* (1250) for Requiem Masses, the *Veni Sancte Spiritus (Come Holy Spirit, Heavenly Dove),* composed by Pope Innocent III, in 1198, for Pentecost, and the *Stabat Mater* (1306). Today the sequence is preceded by a second Gradual or Tract and sung on Sundays, Mondays, Wednesdays, and Fridays of the Lenten season.

The vernacular sequence in praise of Saint Eulalia is preserved in a single MS now at Valenciennes. It is found side by side with the Old High German poem "Einan kuning uueis ih, heizsit her Hluduig," a poem composed in honor of the Battle of Saucourt (August 3, 881), a victory of Louis III over the Norsemen. This German poem refers to Louis as alive and he died on August 5, 882; it must be dated between those two dates; and, as the *Eulalia* is in the same hand and the MS itself is ninth-century, it is usual to place both around 882. A Latin sequence, also in praise of Saint Eulalia, is often compared with the Romance hymn and cited as its model in form and versification. For content the Romance *Eulalia* is indebted to Prudentius (fourth century) who had dedicated a hymn to this young Spanish saint in his *Peristephanon.* Bede's *Martyrologium* may have been a contributing source, as he alone narrates her death by the sword and not by fire.

Saint Eulalia was a girl of noble birth, a native of Merida, Spain; she suffered the death of a martyr on December 10, 304. The dialect of this sequence is seemingly that of Saint-Amand, near Valenciennes—that is, Picard-Walloon. There are fourteen strophe pairs and a concluding line, twenty-nine lines in all.

Two other compositions of equal importance with the *Eulalia* are the *Passion* and the *Life of Saint Leodegar* (or *Saint Ledger*). They are referred to as the Clermont-Ferrand poems because the one MS in which they are preserved belongs to the library of that town. This tenth-century MS is a Latin glossary. For economy's sake a hand, other than the original, filled in the gaps with miscellaneous selections of prose and poetry. After the word *bellum* in the glossary there follows the *Passion;* after *illustris* is the *Life of Saint Leodegar.*

The *Passion,* dating from the first part of the tenth century, was certainly composed in a dialect of northern Gaul, but its original dialect has been considerably altered by a Provençal copyist. There are 129 strophes of four lines each: 516 lines in all. The lines have eight syllables and are in assonanced couplets. The sources are, for the most part, the Gospels of Matthew, John, and Mark. The Apocryphal *Descensus Christi ad inferos* and *Nicodemus* have been utilized to a slight extent.

The *Life of Saint Leodegar* belongs to the close of the tenth century. It, too, was composed in the north, possibly in Walloon territory, but the hand of a copyist introduced Provençalisms—to a lesser degree than in the *Passion.* There are forty strophes, each containing three verse pairs (and not two as in the *Passion*). The lines are octosyllabic, in assonanced pairs. There is a total of 240 lines. Saint Leodegarus was a bishop of Autun. He was blinded and then beheaded by his enemy Ivroïn in 678. There are two Latin lives of this saint, both earlier than the Romance version. The one was composed by an anonymous monk of Saint-Syphorion of Autun, dedicated to Bishop Hermenarius; the other was the work of Ursinus, a monk of Saint-Maxent, dedicated to two patrons —Ansoald, Bishop of Poitiers, and Andulf, Abbot of Saint-Maxent. Both these Latin versions are supposed to come from one source, a contemporary life. The Romance poem is based freely upon the work of Ursinus.

The remaining vernacular work of the Carolingian period is a fragment, of still less literary interest than the *Oaths of Strasbourg.* Bethmann discovered, in 1839, a tenth-century fragment on a strip of parchment which had been used for the binding of a work of Saint Gregory of Nazianzus. It consists of thirty-seven lines, partly in Tironian shorthand, on the *verso;* the *recto* is even less legible. Apparently, this was a portion of a sermon on Jonah, chapters 1 and 4, and it is an odd mixture of Romance and Latin. It is known as the *Jonas fragment* and was published by Génin in his *Roland* edition of 1850. Professor H. F. Muller[2] believes this was by a foreigner—possibly a German—who did not speak Romance as a native.

---

[2] *A Chronology of Vulgar Latin.* Beiheft 78, ZfrPh (1929), p. 132.

# CHAPTER II

## THE ELEVENTH CENTURY

H. O. Taylor, *The Medieval Mind* (4th ed.; New York and London, 1925).
Max Manitius, *Bildung, Wissenschaft, und Literatur im Abendlande von 800 bis 1100* (Crimmitschau, 1925).

The eleventh century in France was a period of enterprise and expansion. Foreign expeditions were carried on by Norman adventurers who sought further conquests in Sicily, Spain, and England. The Normans, or Norsemen, had been resident in Neustria, or northern France, for more than a century, a period sufficiently long to make them Frenchmen in speech and customs, but not long enough to remove the roving, adventurous spirit from their blood. It is a fact of startling significance that those little bands of Scandinavian pirates, who settled in France in the ninth and tenth centuries, did the most towards exalting the French name and language to the supremacy which it has held ever since. The Grandmesnil family and their like in the service of Byzantium, men of the type of Guillaume de Montreuil in Spain, and many others, led the way to that French glory which has been perpetuated in Asia Minor as well as in Europe. The French enterprise of the eleventh century owed much to the activity of the Normans.

Most of the marked improvements in comfort and progress, such as the new Romanesque architecture in stone, the serious beginnings of a popular literature, the increase in trade and pilgrimages, and the improvement of roads and bridges—occurring at this time—were ascribed in former years to the passing of the year 1000, the Millennium. It was supposed that the Christian world, in gratitude for its preservation, sought to beautify the churches, erect additional monasteries, and construct more permanent dwellings of stone. Historians now doubt that there was any panic over the possible end of the world in the year 1000. (Perhaps this panic has been discounted to an excess, for it would be reasonable to expect some joy at the passing of the dreaded Millennium.) The new expansion and progress may be ascribed, they say, to more peaceful conditions, fewer invasions, renewed commerce—especially in the Mediterranean—and less isolation. The fierce Norsemen were finally checked in 943, and the Hungarians in 937. But the tenth century was a hard one, save for the effects that were felt in Germany and in Italy from the so-called Ottonian Renaissance (936-973). This last was the second revival of culture in the Middle Ages. The tenth century was an Age of Iron when strong kings were non-existent in France and when nobles terrorized the land with their rapine and petty wars. The learning revived by Charlemagne had not disappeared, but it had kept within the walls of such monastic establishments as Tours, Fulda, Reichenau, St. Gall, Lorsch, Fleury, Saint-Riquier, and Corbie, or in such cathedral centers as Metz, Cambrai, Auxerre, Rheims, and Chartres, where there was strong civil protection from violence. Gerbert d'Aurillac began his teaching at Rheims in 972. He was undoubtedly an important intermediary through whom the Hindu-Arabic numerals reached Latin Europe from Spain. He was a celebrated mathematician and astronomer who knew the use of many instruments. Occasionally he is given more credit than is due him, by modern historians; for example, he did not invent the water clock, which was known to the ancients. The theory that he urged a Crusade against the infidels is based upon a passage in his Letter No. 28 (ed. Havet) which is no longer so interpreted. It is none the less true that he stood out in his time as one possessed of great intellectual curiosity. A pupil of his was Fulbert, Chancellor and Bishop (1007-1029) of Chartres, who launched the fame of the schools of Chartres—schools which remained in the first rank till the middle of the twelfth century when they were eclipsed by Paris and Orleans.

With the turn of the Millennium, then, there were factors such as the new Capetian dynasty (weak though it was), the power of the German Emperors, the force of the now civilized Normans, and more stable conditions at Rome, after the death of Otto III in 1002, which conspired for more enduring law and order. Since churches were not being burned by the Norsemen, the clergy and the people united to erect more durable buildings of stone, in a modified style called the Romanesque which spread from southern France. This style was thought to be a solution of an age-old architectural problem: how to use the old Roman barrel vault in a building the shape of a cross with nave and transept. Romanesque architecture soon replaced the basilica type; but Romanesque buildings were too heavy. Many of them fell, in the course of a century or so, before a more suitable solution, the northern French or so-called Gothic style, came into being with the middle of the twelfth century. Trade and pilgrimages had not ceased entirely in the ninth and tenth centuries, but they were performed under very difficult circumstances. From 1000 on trade multiplied and travel increased, thus enriching the people of France materially and intellectually. Study of the Latin classics had never stopped among the laity of Italy, particularly in the South. When the Normans first went into Apulia and Calabria in the early eleventh century they opened the road for Byzantine and Arabian culture to travel into France; it did so very slowly, to be sure, but this was a beginning. Pope Nicholas II acknowledged Robert Guiscard, Robert d'Aversa and other Norman leaders in southern Italy, in 1059. In 1091, Sicily also passed under Norman control from the hands of the Saracens.

By the second half of the eleventh century conditions had improved still more. Thanks to the spread of pupils from such men as Gerbert and Fulbert, the cultivation of Latin letters had spread throughout France, particularly to Orleans, Tours, and Liége. The Twelfth-Century Renaissance was really underway by 1050. In this second half of the century we have such charming poets as Hildebert of Le Mans, Baudri de Bourgueil, and Marbod de Rennes. Hildebert (*ca.* 1055-1134) was bishop of Le Mans and later Archbishop of Tours; he was educated at Chartres. His two poems on ancient Rome were considered classical throughout the Middle Ages and even later. They seemed too good for a medieval poet. Baudri was a product of the schools at Fleury; Marbod, of those at Chartres.

The *Digest* of Justinian (reigned 527-565) came to light again by 1076. The *Corpus juris civilis,* which that great emperor ordered the jurist Tribonian to revise, consisted of the *Digest,* or summary of opinions of the notable Roman jurists, the *Code,* or codification of imperial legislation, the *Institutes,* or law text book for use of schools, and the *Novels,* or additional legislation of Justinian. The *Digest* was the most important of these but it had dropped out of sight from 603 to 1076. Bologna became the center for the revived instruction of this civil law, and Pepo and Irnerius (1060 ?-1125 ?) were the lawyers who initiated its study. Berengar of Tours, a pupil of Fulbert of Chartres, emphasized the importance of reason, or dialectic, as opposed to authority, from 1049 till 1088, during his controversy with Lanfranc of Bec. Roscellinus of Compiègne formulated his nominalist doctrine which, though condemned in 1092 by the Church, was to prove the eventual undoing of medieval philosophy in the fifteenth century. Spain was being reconquered from the Moslems; Toledo was won by the Christians in 1085, and Saragossa in 1118. This opened a new road, other than Sicily and southern Italy, for the inroad of Moslem culture and of translations from the Greek. Thousands of northern Frenchmen, particularly Normans, joined in the wars in Spain, and they carried some of this culture northward.

In giving a brief account of the political history of France during the eleventh century, we begin with Hugh Capet, the founder of the Capetian dynasty, who reigned from 987 to 996. Previous to his accession, he was Count of Paris and titular Abbot of Saint Martin's of Tours, of Saint-Denis, and of Saint-Germain-des-Prés. It is supposedly because of his abbot's hood that he gained the title *capet.* Though personally brave, he was modest and retiring, and really held but little more power than some of his nobles. At that, he was stronger than his Carolingian predecessor who had controlled Laon and nothing else. At his death Hugh was succeeded by his son Robert I, or the Pious. Helgaud, Robert's biographer, has left us a pious picture of his master, making him seem more a monk than a king. He tells the story of how thieves would strip the very fringe from the King's cloak when he walked abroad, and how the King would not lift a finger to prevent it. Robert is said to have written a number of Latin hymns which have not been preserved. His life would seem to belie his *fainéant* reputation. He repudiated his first wife, Susanna of Flanders, and married Bertha. This second queen was a distant cousin, a match forbidden by the Church, so Robert was excommunicated. He finally yielded and replaced Bertha by Constance of Provence, in 1003. There is a very charming modern picture, in the Luxembourg Museum of Paris, which represents the mental struggle of Robert and Bertha after receiving the papal interdict. The new queen was rather trying to live with and made her husband miserable. Perhaps some of his monklike resignation was in reaction to her. Robert engaged in many successful struggles while seeking to control his turbulent nobles.

Henry I, who succeeded his father in 1031, was a man of considerable power, though we know very few details of his career. He put down a rebellion headed by his mother. He married for his second wife Anna of Kiev, daughter of Iaroslav I, Grand Prince of Russia (1019-1055), ostensibly to avoid any chance of consanguinity as in the marriage of his father with Bertha. He resisted vigorously the attempts of Henry III, or the Black, of Germany to gain Lorraine. His son, Philip I, became king in 1060, at the age of eight. A more miserable king could scarcely be imagined, unless it be Henry III of France who was to come four hundred years later. Philip engaged in much private scandal; he took no part in the great events of his lifetime; his control over the barons became very weak, particularly his influence with the house of Normandy. He was under an interdict for two years (1102-1104) as a result of his illegal possession of Bertrade de Montfort, Countess of Anjou. Fortunately, the last years of his reign were brightened by his son Louis who had begun the task of quelling the rebellious barons.

The two greatest political events of the eleventh century were the invasion of England and the First Crusade. The Battle of Hastings, or Senlac (October 14, 1066), saw William of Normandy established in England, although it was not till 1071 that his possession was assured. Pilgrims had flocked to Palestine in large numbers, as best they could under adverse conditions, since 359, the date that Saint Cyril announced by letter the discovery of the True Cross. (It was supposedly discovered in 326 by Saint Helena, the mother of Constantine the Great.) The pilgrims suffered a great repulse with the spread of Mohammedanism in the seventh century, but many still ventured the long and hazardous journey for a sight of the Holy Sepulchre. In spite of the destruction of the Church of the Holy Sepulchre in 1010, the pilgrims became even more numerous with the improved conditions of the eleventh century. Twelve thousand souls accompanied Bishop Günther of Bamberg to the Holy Land in 1065. The Seljuke Turks under Alp-Arslan advanced in 1071 after their defeat of the Byzantine emperor; the son of Alp-Arslan, Malak-Shah, captured Jerusalem in 1076. At the same time the Almoravides in Spain were gathering strength and won the decisive victory of Zalaca (1087). Christianity was faced with the gravest of dangers in a renewed advance of the Moslem peoples; access to Jerusalem and to the tomb of Saint James of Compostella was becoming increasingly difficult.[1] The answer was the First Crusade, preached by Pope Urban II at the Council of Clermont-Ferrand, November 18, 1095. The knights set forth in December, 1096, and reached Constantinople after a journey of five months. They were six hundred thousand men. Antioch fell to them in 1098, and Jerusalem on July 15, 1099. Many of the crusaders now returned home, but those who remained to occupy the new Latin Kingdom of Jerusalem captured the seaport Akko in 1104. They renamed it Saint-Jean-d'Acre.

We have noted that the Carolingian period enjoyed a few saints' lives and certain other forms of religious material in the vernacular; the eleventh century saw the rise of the Old French epic or *chanson de geste*. Whether it began shortly before 1000 A. D., or shortly after, will not concern us till a later chapter, but this new literary form achieved its great popularity and much of its conventional structure in the period 1000 to 1100. Nearly all the epics composed during those years have disappeared, all with the possible exception of the *Gormont et Isembart* and the *Chanson de Roland*. There is a reasonable explanation for this. The succeeding century, the twelfth, saw such development in all types of vernacular literature that the earlier compositions were subjected to a vigorous revision, and their primitive forms were intentionally forgotten. Only an occasional lucky find has enabled modern scholars to observe traces of vernacular writing in the earlier eleventh century.

On the last sheet of a MS of the *Liber historiae,* preserved at the Royal Library of the Hague, there is a Latin fragment in prose which gives an account of the besieging of a Saracen city by Christians. Paleographers date it around 1030. Such important epic characters as Ernaut, Ber-

[1] The Shrine at Saint James of Compostella was first established in 860.

nard, and William of Orange appear in the narrative. This fragment, as we have it, was doubtless a schoolboy exercise. The task was to make a prose rendering of a Latin poem; and this Latin poem, in turn, must have had a vernacular original, one of our very earliest *chansons de geste*. Such is the explanation of Suchier. This so-called exercise is commonly called the Hague fragment.

There is a single piece of vernacular literature which has survived, entire, from the first half of the eleventh century, a life of Saint Alexis. It is dated around 1040. A certain Jonas of the Abbey of Fontenelle has narrated to us how in 1042 the bones of Saint Wulfram (d. 693), Archbishop of Sens, were carried through the streets of Rouen to rid the city of a dreadful plague. Among the miracles wrought was the restoration of his failing eyesight to one Tedbalt of Vernon, who had translated from the Latin the lives of several saints and had recast them into the common tongue with much eloquence and a sort of ringing rhythm. On the basis of this meager reference it is inferred that Tedbalt of Vernon might have been the author of our *Saint Alexis*. In any case this evidence proves that saints' lives in the vulgar tongue were not uncommon in the eleventh century. We possess what appears to be the Latin original of the *Life of Saint Alexis*. It is in prose, and is based, in turn, upon a Greek original which has also been preserved.

The poem consists of 125 strophes of five ten-syllable lines each, in assonance. There is a caesura after the fourth beat. The dialect is certainly Norman, though two of the oldest MSS were Anglo-Norman. There are six MSS: the Hildesheim (L), three at Paris (P, S and M), the Ashburnham (A), and another containing only 129 lines (Vatican lat. 5334), recently discovered by Pio Rajna (*ArchRom,* XIII, 1 ff.). He considers the new MS closest to (L), which is of the twelfth century and the best. The plot of this *Life* is as follows: A certain lord of Rome, Eufemiiens by name, has been married for many years and is unblessed with children. He and his wife pray to God with such earnestness that the wife conceives. A son is born and he is called Alexis. When the boy is fullgrown, his father, knowing that they will have no more progeny, determines to marry Alexis off at once that he may see his lineage survive. The wedding is brought about, but Alexis' thoughts have been turning towards higher things. He leaves his wife on the wedding night and sails away to Alsis, a distant city. He continues there as a beggar for seventeen years. God then causes an image to speak, proclaiming Alexis a man of God. To avoid the honor which is to come to him, Alexis once more takes ship, this time for Tarson; but the winds are contrary and he is carried back to Rome. Knowing his father will not recognize him, he demands a pallet under his father's stairs and the leavings from his table. For another seventeen years he dwells in this fashion, reviled and abused by the servants of the household. When he is about to die he asks for ink and parchment and writes the account of his life. The voice of God once more speaks and announces him to be a holy man. The Emperor and the Pope seek him out, his story is read, and he is buried with great honors.

This narrative is somewhat unpleasant to the modern reader because of the utter selfishness of its asceticism—a disregard of the second great commandment, man's duty towards his neighbor. Alexis sees his mother and father, not to mention his wife, sorrowing unceasingly, and yet he keeps his silence to the last. For a more sympathetic appreciation than mine see E. R. Curtius in *ZfrPh* LVI (1936), 113-139. He emphasizes how well the *Life* is written with proper understanding of *exordium, narratio,* and *conclusio.* An interesting testimony of the later popularity of the theme is to be found in the *Chronicon anonymum Laudunense,* a universal history from the year 1 to 1219. The chronicler, an Englishman of the order of the Prémontré, is speaking of Waldo of Lyons, the founder of the Waldensian sect: "Is quadem die domenica cum declinasset ad turbam quam ante joculatorem viderat congregatam, ex verbis ipsius compunctus fuit. . . . Fuit enim locus narrationis eius qualiter beatus Alexis in domo patris beato fine quievit." There are several later versions of this *Life* surviving from the thirteenth century.

Rodulfus Tortarius (1063-1114) was a monk at Fleury-sur-Loire, a monastery famous in the history of medieval writing. Preserved in the Vatican Library is a MS of his works, consisting for the most part of his versification of Valerius Maximus and of the description of his journey to Caen, Blois, and Bayeux. This MS also contains a Latin letter in which he narrates famous friendships, and among them is the tale of Amis and Amiles in 204 hexameter lines. Monteverdi (*Studj romanzi* XIX (1928), 125) dates this letter late in the life of Rodulfus, but it is important as indicating the early spread of a theme which was used in a *chanson de geste.* Perhaps Rodulfus was rehearsing the story from a primitive version of this *chanson.*

*Gormont et Isembart* and the *Chanson de Roland* may have been composed in the second half of this century; but we shall examine them in a succeeding chapter, with the epics as a group.

## EDITIONS

*The Life of Saint Alexis,* ed. V. L. Dedeck-Héry (New York: IFS, 1931); *Vie de Saint-Alexis,* ed. G. Paris-M. Roques (6th ed.; Paris: Cfmâ, 1925)· *Sankt Alexius,* ed. W. Foerster-M. Rösler (Halle: SrT, 1928);

*Vie de Saint-Alexis,* ed. J. M. Meunier (Paris, 1933); still another edition is by C. Storey (Paris, 1934).—

*Amis et Amiles und Jourdains de Blaivies,* ed. K. Hofmann (2nd ed.; Erlangen, 1882), pp. xxi-xxxii.—

The *Song of Burgundofaro* and the *Hague fragment* are in the *Uebungsbuch* of Foerster-Koschwitz, *v. supra.*—

*Rodulfi Tortarii Carmine,* ed. M. B. Ogle and D. M. Schullian (Rome: American Academy, 1933).

# CHAPTER III

# THE BACKGROUND OF THE TWELFTH CENTURY

C. H. Haskins, *The Renaissance of the Twelfth Century* (Cambridge: Harvard Press, 1927).

In 1108, Louis VI, or the Fat, succeeded his father, Philip I, as king of France and continued with vigor a campaign of law and order. By punishing such noble brigands as Thomas de Marle, Anseau de Garlande, Thibaut de Chartres, and Hugues du Puiset, he made it clear that rapine and highway robbery were not to be tolerated in his realm. It is a striking fact that from Henry I on, the Capetian kings seem to alternate in qualities of valor and timidity. Louis VII, or the Young, succeeded to the throne in 1137 because of the death of his older brother Philip in 1132. Louis VII, a few days before his father's death, was united in marriage to Eleanor of Aquitaine, the heiress of that vast district south of the Loire, and thus given direct control of a kingdom greater than that held by any French king since Charles the Bald. Eleanor was the granddaughter of the Provençal troubadour, William IX of Aquitaine (1071-1127), or William VII of Poitiers, as he is variously called. It is only natural that she should have brought with her to Paris a taste for Provençal poetry, language, and customs. The Provençal influence upon northern French literature became an important factor with her marriage to the young Louis.

Louis did not start his reign so auspiciously; he showed some lack of judgment. It was fortunate for him that he had the aid of Suger (1081?-1151), Abbot of Saint-Denis, who had also served his father. As it was, young Louis succeeded in antagonizing his nobles needlessly and in irritating the Church. His wife, Eleanor, was responsible for much of this attitude. At the close of 1146, Louis VII determined to lead a crusade to the Holy Land, the Second Crusade. It was preached by Saint Bernard of Clairvaux at Vézelay. In June, 1147, the French knights set out and were joined by a German army under Conrad III at Ratisbonne. Each army had about seventy thousand fighting men. The campaign in Syria was disastrous, largely due to the treachery of the Byzantine Greeks, and the crusade closed with the defection of the Latin Christians of Syria before Damascus. Eleanor accompanied her husband, but in March, 1148, there was considerable scandal arising about her and Raymond of Aquitaine. She called her husband's attention to the fact that they were cousins in the fourth and fifth degree. Louis returned home in 1150 and a divorce between him and Eleanor was effected in March, 1152; two months later the Queen married the young Henry Plantagenet, who was soon to be Henry II of England and Louis's most formidable adversary. Aquitaine was a loss to France and a gain for England.

During the remainder of Louis's career he was a changed man. He became a devoted son of the Church and a generous and servile host to Alexander III during the Pope's exile in France (1162-1165). Louis received and supported Thomas à Becket, Archbishop of Canterbury, who fled from England in 1164. He brought about the reconciliation between Henry II and Becket in 1170, which was to end with the murder of Becket in the cathedral at Canterbury on December 29 of that year. For all this Louis gained in spiritual prestige and reputation for piety, but he was shamefully outdone by Henry II of England in matter of territory. Louis seemed to turn the other cheek and belie all the warlike energy of the beginning of his reign. He almost suffered an invasion from Frederick Barbarossa of Germany, in 1162. After the divorce from Eleanor, Louis married Constance of Castille in 1154; on her death he married Adèle de Champagne, in 1160. By Eleanor he had two daughters: Marie, whom he married to Henry, Count of Champagne, in 1164, and Alix, whom he gave to Count Thibaut of Blois. His first daughter by Constance, Alix, married the Count of Ponthieu. Adèle gave Louis his only son, Philip Augustus, in 1165; a subsequent daughter, Agnes, was married to the Emperor of Constantinople. Knowledge of these alliances is important for an understanding of the period. The two daughters of Eleanor of Aquitaine shared their mother's taste for Provençal language and literature. The distant marriages with Hungary and Greece give some idea of the prestige of Louis VII in other lands.

When Louis VII died in 1180, he was succeeded by his fifteen year old son, Philip Augustus, or Philip II. As was usually the case with the accession of a new king in the Middle Ages, he had to suppress a coalition of his nobles. Philippe d'Alsace, Count of Flanders, and the new King's uncles, Archbishop Guillaume of Rheims, Count Henry I of Champagne, Count Thibaut V of Blois and of Chartres, and Count Etienne of Sancerre—all brothers of the Queen Mother—disputed the right to advise. Philip Augustus would have nothing to do with any of them. An early act in his reign (1180) was to persecute the Jews and obtain from them a large sum in ransom, fifteen thousand marks. He next turned his attention towards the Plantagenet empire. Henry II, now old, held England, Normandy, Anjou, and Poitou, not to mention his rights in Scotland, Wales, Ireland, and Britanny. Philip, aided by Eleanor of Aquitaine, encouraged the English king's sons in revolt. Henry suppressed them but he was sorely tried. The so-called Young King, Henry, the heir to the English throne, died in 1183. This was a great loss to the troubadours and other *gens de lettres* who had enjoyed favor with the pleasure-loving prince. Philip and Richard the Lion-hearted, the new heir to the English throne, formed an alliance against Henry II; John Lackland, Henry's youngest son, also joined it. This last was a blow that contributed to Henry's death in 1189.

Jerusalem fell to Saladin, or Salah-ed-Dîn, on October 2, 1187; Saint-Jean-d'Acre was also taken. Both Philip Augustus and the new English king, Richard I, received the cross. They did not reach Syria till 1190, recapturing Saint-Jean-d'Acre in 1191. Jerusalem was never to be recovered from the hands of the Moslems. Philip grew sick, quarreled with Richard, and left for home. Richard remained a little longer; on his return, in 1192, he was taken prisoner by Duke Leopold of Austria whom he had grievously insulted. His person was delivered to Henry VI, Emperor of Germany, who finally freed him in January of 1195, after a captivity of a year and a half. The English paid a ransom of one hundred thousand pounds, and Richard had to recognize the German emperor as his suzerain! Philip had conspired to keep Richard in prison; henceforth there could be no peace between the two. The renewed war lasted till 1199 when Richard was killed in southern France while besieging a castle in search of treasure. War was renewed with John as the English king in 1202. In April, 1204, the famous Château Gaillard fell and Normandy was once more in the hands of a French king. The Battle of Bouvines (July 27, 1214) confirmed Philip in his new possessions and left to England, on the continent, only a section of Poitou.

This historical sketch may seem overlong to the literary student but many of the facts given reflect themselves in the vernacular literature of the period. For handy reference we shall now recapitulate and add a table of the rulers in France, England, and Germany during the twelfth century.

| FRANCE | | ENGLAND | | GERMANY | |
|---|---|---|---|---|---|
| Philip I | 1060-1108 | Henry I | 1100 | Henry V | 1098 |
| Louis VI | 1108 | Stephen | 1135 | Lothair | 1125 |
| Louis VII | 1137 | Henry II | 1154 | Conrad III, the | |
| Philip | | Richard I | 1189-1199 | first Ghibelin | 1137 |
| Augustus | 1180-1223 | | | Frederick | |
| | | | | Barbarossa | 1152 |
| | | | | Henry VI | 1190-1197 |

Among the popes let us mention Hadrian IV (1154-1159), the only Englishman who has ever occupied the papal throne. His secular name had been Nicholas Breakspear. He was succeeded by Alexander III (1159-1181), an Italian, whose stay in France was so welcomed by Louis VII. On April 20, 1159, Hadrian gave the famous bull *Unigenitus* which either did or did not authorize Henry II to take possession of Ireland. Some say that it did not, and that it was altered by Henry to suit his purpose. Innocent III (1198-1216) brought the papacy to its highest level in the Middle Ages.

France and England, using the same language, were bound by such close ties in the twelfth century that we must consider their literature together. There was an unfailing supply of public singers, jongleurs of the higher type, who moved about in these two countries and who later carried their wares into Italy and Spain. Many of these minstrels were Celts who sang in French. They put into general circulation certain of their native legends; there was a constant flow of Celtic material moving from Ireland to Cornwall, from Cornwall to Wales or Brittany, and thence into the French vernacular. The monastery of Saint David's in Wales had direct communication with ten important Irish monasteries: Tallaght, Clonfertmulloe, Ferns, Cork, Tascoffin, Emily, Ardmore, Scattery Island, Timoleague, and Clonard. (Clark Slover in "Early Literary Channels between Ireland and Britain," *UTexSE*, 1927.) Perhaps some of this legendary material did not begin with Ireland but was native to Cornwall and other Celtic districts.

Society at this time must be considered very definitely in two groups: the clergy who used Latin, and the rest of the population who understood and spoke only French. Not all the clergy were ordained priests. The majority did not say Mass but were members of the learned professions and were in minor orders in the Church, as part of the international Latin-speaking world. They had a literature of their own, in Latin, which was immense and which has only begun to be properly estimated by our scholars of today. Very often the French literary forms were modelled upon the Latin, in which case we say they were aristocratic in origin. This Latin-speaking clergy was an aristocracy of letters, taking their material in turn from the ancients, although many of the individual clerics came from the peasant class. The vernacular public was subdivided into two groups, those who could read and those who could not. A large part of the wealthy middleclass men and of the nobles were able to read, and often their women had a similar education. It is likely that the reading public was increasing considerably at the close of the twelfth century. This is suggested by the increase in prose literature around 1200, for prose was not so well adapted for oral recitation. Those who could not read were dependent upon the minstrels who preferred to chant in verse.

In this history of ours we cannot neglect entirely the aristocratic models offered by the Latin-speaking society, but our chief concern will be with the vernacular. Often the jongleurs who composed in French were men of clerical training who knew and used the best Latin sources.

The cathedral towns were the main centers of learning in the twelfth century, such towns as Chartres, Orleans, Rheims, Laon, Canterbury, and Paris. The monasteries were becoming less influential as schools of letters. They had done their part in bridging the gap from the ninth to the eleventh century. The celebrated Abbey of Cluny and the Norman monastery of Bec still had great influence but their star had begun to set. The feudal courts of kings and nobles often had a following of Latin poets and scholars, and it was at such courts that Latin material first passed into the vernacular. Henry II of England had a personal retinue of men of letters, and his son, the Young King (d. 1183), also encouraged them. The court of the Norman kings in Sicily was a fertile field for Latin-speaking scholars and there they met with the learning of Greece and Arabia.

After the middle of the century the school at Chartres began to wane and Paris became increasingly prominent. The interest then turned away more from *belles lettres;* canon or Church law, theology, and dialectic were the chief subjects at Paris. Students came from all countries to follow this curriculum. The reputation of Louis VII for piety and paternal care was so great that fathers would send their sons to him with letters asking his personal solicitude in their sons' interests. Civil or Roman law was taught at Bologna and at Montpellier. The latter was also famed for its medical school which was in existence by 1159, and probably much earlier. It was second only to Salerno in Italy, near Naples. Elementary instruction was given by the family chaplain, sometimes in schools presided over by a young cleric. The trouvères and jongleurs had their schools where they learned new poems for recitation and where they studied reading and writing in the vulgar tongue. Leading schools of this nature were at Beauvais and at Rheims. These did more for the standardizing of Old French spelling and for the rules of composition than is usually credited to them.

What authors did the Latin speakers study and read in their schools? Their primers were the *Disticha Catonis,* the Fables of Avianus, the love elegies of Maximianus, a so-called eclogue of Theodulus, and the *Ilias latina.* The distichs of Cato, which taught moral precepts to the youth, were really composed in the third or fourth century A. D. and had nothing to do with the austere old Cato the Censor of the third and second centuries B. C. The eclogue of Theodulus was written by Godescalc of Fulda (805-869). The Latin Homer or *Ilias latina* is a condensation of the material in the Greek *Iliad,* made before 69 A. D. for school use. It has 1,070 hexameters. It retells the earlier books of the *Iliad* in sections of some hundred verses to each book, but the résumés of the later portions of Homer's great poem are occasionally reduced to three lines to a book.

Having digested this pabulum, the students were ready for a more varied program. The favorite poets were Vergil, Ovid, and Horace. They also read Persius, Lucan, Juvenal, Statius, and, very slightly, Lucretius and Martial. Among the prose writers they were fond of Sallust, Cicero, Caesar *(Civil Wars),* Seneca, Aulus Gellius (always called Agellius), and Valerius Maximus. Suetonius and Quintilian were not cited frequently. The learned men of this age were conscious of Greek. Even an occasional writer in the vernacular, such as Philippe de Thaün, could cite an odd Greek word or so, very much corrupted, but not one could read the language. A few MSS were brought as curiosities from Byzantium, notably to the Abbey of Saint-Denis by William of Gap (1167). The Greek writers that were available in fragmentary Latin translations were Plato, Aristotle, Hippocrates, Galen, Philo the Jew, and Josephus. Plato was known through the translation by Chalcidius of Cordova (fourth century) of one-half of the *Timaeus,* and through citations in Macrobius, Boethius, Apuleius, Saint Augustine, and Cicero. There may have been a translation of the *Timaeus* by Boethius if we can trust a solitary entry in a twelfth-century catalogue of the library at Bec. The versions of the *Meno* and the *Phaedo* made by Aristippus of Catania in 1156, or later, were not well known for some years. The school at Chartres was enthusiastic for Platonic doctrine.

The four Greek treatises ascribed to Dionysius the Areopagite—the Dionysius who was converted by Saint Paul at Athens (Acts 17:34)—were in reality compositions of a Christian auditor of Proclus, the neo-Platonist, and were written in the sixth century. These treatises were actively known in Latin translation throughout the Middle Ages and must have informed many clerics of certain neo-Platonist doctrines. Of Aristotle, the twelfth century had the *Old Logic (Categories* and *De interpretatione),* and the *New Logic (Prior* and *Posterior analytics, Topics, Elenchi).* These six treatises form the *Organon;* they were translated into Latin by Boethius. It was not till after 1159 that Aristotle began to be appreciated fully. Translators from the Arabic were flourishing in Barcelona, Tarazona, Segovia, Toulouse, Narbonne, Toledo, in the second quarter of the century. The greatest of all was Gerard of Cremona, whose work was done in Toledo. But the translations were mostly of philosophic and scientific works, such as Ptolemy's *Almagest,* Aristotle's *Physics* and *Metaphysics,* and the works of Avicenna and Averroës, and they did not spread far until the thirteenth century. Similarly, in Sicily and southern Italy translators were busy with work from the original Greek.

The Arabic Koran was translated, but it was read by very few. Most men of the twelfth century continued to think of the Saracens as worshipping a trinity of idols, Apollin, Mahom, and Tervagant. Peter the Venerable, Abbot of Cluny, appointed a commission of three Christians and one Arab to translate the Koran, a *Life of Mohammed,* and a certain dialogue on Mohammedanism. The work was executed after 1143 and Peter's purpose was to refute the doctrine.

In the list of Latin authors popular at this time, we have not included those who were read for scientific purposes. They were: for grammar and rhetoric, Macrobius, Victorinus, Donatus, Martianus Capella, Priscian, Phocas; for natural history and geography, Pliny the Elder and Solinus; for astronomy, Hyginus and Aratus; for architecture, Vitruvius; for agriculture, Palladius and Apuleius; and for military art, Vegetius and Frontinus.

We must not be deceived by this classical learning into the belief that the twelfth century was a humanistic era. The men of that day read their Cicero and their Vergil, but they did not do so in the sense of critical humanists. The medieval man was a modernist: he read the classics for the bearing they had upon life in his own day. The classics were authorities to be followed because it was a tradition that, save for Christianity, they taught the truth in a way not to be surpassed. The medieval man believed in the eternal values of Truth, whether it were in the matter of salvation for the soul, in ethics, or in the choice of a proper literary style. There was no temporizing, no relativity, no desire for approximation; he chose the best authority and followed it blindly. Nearly every one, in northern France at least, had as an ultimate object the salvation of his soul. An individual might be a gay dog in his youth, even a ravisher and a murderer, but his eye was ever cast in the direction of Truth—of the Church—for fear that old age or accident might catch him napping. This blind trust in authority of every kind is a basic medieval trait. There was no desire for experimentation or observation, and very little for speculation, save on those subjects which authority did not cover. With such an attitude experimental science could not exist, nor could history, as an exact science. To the individual of the twelfth century the past was a shadowy substance reflected in a mirror, with no concept of distance or complete outline. The observer might concentrate upon one such area that pleased him and chanced to win his attention, but he would further surround it with a cloud of mist of his own imagining. Just how many years Charlemagne lived, what he was really like, no one cared to know critically or exactly. So much for history. The contemporary world was full of surprises, even when one followed the authorities and the rules. The goddess Fortuna could turn her wheel at any time and, irrespective of merit, bring down the mighty or raise the humble on high. This pagan conception fluctuated with the more orthodox belief that virtue brought rewards on earth and that misfortune was a punishment from God. In view of this, mortal man was but a sport for supernatural forces, including the Divine, and it was needful to take a sporting view of things. The medieval man knew how to die and that is much of knowing how to live.

In seeking causes for the mental prosperity of the twelfth century we must not forget economic conditions. Since the First Crusade, Europeans were engaged in active commerce with Africa, Syria, and Byzantium, importing spices, incense, ivories, pearls, precious stones, silks, cotton, and such dye-stuffs as bresil, lakka gum, indigo, and alum. Between 1134 and 1154 the Normans in Sicily were in a fair way to organize a colonial empire in Algeria, Tunisia, and Tripolitana. The Genoese and Pisan fleets carried goods from Gibraltar to the Nile. The Venetians had a monopoly arranged with the ports of Alexandria and Cairo. Much of this wealth and commerce poured into France and England; it meant prosperity for the artisan, leisure for others, and time for many to travel or devote themselves to books. In order to bring crowds and prosperity to certain towns the kings appointed and regulated many fairs which lasted for a week or more and which were attended by merchants from distant regions. Notable among these fairs was the Endit, or Fair of St. Denis, founded in 1108; the Count of Champagne had another important one at Provins, a center for the wool trade.[1] At the fairs there were numerous jongleurs or entertainers who sang popular literature to the public.

## EDITIONS

*Dicta Catonis quae vulgo inscribuntur Catonis disticha de moribus,* ed. Geyza Nemethy (Budapest: *Sumptibus Academiae Litterarum Hungaricae,* 1895); also ed. F. Hauthol (Berlin, 1869).—*Homerus latinus,* ed. F. Vollmer (Leipzig: Teubner, 1913).—*Theoduli ecglogam etc.,* ed. J. Osternacher (Ripariae prope Lentiam, 1902).—*Elegies of Maximianus,* ed. R. Webster (Princeton, 1900); *Maximiniani Elegiae,* ed. M. Petschenig (Berlin, 1890).—*Platonis Timaeus interprete Chalcidio,* ed. J. Wrobel (Leipzig: Teubner, 1876).—The treatises of the pseudo-Dionysius the Areopagite, translated by John Scotus Erigena, are in Migne, *PL,* CXXII. A splendid study on John Scotus' knowledge of Greek and on the value and methods of his translation has been published by the Reverend Father P. G. Théry in *ALMA* VII (1931), 185-278.

[1] F. A. G. Cowper in *R Rev* XXII, 291-300.

# CHAPTER IV

## BIBLICAL TRANSLATIONS, SERMONS, LIVES OF THE SAINTS, AND OTHER ECCLESIASTICAL LEGENDS

Paul Lecoy, *La chaire française du moyen âge* (Paris, 1868).
L'Abbé L. Bourgain, *La chaire française au XII<sup>e</sup> siècle* (Paris, 1879).
Samuel Berger, *La Bible française au moyen âge* (Paris, 1884).
Jean Bonnard, *Les traductions de la Bible en vers français au moyen âge* (Paris, 1884).
Paul Meyer in the *Histoire littéraire de la France*, Vol. XXXIII [a valuable list of saints' lives].

France in the twelfth century was a seething cauldron of religious thought and activity. Among other questions, the doctrine of transubstantiation, clearly defined in 831 but not promulgated till 1215, was a matter for reflexion and argument. The same was true for compulsory auricular confession, which was not proclaimed till 1265. In the midst of this activity in thought, the pulpit was an instrument: bishops, monks, and hermits used it vigorously against the heretics, as well as for those souls already consecrated to the Faith. The heretics themselves were busy. Among them we must be careful to distinguish Peter Waldo, the merchant of Lyons, whose sect has continued in small numbers to the present day. Tachelme (d. 1123), Peter of Bruys (d. 1147), and Henry (d. 1148) were unscrupulous men who did little but stir the public momentarily. The Albigensian or Manichean heresy, which had sprung up in Arras and Orleans as early as 1023, was by this time centered around the town of Albi in Provence; it was a dark cloud on the horizon. It had made considerable headway in the South, and required the intervention of such a powerful preacher as St. Bernard of Clairvaux. The tide was too strong for him. There were more than three hundred *concilia,* or church councils, in the twelfth century for the correction of abuses. In spite of schisms and an antipope, the faithful were "enthousiastes de la foi."

Though the *concilium* of Toulouse (1129) pronounced against Bible translations, many fragmentary ones were made, in prose as well as in verse. The latter were necessarily paraphrases. The earliest of the verse translations is that of the *Song of Solomon,* dating in the neighborhood of 1100, or perhaps in the last years of the eleventh century. This enigmatical song was a fruitful source of commentary in the Middle Ages.

The paraphrase consists of thirty-one strophes of a rather peculiar structure: each strophe was formed by two verses in rhyme of ten syllables each and a third line of four syllables which makes neither rhyme nor assonance. The dialect cannot be stated with certainty.

At approximately the same date (1100) there was made a translation into prose of the psalms, now known as the *Oxford Psalter,* or the *Psalter of Montébourg.* This early Norman version enjoyed great popularity and it has been stated that it continued in use till the sixteenth century; further, that many of the hundred or more later versions of the psalms were mere rehandlings of this early translation. A few years later, still in the early twelfth century, another translation, written between the lines of a Latin *Psalter of St. Jerome,* was made at Canterbury. This is referred to as the *Cambridge Psalter.*

Other prose translations are fragments of the so-called Waldensian Bible, or translation of Peter Waldo, and above all there is the *Quatre livre des rois,* from the second half of the century. This last has survived complete. The original dialect was probably Norman. We do not have preserved any other extensive translation in prose until the complete translation of the *Macchabees* in the early thirteenth century. At that time (1220?) there was an effort to form an entire Bible in translation, supposedly for the use of Knights Templar and Hospitalers in the Holy Land. It consisted of:

a. An abridgement of the Pentateuch
b. Joshua
c. Judges
d. Kings
e. Judith
f. Esther
g. Job
h. Tobias
i. Ecclesiastes, or Le Sage
j. Macchabees
k. Ruth

Doubtless this was made up as far as possible from existing prose translations (see Berger, *op. cit.,* p. 101).

To return to the twelfth century, translations in verse were: the version of Genesis (*ca.* 20,000 octosyllables) by one Everatus, dedicated to Marie de Champagne in 1190; and the ambitious Old and New Testament of Herman of Valenciennes. This last was a meager summary composed at the end of the century. A metrical version of the forty-fourth psalm, the *Eructavit,* was written for Marie de Champagne in the last quarter of the century.

Sermons were delivered in Latin before monastic and clerical assemblages; in French before the laymen, since the Council of Tours (913). Unfortunately, nearly all the surviving sermons are mere Latin abstracts which were embellished by the preacher into Latin or French as the case required. Among the monastic preachers who have left sermons in this form are two Benedictines, Guibert de Nogent (d. 1124) and Pierre de Celle (d. 1183), also Abelard (d. 1142), the Cistercian Alain de Lille (d. 1202), Saint Bernard of Clairvaux, and Hugh of St. Victor (d. 1141). Among the secular clergy there are sermons by Saint Anselme (d. 1109), Bishop Marbod of Rennes (d. 1125), Bishop Hildebert of Mans (d. 1134), Peter Lombard (d. 1160), and Maurice de Sully, Bishop of Paris (d. 1196). Several of these men were celebrated for other forms of writing. Beside the surviving Latin abstracts of Bishop Maurice de Sully, which were intended as time savers or a manual of homiletics for the clergy of his diocese, we possess some French elaborations of these same sermons, doubtless the work of other preachers who were using the manual. In addition, there are extant French versions of some forty-five sermons of St. Bernard of Clairvaux. These begin at the Advent season and stop with the Annunciation. The French sermons of St. Bernard are preserved in a thirteenth-century MS (BN fr. 24768).

Further, there exist some rhymed sermons in French for the "simple gent." There is no reason for suspecting that these were not delivered from the pulpit. Even in Latin sermons of the time we occasionally find interspersed specimens of rhymed prose. This was to touch the hearts and flatter the ears simultaneously. Here is the beginning of a Latin sermon on the Assumption of the Blessed Virgin, by Saint Anselm:

> In illo tempore Maria stabat ad monumentum foris, plorans.
> Audivimus, fratres, Mariam ad monumentum foris stantem,
> audivimus Maris foris plorantem:
> Videamus, si possumus, cur staret,
> videamus et cur ploraret.
> Prosit nobis illius illam stare,
> prosit nobis illius illam plorare, etc.[1]

One of the French rhymed sermons is the Norman *Grant mal fist Adam*, which dates from the beginning of the twelfth century. It is in stanzas, with six five-syllable lines each. The rhymes are *aabccb*. This somewhat unusual versification was certainly intended to facilitate memorizing. The author is unknown. A similar sermon in the vernacular, also by an unknown author, is the Anglo-Norman *Deu le omnipotent*. It is some years later than the other; its verse scheme is similar. A sermon of 1923 verses was composed by Guischart de Beaulieu (Hampshire) towards the close of the century. This priest knew the *Grant mal fist Adam* and his subject was identical: the inheritance bequeathed to man by Adam and Noah. Guischart also knew some form of a dialogue between body and soul and the *Life of Saint Alexis*.

[1] Bourgain, *op. cit.*, p. 373.

The saints' lives and legends of the Virgin form a rich collection at this time, both in Latin and in French. We shall discuss only those written in the vernacular. One of the most important is the *Voyage of Saint Brandan*. Saint Brandan was an Irish saint of the sixth century and there is a Latin narrative, the *Navigatio Sancti Brendani* (ninth century), on which the French version is dependent. The Latin voyage, in turn, goes back to Irish tradition. We possess an Irish *Echtra Brain maic Febail* which is nearer still to the source. The French poem was composed by a certain monk named Benedict for the second queen of Henry I of England, Aaliz de Louvain. It is consequently posterior to 1121, the date of her royal marriage. The versification is unique: it is in strophic form, each strophe containing two rhymed couplets, the masculine lines possessing eight syllables but the feminine only seven (plus the final mute *e*)! In brief, the feminine *e* is counted as a syllable. The theme is the voyage of Brandan to the Island of the Blessed. He and his companions see sheep as big as stags; they mistake a giant fish for an island; they behold the birds' paradise; they see a battle between two monster fishes, and another waged by a dragon and a griffin. They behold Judas Iscariot and others on a rock in the ocean. At last they reach the earthly Paradise. This legend is obviously a Celtic *immram,* a type in which the hero sails about on a difficult quest, meeting with many adventures. But the Celts themselves were tireless borrowers from classical tradition. The *immrama* were perhaps inspired by the *Quest of the Golden Fleece,* by Books III, IV, and V of the *Aeneid,* and by similar classical voyages. It is a question whether the Irish knew Oriental traditions, notably the Sindibad story.

There are two versions of a *Life of Saint Gregory* extant today, and both were remade in the thirteenth century from an original of the early twelfth. It was Mario Roques who demonstrated that the eight-syllable rhymed couplets of these later poems were a making over of an earlier life in monorhymed stanzas (*Rom* XLVIII, 41-61), a verse scheme that was particularly popular in the first half of the twelfth century. The Saint Gregory in question is a legendary character who cannot be identified among the popes. The story is a folk theme (Mt. 933, *FFC,* 74) of Oriental, possibly Byzantine, source. The child Gregory is the son of a brother and a sister. He is reared far from his parents with no knowledge of his incestuous birth. He is knighted and, after a successful combat, marries his mother. This is the Oedipus motif. On the discovery of his crime he spends seventeen years of penitential solitude on a rock in the sea. "The sins of the fathers are visited upon the children unto the third and fourth generations." At the close of this penance a divine voice proclaims him pope. Hartmann von Aue, the Middle High German poet, based his *Gregorjus* (1190-1200) upon another French version of this legend which is not extant.

Wace, a professional poet among the clergy, of whom more will be said, composed a number of hagiographic accounts, probably between 1140 and 1150. Of these there have survived a *Life of Saint Nicholas*, a *Conception Nostre Dame*, and fragments, known as the Tours fragments, of a *Life of Saint Marguerite*. It is suggested that a *Life of Saint George*, which we have, was also by him; there is little proof of this. The *Conception* appears to have been propaganda for the establishment of the Feast of the Immaculate Conception in Normandy, a feast which was definitely authorized in 1145. This poem begins with a life account of the Virgin and then narrates how Abbot Helsin of Ramese was told by an angel to urge the establishment of the Feast for the eighth day of December. The poem has some 1,800 verses. The sources were a *Miraculum de conceptione Sanctae Mariae* attributed to Anselm, a *Liber de transitu Sanctae Mariae* of one Meliton, and certain of the Apocrypha. Wace's *Life of Saint Nicholas*, preserved in five MSS, has 1,491 lines. It would appear to have been very popular. It was based upon the *Laudatio Sancti Nicolai* of Methodius (ninth century) and upon another account by John the Deacon. Saint Nicholas was a bishop of Myra who died December 6, 347. His bones were stolen and removed to Bari, in southeastern Italy, in 1087, where his shrine has always been a favored spot for pilgrims. The Tours fragments of a *Life of Saint Marguerite* are concerned with one of the best known patron saints of women. Saint Marguerite of Alexandria was beheaded on July 20, in the third century.

Herman de Valenciennes, whom we have mentioned for his rhymed Bible, composed an *Assomption Nostre Dame* in monorhymed alexandrine *laisses*, at the close of the century.

Marie de France, whose chief fame depends upon writings of a different sort, wrote an *Espurgatoire Saint Patriz* (1190). This is one of seven versions, by seven different Old French poets, which are based upon the Latin *De purgatorio Sancti Patricii* of Henry of Salisbury, which itself was written only a short time before 1190. These voyages of a living man to Purgatory or Hell, one of the most active legends in literature, may have begun with the apocryphal *Apocalypse of Saint Paul*. Consult G. P. Krapp, *The Legend of Saint Patrick's Purgatory; its later Literary History* (Baltimore, 1900). The legend was removed from the Roman Missal in 1522-1524. Marie's poem is in eight-syllable rhymed couplets.

An important biography of a twelfth-century saint is the *Life of Saint Thomas Becket* by Guernes (or Garnier) de Pont-Sainte-Maxence. This poem of 6,180 lines was composed between 1172 and 1174; the sources were oral tradition of those present at the events, and the Latin biographies of Becket by Edward Grim (1172), William of Canterbury (1173-4), and perhaps that of Benedict of Canterbury (1173 or 1174). Guernes tells us that immediately after the murder of Thomas Becket, on December 29, 1170, he began a biography with which he was not satisfied. He hastened to Canterbury and composed the life which we now have. The verse form is strophic with monorhymed alexandrine strophes of five lines each. Guernes was perhaps a *clericus vagans* who peddled his literary wares for a livelihood. An analysis of the *Life* is as follows:

Thomas Becket, chancellor of Henry II of England, was elected Archbishop of Canterbury (on June 3, 1162). Conflict with Henry over the liberties of the Church in England began almost immediately. After the Constitutions of Clarendon (1164), Archbishop Thomas was forced to take refuge in France. He was loyally supported by Louis VII, who did all in his power to reconcile his guest with the English king. The inevitable result was intermittent warfare between France and England. On July 22, 1170, peace was at length declared between King and Archbishop; but Thomas was scarcely reinstated at Canterbury (December, 1170) when the final tragedy fell. Henry, in residence near Bayeux, troubled by reports against the Archbishop, cried out "Li duels m'en vait al cuer, nuls ne m'en a vengié (v. 5035)." Certain of his knights embarked soon thereafter and Thomas was slain in his cathedral on December 29. Edward Grim stood by and did his best to prevent the tragedy. The furor which arose needs no description. Becket was canonized (1173) and the English king's power received a shock from which it did not recover completely. His public humiliation and his pilgrimage to the tomb (1174) are described very briefly by Guernes, perhaps as an addition.

Towards the close of the century, Guillaume de Berneville made a free translation of a Latin *Vita S. Egidii;* namely, his *Vie Saint Gilles* (3,794 verses). Simund de Freine, a canon of Hereford and a friend of Giraldus Cambrensis, adapted a *Vie Saint Georges* from the Latin, in 1,711 lines, naming himself in an acrostic. Adam de Ross was responsible for a *Vision Saint Paul* (427 verses) and the nun Clemence of Barking wrote, around 1160, a celebrated life of Catherine of Alexandria, in 2,688 verses. All of these poets were Anglo-Normans, writing in England. The *Life of Saint Edmund, King of East Anglia,* by Denis Piramus, is especially well-known today because its author mentions the fame of Marie de France (vss. 35-65). As Haxo (*MPhil,* XII, 345, 559) has shown, fairly conclusively, this Denis was a continental Frenchman, from Maine(?), who was a monk at Bury St. Edmund's. He is named four times in Jocelin's *Chronicles:* for the years 1176, 1182, 1191, and 1200. He was probably dead by 1214. This *Life* was written in 1170-

1180, in 4,032 octosyllables. Another work with similar theme is an Anglo-Norman *Passiun de seint Edmund* (424 four-line stanzas), composed early in the second half of the twelfth century.

Not so easy to date are certain vernacular pious tales which can be placed equally well in the late twelfth or in the early thirteenth century. We refer to a *Life of Saint-Laurent* (950 verses), which is Anglo-Norman, to a life of the Irish Saint Modwenna (8,000 verses), and to a *Life of Sainte-Geneviève*, by Renaud. There is a *Life of Saint-Remi* by Richier and a *Life of Sainte-Euphrosine*, which are presumably twelfth-century. A poet named Rogier composed a *Vie de Saint-Julian* (4,860 octosyllables) which we also place here, with some hesitation as to date. There is a group of four fragmentary poems: a *History of Jesus and Mary*, a *Passion*, a *Descent of Jesus into Hell*, and the *Pénitence d'Adam* (consult P. Meyer in *Rom, XVI*, 253) which occur together in order and which are adaptations from the apocryphal *Evangelium Nicodemi*. A *Life of Mary of Egypt* (1,534 octosyllables), and a *Life of Saint Thaïs* (*ca.* 320 verses) belong to the close of the twelfth century. The Thaïs poem was inserted later into the *Poème moral* (vss. 107-426), a moral satire composed at Liége.

Of considerable importance is the Placidus-Eustachius legend which goes back ultimately to an Oriental Buddhist theme (Mt. 938, *FFC*, 74). It is found in a Greek version as early as the eighth century; it was adapted into Latin by the tenth century.[2] In the Old French language we find eleven poems and thirteen prose narratives inspired by this legend, most of them dating from the thirteenth century. It is not unlikely that one version, preserved in B. N. MS. 1374, belongs to the late twelfth century. This particular poem consists of 393 four-line strophes in decasyllables. Its chief source is a Latin account now found in the *Acta Sanctorum* for September 6. The plot of the legend is worthy of our attention. Placidus a virtuous pagan, is commander of the horse, under Trajan. While hunting, he becomes separated from his companions in the pursuit of a stag. The stag climbs to a high rock, a cross appears between its horns, and it speaks with the voice of the Lord, urging Placidus to be baptized. Placidus does so and is renamed Eustachius; his wife and two sons also receive the sacrament. Christ, still in the form of the deer, offers Eustachius his choice; to be tried as was Job, immediately or later. Present suffering is more acceptable to the new convert. Soon thereafter his servants die, his beasts and cattle perish, and his house is robbed. The family leaves for Egypt to avoid the emperor's displeasure. The sea-captain is a barbarian. He hurls Eustachius and his sons overboard but retains the wife. They win to shore, but later a lion carries off one

[2] Cf. *Nuovi studi medievali*, III, 223-258.

son, a wolf the other. Eustachius becomes domiciled in the town of Dadissus. His wife will not yield to the captain and so she is taken to the barbarian's land. The king of these barbarians makes war on Trajan, many years later. The emperor sends messengers to seek his old master of the horse. Eustachius is found and his two sons, who had been rescued by peasants, serve him, unknown to all, as military aids. The barbarian king is defeated, Eustachius recovers his wife by chance and recognizes his sons. When all return to Rome, Trajan is angry because the reunited family will not sacrifice to the pagan gods. They are thrown to the lions who will not hurt them. They are then encased in an idol of heated metal. God preserves their bodies from the flames but causes them to die. They are buried in odor of sanctity. Note the resemblance to the theme of *Apollonius of Tyre*.

William of Malmesbury was the author of the Latin *Miracula Dei genetricis*, a series of miracles performed by the Blessed Virgin. This collection was made by him, from various sources, in the first half of the twelfth century. A clerk named Albri used William of Malmesbury as source for another Latin collection and this book by Albri came into the library of Saint Paul's at London. There it was utilized, along with the original of William, by master Adgar, who turned portions of both into French. For detail on Adgar's sources, and on Virgin miracles in general, consult A. Mussafia in his *Studien zu den mittelalterlichen Marienlegenden* (Vienna, 1886-1889). The extant MSS. of Adgar's French collection are fragmentary; one contains forty miracles, another twenty-two, and the third, the Dulwich fragment, is very small indeed. The four most venerable of the legends which occur in these collections are the tales of the *petit juitel*, the story of Theophilus, the tale of the pregnant woman rescued from the sea, and the narrative of the death of Julian the Apostate. These are often called the element miracles, because the Virgin appears there in or on the four elements: fire, air, water, and earth, respectively.

## EDITIONS

*Libri psalmorum versio antiqua gallica* [Oxford or Montébourg Psalter], ed. F. Michel (Oxford, 1860).—*Livre des psaumes . . . d'après les manuscrits de Cambridge . . .* , ed. F. Michel (Paris, 1876).—Waldensian Bible, ed. Salvioni in *Archivio glottologico italiano*, XI.—*Li quatre livre des reis*, ed. R. Curtius (Halle: GrL, 1911).—*Eructavit*, ed. T. A. Jenkins (Halle: GrL, 1909). —Herman de Valenciennes, *Passion (extrait de la Bible)*, ed. P. Meyer in *Bull. SATF*, XV, 83 ff.—*Reimpredigt*, ed. H. Suchier (Halle: Niemeyer, 1879).—*Voyage of St. Brendan, by Benedeit*, ed. E. G. R. Waters (Oxford Press, 1928).—*Vie du Pape Saint-Grégoire le Grand*, ed. Luzarche (Tours: Bouserez, 1857).—Wace, *Life of Saint Nicholas*, ed. M. S. Crawford (Philadelphia: UPSR, 1923); *La vie de Sainte-Marguerite*, ed. A. Joly (Paris, 1879);

*La conception*, ed. V. Luzarche in *La vie de la vierge Marie* (Tours, 1859); ed. W. Ray Ashford (University of Chicago Press, 1933).—Marie de France, *Espurgatoire Saint Patriz*, ed. T. A. Jenkins in the University of Chicago Dicennial Publications (University of Chicago Press, 1904); also ed. K. Warnke (Halle, 1936).—Guernes de Pont-Sainte-Maxence, *La vie de saint Thomas le martyr*, ed. Walberg (Lund: *Acts of the Royal Society of Letters*, 1922); also in *Cfmâ*, 1936. For further editions and bibliography consult Walberg in *La tradition hagiographique de saint Thomas Becket* (Paris, 1929).—Guillaume de Berneville, *Vie Saint Gilles*, ed. G. Paris-A Bos (Paris: *SATF*, 1881). —Simund de Freine, *Oeuvres*, ed. J. E. Matzke (Paris, *SATF*, 1909).—Adam de Ross, *Vision saint Paul*, ed. Kastner in *ZfrSL*, XXIX, 274.—Clemence of Barking, *Catherine of Alexandria*, ed. Jarnik in *Due verse starofrancouske legende o sv. Katerine alexandrinske* (Prague, 1894).—Denis Piramus, *La vie seint Edmund le rei*, ed. F. L. Ravenel in *Bryn Mawr College Monographs* (1906); also ed. Hilding Kjellman (Göteborg, 1935).—*Vie de Saint-Laurent*, ed. Söderhjelm (Paris, 1888).—*Life of St. Modwenna—An episode*, by A. T. Baker in *A Miscellany of Studies in Romance Language and Literature.*—An edition of the *Vie Sainte-Geneviève* is in preparation.—*Vie Sainte-Euphrosine*, ed. R. T. Hill in *RRev* X, XII.—*Vie de Sainte-Marie l'Egyptienne*, ed. A. T. Baker in *Rlr* LIX.—The *Life of Thaïs* is included in the *Poème moral;* q.v.— *Das altfranzösische Eustachiusleben*, ed. C. Ott in *RFor* XXXII, 481 ff.— *Adgars Marienlegenden*, ed. C. Neuhaus (Heilbronn: *AfrB*, 1886). Three of Adgar's miracles are rendered very charmingly into modern French by the late Mme Lot-Borodine in her *Vingt miracles de Notre-Dame* (Paris, 1929).—*Li sermon Saint Bernard*, ed. W. Foerster (Erlangen: Deichert, 1885); *Predigten des h. Bernhard in altfranzösischer Uebertragung*, ed. A. Schulze (Tübingen, 1894).—The *Cantique des cantiques* is published diplomatically in the Foerster-Koschwitz *Uebungsbuch;* q. v.; see also G. Paris in *Rom* XV, 448 ff.—Rogier, *Vie de Saint-Julian*, ed. Tobler in Herrig's *Archiv*, CI, CII.—There is a notable need for editions of Everatus and of Herman of Valenciennes.—*Poème moral*, ed. A. Bayot (Bruxelles, 1929). New editions are in preparation of the lives of St. Modwenna, St. Catherine, and St. Margaret, of the *Passiun de seint Edmund*, and of the Oxford and Cambridge *Psalters* for the Anglo-Norman Text Society.

# CHAPTER V

## ORIGINS OF THE DRAMA

Karl Young, *The Drama of the Medieval Church* (Oxford Press, 1933), 2 vols.
W. Creizenach, *Geschichte des neueren Dramas* (3rd ed.; Halle, 1920), Vol. I.
E. K. Chambers, *The Mediaeval Stage* (Oxford, 1903, 2 vols.).
G. Cohen, *Le théâtre en France au moyen âge,* Vol. I, *Le théâtre religieux* (Paris: Rieder, 1928).
G. Cohen, *Histoire de la mise en scène dans le théâtre religieux français du moyen âge* (2nd ed.; Paris: Champion, 1926).
L. Petit de Julleville, *Les mystères* (Paris: Hachette, 1880, 2 vols.).
Marius Sepet, *Les origines catholiques du théâtre moderne* (Paris, 1901).
C. Lange, *Die lateinischen Osterfeiern* (München: Stahl, 1887).
Léon Gautier, *Histoire de la poésie liturgique en France au moyen âge: Les tropes* (Paris: Palme, 1886).

Greek tragedy and comedy, which were introduced into Rome by Livius Andronicus in 240 B.C., never enjoyed there a great popularity. They were artificial in their new environment. They satisfied certain religious needs and ideals among the Greeks which did not exist with the Romans. The Latin citizens preferred spectacles of grandeur, displays of wild beasts and gladiatorial combats, which became more and more frequent during the first century B.C. The year 45 B.C. is often cited as the last recorded date of a tragedy performance at Rome. Seneca's tragedies, written in the first century A. D., were widely read but were presumably not produced. Comedy, on the other hand, did not disappear quite so quickly; plays of this sort were given during the first centuries of the Empire, but they, too, were forced to yield, eventually, before mythological spectacles and combats. The early Christian Fathers gave a *coup de grâce* to an already ailing victim. Terence and Plautus continued to be read, but they were understood as non-dramatic poems. (Such an authority as Gustave Cohen disputes this assertion, that the dramatic nature of Latin comedies was misunderstood during the Middle Ages.) Perhaps there were a few enlightened readers, but many doubtless agreed with the twelfth-century Honorius (d'Autun ?) who defined tragedy as a poem treating of wars, in the manner of Lucan; comedy as a nuptial song, in the manner of Terence; satire as a corrective poem, and the lyric as a eulogy of the gods or of kings (Migne, *PL,* CLXXII).

But the dramatic instinct still remained with the people and the Church was the chief group to utilize this. The very Mass itself was a memorial couched in dramatic form, recalling vividly the Sacrifice of Our Lord; later it was realized to be no memorial at all but the Sacrifice itself, by the doctrine of Transubstantiation. The priests in the medieval era often heightened the effects of their sermons by delivering them in dialogue form. The Gospels in the offices or services were sometimes read on festal occasions, by two or more priests, each reading a special rôle in the dialogue. This custom is retained today among certain of the religious orders. The dialogued or dramatized form was, and has always remained, one of the vivid means of instruction. The reader must understand that, at the outset, these clerics were not conscious of such a formulated thing as drama. They were merely using devices which rendered the Mass, the Gospels, and their sermons, more living to a non-reading public.

During the early centuries of the Church unauthorized tropes, or liturgical hymns, came to be inserted into the Mass. On special occasions a trope, which either summarized the contents of the Psalter for that day or which gave additional coloring to the festal office, would begin the service. The dialogue form was used here. The trope would be sung antiphonally by two groups of singers. Doubtless as a result of the reform, of the liturgy, which began in the eighth century and which was confirmed, in France, by Charlemagne, such antiphonal tropes were transferred to Matins. Here it was possible for special persons to be assigned parts in the dialogue. This final transition from the trope to a dramatic form was first accomplished in monastic churches, and it is not improbable that it was first made at the Monastery of Saint Gall in the early tenth century. This religious house was distinguished, among other things, for its choir school. Apparently it was the Easter Sunday trope which first lent itself to drama. The simplest form of this trope is found in a MS. of Saint Gall, No. 484, fol. 4:

> Quem quaeritis in sepulchro, Christicolae?
> Iesum Nazarenum crucifixum, o caelicolae.
> Non est hic, surrexit de sepulchro.
> Ite, nuntiate quia surrexit de sepulchro.
>                    Resurrexi, etc.

It is probable that this dialogue was first sung antiphonally and then came to be chanted by two priests with no attempt at actual impersonation. Today we possess forty-odd examples of this undramatized dialogue, some of them a few lines longer, but all similar. But when this Easter dialogue was transferred to Easter Matins, in a position immediately before the *Te Deum*, after the third responsory, it was elaborated further and given a genuine dramatic setting. The religious drama of the

Middle Ages was then created! In this enlarged dramatic form we call
our dialogue the *Visitatio sepulchri,* or Easter Play. There are four hundred and sixteen texts of this *Visitatio,* as opposed to the forty-odd examples of the simple Easter trope, which have been preserved. The
*Visitatio* was carried to the Holy Land quite early and produced each
year at the Manger, a fact which led Joseph Klapper to insist that it originated there between 500 and 750 *A.D.* Karl Young corrected this (*Spec*
I, 71-86).

This explanation of the origins of the medieval religious drama within
the Church liturgy was suggested and elaborated by such men as Heinrich Hoffmann, F. J. Mone, Milchsack, Marius Sepet, and particularly by
C. Lange and Karl Young (*PMLA* XXIX, 1-58). Jacob Grimm believed that it began with heathen folk plays at the summer, winter, and
sword dance festivals, a supposition that is not devoid of interest in the
history of medieval comedy, but which can hardly be related to the medieval religious theater. Oscar Cargill (*Drama and Liturgy,* New York,
1930) has again sought to trace the religious drama to secular minstrels,
but he has been well answered by G. R. Coffman in a most informative
review (*Spec* VI, 610-617). Attention should also be given to Coffman's
suggestion that there is need for more study of the early drama in the
light of cultural environment (*MPhil* XII, 239-271).

The *Concordia regularis* of Bishop Ethelwold of Winchester, drawn
up in the reign of Edgar (959-979), tells of the dramatic action which
was used. A priest, vested in an alb, stood by the "sepulchre," or representation of Christ's tomb, with a palm in hand. Three priests, also in
vestments with amices and copes, drew near with thuribles of incense,
representing the Three Marys: the Virgin, Mary Magdalene, and Mary
Salome. The angel chanted the first line of the *Quem quaeritis* dialogue
and the three Marys the second. The angel replied with the final two
lines. Then the Marys turned to the choir and sang *Alleluia! resurrexit
Dominus!,* followed by one Mary alone who sang the anthem *Venite et
videte locum,* showing the empty cloths in the sepulchre to the others.
Then all sang the anthem *Surrexit Dominus de sepulchro* and laid the
cloths upon the altar.

We must say something of the device that was used for a sepulchre.
It was often an altar in a side chapel with something laid upon it that
could be opened and shown to be empty. Gradually it became the custom to construct a permanent tomb with a hollow top that could be
opened and viewed. This was placed in the northern transept of the
nave; sometimes it was in a special chamber. In the eleventh century there
was added to the *Visitatio* a scene in which the apostles Peter and John
race to the grave, after hearing the announcement made by the three

Marys. John reaches the tomb first but Peter enters the tomb and shows the cloths to the others. By the twelfth century another occasional addition was the scene of Christ appearing as a *hortulanus,* or gardener, to Mary Magdalene, when he says *Noli me tangere.* A secular or profane element which also came to be added later was the merchant scene in which the three Marys stop on their way to the tomb and buy ointment from a merchant. This has no scriptural basis and was intended to be somewhat humorous. The Easter play, in some form or other, survived well into the sixteenth century.

By the eleventh century there was devised a similar dramatized trope for the third Christmas mass, transferred to the Matins *after* the *Te Deum.* This is referred to as the *Pastores* and it was performed at the *crèche,* or *praesepes,* the representation of the manger. The Church Sta. Maria Maggiore at Rome had a permanent *praesepes* since the eighth century, and the custom of constructing a temporary one every Christmas soon spread. This *Pastores* drama never achieved great popularity, but it must have given rise to the *Stella* by the close of the eleventh century. The *Stella* was a trope of the three Magi, or Wise Men, for Epiphany Sunday, and it enjoyed great vogue. I have seen a dramatized *Stella* performed today in the Episcopal Church service at the negro College of Saint Augustine, in Raleigh, N. C. It was instituted there by the Rev. Dr. Hunter some forty years ago, in imitation of the custom still preserved in Italy. A *Rachel,* representing the Massacre of the Innocents, was rarely added to the *Stella;* by the twelfth century the *Quem quaeritis* was also the suggestion for another drama, the *Peregrini,* or procession to Emmaus with the supper eaten there. The *Passion* is not found in dramatized version until 1200 at Siena, Italy (Grace Frank in *PMLA* XXVIII, 464-483).

The two patron saints of the student clerics were Saint Nicholas and Saint Catherine of Alexandria. There were over two thousand centers of the Saint Nicholas cult—mostly in Germany and in France—with four hundred and thirty-seven in England. A great impetus to this interest in Saint Nicholas was given by the transfer of his relics to Bari in 1087. Once the custom of the dramatized trope had become established, it was not long in the eleventh century before dramatized legends of that Saint were performed on his feast-day, December sixth. These were drawn from earlier Latin and Greek accounts, but the ultimate source is impossible to trace. Perhaps Saint Nicholas was associated in early times with vegetation and even Poseidon myths. There are four of these legends which were popular in the Middle Ages, the *Tres filiae,* the *Tres clerici,* the *Iconia Sancti Nicholai,* and, much less so, the *Filius Getronis.* In the first of these the Saint saves three dowerless daughters from a life

of shame by pitching a bag of gold down the chimney, on three successiv
nights. There is a twelfth-century baptismal fount in Winchester Cathe
dral with scenes carved from this legend. In the *Tres clerici* three stu
dents are resurrected who have been slain by a murderous innkeepe
and hurled in small pieces into a salting vat. The third we shall tell be
low in more detail: the image of Saint Nicholas protects treasure anc
forces thieves to return what they have stolen. In the fourth legend th
Saint whisks away a stolen boy, before the eyes of his captor, and re
stores him to his home. The reader will have no difficulty in recognizing
in the *Tres filiae* the origin of the Santa Claus myth. The German anc
Dutch children still place their shoes in the chimney place to catch th
candy that Saint Nicholas will throw down the chimney on Decembe
5th.

In British Museum Add. MS 22414, known as the Hildesheim MS
there are versions of the *Tres filiae* and *Tres clerici* in Latin, from th
eleventh century. A fragmentary version of the *Tres clerici*, also in Latin
is found in Einsiedeln, Stiftsbibl. MS 34. An interesting MS for th
Latin liturgical drama is in the public library at Orleans, MS 201, th
so-called Fleury manuscript. It contains Latin versions of all four of th
above mentioned legends. This manuscript as well as the entire subject o
Saint Nicholas in the liturgical drama, has been studied most compre
hensively by Otto E. Albrecht (*Four Latin Plays of St. Nicholas*, Phila
delphia: *UPSR*, 1935).

The twelfth century saw a Christmas dramatization of the pseudo
Saint Augustine's *Sermo contra Iudaeos, Paganos, et Arianos, de symbol*
which could not have been composed before the sixth century. This ser
mon was read as a lesson at Matins, either on Christmas day or imme
diately preceding. *Vos, inquam, convenio, O Iudaei*, says the reader anc
the Jewish prophets from Isaiah to John the Baptist then appear one by
one and give their testimony for Christ. This drama is commonly re
ferred to as the *Prophetae*.[1] In some of the dramatized versions the epi
sode of Balaam and his ass is added at the close. This does not appear in
the Latin sermon; E. K. Chambers thinks it was added as an apolog
for the appearance of an ass in church during the *Fête des Fous*. Thi
last was one of the four frolics allowed the minor clergy on the feast
just following Christmas. The *tripudia*, as these frolics were called, fel
upon Saint Stephen's day (for the deacons), Saint John the Evangelist'
(for the priests), Holy Innocents' (for the choir-boys), and upon th
Feast of the Circumcision (for the sub-deacons). The last occasion bor
the name *Fête des Fous*; it is first mentioned at the close of the twelft

---

[1] See Karl Young, *Ordo prophetarum* (*Trans. Wisconsin Acad. Sci., Arts, Lett.*, vol
XXVI, 1921).

century by Joannes Belethus of Paris. The first three *tripudia* are attested for the Monastery of Saint Gall as early as 911. A number of excesses, such as the burning of sausages and meat puddings instead of incense, the bringing of a braying ass into the church, etc., were indulged in, against the protests of the higher clergy.

At the end of the first quarter of the twelfth century, Hilarius, an Englishman (?) and a former pupil of Abelard at Nogent-sur-Seine, composed three plays, which it is assumed were written for the repertory of a band of wandering clerics which Hilarius had either organized or joined. These were a Saint Nicholas play, a *Suscitatio Lazari,* and the story of Daniel. The miracle of Saint Nicholas which is here dramatized is the *Iconia Sancti Nicholai.* The *Suscitatio* was appropriate for Easter Week; the *Daniel* would be an extension of the *Prophetae* drama and was doubtless performed at Christmastide. Hilarius was also the author of some Latin lyric verse, of an amorous and jesting nature, which is a good indication that he was a professional minstrel devoted to the clerical, or Latin-speaking public.

The Saint Nicholas play and the *Suscitatio Lazari* of Hilarius have refrains in French. It is not the first time that we note a tendency to "stuff in," or *farcir,* vernacular lines into the Latin service of the Church. We have observed the *Eulalia* sequence; mention must also be made of an epistle used on the Feast of Saint Stephen (December 26), of which we have a version preserved from the early twelfth century, where each Latin verse of the epistle is followed by one or more strophes in French, giving a free translation. The French verses are in ten-syllable meter. This practice was not at all uncommon for the epistle on feast days; we have preserved from a later date the same type of *épître farcie* for Saint John's day, the Epiphany, and the Feast of the Holy Innocents. The few lines of vernacular which were inserted made it possible to hold the attention of the laity, even when they were nothing but a refrain. This gradual introduction of French into the Latin liturgy is considered the beginning of a transition to liturgical drama wholly in the vernacular.

From the first half of the century we have a drama of the coming of the bridegroom, the *Sponsus.*[2] It is a step farther on our road than the pieces of Hilarius, for, in addition to French refrains, some of the speeches are wholly in that language. The dialogue is based upon Matthew 25:1-12. The bridegroom speaks first in ten Latin verses, announcing his coming. Then the prudent virgins speak, in four French strophes of three rhymed verses each, with a two-line refrain. Their speech is an elaboration and paraphrase of what the bridegroom has just said. The

---

[2] The student should consult the study of the *Sponsus* by L. F. Thomas in *Rom* LIII, 43 ff.; LV, 45 ff.; and especially that of Franz Rauhut in *RFor* L, 21-50.

foolish virgins appear and beg for oil, in three monorhymed Latin strophes
of four lines each, plus a French refrain (*Dolentas! Chaitivas! Trop i
avem dormit!*). The *Prudentes,* or prudent virgins, speak again, this
time in Latin, in the same verse scheme, and with the same refrain that
the foolish virgins have used. The *prudentes* refuse oil and urge their less
fortunate sisters to go and buy. Once more the *fatuae,* or foolish virgins,
ask for oil, also in Latin with French refrain. The wise maidens now
give the same advice as before, but in French. Merchants speak up in
French and refuse to sell. The *fatuae* lament in two Latin strophes;
Christ comes and rebukes them in two lines of Latin, and sends them
to eternal fires with three lines of French. The final stage direction is
*Modo accipiant et praecipitantur in infernum eas daemones.* There are
forty-eight Latin verses and forty-six French, so the division between languages is nearly half and half. The French is of the dialect of Angoumois,
on the Provençal-speaking border. It is necessary to explain the manner of this mixture of Latin and French. Probably the audience was
composed of both clerics and laymen. It is not probable that this play
was performed on some special day; it is more likely that it was suitable for any time in the Christian calendar. It is interesting to note that
it was performed, with the original music, in Brussels on November 21,
1924, in a church.

Gustave Cohen discovered, more than fifteen years ago, two nativity
plays in the Walloon dialect, with no Latin (*Mystères et moralités
du manuscrit 617 de Chantilly,* Paris: Champion, 1920). He dates these
as belonging to the twelfth century, although the proofs are not absolutely certain. They are very naïve in content and form.

There are but two remaining dramas in French which date from
the twelfth century. They are the *Jeu d'Adam* and the *Jeu de Saint-
Nicholas.* The *Jus* or *Jeu d'Adam* was probably written about 1150-1160,
in Normandy. It is an elaboration of the Christmas *Prophetae* type which
has been mentioned above. Though composed in Normandy, the play
survives in an Anglo-Norman MS. There are three divisions: first, the
story of Adam and Eve—the Fall of Man (in 600 verses); then, the murder of Abel by Cain (600 verses); and lastly, the *Prophetae* proper, the
procession of the prophets, one by one, from Abraham to Nebuchadnezzar
(*sic*), announcing their message of the Messiah (200 verses). This procession must have continued as far as John the Baptist; so we assume
that the remainder of the play is lost. The name *Jeu d'Adam* is not a
good one: it designates only the first episode while the last attracted the
chief interest in the twelfth century. We find the dialogue between Eve
and the serpent highly diverting; it shows a keen knowledge of feminine
psychology on the part of the serpent, and, shall we say, on the part of

the author! This character of Eve was worthy of a Rachel or of a Sarah Bernhardt! The demons are active and drag Adam and Eve, as well as Cain, into everlasting torment, at the appropriate moments. God moves about the stage and is designated as the *Figura*. The verse scheme is the eight-syllable rhymed couplet. Though all the spoken lines are in French, the stage directions are in Latin. The play was played by Latin-speaking clerics for the benefit of the common people.

The early Latin liturgical dramas were first played in the monastic churches. Just when they were transferred to more secular settings, such as the chapter house or refectory hall, we cannot say. They must have been transferred soon to the chancel of non-monastic churches, and eventually to the steps and outside portal of the church. A play such as the *Adam* would draw a large crowd. The fact that its scenery was rather complicated is evidence that it was played out of doors.

The remaining drama in the vernacular, assigned to this century, is the *Jeu de Saint-Nicholas,* by Jean Bodel (d. after 1202). Jean Bodel was a poet active in other types of literature, notably epic and lyric poetry. The subject of his drama is a well-known Saint Nicholas miracle to which we have already referred, the *Iconia Sancti Nicholai.* Jean Bodel enlivened it with a few profane scenes. His play is invaluable for a study of medieval dicing and of thieves' slang (*Rom* LVII, 436-437).[1] Surely it could have been played nowhere but outside the church. The Christians have invaded the realm of a Saracen king who sends a messenger, Auberon, to summon all his vassals. En route Auberon stops at a tavern for a drink and a throw at the dice. The vassals answer the summons and a desperate battle ensues between pagans and Christians; the Christians are outnumbered and slain to all but the last man. This lone survivor, a *vieillard,* is found invoking aid before an image of Saint Nicholas. The Saracen king scorns this *Mahom cornu* (with reference to the mitre on the saint's head) and throws the Christian into prison. As a last concession the king agrees to expose his treasures in the guard of this image; if they are not stolen the old man shall go free. Once more the scene shifts to the tavern. Three thieves with the shady tavern-keeper and his drawer give a most interesting picture. They resolve to steal the treasures. They do so. The king discovers his loss and would put the Christian to death. It is then that Saint Nicholas appears in person and forces the robbers to restore the stolen goods. The Saracens are converted by this miracle, the old man is freed, and the idol Tervagant (one of the Saracen gods) vents his wrath in a strange language, a language existing only in the head of Jean Bodel. The drama is in the Picard dialect, in eight-syllable rhymed couplets. Bodel used the legend,

[1] See also Grace Frank in *MLN* L, 9-13; C. Knudson in *Rom* LXIII, 248-53.

as well as certain of the *chansons de geste*, particularly *Fierabras*, as sources.

Some authorities speak of this play by Jean Bodel as though it belonged to the thirteenth century. Since we know from his *congé*, or leave-taking poem, that Jean retired to a leper hostel in 1202 it would seem that we are not incorrect in discussing all of Jean Bodel's work as representative of the close of the twelfth century. Needless to say, the distinction by centuries is often arbitrary.

## EDITIONS

Karl Young, *op. cit. supra.*—Du Méril, *Les origines latines du théâtre moderne* (in the Collection de reproductions en fac-similé, No. III, Leipzig and Paris: Welter, 1897).—*Die lateinischen Osterfeiern*, ed. C. Lange (München: Stahlt, 1887); Neil C. Brooks, *The Sepulchre of Christ in Art and Liturgy* (Urbana: UIS, 1921); for further publications of dramatized tropes see the review by G. R. Coffman in *Spec* VI, 610-617.—Foerster-Koschwitz *Uebungsbuch, etc.*, contains the *Sponsus* and a *Stopfepistel* for Saint Stephen's day. L. F. Thomas (*Rom* LIII, 43 ff.; LV, 45 ff.) improves the text of the *Sponsus*. Other semi-vernacular epistles from the Middle Ages are reproduced in *ZfrPh* XI, in the *Bull. hist. et phil. du Comité des trav. hist.* (1887), and in the *Språkvetenskapliga sällskapets i Upsala förhandlingen*, ed. P. A. Geyer (1887).—*Hilarii versus et ludi*, ed. J. B. Fuller (Henry Holt, [1929]).—*Jus d'Adam*, ed. P. Studer (Manchester, 1928); *Adamsspiel*, ed. K. Grass (2nd ed.; Halle: *RomB*, 1928).—Jean Bodel, *Jeu de Saint-Nicholas*, ed. A. Jeanroy (Paris: Cfmâ, 1925). M. Henshaw and F. Sullivan will publish an edition of Hilarius' plays.

# CHAPTER VI

## DIDACTIC MATERIAL

George Sarton, *Introduction to the History of Science*, II, part I (Washington: Carnegie Institution, 1931).

F. Lauchert, *Geschichte des Physiologus* (Strassburg, 1899).

Both the saints' lives and the medieval drama were intended to instruct, but there are still other types of a purely didactic nature, such as scientific treatises, proverbs, and poems of moral instruction. The Middle Ages had a vast amount of didactic material composed in Latin, destined for the clergy and learned men, for which I refer the reader to the reference by George Sarton and to the bibliography listed therein. In the twelfth century a few popularized treatises in the French vernacular began to appear for the use of royalty, nobles, and bourgeois who had an interest in such matters but who could not read the language of science. Some of the lower clergy were poor Latinists who read nothing in Latin save the canon of the Mass. They also required French books, but they were not encouraged in their ignorance and it was taken for granted that all the clergy could use Latin.

Perhaps intended for the ignorant clergy was the *Cumpoz* of Philippe de Thaün, an ecclesiastical calendar with a list of festivals, the phases of the moon, the zodiac, etc. It contains a good bit of allegorical interpretation. The chief sources were Bede's *De temporum ratione*, Gerland's *Computus*, and the *Computus* of Helpericus, a monk of St. Gall. Use was also made of a lost treatise by Thurkil and of another by Nimrod the Astronomer. The verse, as we should expect in a naïve poem of this nature—intended to be memorized easily—is in six-syllable rhymed couplets. The date must be either 1113 or 1119, probably the latter. These two dates can be computed with absolute accuracy since Philippe records the *concurrent* number of the current year as 2 (that is, the Sunday Letter *E*) which can apply to the two years mentioned. Philippe de Thaün was an Anglo-Norman writing at the court of Henry I. His name was derived from a property three miles out of Caen in the diocese of Bayeux.

Philippe de Thaün's most famous work is a *Bestiaire*, a description of marvellous beasts, with a Christian allegorical interpretation for each one. He added, as well, a list of birds and of stones; the poem is probably not complete in its surviving form. Certain beasts are likened to

Christ (lion, unicorn, panther, deer, etc.), others to men (ant, beaver, hyena, weasel, elephant, etc.), and still others to the devil (porcupine, fox, monkey, etc.). The same comparisons are made with the birds and stones. The pelican which feeds its young on its own blood is Christ, and so is the diamond, of insuperable hardness. The immediate source was the *Physiologus*, a natural history of Christian interpretation, which was compiled at Alexandria in the second century A. D. A Latin adaptation of the *Physiologus* was certainly made in the fourth or fifth century and this became current in Western Europe. The sources of the Greek original were the Bible, Aristotle, oral tradition, and possibly the *Historia naturalis* of Pliny the Elder. Philippe may have consulted Pliny, Solinus, and Isidore of Seville. The first 2,888 lines of his poem are in six-syllable rhymed couplets; the meter then changes to eight-syllable couplets. The date must be after 1121 when Henry I married Aaliz of Louvain to whom the *Bestiaire* is dedicated. This Aaliz did not cease to have the title of Queen till after 1139 when she married Guillaume d'Albini, Earl of Arundel; but, all things being considered, it is usual to suppose that Philippe completed this *Bestiaire* by 1125. In an Oxford MS (No. 249 of Merton College) the poem occurs with a second dedication, to Eleanor, the Queen of Henry II after 1152. It is not impossible that Philippe lived to a ripe old age and changed the dedication himself.

Lapidaries, or lists of precious stones, enjoyed a particular vogue. Their miraculous and symbolical properties went back ultimately to the authority of the Bible, for in Exodus 28: 17-20 there is a description of the stones on the breastplate of the high priest, and in Apocalypse 21: 19-20 the foundations of the New Jerusalem are described. Bede and some of the other lapidary authorities of the Middle Ages discussed no stones except those listed in Exodus. Unfortunately the Hebrew names are not clear and so the Biblical translations vary among themselves in identifying the stones. The chief scientific discussion of precious stones and minerals was in Book 37 of the *Historia naturalis* of Pliny the Elder, where there was a remarkable synthesis of all that had been written before. Saint Isidore of Seville utilized this freely in Book 16 of his *Etymologiae* but he arranged the minerals in groups according to prevailing color: green, red, white, black, golden. During the Hellenistic age stone books of a magical and mystic sort began to appear at Alexandria, in the Greek language. One of these, which is commonly called the Damigeron, may have been translated into Latin as early as the first century A. D. It was exceedingly popular in Western Europe.

Between 1067 and 1101 Bishop Marbod of Rennes wrote a Latin poem *De lapidibus*. His immediate sources were Pliny, Isidore, Damigeron, and, of course, the Bible. There is considerable internal evidence that Marbod had seen very few of the minerals that he discussed, but his book obtained great authority. There are over a hundred and fifty MSS extant of the Latin text and the poem was adapted into French, Provençal, Italian, Irish, Danish, Hebrew and Spanish. It is the oldest French version which now concerns us. This first French version was made before 1150 and was probably of Anglo-Norman origin. There are 967 verses in octosyllabic rhymed couplets. The poem begins with a frame story. Evax, king of Arabia, is so wise and rich that Nero has asked him for a book on the properties of precious stones. This is the book. The *incipit* of the Damigeron is the source for this prologue in Marbod. There are fifty-nine mineral substances discussed, not all of them precious stones. It is possible to identify most of them with some accuracy. Descriptions are given, with marvellous properties, of achates (agate), adamas, aetites (clapperstone of limonite), alabandica (ferric aluminum garnet), alectorias (silicate pebble in a chicken's craw), amethyst, androdamas (andalusite), apsyctos (?), asbestos (chrysotile), beryl, carbuncle (large, thick magnesium garnet), ceraunius (prehistoric axehead), chalazias (white flint pebble confused with hail stone), chalcedonius (chalcedony), chalcophonos (phonolite), chelidonius (pebble removed from a swallow's craw), chelonitis (toad-stone), chryselectrum (essonite garnet), chrysolite, chrysopace (chrysoberyl), chrysoprase (leek-green prase), coral, carnelian, rock crystal, diadocos (euclase), dionysias (jasperlite), enhygros (chalcedony with water center called a *Wasserstein*), gagates (jet), gagatromaeus (grayish chalcedony, or corundum), galactites (milk-white quartz), haematite, heliotrope (bloodstone)[1], hephaestites (spinel), hexacontalithos (fluorite), hieracites (onyx marble), hyacinthus (zircon), hyaenia (?), iris (iridescent crystal), jasper, liparea (pumice stone ?), lyncurium (amber), magnetite, pearl, medus (jasperlite), malachite, opal, critis (siderite), paeanitis (same as aetites), pyrite, pantheros (serpentine of a spotted ash-color), prasius (chrysoprase of an apple-green shade), sagda (a greenish barnacle), sapphire, sard, sardonyx, selenites (green muscovite), smaragdus (emerald, green andradite garnet, or dioptase), tecolithos (Jew stone), topaz.

The first Anglo-Norman prose lapidary also belongs to the twelfth century. It is an abridgment of the above mentioned verse translation of Marbod, although the Latin original may also have been consulted. Philippe de Thaün, author of the *Cumpoz* and of the *Bestiaire,* had an interest in stones also. He added a few stones to the close of his *Bestiaire* and he was doubtless the author of an alphabetical lapidary (1,710 octosyllables) and possibly of what is called the apocalyptic lap-

---

[1] In Europe the haematite is called bloodstone. By this term I mean green chalcedony speckled with red jasper.

idary (297 octosyllables) in MS 87 of Pembroke College (Cambridge). At the end of the alphabetical version, where the stones are arranged in alphabetical order, Philippe promises a work of more celestial significance which may well be our apocalyptic version. These poems by Philippe would antedate 1130. Philippe's sources for these would be Damigeron and Marbod direct. The *Lapidary of Modena* and the *Lapidary of Berne* are continental versions of Marbod, independent of the early French version. They are fragmentary, preserved in only one MS each.

No vernacular herbal, or discussion of medicinal plants, was written during this century. Beside Pliny, Isidore, and Solinus the chief botanical authority of the day was the *De herbarum virtutibus* (Latinized in fifth century) of Apuleius Barbarus. An Oxford MS of this work (Bodleian 130), executed at Bury St. Edmund's not long after 1120, contains some interesting drawings of plants, made from nature!

The Proverbs of the Bible were always popular. In England they were rendered into Anglo-Norman French by Samson of Nanteuil, in an elaborate manner. We have mentioned the *Disticha Catonis,* a compilation of the fourth century *A.D.* which was so popular as a primer in the schools. These were translated into French, into six-syllable rhymed couplets, by Evrard de Kirkham, an Anglo-Norman. Elias of Winchester put them into eight-syllable verse. There are still other French translations of these *Disticha.*

At the court of Philip of Flanders, in the last quarter of the twelfth century, an independent, original compilation of popular sayings was made and called the *Proverbe au vilain.* Here each adage is commentaried in a strophe of six six-syllable lines with the refrain "Ce dit li vilains." This must have contained, in its earliest form, two hundred and eighty proverbs. Of the compiler we know nothing except that he had some clerical education and that he was a ne'er-do-well. The proverbs reflect his personal philosophy: resignment to poverty, thrift, suffering, and disillusionment.

There are some twenty-nine collections of proverbs in French prior to 1400. Nearly all of them are based upon the *Proverbe au vilain,* a good gauge of its popularity. There are two other collections, the *Proverbe au conte de Bretagne* and that preserved in MS Sainte Geneviève 550, fo. 282, which are also original in content. Their date is not certain, but they may belong to the twelfth century.

The *Proverbe au vilain* makes mention of the legend of *Salomon et Marcolfus,* which is first attested by Notker Labeo, a monk of St. Gall (952-1022). King Solomon meets the insolent dwarf, Marcolfus, and his equally hideous wife. There ensues an altercation in which Solomon utters a saying and Marcolfus contradicts it with another. Marcolfus always gets the last word. There are several such scenes in which Marcolfus compensates for his insolence by his wit. At length he is shown great honor by the King. It will be observed that the main portion of this tale is a collection of proverbs. The origin of the frame story may be sought in Byzantium, although such western sources as Macrobius and Diogenes Laërtius may have been used. The title given above is that of the Latin version composed in France in the twelfth century. There is a much reduced French version (59 strophes) of the same period with the title *De Marcoul et Salemon*. This Marcolfus, or Marcoul, is perhaps the Jewish name Marcolis, found in the *Mischna*. It is certain that the proverbs themselves, all of popular origin, existed before the frame story. The Solomon and Marcolfus frame story is also found in England, Roumania, Germany, Italy, Portugal, and Slavic countries. The name of Marcolfus underwent changes in the various versions.

Although didactic is hardly a term to describe it, we must classify under serious literature the translation of the famous Latin letter of Prester John, made by Roau d'Arundel in Anglo-Norman verse, in 1192. The legend of a Christian priest-king in central Asia reached the West for the first time in 1122. Between 1165 and 1177 a letter from this King Prester John, to the Byzantine emperor, Manuel Commenos, circulated freely. This forged letter, whether first written in Greek or Latin is uncertain, described the marvels of Prester John's country: strange beasts, streams of milk and honey, pigmies, precious stones and pepper. For two hundred years men continued to believe such marvels; then, in the fourteenth century, the land of Prester John was associated with Ethiopia. It is probable that the foundations of this legend are to be sought in the Nestorian Mongols in south central Asia. King John himself may have been the Mongol prince Yeliu; the name John may well be a corruption of the Chinese word *wang*, 'lord' (Zarncke in *Abhandlungen der k. sächsischen Gesellschaft der Wissenschaften*, VII, 837 ff.).

The *Roman des romans* is not a romance but an Anglo-Norman poem of moral content, composed about 1150. The 1,028 verses, in monorhymed stanzas of four ten-syllable lines each, are filled with pessimism. They contain a great deal of censure for the clergy. Hélinant (d. 1227), monk of Froidmont and native of Beauvaisis, composed the *Vers de la mort* between 1194 and 1197. This is a warning, in true medieval fashion, of approaching death. His dialect is very similar to that of central France. In the years 1182-1185 Hélinant was a singer and poet at the court of Philip Augustus. The meter of the *Vers de la mort* became famous and was adopted later by numerous thirteenth-century poets, especially by those who wrote on a similar theme. This meter, invented by Hélinant, is the twelve-line strophe with rhymes *aab aab bba bba,* which is No. xxxvi in G. Naetebus, *Die nichtlyrischen Strophenformen des Altfranzösischen* (Leipzig, 1891).

Etienne de Fougères, chaplain of Henry II of England, was consecrated bishop of Rennes in 1168. Robert de Torigni, the chronicler, tells us that Etienne composed many things in poetry and in prose, but that he sobered down a bit before his death in 1178. His writings were mostly in Latin, as are his surviving lives of St. Firmatus and Abbot Vitalis, and his account of the embellishment of the cathedral of Rennes. There has come down to us one French poem under his name, the *Livre des manières*, a moral work in monorhymed quatrains of eight-syllable lines. The dialect is pure Norman. This poem is preserved in a single MS (Angers No. 295, fol. 141 ff.) and was probably composed in 1174-1178. The dedication was to the Countess of Hereford, a lady who had lost her children and needed to be consoled. Etienne's sources are difficult to trace: perhaps he used John of Salisbury's *Polycraticus* and certain portions of the Alexander romance of Lambert le Tort. He was a crude, though powerful, poet. Simund de Freine (b. before 1147—d. after 1203) was a canon of the cathedral at Hereford. He was a great admirer of Giraut de Barri for whom he wrote several Latin poems; we know him best as the author of the *Roman de philosophie,* a French poem based freely upon Boethius' *Consolatio philosophiae.* It has 827 rhymed couplets.

In *Li ver del juise,* which has the flavor of a sermon, are a vision and the remarks of a soul concerning the last judgment. Of special interest is the *Evangile aux femmes,* which deals with a topic dear to the heart of the medieval ascetic, the evils of womankind. The form of satire is very clever. There are four alexandrine lines to each stanza. In the first three the poet pretends to praise women; in the fourth line he reverses it all with a clever twist. This was composed at the end of the century.

A poem of allegorical and theological content is the anonymous *De David li prophecie.* It is superficially an account of the siege of Jerusalem by Nabazan, with an interpretation of Jerusalem as the human heart, and of the Assyrian invader as the devil. There are some 1,550 verses and the poem is definitely dated 1180; the author says, "Mil ans ot et.c. e hoitante Cant a travaillier mit s'entente." This is a rare courtesy on the part of a twelfth-century poet.

Probably between 1182 and 1185 Thibaut de Montmorency, Seigneur de Marly, wrote his *Vers de la mort.* There are resemblances here to the sermon of Guischart de Beaulieu. Thibaut de Marly became a Cistercian monk and died after 1190 (R. Reinsch in Herrig's *Archiv,* LXIII).

Philippe de Thaün, *Li cumpoz*, ed. E. Mall (Strassburg, 1873); *Bestiaire*, ed. E. Walberg (Paris: Welter, 1900); *Lapidaire*, ed. Paul Meyer in *Rom* XXXVIII, 484 ff.—*Anglo-Norman Lapidaries*, ed. P. Studer-J. Evans (Paris, 1924).—*Les lapidaires français du moyen âge*, ed. L. Pannier (Paris, 1882).— Everard de Kirkham, *Traduction des disticha Catonis*, ed. Furnivall in *The Minor Poems of the Vernon MS* (*EETS*, No. 117, 1901), a new edition is in progress for the Anglo-Norman Text Society.—Elies de Wincestre, *Uebertragung der Disticha Catonis*, ed. E. Stengel (Marburg, 1896).—Adam de Suel, *Distiques de Caton*, ed. J. Ulrich in *RFor* XV, 107.—Jehan Le Fèvre, *Traduction des disticha Catonis*, ed. J. Ulrich in *RFor* XV, 70.—*Marcoul et de Salemon*, ed. Crapelet in *Proverbes et dictons* (1831).—*Proverbes français antérieurs au XVᵉ siècle*, ed. J. Morawski (Paris: Cfmâ, 1925).—*Diz et proverbes as sages*, ed. J. Morawski (Paris: Presses Universitaires, 1929).—*Li proverbe au vilain*, ed. A. Tobler (Leipzig, 1895).—Roau d'Arundel, *Die anglo-normannische Versversion des Briefes des Presbyters Johannes*, ed. A. Hilka in *ZfrSL* XLIII, 100-111.—Hélinant, *Vers de la mort*, ed. E. Walberg (Paris: *SATF*, 1905).—Etienne de Fougères, *Livres des manières*, ed. J. Kremer (Marburg, 1887).—Simund de Freine, *Oeuvres*, ed. J. E. Matzke (Paris: *SATF*, 1909).—*Li ver del jüise*, ed. V. Feilitzen (Upsala, 1883).—*Evangile aux femmes*, ed. M. Constans in *Marie de Compiègne d'après l'Evangile aux femmes* (Paris, 1871); also ed. G. Keidel in *Romance and Other Studies* I (Baltimore, 1893).—*De David li prophecie*, ed. G. E. Fuhrken (Halle, 1895). —*Le Roman des romans*, ed. I. C. Lecompte (Princeton: *EM*, 1923); also ed. F. J. Tanquerey in *Fünf anglonormannische Texte* (Paris: Champion, 1922).— *Les vers de Thibaut de Marly*, ed. H. K. Stone (Paris: Droz, 1932).

# CHAPTER VII

## THE ORIGINS OF THE *CHANSON DE GESTE*

M. C. Nyrop, *Storia dell' epopea francese nel medio evo,* tr. E. Gorra (Florence, 1886).
Joseph Bédier, *Les légendes épiques* (3rd ed.; Paris, 1926-29).
Léon Gautier, *Les épopées françaises* (2nd ed.; Paris, 1878-92), 4 vols.
Pio Rajna, *Le origini dell' epopea francese* (Florence, 1884).
Gaston Paris, *L'histoire poétique de Charlemagne* (1865; 2nd ed. 1901).

The Old French epic or *chanson de geste* was a narrative poem of moderate length, averaging four thousand lines, usually in ten-syllable verse, with assonanced or rhymed *laisses.* Its theme was the glory of the Franks, the Christian religion, and the deeds of certain famous knights who owed allegiance to Charlemagne, or to his son Louis the Pious. Only rarely did these poems center about Charles Martel or Clovis. The subject matter, and most of the characters were legendary, not to say outright creations of the jongleurs, but the audiences of the twelfth century regarded most of them as true history. With the possible exception of *Gormont et Isembart* and the *Chanson de Roland* none of the epics which we possess are older than 1100 in their existing form. That many of them were current fifty or sixty years before that date no one will deny. The earlier versions have disappeared. It is important to conjecture just how and when this type of literature came into being.

Four important theories have been suggested to explain the origin:

1. The cantilena theory (Gaston Paris, Léon Gautier, Robert Fawtier),
2. Theory of Germanic origin (Pio Rajna, G. Gröber, L. Jordan),
3. Theory of saga or prose tradition (H. Suchier, C. Voretzsch, Paul Meyer),
4. Theory of recent French origin (P. A. Becker, Joseph Bédier).

The names in parentheses indicate some of the foremost exponents of each theory.

At the beginning of the nineteenth century, Fauriel, Raynouard, others in France, and in particular the German Romanticists, conceived a remarkable theory with regard to epics in general. W. Grimm may be considered their spokesman when he said, "It is the people as a whole who create the epic. It would be absurd for an individual to wish to compose one, for "jedes Epos muss sich selbst dichten, von keinem Dichter geschrieben werden" (*Kleinere Schriften,* IV, 19). After the battles of

Charlemagne, lyric poems arose on the field of action and were chanted by soldier and jongleur to posterity. These lyric poems, when they dealt with the same or consecutive events, were one day put together; that was the making of an epic. In 1835, the word *cantilena* was brought to light from a Latin source, and it was believed to be the medieval term for one of these soldier lyrics. This is the *cantilena* theory as it was conceived in the first half of the nineteenth century. It remained for Gaston Paris to solidify and rationalize this theory in his *Histoire poétique de Charlemagne* (1865). His innovation was that he no longer believed in a spontaneous rising from the soil, in the composition of *cantilenae* by the great voice of the multitude. He, unlike Grimm, sought for authors and dates. In his opinion these *cantilenae* were the work of individuals who composed them immediately after the events in question. This thesis has been supported very recently by Robert Fawtier (*La chanson de Roland,* Paris: De Boccard, 1933) who has made evident some of the weaknesses in the Bédier solution of the problem without, however, succeeding in reëstablishing plausibly that of Gaston Paris. Léon Gautier, in the *Epopées françaises,* upheld substantially the same thing, though he asserted that the *cantilenae* had been composed in German and not in Romance (*op. cit.,* I, 182).

In 1884, Pio Rajna published his *Le origini dell' epopea* to announce his belief in the Germanic origin of the French epic. The German epic is very old; indeed, it is said to have begun at the time of the migrations of the people, by the fifth century *A.D.* Rajna called attention to certain similarities between the French epic and the German poems of this type. They are:

1. naming of swords and horses;
2. status of king among the nobles, his constant asking for advice;
3. giants, etc.;
4. legal institutions;
5. common occurrence of the number twelve; e.g., twelve peers;
6. the *Brautfahrt,* or motif of the quest for a bride.

These parallels are all open to contention. Most of them occur in the popular literature of peoples who have never undergone Germanic influence. Add to this the fact that the German and French epics differ greatly in form, alliteration as opposed to the *laisse,* and that the Germans had nothing similar to the *laisse similaire.* Further, the spirit of the German epic is pagan, even in the Old Saxon *Heliand* which has Christ as its central figure; but the French *chansons de geste* are nothing at all if not Christian. One of the favorite devices of the French epic poet was the long prayer which is said by an individual immediately before battle or upon some similar occasion. This frequently begins with

"O God, Thou who didst . . ." introducing a summary of main events of the Old or New Testament, followed by a request for personal victory or salvation. (A variation was the invocation of a saint, with mention of his or her acts and miracles.) There is no parallel to this in the Germanic epic. Might we mention also the prophetic dreams in which an angel appears to Charlemagne or to one of the knights? These are not found in the German poems.

The third theory, which is little more than a modification of that of Gaston Paris, is one of prose tradition. According to this, the soldiers and eyewitnesses of the historic battles narrated their experiences which were thus passed down through successive generations. Eventually a considerable portion of this prose tradition was collected and put into poetic form (in the ninth and tenth centuries). This differs essentially from the *cantilena* theory only in the use of saga or prose tradition rather than verse. Voretzsch and many other distinguished scholars of today hold to this theory. It is certainly the most plausible after that of Bédier. It was suggested by Paul Meyer in his *Recherches sur l'épopée française* (1867).

All three of these theories are alike in one feature: they admit the existence of French epic themes for two or three centuries prior to those we possess. The subject matter would go back to eyewitnesses or contemporaries of the deeds celebrated. Foerster and Koschwitz have published thirty-two odd passages from Tacitus (55-120 A.D.), Venantius Fortunatus (530-609 A.D.), Cassiodorus (468-562 A.D.), Eginhard's *Life of Charlemagne,* Ermoldus Nigellus, and others, which are commonly cited as proof of age for the Old French epic. These are all refuted in detail by Bédier, to whose work cited above we can do no better than refer the student. It should be perfectly clear to anyone that mere mentions of singing in the vulgar tongue are not sufficient to prove the existence of battle *cantilenae,* composed by eyewitnesses, or of full fledged copies of a German model. Singing and chanting of some sort are as old as the hills. Mentions of folk music among the ancients and early medieval writers will never demolish the theory of Joseph Bédier. However, two of the passages cited by Foerster and Koschwitz are more important than the others: the *Song of Burgundofaro* and the *Hague fragment.* They will be discussed at the close of our presentation of Bédier's theory.

The fourth theory, developed so fully by Bédier, was first broached by Daunou as early as 1824, in his *Discours sur l'état des lettres en France au XIIe siècle* (in the *Histoire littéraire de la France,* Vol. XVI). Philip A. Becker, of the University of Leipzig, then at the University of Vienna, took up this view in earnest and refuted successfully many of his opponents' arguments. Becker claimed that our *chansons de geste* were based upon chronicles, and did not exist in a form prior to those which have survived. But it remained for Professor Joseph Bédier, of the Collège de France, to develop this thesis brilliantly and more convincingly in 1904. His final conclusions can be briefly told. The epics are a mere extension of that type known as the saint's life. The latter was sung in or before the church, sometimes in the market place, or at the shrine of the saint in question. This was permitted and encouraged by the local clergy as it gave fame to the shrine and brought material advantages. Many churches, monastic and secular, had the bodies of their founders or of some other pious knight, many of whom had seen good service under the banners of Charlemagne or of his successors. The monasteries also possessed foundation charters, or chronicles, which gave a meager fact or two about these heroes. Some ingenious *jongleur,* not earlier than the year 1000, conceived the idea of obtaining a shred of information from the clergy of a church which possessed such a tomb and of expanding it into a long heroic narrative, keeping in mind that Charlemagne lived in men's hearts as the patron of Christianity and as the greatest of French kings. The resulting poem achieved local popularity to the advantage of both the jongleur and the foundation in which the hero's tomb lay. When the jongleur moved about with his poem it attracted still more interest and pilgrims began to flock to that tomb.

These are the conditions under which the first *chanson de geste* was written, says Bédier. The idea must have spread almost instantaneously. Other jongleurs exploited other tombs, and some of the less scrupulous clergy even invented heroes, as well as the necessary documents for giving facts about their lives. This species of advertising was more successful along or near the great pilgrim routes. Pilgrims were willing to go a few miles out of their way to visit some shrine of pious fame. Thus it came about that Ogier the Dane was venerated by pilgrims in the Church of St. Burgundofaro at Meaux, Roland in Saint-Romain of Blaye, and William of Orange at Saint-Guilhem-le-Desert. Girart of Roussillon was the patron of Vézelay. Just what connection these individual heroes had with their particular shrines will be discussed by us under each *chanson de geste.* The three major pilgrimages were those of Jerusalem, Rome, and Saint James of Compostella in Galicia. The first two, due to their difficulty, were not so often travelled as the third. There were a number of highways through southern France to Compostella. It was only natural that epics should have been used to attract pilgrims to one road rather than to another. Though the element of advertising may have been strongest at the beginning, the epics soon came to be looked upon as an incomparable form of entertainment. Wilmotte has suggested that this love of epic literature existed from the very origin, that the clerics had their imaginations stimulated by the ancient epic and by certain Low Latin poems.[1] This would remove some of the utilitarianism and suggest that it was a cleric rather than a jongleur who first conceived the idea. In any case, the epics were soon a combination for great amusement and great profit to those shrines which could claim heroes as their own.

Such, in brief, is the theory of recent French origin. The poems do not date before the year 1000 and they are all of semi-learned extraction. In disposing of the opposing evidence Bédier has been fairly convincing; yet there are two documents which Bédier has not been able to explain away so easily and which must lead the way to some modification of the theory. The *Song of Burgundofaro,* which had been brought forward as evidence by so many of Bédier's predecessors, is preserved in the Latin life of Bishop Burgundofaro of Meaux. An extract reads:

. . . Ex qua victoria carmen publicum juxta rusticitatem per omnium paene volitabat ora ita canentium, feminaeque choros inde plaudendo componebant:

> De Chlothario est canere rege Francorum,
> Qui ivit pugnare in gentem Saxonum.
> Quam graviter provenisset missis Saxonum,
> Si non fuisset inclytus Faro de gente Burgundionum.

Et in fine huius carminis:

> Quando veniunt missi Saxonum in terram Francorum,
> Faro ubi erat princeps, transeunt
> Instinctu Dei per urbem Meldorum,
> Ne interficiantur a rege Francorum.

Hoc enim rustico carmine placuit ostendere, quantum ab omnibus celeberrimus habebatur. . . .

This fragment of a song, celebrating the war of Clothair against the Saxons, is supposed to prove the existence of the epic form in the seventh century. (Paulin Paris, Léon Gautier, E. Böhmer, and Hermann Suchier were so convinced that these verses were a translation from a seventh-century Romance original that each, on various occasions, published a translation of the lines into twelfth-century Old French, more or less good!) Bédier believes that this *cantilena,* like the rest of Hildegarius' *Life of Burgundofaro* was manufactured out of whole cloth in the ninth century and had no source contemporary with Faro. His arguments are convincing for the date of the life as a whole, but they are not so strong when he dismisses the verses as worthless for the history of the epic. Hildegarius was writing *in the ninth century;* certainly these lines are

[1] *De l'origine du roman en France (La tradition antique et les éléments du roman)* (Paris: Champion, 1923).

not an idle dance song. There is direct mention of Clothair and of his Saxon war, even though the doings of Saint Burgundofaro are the main theme preserved in this fragment. We do not know what the remainder of the song contained. This shows beyond any doubt that a Frankish king and his wars could be sung about in the ninth century, however crude and unformed the result might have been.

The other document with which Bédier has difficulty is the *Hague fragment.* The MS on which this epic fragment is preserved is correctly dated by Charles Samaran between 980 and 1030 (*Rom* LVIII, 190-205). Bédier himself admits the date 1040 and that this Latin fragment is a prose rendering of a Latin verse epic, which in turn was translated from a vernacular *chanson de geste.* With these points in view Bédier still contends that they do not contradict his belief that no vernacular epics existed before 1000. But the original of this fragment (belonging to the cycle of Garin de Monglane) must have been a well developed specimen, to judge from the Latin prose extant, and this original must have antedated what is preserved by from fifteen to twenty years. If Suchier was correct in calling the Latin prose a schoolboy exercise it is probable that the French original was a familiar and wide-spread composition. The action portrayed in the fragment is the siege of a town, either Narbonne or Gerona. Some of the phraseology is reminiscent of Vergil, Lucan, and Ovid.

In view of the difficulties presented by the *Song of Burgundofaro* and by the so-called *Hague fragment,* and particularly in view of some of the recent research of Ferdinand Lot,[1] we are disposed to be a little less strict than M. Bédier in his theory of epic origins. That most of the extant epics were moulded into what would be a form recognizable to us after 1000, and that they were mostly due to a combination of jongleur and cleric, we cannot deny. But, as Wilmotte has said, there is epic material and epic way of thinking in the chronicles and saints' lives of the early Middle Ages in France: in the *Vita Karoli,* in the poem of Ermoldus Nigellus, in the song of Waltharius, etc. "Le Français a la tête épique." There was also a certain amount of popular tradition and legend. It seems impossible to admit that folktales could exist, be repeated from generation to generation by the people, and then deny that memories of great battles, traditions concerning celebrated individuals, could be passed on in the same way, suffering extensive alterations as they went. One might add to Bédier's theory, therefore, the belief that battle songs, saints' lives, *chansons de geste* in a primitive form, and forms existing in popular tradition, *did* exist in a scattered way in the tenth and possibly in the ninth centuries. Also there was some popular

[1] See *Rom* XXVII, 1-54; LII; 75-133, 257-95; LIII, 325-42, 449-73; LIV, 357-78.

tradition passed on from father to son concerning the warriors in certain tombs, the invasions of Norsemen and Saracens.  But, we will admit with Bédier that no definite program of epic construction, no systematic exploitation of the legends, existed till the eleventh century—that great period which saw a rebirth of activity of a national and popular nature.  At that time no jongleur, composing what passed for history, would have failed to check the important part of his theme with the local chronicle, and the cleric, as Bédier has so brilliantly shown, made a profitable partnership with the vernacular poet.  We must admit that the *chansons de geste* grew best along the well-known pilgrim routes and brought much profit to those who fostered them.  But soon the public loved them for their own sakes; and, in the second stage of epic development, the close of the twelfth century till after 1300, some new themes came into use which were not an exploitation and the epic passed to a conventional form of literature.  Epics were then colported about to other countries such as England, Spain, Italy, and Germany.  The eleventh century productions were all revised or rearranged to suit more developed tastes and the early forms disappeared.  Poets became conscious of families of heroes, of similar themes and situations, and they welded all this material into definite cycles of plot, filling out gaps in a hero's career or telling about his father and his brother with new epic compositions.  Such are the origins of the *chanson de geste,* one of France's greatest contributions to medieval literature.[2]

## EDITIONS

Materials relating to the origins of the epic are in the Foerster-Koschwitz *Uebungsbuch,* col. 247-266.  The *Hague fragment* has also been published, with French translation, by Suchier in his *Les Narbonnais* (Paris: *SATF,* 1898), II, 168 ff.

[2] A. Pauphilet also adheres to Bédier's theory, but with some modification in a direction opposite to that of Lot.  He admits less popular tradition than even Bédier does (*Rom* LIX. 161 ff.).

# CHAPTER VIII

## THE *GESTE DU ROI*

E. Faral, *La chanson de Roland* (Paris: Mellottée, 1934).
Jean Györy, *Etude sur la Chanson de Roland* (Paris: Droz, 1937).

Bertrand de Bar-sur-Aube, who composed the epic *Girard de Vienne* (1200-1220), gave us a system of classification for the *chansons de geste* which we still follow. He said (vs. 1448 ff.):

> N'ot que trois gestes en France la garnie
> *Du roi de France* est la plus seignorie
> Et de richesce et de chevalerie;
> Et l'autre apres, bien est drois que je die,
> Est *de Doon* a la barbe florie
> Cel *de Maiance* qui tant ot baronie
>
> . . . . . . . . . . . . . . . . . . . . . . . . .
>
> La tierce geste ke moult fist a proisier
> Fu *de Garin de Monglane* le fier.

Briefly, there are three *gestes,* that of the king, that of Doon de Mayence, and that of Garin de Monglane. We shall examine each of these cycles in their order. There are eighty or more extant *chansons de geste* of which some thirty belong to the *geste du roi.*

In the *geste du roi,* or cycle of the king, the king or emperor of France, usually Charlemagne, forms the background with his faithful and immediate vassals. The vassals are more active than the king, who is frequently little more than a court of appeal or their accepted leader in peace and battle. It is at his court or in his camp that the action passes. Charlemagne was "by his very definition an immutable majesty." Though a German in race and language, he was the traditional hero of the French. The Germans themselves never celebrated him in poetry, save through translations from the French. He was the embodiment of Christianity successful before the Saracen, the great Emperor of the West whose memory was a heritage to the continental French.

This brings us to the first *chanson de geste* of this cycle, which is the most famous and probably the oldest of all the Old French epics now extant: the *Chanson de Roland.* Its form as found in the Oxford MS may be dated with reasonable certainty 1098-1100. On the other hand Giulio Bertoni, and others associated with him, prefer an earlier dating, 1066-1096 (see Michele Catalano in *Arch Rom* XVIII, 381-90). The late

Boissonnade preferred so extreme a date as 1120-25: this we believe is hardly possible.

The Saracen king, Marsilies, worried by Charlemagne's seven years of continuous war in Spain, holds council with his peers. They determine to send hostages with false promises of submission, in order to induce the Franks to return home. An embassy, headed by Blancandrins, sets out with rich presents to bear the message to Charles before Cordova. Their offer is accepted by Charles after some debate, and Ganelon is suggested by Roland as the returning messenger to the Saracen camp. Ganelon is Roland's step-father. He already hates Roland, presumably because his step-son had outdone him in some financial transaction *(lui forfist en aveir)*. He goes on the dangerous mission and delivers Charlemagne's message like a man; but later he arranges for the pagans to massacre the rear guard at the pass of Roncesvalles; he assures the Saracens that Roland, their deadly enemy, will be there. Charlemagne's army moves northward and the rear guard follows as prescribed. In it are Roland and the twelve peers of France. The Saracens fall upon them but the Franks sell their lives dearly. Oliver begs Roland to blow his horn and summon the main army, but he refuses through false pride till it is too late: all his comrades are slain. He, too, dies after the pagans have retreated, but only as a result of his mighty blast upon the horn, not by the enemy hand. Charlemagne, who has heard the horn, hastens back. Now begins the so-called Baligant episode. The Emperor is met upon the field of Roncesvalles by the emir Baligant, with another huge army. The Saracens are defeated by the Christians, Marsilies dies and Spain is conquered. Charlemagne returns to Aix-la-Chapelle where Ganelon is judged a traitor, through trial by combat, and drawn by four horses.

Such is an outline of the fairest poem of the French Middle Ages. It is 4,002 lines in length, in the usual epic ten-syllable verse, with caesura after the fourth syllable. Of the 290 *laisses* there are 158 which close with the refrain *Aoi;* there are twelve in which this word is found in the interior, a position hard to explain, unless the refrain were misplaced by a copyist.[1] The poem ends with a verse which has been the subject of some controversy:

> Ci falt la geste que Turoldus declinet.

The late Professor Holbrook suggested (*MPhil* XXI, 155-164) that this be translated,

> Here ends the tale for Turoldus grows old.

[1] I agree with Grace Frank (*PMLA* XLVIII, 629-35) and others that this *Aoi* had to do with the musical presentation.

This translation was also held by Professors T. A. Jenkins and Lucien Foulet, independently of Holbrook, although Foulet has since relinquished the theory. This reading would indicate that Turoldus was the poet who was forced to break off through the infirmities of age. Still other translations for this line are:

Here ends the [source] chronicle which Turoldus completes (L. Gautier, op. cit. III, 497).

Here ends the epic which Turoldus recites (G. I iris, Rom XXIV, 632).

Here ends the chronicle which Turoldus narrates (P. Rajna, Rom XIV, 405).

Here ends the geste which Turoldus amplifies poetically (L. Olschki, Arch Rom XIX, 425-31).

Joseph Bédier does not translate this line in his version of the poem. Herbert K. Stone (MPhil XXXIII, 337-50) demonstrates that the usual meaning of decliner in French and Provençal is exposer. V. Crescini took a similar view in his L'ultimo verso della canzone di Rolando (Rome, 1895).

Immediately following this last verse, in the Oxford MS, there is evidence of erasure which once gave hope of further explanation. This erasure has since been read by Charles Samaran, with the aid of the violet ray (Rom LV, 401-410). The Roland was followed here by the Chalcidian translation of Plato's Timaeus.

This Turoldus, whether he be poet or jongleur, is a mysterious figure. On the Bayeux tapestry there is a representation of a dwarf who is so named, and be it noted that other individuals are seldom named in the tapestry. Tavernier, in his Vorgeschichte des altfranzösischen Rolandslieds (Berlin, 1898) identifies Turoldus with Thorold of Envermeu, a monk of the Abbey of Bec and at one time Bishop of Bayeux. Professor Jenkins agreed with this in his edition of the poem. In this event the Chanson de Roland would be the work of no ignorant jongleur but of a cultivated Norman cleric whose greatest vice, perhaps, was his worldliness. This identification is an interesting one, but it is far from certain in our present state of knowledge. Boissonnade suggested that the poet of the Roland was a Norman jongleur who had participated in the crusades into Spain, probably Guillaume Turold who was established at Tudela in 1128.[1] F. Lot does not believe the poem to be the work of a Norman.[2] If we accept an early dating it may be that this chanson was composed with the purpose of calling attention to the Saracens and the plight of Jerusalem, or perhaps to the Moorish advance in Spain, for Alfonso VI was decisively defeated at Zalaca in 1087.

The oldest and best MS, preserved at Oxford with the classification

[1] Du nouveau sur la Chanson de Roland (Paris, 1923), p. 481 ff.
[2] Rom LIV, 379. Ivan H. Petkanov (Arch Rom. XX, 289-97) examines all these theories and demonstrates that they are inconclusive.

Digby 23, was made in England between 1130 and 1150. This is the date given by Charles Samaran. Another MS in the National Library of Saint Mark's in Venice (V⁴), belonging to the thirteenth century, is somewhat italianized. In the same library there is still another version in rhyme, with many interpolations (V⁷). The (V⁴) supposedly has some value alongside the Oxford MS for a study of the text. The (V⁷) is worthless. Equally padded and unauthoritative are MSS preserved at Chateauroux (C), Paris (P), Lyons (L), and Cambridge (T). All the MSS other than O are held to be derived from a lost version designated as β.

The historical *départ* for this poem was a passage in Eginhard's *Vita Karoli*, narrating how, on the return of Charlemagne's first expedition into Spain (778), the rear guard was attacked by the Basques at a mountain pass. The Val de Cize, or the Col de Ibañeta, the pass which is used between Pamplona and Saint-Jean-Pied-de-Port, is not named as the scene of this skirmish, but there is no reason for supposing that it did not occur there. This pass has always been commonly known as the Pass of Roncesvalles. There is an excellent study of its topography by E. Lambert, in *Rom* LXI (1935), 17-54. Albert Pauphilet has argued, however, with considerable conviction that no legend or tradition was preserved at this pass, or anywhere else, concerning Roland, until after the composition of the *Chanson de Roland* (*Rom* LIX, 161-98). The passage in Eginhard reads:

In quo proelio Eggihardus regiae mensae praepositus, Anshelmus comes palatii et Hruodlandus Brittanici limitis praefectus cum aliis compluribus interficiuntur. Neque hoc factum ad praesens vindicari poterat, quia hostis, re perpetrata, ita dispersus est ut ne fama quidem remaneret ubinam gentium quaereri potuisset.

An epitaph of the Eggihard who was slain tells us that the battle occurred on August 15, 778. The version of the *Chronicle of Lorsch* (after 1179), preserved in the abbey library of Moissac, is our authority that the day was a Sunday and that the battle was at three o'clock. (We are better informed today and know that the day was a Saturday!) With the one historical passage, and possibly a small amount of floating legend, the poet constructed his original poem. He imagined, or perhaps he had heard, that the attack was avenged with great slaughter and that the enemy were not insignificant Basques, but Saracens. The part about Ganelon he introduced from his own creation, although he may have heard of the traitorous Wanilo, Archbishop of Sens (837-865).

May certain monasteries not have aided in fostering this Roland poem? The Abbey of Saint Foy at Conques (Aveyron) has the name *Rotlandus* in its charters as early as 959; it secured possession of the almshouse at

Roncesvalles before 1104. The Abbey of Conches, or Castillon, in Normandy (Eure) has relics of Saint Foy. The first of these foundations is on the *via franca*, pilgrim route to Compostella. Along the *via franca* (Bordeaux, Dax, Saint-Jean-Pied-de-Port, Roncesvalles, Pamplona) fourteen expeditions of northern Frenchmen had moved into Spain, during the eleventh century, to fight the Infidel. There were fifteen more such expeditions in the twelfth century, and five in the thirteenth. Roland's supposed tomb was shown to travelers at Saint-Romain de Blaye, and his horn at Saint-Seurin of Bordeaux. It was in connection with this *via franca* and its ecclesiastical foundations that the *Chanson de Roland* could most easily have come into existence. Saroïhandy (*Homenaje a Menéndez Pidal*, Madrid, 1925, II, 259-284) proposed a definite reason for the composition of the *Roland* other than the general stimulus of the pilgrim route. He said that Bishop Pierre d'Andouque founded the almshouse at Roncesvalles in 1101-1102, and that the *Chanson de Roland* was composed mainly for the purpose of exploiting this hospice to the profit of the canons at Pamplona and the monks at Conques, as a rival of the celebrated hospice of Ibañeta which belonged to the monks of Leyre. Bishop Pierre's immediate predecessors, as bishops of Pamplona, had been also abbots of Leyre, and Bishop Pierre was elected to break that tradition. Leyre was dominating the entire Church in Navarre. That happy jongleur Turoldus, if such were his name, was in the employ then of Pierre d'Andouque. This would place the date of composition more precisely at 1101-1102; but this is rather late.

Karl Heisig seeks to demonstrate that the poem of the *Roland* owes much to the Pseudo-Methodius (late seventh century) and other "end-of-the-world" types of writings, which we may call Sybilline prophecies. The Saracens were the Antichrist and the Christians were God-inspired to die as martyrs (*ZfrPh* LV, 1-87). The Cluniac monks, he says, were influential in inspiring this epic of the *Roland*. Heisig has written some interesting pages but his theory goes too far afield. Charles Knudson (*Rom* LXIII, 48-92) argues very convincingly that the poem is the unified work of a conscious artist and that the MS O preserves the original version. He believes, however, that there has been some slight retouching of the order of verses and language in O.

Traces of a different version of the Roland story, earlier than the Oxford MS at least, are in two Latin compositions, the *Carmen de proditione Guenonis* and the *Historia Caroli magni et Rothlandi* or *Pseudo-Turpin*. The *Carmen*, sometimes ascribed to Walter the Englishman, may have been a scholastic exercise. It dates from the middle of the twelfth century, has 241 Latin distichs, and is preserved in a single fifteenth-century MS of the British Museum. It lacks the embassy of

Blancandrins, the Baligant episode, and the trial by combat for Ganelon's life. The other Latin work is in prose, narrating Charlemagne's legendary Spanish war from beginning to end. The material of the *Chanson de Roland* is covered in Chapters XIX to XXVII. The Archbishop Turpin is represented as having survived the famous battle and lived to an old age when he composed this account. It is now generally recognized that this *Pseudo-Turpin* (middle of the twelfth century) was the fourth part of a *Book of Saint James of Compostella,* a work intended to promote that pilgrimage. Its vogue was enormous. The Roland windows of the basilica of Saint-Denis and the cathedral at Chartres are based upon the *Pseudo-Turpin* and not upon the French epic version.

Chapter XI of the *Pseudo-Turpin* bears close resemblance to another epic of the Charlemagne cycle which survives in a single fragment of 160 lines. Paul Meyer discovered this sheet at the University of Cambridge where it is designated as additional MS 3303 (*Rom XXXV,* 22-31). The poem may be dated in the last years of the twelfth century, but the inclusion of the story in the *Pseudo-Turpin* would argue for a still earlier version—probably of the early twelfth century. Meyer named this *Chanson* after its chief Saracen character, Agolant. This *Chanson d'Agolant* narrates certain episodes of Charles's war in Spain, in particular a combat between Ogier and Agolant. The *Pseudo-Turpin* omits this particular combat.

There are two Provençal poems of *Ronsasvals* which retail the famous battle at the pass. They are quite late, as the character Galien appears in them. See M. Roques in *Rom XLVIII,* 311-13, and his edition of one of them in *Rom LVIII,* 1 ff.

Next to be considered is the *Pèlerinage de Charlemagne,* a poem of 870 lines in twelve-syllable *laisses,* composed between 1109 and 1150, to be sung at the *Lendit* or Fair of Saint-Denis. It is the oldest piece of literature of which we possess a trace, emanating from the city of Paris. The spirit of it is truly Parisian. The city which vacillated from Armagnac to Burgundian, in the fifteenth century, which started so many revolutions and mocking heresies, might well have given life to this little epic poem. It is filled with a hearty humor from first to last, a humor which some critics have misunderstood.

Charles with his twelve peers and a thousand knights of France sets out for Constantinople. His queen has told him that Hugh the Strong, Emperor of Constantinople, is more noble and wears his crown more loftily. Charles is beside himself with anger and has vowed to slay her if the statement is not true. They arrive first at Jerusalem. The patriarch gives them a magnificent reception and bestows upon them many relics: the arm of St. Simon, the head of St. Lazarus, some of St. Stephen's blood, a bit of the shroud of Our Lord, the chalice of the Last Supper, and seven other relics equally powerful. The cavalcade moves on to Constantinople. There they are well received by the King whom they find ploughing with a golden plough. They marvel at the rich palace, which revolves in the wind, and at the automatons and other wonders of the city. They are lodged that evening in a noble chamber where there are twelve beds ranged around a thirteenth for the King. (It is a question only of the peers: the thousand knights play well into the background). They drink deeply and feel the effects. They begin to boast or *gaber,* for the sake of amusement; but Hugh has hidden in a hollow pillar a spy who takes all these foolish boasts to heart. Charlemagne boasts that with one stroke he can split clean through Hugh's best knight clad in reïnforced armor and mounted on a stalwart charger, and bury his sword in the ground. The others make similar vaunts of strength and skill, all save Olivier whose boast is of an amorous nature. The spy reports to his master and Hugh is enraged. The following morning he informs the now sober Franks that they must fulfill their *gabs* or die. They pray devoutly for God's aid and an angel appears and promises success in their undertakings. Strangest of all strange things Olivier is the first to be put upon trial! God will not aid him in a trial of so lustful a nature, but he is saved by a falsehood of Emperor Hugh's daughter. Several of the others, with divine aid, fulfill their *gabs* to the letter. Hugh has had enough. He makes his peace and the two emperors wear their crowns side by side, though Charlemagne's is admittedly a little higher. The Franks return with their relics, and through the generosity of Charles the queen is pardoned her misdemeanor.

The work is a caricature of the official story which was, in turn, forged to explain the existence of certain relics in Saint-Denis. The official written version may have been known to the poet, or it may have been composed later. The poet could have secured all the necessary information verbally from monks at Saint-Denis. The official Latin narrative was entitled the *Descriptio qualiter Karolus Magnus clavum et coronam Domini a Constantinopoli Aquisgrani detulerit qualiterque Karolus Calvus hec ad Sanctum Dyonisium retulerit,* known for brevity's sake as the *Descriptio* or *Iter Hiersolimitanum,* and has been preserved to-day in three slightly differing versions. It was retold by a number of medieval chroniclers, Philippe Mouskés, Michel de Harnes, Sigebert de Gembloux, Gui de Bazoche, and in the *Grandes chroniques* (see *Rom* LVI, 193-211). The *Pèlerinage,* a vulgar derivative of this official story, was not only entertaining to the visitors to the Fair of St. Denis, but it also rendered popular the story of the relics. It was not the only popularization of the *Descriptio.* There was a series of them, all explaining

more or less the translation of certain relics to Saint-Denis, and all interspersed with a large amount of extraneous detail. These "relic poems"
have even been dignified by the term "cycle"—"cycle of the relics". In the
*Mort Aymeri de Narbone* we read:

> Charles li rois, a la barbe florie,
> De Jerusalem aporta les reliques
> De cel saint fust ou Deus soufri martire,
> Et la corone qu'il ot el chief, d'espines,
> Et les sains clous, et la sainte chemise
> Qu'empres sa char avoit sainte Marie
> Quant elle fut de son chier fil delivre
> Ce aporta en France la garnie. . . .
>             Ce fu une des gestes (vs. 3063 ff.)

Nearly all of the poems of this minor cycle have been lost, so we give
it only brief mention here. Two of the later ones were related by Jean
d'Outremeuse (fourteenth century) in his *Myreur des histoires.*

T. P. Cross has shown (*MPhil* XXV, 349-354), after Thurneysen and
K. G. T. Webster (*Englische Studien,* XXXVI, 351-61), that some of the
famous *gabs* of the *Pèlerinage* (which form the more entertaining part
and which suggested to Anatole France his *Le Gab d'Olivier*) are reminiscent of Celtic material. We have observed how Celtic folklore and
legend were current in France through minstrels from Brittany, Wales,
and Cornwall; these, in turn, had some contact with Ireland. So commonplace were the Celtic songs that one of the authors of the amusing
*Roman de Renart* (thirteenth century) puts a Welsh song into the mouth
of an animal minstrel, Ferrant the horse:

> Et le roncin sire Ferrant
> Harpera, tiex est mon plesir,
> Un *son galois* tout a loisir (ed. Martin, II, 225).

There was probably intended an uncomplimentary resemblance to the
neighing of a horse. The *gab,* or feat, of Archbishop Turpin is very
like the *uballchless* feat of Cuchulain; the feat of Garin resembles the
play of the young Cuchulain with his *lorg áne;* Berengier's *gab* is similar
to an episode in the *Tochmarc Emire,* "Wooing of Emer." Mrs. Laura
Hibbard Loomis (*MPhil* XXV, 331-349) goes still farther and attributes
the episode of the twelve beds around a central bed, the room lighted by
a carbuncle, and even the twelve peers of Charlemagne themselves, to a
survival of Celtic tradition. These resemblances are too close to be passed
over lightly. Until new evidence appears to the contrary we may well
accept these conclusions of Cross and of Mrs. Loomis. Permit me to
add that the presence of these Celtic descriptions in the *Pèlerinage* would
show that they were not taken seriously by the French speaking public.
Indeed, it may have been to ridicule them, as in the above episode of the

horse minstrel, that such descriptions were inserted in the *Pèlerinage*. Schofield, Webster, and Loomis are more explicit and suggest that the "advertiser of Saint-Denis" seized upon an early Arthurian legend and substituted epic characters (*Spec* III, 25). Similarities of detail are to be found in the *Pèlerinage* and in later Arthurian tales such as *Diu Krone, Rigomer, Arthur and Gorlagon.*

To return to the *geste du roi*, another poem is *Fierabras*, of which the surviving form was composed about 1170. There are 6219 verses, in the usual epic metre and in Picard dialect. As the unknown poet tells us (vs. 6207 ff.), the action was supposed to have occurred three years before the events of the *Chanson de Roland*. It begins with a combat between Oliver and the pagan Fierabras of Alexandria. The father of Fierabras, the emir of Spain, has taken possession of Rome and carried off the holy relics. Among these are the crown of thorns and the ointment with which the body of Our Lord was anointed. This ointment has the miraculous power of making whole any wound, no matter how serious. Charlemagne has attacked the despoilers. The giant Fierabras has marched before the Christian camp and has ordered them to send a champion. Oliver alone accepts, though he is badly wounded. The pagan is defeated and baptized but Oliver is captured, and with him four others: Berart de Montdidier, Aubri the Burgundian, Geoffrey of Anjou, and William the Scot. The seven other peers, among whom are Roland, Ogier the Dane, Naimes of Bavaria, etc., are sent by Charlemagne to rescue their companions, but they, too, are captured. The sister of Fierabras, Floripas, falls in love with one of them, Guy of Burgundy. Her aid sets them free and gives them arms; after many combats they are freed by Charlemagne. The Emir is slain, for, unlike his son, he will not become a Christian. Floripas marries her lover and Spain is divided between Guy and Fierabras. As Gaston Paris had occasion to remark (*Histoire poétique de Charlemagne*, p. 251), this epic *Fierabras* is probably the rehandling and continuation of another, now lost, describing the fall of Rome at the Emir's hands. Gaston Paris entitled this lost epic *Balan,* the name of the Emir. Material from this *Balan* was worked into a preface (1507 alexandrines) to the *Fierabras.* This preface, found in two variant MSS, is known as the *Destruction de Rome* (See Stimming in *ZfrPh* XL, 550-88, and H. M. Smyser in *HSN* XIV, 339-49). These poems were sung on the pilgrim routes to Rome, and the basic substance was doubtless obtained at Rome itself, in the Church of St. Peter. This substance or *point de départ* is knowledge of the fact that the Saracens sacked Rome in the year 846. The rest was the poet's imagination.

The epic *Floövant* was composed at St. Denis, though it makes no mention of the relics. It has survived in a late twelfth century version, 2533 lines long. It is the only *chanson de geste* to center about Clovis.

Floövant (Hlodoving?) is the eldest of Clovis' four sons. As a youthful prank he one day clips the beard of his preceptor, a baron of high rank. We are given to understand that at that time only criminals suffered this indignity. Clovis is so angry that he would have slain his son save for the intervention of the queen and the clergy. Floövant is sentenced to seven years' exile, during which he wins glory in arms and goes in search of a wife (the *brautfahrt* motif). The content of this poem is the story of young Dagobert (seventh century) as narrated in the *Gesta Dagoberti*. This Latin original also included the founding of Saint-Denis. Dagobert in his flight took refuge in an obscure chapel where reposed the bones of St. Denis, St. Eleutherius, and St. Rusticus. When he became king he raised upon the site the Abbey of Saint-Denis, to show his gratitude. This was the account with which the monks at Saint-Denis were familiar; the French poem is a vulgarization of the history, although it omits the account of the founding of the Abbey.

*Aquin* is preserved in a single fifteenth century MS, though there is but little doubt that it was composed in the last quarter of the twelfth century. The first sheet of the MS has been lost and the scribe did not complete the copy, so fifty-four verses are missing at the beginning and perhaps an equal number at the end. There are 3,087 verses which have survived. The whole was composed in the Francian (Ile-de-France) dialect.

For thirty years Brittany has been held by the Saracen Aquin, who seized it during one of Charlemagne's enforced absences from France. Aquin's chief strongholds are Quidalet (Aleth), Gardoine (legendary), and Dinard. From these points he threatens to invade further territory, Paris and the Ile-de-France! Dol is still in Christian hands, and at the opening of the poem the Bretons have called upon Charlemagne for aid. He responds at once, and after battles, sieges, etc., he forces the Saracen's strongholds and drives him to Mene-Hom. The end of the poem should have narrated the final expulsion of the Saracens.

The author of *Aquin* shows a faultless acquaintance with his terrain. He knows fords, islands, and roads, and he has taken the trouble to present them all with accuracy. He was a Breton and, as we shall see, perhaps a resident of Dol. The Archbishop of Dol, since the tenth century, had been trying to assert his independence from the See of Tours. By 1120 only three bishops recognized the Archbishop of Dol, those of Saint-Briève, Tréguier, and Aleth, the last being the most important. But the Bishop of Aleth also went over to the Archbishop of Tours during the succeeding ten years, and this was very keenly felt. Henry II of England, Pope Hadrian IV, and his successor, Alexander III, all encouraged the Breton Archbishop, and he began once more to assert his pretensions. It was at this time, says Bédier, that *Aquin* was composed. "Il n'est rien qu'une œuvre d'actualité, destinée à établir la précellence du siège de Dol . . . la vassalité du siège d'Aleth ou de Saint Malo." (*Lég. épiques*, II, 124). The *Chanson d'Aquin* is authority that it was Archbishop Ysoré of Dol and Charlemagne who first constructed churches in the territory of Aleth. *Ergo*, as this district had been Christianized by Dol, it was subordinate to that See. Such was probably the *raison d'être* for this *chanson;* it was the combined work of a jongleur and the See of Dol.

*Aspremont* dates from the last decade of the twelfth century. It is unusually long for a *chanson de geste* (11,376 lines) and it is in ten-syllable monorhymed *laisses*. The Saracen king, Agolant, sends a messenger to Charles from Italy, giving defiance. Charles in his anger seeks to slay the messenger, Balant; he is checked by Naimes. The Franks set out for Calabria, and with them is the young Roland who has not yet won his spurs. Roland is the protagonist, if there is any, in this long rambling poem. He saves Charlemagne's life, and wins among the spoils the famous sword Durendal. After a great deal of desultory fighting and lamenting on the part of Agolant, the Christians are victorious. The Christian camp is at Aspremont, which accounts for the name of this *chanson de geste*. It contains material from an eleventh century epic, *Girart de Frete* (the ancestor of the *Girart de Roussillon*). R. van Waard suggests that the poem was composed in 1188 as propaganda for the Third Crusade. It is closely dependent upon the *Chanson de Roland* and stresses the unity of Christendom against the threatening Infidel. Calabria was a stop on the route to Jerusalem; a legend of an expedition by Charlemagne into Calabria had been in existence since the tenth century. The author of *Aspremont* was familiar with his terrain (*Etudes sur l'origine et la formation de la Chanson d'Aspremont,* Groningen: Wolters, 1937).

Contemporary with *Aspremont* is another long epic, *Huon de Bordeaux* (after 1191). It has 10,495 verses, but its versification is the regular ten-syllable assonance. The classification is very difficult. It shows considerable influence from the romances, and it could be placed in the cycle of Doön de Mayence (the rebellious vassal cycle) as well as in the *geste du roi*. Guessard and Grandmaison say of it in the Preface to their edition:

On a evidemment composé *Huon de Bordeaux* à l'époque où la veine héroïque commençait à s'épuiser, où les contes bretons [the romances] s'emparaient déjà de la faveur réservée jusqu'alors aux . . . chansons de geste. Cette époque, selon nous, comprend la fin du 12ᵉ et les premières années du 13ᵉ siècle. . . .

On the death of Séguin, Duke of Bordeaux, his sons Huon and Girard fail to go to Paris to do homage for their fief. An evil traitor, Amauri de la Tour de Rivier, covets their land and proposes that they be dispossessed as rebels. Naimes, their uncle, intercedes and recommends that they be summoned. Amauri suggests mischief to Charlemagne's unworthy eldest son, Charlot, and he lays an ambush for them. He is slain by Huon. Charlemagne's wrath knows no bounds at the death of his heir. It is only when his peers renounce Charlemagne that he spares Huon's life—provided he make a long and perilous journey into the country of the Saracens. Girard is allowed to stay at home and administer the fief. There then follows a series of adventures, in one of which Huon is aided unfailingly by the fairy king Auberon, second son of Julius Caesar and the fairy Morgan. He returns safely, but alas! he discovers that his brother Girard has betrayed him and is usurping the fief. Auberon appears once more, brings about the hanging of Girard, and reconciles Huon with the Emperor. Huon marries Esclarmonde, the beautiful princess he has won among the Saracens. Auberon departs but he promises to give Huon the crown of fairyland in three years.

X. Pamfilova (*Rom* LIV, 484-492) agrees that the connections and circumstances of origin of this poem are not yet understood but she brings into discussion the little Abbey d'Eysses in the town of Villeneuve-sur-Lot, on the road from Agen to Périgueux. The reputed founder was Seguinus, Viscount of Bordeaux. The legend tells that Seguinus, an idolater, killed his son, and was sent by a doctor to Rome, to Pope Sylvester. When his soul was cured by the pope he returned to France and founded the Abbey. This Seguinus is, beyond a doubt, the Duke Séguin of the epic poem. The remainder, however, is little more than an adventure romance based upon folk motifs (Mt. 461 IIa, IVa, *FFC*, 74; Mt. 461A, *FFC*, 78; Mt. 461, *FFC*, 81). Professor Brugger's suggestion (*MLR* XX, 158-173) that the *Fergus* was used as a source is very probable. Whence the name *Auberon?* It occurs at this same date in Jean Bodel's *Jeu de Saint-Nicholas*. Shakespeare derived his Oberon, the fairy king in *A Midsummer Night's Dream*, from Lord Berner's translation of a late prose version of *Huon de Bordeaux*.

Carl Voretzsch and D. Scheludko have proposed certain other folk themes as a basis for this *chanson de geste*. Voretzsch suggests the Two Brothers (Grimm no. 60), the Elves (*ibid.*, no. 91), the Skilful Huntsman (no. 111). Scheludko names as source the Water of Life (Grimm no. 97) and the Golden Bird (no. 57). A. H. Krappe, on the other hand, believes that the author drew upon certain Celtic tales such as the *Cath Maige Tured*, etc.; that he used also the Eastern legend of the Two

Roads to Babylon. This material, Krappe says, was embellished with contemporary coloring and figures. Auberon he believes to be reminiscent of Duke Alberich of Elbenland, who is also celebrated in the Middle High German *Ortnid*. (See Krappe in *ZfrPh* LIV, 68-88; Voretzsch in his *Die Composition des H. von B.*, Halle, 1900; and Scheludko in *ZfrPh* XLVIII, 361-97.)

We do not possess any French version of *Basin*, a *chanson* of the youth of Charlemagne. It is accessible in the Norse prose collection known as the *Karlamagnussaga,* an adaptation made for King Haakon V of Norway, in 1300, of the Old French epics dealing with Charlemagne. *Basin* may well have been composed in the first half of the twelfth century. This is the story: After the death of Pepin, Charles is warned by an angel to flee for his life. He takes refuge in the forest of Ardennes and is bidden by the angel to go and rob with Basin, a notorious thief of those parts. In this way he will save his life. Charles obeys. While hidden as a thief in the castle of the traitor Rainfroi, in the Ardennes forest, he learns of a plot to slay him. Rainfroi shall be emperor and Helpri duke. On his coronation at Aix-la-Chapelle, with the aid of Basin, Charlemagne ferrets out the traitors. Basin, the thief, is rewarded with Rainfroi's wife and castles.

Rainfroi and Helpri are unquestionably the Raginfredus and Chilpericus who were defeated by Charles Martel at Amblève, Belgium, on March 21, 717. The epic poem *Basin* is pure fiction save for the names of these two chief characters; it may be based upon a folktale (Mt. 951A, *FFC*, 74 and 81). Twelve miles from Amblève was the monastery of Stavelot, founded around 650. At the close of the eleventh century a monk of Stavelot wrote the *Passio Agilolfi,* in which is told how the pious abbot Agilolfus was slain at Stavelot by the traitors Raginfredus and Chilpericus. Bédier is able to show excellent evidence that the author of *Basin* was familiar, directly or indirectly, with this *Passio Agilolfi.* He had a thorough topographical knowledge of the district near Stavelot, and he could not very easily have obtained elsewhere the names of the two traitors. Perhaps the poet's knowledge of the *Passio* was not a personal one; he may have heard the names in the sermon of some monk of Stavelot. Who can tell?

*Basin* lent the names of these same traitors to two other poems which treat of Charlemagne's youth: *Mainet* and *Berthe aus grans piés*. There existed versions of both of these at the beginning of the twelfth century, but our oldest extant *Mainet* belongs to the close of that century and *Berthe aus grans piés* does not survive earlier than the thirteenth. The latter will be discussed in a later chapter.

We possess only 1,328 fragmentary verses of *Mainet* which, when
entire, Gaston Paris estimates to have had five thousand lines. The fragments, as we know them, are in twelve-syllable *laisses,* part in rhyme and
part in assonance. Gaston Paris' theory with regard to this mixture is
this: ". . . il est probable que la forme que nous avons sous les yeux est
le produit d'une tentative faite pour ramener à la rime pure un poème
en assonances: le remanieur a renoncé à la tâche quand elle était
trop difficile. . . . A en juger par l'allure générale du style, notamment
dans les laisses assonantes, l'œuvre primitive était de la première moitié
du 12ᵉ siècle, le travail de remaniement . . . n'est pas postérieur à la fin
de ce même siècle." The MS fragments were discovered by A. Boucherie,
in use as a covering for a cardboard box. Aside from the two names
drawn from *Basin,* it has been impossible to determine anything concerning tne origin of this epic. There may have been some circumstance
in connection with Stavelot which caused the monks there to narrate the
childhood of Charlemagne. It seems significant that the three poems
which deal with the youth of Charlemagne are related and can be attached
to Stavelot. More cannot be said until we possess all three poems intact.

The plot of *Mainet* is interesting:

Helpri and Rainfroi, the sons of a female serf who had impersonated
Pepin's wife, Berthe "as grans piés," have poisoned the royal pair. Rainfroi, who was appointed regent by the dying king, has relegated their son
Charles to the kitchen. He and Helpri plot the boy's destruction. Charles
flees with some comrades, among them David, a faithful servitor. They
go to Spain and take service with the Saracen king Galafre. There
Charles distinguishes himself and wins the love of Galafre's daughter,
as well as the spite of her brother, Marsilies. From Spain Charles goes
to Italy and thence to France where he slays his enemies and is crowned
king.

Of the *Chanson des Saisnes,* composed not long before 1200, we are
fortunate enough to know the author. He was that same Jean Bodel
whom we have already mentioned, the author of the *Jeu de Saint-
Nicholas.* He also wrote lyric poetry; one of his lyric poems, a *Congé*
(1202), was written on the occasion of his withdrawing into a leper
colony. This would justify us in treating his major work as twelfth
rather than thirteenth century. The *Chanson des Saisnes* is in twelve-
syllable *laisses* with a mixture of rhyme and assonance. There are about
7,650 verses.

The poem begins with a brief history of Charlemagne's predecessors
to the throne of France:

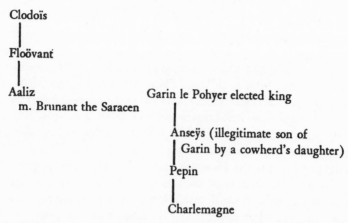

Clodoïs
|
Floövant
|
Aaliz          Garin le Pohyer elected king
m. Brunant the Saracen
                          |
                          Anseÿs (illegitimate son of
                          |    Garin by a cowherd's daughter)
                          Pepin
                          |
                          Charlemagne

The narrative proper now begins. Guiteclin the Saxon, recently married to Sebille, has heard of the death of the twelve peers at Roncesvalles. Believing France undefended, he destroys Cologne. Charlemagne, who has just returned from Spain, is desirous of avenging the massacre at once. His own barons refuse to follow, unless the Hurepois (Normans, Angevins, Bretons, and knights of Maine and Tours) are forced to pay tribute and give service. The Hurepois will not pay but they promise to follow and aid him. There is a most dignified statement of their rights. Charles sets out for the Rhine and camps on the left bank. Here follows the love affair of Sebille and Baudouin, brother of the dead Roland, in addition to numerous other episodes. At last the Frankish army crosses the Rhine upon an improvised bridge and the Saxons are defeated. Guiteclin is slain; Baudouin and Sebille are married and granted the fief of Saxony. Charlemagne departs. Unhappily the pagans, led by sons of Guiteclin, take up arms once more, and slay Baudouin. Charles returns and the kingdom is then bestowed upon Dyalas, a converted son of Guiteclin. Sebille retires to a monastery.

There is nothing historical in this *chanson* save the names Guiteclin and Charlemagne. Bodel professed to have obtained his material from St. Burgundofaro's Church at Meaux. If Bodel had consulted the *Chronicle of the Monk of St. Gall*, or the *Life of Burgundofaro* by Hildegarius, he would surely have utilized some of the details upon Charlemagne's Saxon campaign given there. This is Bédier's belief. The pretense of securing material at Meaux was due to vague knowledge on Bodel's part that Burgundofaro of Meaux was a reputed eyewitness of the Saxon campaign. This *chanson de geste* was doubtless an original composition of Jean Bodel and not a revision of a previous poem. So far as we know it had no connection with any ecclesiastical foundation. Whether it had any propaganda as its motif, or incidentally, it is difficult to determine. There

:s one point which has suggested itself to me. Who were these Hurepois who finally promised service to Charles, provided their ancient rights were secured? They were those same counties of Maine, Anjou, Normandy, and Brittany which Philip Augustus was at that moment seeking to snatch from John Lackland. Philip actually invaded Maine in 1199; the conquest of all this territory, save Brittany, was established by October, 1206. Perhaps as a well-known and influential poet Jean Bodel wished to remind the French that such a political change would take time, and that the Hurepois must not be exploited excessively. If this is correct it would account for the Hurepois episode, which, indeed, appears to be a digression. The first suggestion of the complete poem may have come to Bodel from the close of the *Roland*. After Charlemagne's vengeance upon Ganelon, while still grieving for Roland and his peers,

> Li reis se colchet en sa chambre voltice,
> Sainz Gabriël de part Deu li vint dire:
> Charles, somon les oz de ton empirie,
> Par force iras en la tere de Bire;
> Rei Vivien si socorras en Imphe
> A la citet que paien ont asise.  (*Roland*, vss. 3992-3997)

It is probable that Bodel knew nothing of either Bire or Imphe, although Bire or Bile does occur elsewhere as a Saracen country. No other poet had taken advantage of this opportunity for a new theme suggested by the close of the *Roland*,

> Encontre mei reveleront li Saisne (vs. 2921).

It is not unlikely that Bodel determined to continue the *Chanson de Roland* by substituting the more familiar town of Cologne for the unknown Imphe.[1] In all events, it *is obvious* that Bodel was continuing the older poem.

Léon Gautier was unusually severe upon this *chanson de geste*. We find it smooth and well written with many a touch of humor. The scholars of Gautier's day were more wont to look for high exaltation of treatment, the patriotic outpourings of a victorious people, in the Old French *chanson de geste*. This accorded with their theory of mass origin and composition by the people under emotional stress. Jean Bodel was a capable writer and a clever mind; to us he appears almost twentieth century in his point of view.

The other epics in the cycle or *geste du roi* are: *Berthe aus grans piés, Otinel, Enfances Ogier, Gui de Bourgogne, Gaydon; Anseis de Carthage, Macaire, Guiteclin de Sassoigne, Entrée en Espagne, Prise de Pampelune,*

[1] F. A. G. Cowper intends to publish a paper identifying this *Imphe* with *Imphy* in Nièvre.

*Enfances Roland, Simon de Pouille,* and *Jehan de Lanson.* They belong to the thirteenth and fourteenth centuries, and some of them will be discussed in a later chapter

EDITIONS

*La Chanson de Roland,* ed. T. A. Jenkins (rev. ed.; Heath, 1929); ed. Joseph Bédier (Paris: L'Edition d'Art, [1921-1927], 2 vols.); ed. Giulio Bertoni (Florence: Olschki, 1935); ed. A. Hilka, *Das altfranzösische Rolandslied* (Halle, 1926).—*La Chanson de Roland, genauer Abdruck der Venetianer Hs. IV,* ed. E. Kölbing (Heilbronn, 1877).—*Das altfr. Rolandslied, nach den Hsten von Chateauroux und Venedig VII,* ed. W. Foerster (Heilbronn, 1883). —*Das altfr. Rolandslied, nach den Hsten von Paris, Lyon, und Cambridge,* ed. W. Foerster (Heilbronn, 1889).—*Rolandsliedmaterialien,* ed. A. Hilka (Halle: *SrT,* 1926).—*Rencesval,* ed. E. Böhmer (Halle: Niemeyer, 1872).—Pseudo-Turpin or *Codex quartus Sancti Jacobi de expedimento et conversione Yspanie et Gallecie editus a Beato Turpino Archiepiscopo,* ed. Ward Thoron (Boston: The Merrymount Press, 1934).—A phototype reproduction of the Oxford Roland MS, with a study by Ch. Samaran, has been issued by the *SATF* (Paris, 1933).—*Le Pèlerinage de Charlemagne,* ed. Anna J. Cooper (Paris, 1925); *Karls des Grossen Reise nach Jerusalem und Constantinopel,* ed. E. Koschwitz-G. Thurau (6th ed.; Leipzig: Reisland, 1913). The only MS, BM 16 E VIII, was mislaid in 1879.—*Fierabras,* ed. M. F. Guessard (Paris: *APF,* 1860).—*Aquin,* ed. Joüon des Longrais (Nantes: Soc. Bibliophiles Bretons, 1880).—*Chanson d'Aspremont,* ed. Louis Brandin (2nd ed.; Paris: *Cfmå,* 1923-1924).—*Huon de Bordeaux,* ed. M. F. Guessard-C. Grandmaison (Paris: *APF,* 1860).— *Karlamagnus Saga ok Kappa hans,* ed. C. R. Unger (Christiania, 1860). *Mainet,* ed. G. Paris in *Rom IV,* 304 ff. Jean Bodel, *Chanson des Saisnes,* ed. F. Michel (Paris, 1839); ed. F. Menzel—E. Stengel, Marburg, 1906-1909.—*La Destruction de Rome,* ed. G. Gröber in *Rom* II, 1-78; see also L. Brandin in *Rom* XXVIII, 489-507. Brandin is studying the Egerton variant of *Fierabras* and the *Destruction de Rome.*—Another edition of the *Pseudo-Turpin* is by Cyril Meredith-Jones, *Historia Karoli Magni* (Paris: Droz, 1936).

CHAPTER IX

## THE *GESTE* OF DOÖN DE MAYENCE AND THE FEUDAL EPICS

Et l'autre apres, bien est drois que je die,
Est *de Doön* a la barbe florie
Cel *de Maiance* qui tant ot baronie
(Bertrand de Bar-sur-Aube, *op. cit.*)

This *geste* of Doön de Mayence is frequently referred to as the rebellious vassal cycle. In each poem commonly grouped under this heading, Charlemagne is forced to pursue and quell some revolting baron who has renounced allegiance, or who has harmed a member of the Emperor's immediate household. According to our modern standards Charles appears here constantly in a disagreeable light. He shows himself unrelenting in the pursuit of feudal enemies long after they have ceased to do him harm. Many of the revolts are caused by Charles's own selfishness, in the face of which the rebel seeks to save his self respect. The poets are aware of this in preliminary discussion; but once a revolt has begun, Charles is again the matchless hero and we are left with only pity for the revolting vassals. We must seek an explanation for such an attitude in the medieval conception of the kingship (see *Spec* I, 308-337). The king could only function when chosen by God, and that God was with Charlemagne no one ventured to doubt. If this divinely chosen king became a tyrant, and God was still on his side, the tyranny was a punishment for the wicked people. Charles may seem tyrannical, but it is because the family of the victim has sinned and is accursed. In this chapter we shall also include several miscellaneous feudal epics in which the vassals are warring against one another, with the king as a more or less quiet partisan of one faction. The spirit of this second group is nearly the same as in those where Charlemagne is the injured and active party. These will be placed at the close of the chapter.

Chief among the rebel vassals was Doön de Mayence, who has given his name to the cycle. Unfortunately, the *chanson* dedicated to his revolt has survived only in a late thirteenth-century form. The testimony of Bertrand de Bar-sur-Aube would prove the existence of this epic by 1215; but a passage from the *Quatre fils Aymon* sets it still earlier by fifteen or twenty years. There is no reason for doubting that such an epic existed at the beginning of the twelfth century, perhaps even in the eleventh;

unfortunately, we lack positive proofs. It would be well to cite the passage in question from the *Quatre fils Aymon:*

> Membre vus de Doön, vo frere le guerrier.
> Entre lui et Girart ki mult s'avoient chier
> Assés le [Charlemagne] guerroierent au fer et l'acier,
> Mais a la pardefin ne porent avancier.
> Fuir les en covint et le païs vuidier.
> Par l'esfors des amis les fist il repairier,
> Par la proiere d'aus n'en quist autre loier (vss. 475-81).

Following the usual tendency of the later jongleurs, the author of the *Quatre fils Aymon,* in its surviving form, tried to knit the cycle more closely together by giving the family tree and showing the blood relationship of all heroes of the cycle. There is no likelihood that this poet was the first to establish this epic "brothership and cousinhood." A jongleur composing a *chanson de geste* with some new characters found it profitable to relate them with heroes already popular. Such a family tree may be called a gradual accretion.

The poems of the rebellious vassal cycle are characterized by their unusual length. Whereas the other epics average four thousand verses, with an occasional seven or ten thousand, these have an average of ten thousand, running as high as twenty thousand in a few instances.

The oldest epic of the group, another not included by the author of the *Quatre fils Aymon* in his composite family connection, is *Gormont et Isembart,* which most authorities believe to be slightly younger than the *Roland* but belonging to the late eleventh or early twelfth century. Ferdinand Lot, on the other hand, considers it the oldest of all, dating it as far back, in its surviving form, as 1068. Only a fragment of this poem has been preserved, in two parchment sheets used in the binding of a book. These sheets, now in the Bibliothèque Royale of Belgium, were copied in the thirteenth century by an Anglo-Norman hand. The meter of this epic is curious: eight-syllable rhymed *laisses.* Only 661 lines are extant. The original dialect is judged to have been that of central France, southeast of Paris. The entire plot can be reconstructed since it was incorporated into later works, among them the *Chronique rimée* of Phillippe Mousket and the German *Loher and Maller* (1437). This last was a translation from a lost French *Lohier et Mallart* (1405). There is also a brief summary in the *Chronicon Centulense* of Hariulf, a monk of Saint-Riquier in Ponthieu, written in 1088 and revised in 1104. This attests an early date for some version of the *Gormont et Isembart.*

Isembart, a rich young vassal of King Louis, Charlemagne's son and successor, is opposed at court by an enemy faction. Louis, weakling that

he is, sides with the opposition and, after an armed struggle, Isembart
is forced into exile. He is received kindly in England by Gormont, a
Saracen king. (At this time the term Saracen was used indiscriminately
for any non-Christian.) Gormont converts Isembart to the Saracen faith
and raises an army which Isembart leads into France. He attacks Vimeu
and Ponthieu, which were his own confiscated fiefs. The final battle is
at Cayeux and it is here that the fragments of the French original take
up the story. King Louis himself slays Gormont, but, in so doing, he
receives an internal injury which causes his own death, in thirty days.
Isembart remains in command of the Saracens but he, too, meets death,
returning to the Christian belief before he expires.

What were the sources and what was the motive of this *chanson de
geste?* Hariulf is witness that the poem existed in the eleventh century.
All we can say of our extant fragment is that it was composed prior to
1130. The source, according to Bédier, is to be found in a knowledge of
a few historical facts. The Norseman Godrun crossed from England
and invaded Vimeu and Ponthieu in 880-882; he burned the Abbey of
Saint-Riquier and was finally defeated by Louis III at Saint-Valéry.
Louis died of pneumonia shortly after the battle. These facts could have
been gleaned from Asser's biography of King Alfred, or from the Annals
of St. Vaast. Bédier has remarked that the tradition of this invasion
existed, and still does in part, around the Abbey of Saint-Riquier at
Abbeville. Saint-Riquier was the third stop on the pilgrim route from
London to Jerusalem. Further, a fair at Saint-Riquier was held annually,
beginning the ninth of October. "Ces chevaliers assemblés autour du
saint comme autour de leur seigneur, ces pèlerins, ces marchands attirés
par la foire, voilà les premiers auditeurs de la chanson de *Gourmond et
Isembard.* Cette légende s'est formée pour eux et par eux."[1] Pauphilet,
and after him, F. Lot (*Rom* LIII, 325-342), deny the possibility of the
poems arising at Saint-Riquier. Lot says that the source was a Norman
saga transmitted to the continent in the ninth and tenth centuries which
was adopted later by the Abbey of Saint-Riquier. There is something to
be said for this, although absolute proof for either side of the case probably will always be lacking.

The epic known as *Girart de Roussillon,* or more properly *Girart de
Rossilho,* survives in the Franco-Provençal dialect and is often regarded
as belonging to the literature of Provence. It is another *chanson de geste*
where Bédier and F. Lot are in disagreement over the conditions of
origin. The existing form was made after 1155, probably between 1160
and 1170. It is quite long, around 10,000 lines in length, in ten-syllable
rhymed *laisses.* The caesura falls, oddly, after the sixth syllable.

[1] *Lég. épiques,* IV, 90.

The hatred of Girart and Charlemagne began over the younger daughter of the Emperor of Constantinople. She had been promised to Girart, while Bertha, the elder and less beautiful, was to belong to Charles. But Charles wanted Elissent, the younger. In recompense he was forced to grant Girart his feudal independence, which he did with keen regret. Girart marries Bertha, and Charles marries Elissent. Time passes by and the Emperor determines to break his faith; he encamps before Girart's castle and demands his allegiance. The ultimate result is a huge battle in the plain of Valbeton, two miles south of Vézelay.[2] Finally the fighting is checked by a divine miracle and the two enemies are put in accord. Five years intervene and the feud breaks out afresh. There is battle after battle and Girart at last meets defeat, for he has become cruel and earned God's wrath. At length he must seek refuge in the Ardennes forest, alone with his wife Bertha. A hermit absolves him from his sins. The pair wander into Germany where they labor as charcoal vender and seamstress at Orliac-sotz-Troïlon. There they remain twenty-two years. Eventually they return to France and, through the pleading of Elissent, are restored to their ancient estate. War breaks out again between Girart and Charlemagne; seven more years pass by and Girart submits another time. He and Bertha send overseas to obtain the body of Mary Magdalene, and found the monastery of Vézelay in honor of this relic. They die and are buried with their son in the valley of Roussillon, at the Abbey of Pothières.

Rossilho, or Roussillon, was apparently a castle lying at Isère, near Vienne, between Valenciennes and Avignon. It belonged to a noble known as Girart de Fraite (or Frete) who was at one time in revolt against Charles the Bald. Lot assures us that the tradition of this revolt hung on and was incorporated into a *chanson de geste* by the close of the eleventh century. This *chanson de geste* he refers to as the lost *Girart de Frete* or *Girart de Vienne*. Dr. Jean Mizrahi (*PMLA* LI, 8-12) proposes that no castle by the name of Roussillon was associated with Girart. He believes that Girart was traditionally a "red-head" and that he was commonly called "Girart le roussillon" which was corrupted into "Girart de Roussillon." This, of course, remains only a conjecture.

Since 1040 the Abbey of Vézelay claimed to possess the body of Mary Magdalene. Three times a year, Easter, Pentecost, and on the Magdalene's Feast Day (July 22), pilgrims flocked by the thousands to Vézelay, a point easily accessible in the center of France where all roads converged. Nearby was the Abbey of Pothières which possessed the bodies of a certain Girart, and of his wife and son. They were the actual founders of the two abbeys, Vézelay and Pothières. According to Lot, a

---

[2] See further, on Valbeton, René Louis in *Rom* LXII, 173-95.

jongleur was attracted by the records of these two abbeys and moved the location of the existing poem, *Girart de Frete*, to this district after 1155, thus composing the *Girart de Roussillon* of which we have an extant version. It is reasonable to suppose that the two abbeys helped in this transfer of location, as it would lend support to their relics and call attention to the tombs at Vézelay. Bédier does not admit the tradition at Isère near Vienne, nor does he believe that the location of the later poem at Vézelay was due to the jongleur. He thinks that the epic in earlier and later forms was a deliberate attempt on the part of the abbeys to advertise their relics and tombs. There are Carolingian ruins on Mount Lassois above Pothières. These and the tombs of Girart and his family, along with monastic records about this Girart, were the sole existing material utilized by the poet. The rest was imagination and convention. Lot has strong evidence for his case which, after all, only supplements material which Bédier had so brilliantly developed. The Latin life of this Girart de Roussillon, composed in 1120 and preserved at Pothières, is based upon an early version of the epic. E. S. Murrell supposes that the primitive version, *Girart de Frete,* gave the life-in-the-forest theme to the Tristan legend (*ca.* 1154), and that the Tristan story, in turn, gave the love theme of Elissent and Girart to the later form of *Girart de Roussillon*. The second of these suppositions may be correct. E. B. Ham defends the Montpellier MS. H-349 (Fac. de Méd.) as the best for an edition of this epic (*MPhil* XXXIII, 1-12).

*Renaus de Montauban,* or the *Quatre fils Aymon,* has long been one of the most popular of the Old French epics. Rendered into English, Italian, German, Scandinavian, and modern French, it is still current today. The oldest existing version, which is not necessarily the first, is an Old French epic dating from the very close of the twelfth century. There are 18,489 twelve-syllable verses, which make this poem one of the longest of its kind. The *laisses* are in assonance as far as verse 12,120; from that point on to the end they are in rhyme. There are six MSS of which the best is B.N.fr. 24,387, known from its previous classification (La Vallière 38) as the La Vallière MS.

The poem begins with a prologue. Bueves of Aigremont has refused homage to Charlemagne. Of the messengers whom he slays one is Lohier, Charlemagne's son. There is some fighting, with Doön de Mayence and Girart de Roussillon on the side of their brother, Bueves, but eventually all three submit to Charles. Beuves of Aigremont is slain by treachery while on the road to Aix to pay his homage.

Aymes, or Aymon, the third brother of Bueves, brings to Charles his four sons, Renaut, Aalars, Guichars, and Richart. They are well received by Charlemagne and are armed knights on the following day. Then comes tragedy. Renaut slays Bertolai, a cousin of Charles, in a quarrel over a chess board. The four brothers are outlawed and hounded to the bitter end. They build a castle in the Ardennes and call it Montessor; but after an interval of five years, word of this is carried to Charlemagne by a pilgrim from the shrine of Saint-Remacle (at Stavelot). They are besieged and driven forth, penniless, to wander about in the Ardennes woods. It is there that their father finds them, and he is forced to fight them as rebels. This misery lasts for three whole years. They then return to their father's castle and beg for aid, which is granted by their mother. With gold and silver they set forth and travel to Bordeaux, the city of King Yon of Gascony. They serve him and found the castle of Montauban ("alien's mount"). Renaut weds Yon's daughter and she bears him two sons. The four brothers are once more discovered by Charles as he is returning from Galicia. He lays siege with a huge army, but they are now aided by their cousin Maugis, a magician, son of Bueves of Aigremont. It is he whom Charles detests most of all, and he promises a reconciliation if the magician be given up. The brothers refuse, and as things become more than desperate they discover a subterranean exit and flee. They proceed to Tremoigne (Dortmund, Westphalia) where they submit to siege once more. But Charles's barons are now tired; they insist upon the granting of terms. This is done, provided Renaut make a pilgrimage to the Holy Land. On his return he bids farewell to all and repairs to Cologne where he, a humble porter, seeks to expiate his sins. He is murdered by jealous comrades, then worshipped as a saint. He is buried at Tremoigne.

We have already mentioned the double Abbey of Stavelot-Malmédy, which lies in the two dioceses of Liège and Cologne. The *Passion* of its patron saint, Saint Agilolfus, was of some moment in the formation of the epics of the youth of Charlemagne. This same *Passio Sancti Agilolfi* certainly furnished the historical data for our present poem: that a French king Charles (Charles the Bald) had warred in the Ardennes, and that he had fought against a Gascon king, Yon. The remainder is imagination or, perhaps, legend. Montessor, supposedly at the junction of the Meuse and the Semy, lay close to Stavelot. Montauban in Gascony we owe to the presence of Yon. Tremoigne, or Dortmund, was in close relations with Cologne and Stavelot-Malmédy, due partly to their common patron, Saint Agilolfus. It is very possible that *Renaus de Montauban* was composed at Stavelot, probably to advertise the district and to exploit its legends. This was a foyer of *chansons de geste*. It is generally believed that the second, or rhymed, part of the poem was written by a slightly later poet. It is from this second part that has arisen the cult of Saint Renaud. Saint Renaud goes no deeper than the hero of this *chanson de geste*.

An epic dealing with Ogier the Dane already existed in 1160, to judge from a passage in the *Quirinalia* of Metellus of Tegernsee: "[Occarius] Quem gens illa canens prisca nunc Osigerium." Likewise in the composition known as the *Pseudo-Turpin* (middle of the twelfth century): "De hoc [Ogerius] canitur in cantilena usque in hodiernum diem." The *Chevalerie Ogier de Danemarche,* the surviving version of the rebellion of Ogier, dates from 1192-1200. (Emile Roy in the *Mél. Jeanroy*, p. 415 ff.) An edition based upon MS 938 of the *Bibliothèque municipale* at Tours, prepared by Dr. R. W. Linker, has 12,260 verses in assonanced *laisses.* The author of this is unknown, but a certain Raimbert de Paris undertook to rewrite this *chanson* and stopped at line 1370. His name occurs in MSS D. and P. Ogier the Dane is frequently mentioned in the *Roland* and elsewhere as a companion of Charlemagne. The appellative *li Danois* 'the Dane' is perhaps a corruption of *l'Ardenois*— 'from the Ardennes.' The *Chevalerie* poem is not consistent on this point and speaks of Ogier as a native of Denmark.

Gaufrei, Duke of Denmark, has grossly insulted four of Charlemagne's messengers. The Emperor vows vengeance, which is easily obtainable since the Duke's son, Ogier, is a hostage at his court. The barons plead in vain: Ogier must die. At this time a message from Rome summons Charles into Italy to defend the Holy City against the Saracens; Charles postpones his vengeance. Before leaving Paris with the king, Ogier engenders a son, Baudouinet. In Italy, Ogier slays Brunamon de Misor, the Saracen champion, thus freeing Rome and winning his own knighthood. He is pardoned by Charlemagne. When they return to France he finds his son grown to the age of a squire. Charlot, the son of Charlemagne, quarrels with Baudouinet in a game of chess and slays him in anger. Ogier demands the life of Charlot as atonement for the murder. It is refused. The unhappy father swears unending war till he shall slay Charlot with his own hands, and he goes forth to the court of Desier, King of the Lombards. He is forced to move on and finally seeks refuge in his own castle, *Chastel Fort.* After much warfare Ogier is at length captured by Archbishop Turpin who comes upon him asleep, as the Archbishop is returning from Rome. Charles refuses to pardon him and he is put in the custody of Turpin, to be starved to death. His jailer preserves him from starvation by a stratagem. When news of Ogier's supposed death reaches the Saracens they march into France as far as Laon. Ogier alone can drive them back. Ogier is pardoned; but he demands first the life of Charlot. The Emperor must give in, but an angel stays the falling hand of Ogier; the boy receives a slight buffet in satisfaction for the famous oath. Ogier, of course, drives back the enemy. The scenes of this poem lie on the pilgrim route to Rome. A French jongleur, with the help of Lombard clerics, composed it. What little history it contains, and this was very little, could have been obtained from the *Vita Hadriani*. In the year 772, after the death of Carloman, joint ruler with his brother Charles, Carloman's widow and sons went to Desier, King of the Lombards, under the protection of a Count Ogier. Charlemagne in pursuit finally secured possession of them. That an Ogier, rebel against Charles, fled to King Desier—that he was eventually captured—that is the historical basis of the prototype of the *Chevalerie Ogier le Danois* of Raimbert de Paris.

This brings us to those *chansons* which are generally called feudal epics, but which I consider similar in theme to the *geste* of Doön de Mayence.

*Raoul de Cambrai*, as we have it, belongs to the end of the twelfth century. It has 8,726 verses, of which the first 5,555 are in rhymed *laisses* and the remainder in assonance. It is usually stated that this second portion was a later addition by another poet. Dr. Levin, in a series of two articles, has vigorously opposed this (*RRev* XVII, 116-128; *MPhil* XXI, 274 ff.). According to him a later poet undertook to revamp the original assonanced poem into rhyme but did not complete the task. Levin's arguments are good, and he has been able to show similarities in expression as well as in treatment of theme between the two portions of the poem. In vss. 2442 ff., a certain Bertolai of Laon is named as author and is purported to have been an eyewitness of the events. Obviously the composer of this twelfth-century version looked upon Bertolai as a contemporary of Charlemagne. Bédier denies his existence and considers him a manufactured proof for the verisimilitude of the poem. Lot is able to show quite conclusively (*Rom* LII, 75-133) that Bertolai did exist and in that case it is probable that he was the author of an earlier version of this *chanson*. Here follows an outline of the plot:

Three years after the death of Raoul Taillefer, Count of Cambrai, his young son, Raoul, is disinherited by the pusillanimous King Louis that a certain knight might be awarded the fief. The wrath of Raoul's mother, Aalis, and of his uncle, Guerri le Sor, is unquenchable. The boy grows to manhood, is knighted, and is named the king's seneschal. His uncle reminds him that he must demand back his fief. His request is refused, but Louis swears upon the saints that Raoul shall have the land of the next count to die. This chances to be Herbert of Vermandois, who has four grown sons. Raoul cannot be persuaded to wait for other land: he holds the King to his oath. His own mother begs him not to dispossess others as he himself was dispossessed. He will not listen, and as he leaves her she calls down upon him her curse. This is his nemesis; he is now given over to cruelty. He invades Vermandois and burns the monastery of Origni with all its nuns. It was founded by the sons of Herbert. Among the flames perishes the abbess, mother of Bernier, a faithful vassal of Raoul. The father of this Bernier is Ybert of Ribemont, one of the four sons of Herbert. On further injury received, Bernier absolves himself from homage to Raoul and passes over to his father and his uncles in this feudal war. He slays Raoul in open battle. Guerri le Sor continues the combat but is defeated; he carries the body of his nephew back to Cambrai. There Gautier, a nephew of Raoul, swears over the dead man's body to avenge his death. Five years later this same Gautier leads his men against Bernier. The war is long but is finally concluded at the court of King Louis in Paris. Bernier and Gautier are judged to a combat in which neither conquers; they both survive half dead. Bernier and his men beg forgiveness from the old mother of Raoul. It is granted. This is the conclusion of the rhymed portion. The remainder carries on the story as follows. Bernier marries a daughter of Guerri le Sor and the former enemies live in perfect peace. But Bernier and Guerri le Sor go on pilgrimage together to St. James of Compostella. On their return journey Bernier is reminded of the fate of Raoul, at Origni. On mention of this to Guerri the old man is so disturbed that he kills his companion with a stirrup as he drinks at a spring. War breaks out again. Guerri is besieged by his grandsons, Bernier's offspring, at Arras. When they refuse him their pardon he rides off alone into the night. He is said to have become a hermit.

We now give the account of the origins of this epic as established by Bédier. The historical content was obtained from the *Annals of Flodoard* (894-966). The following lines furnished the most of it: "Herbertus comes obiit, quem sepelierunt apud sanctum Quintinum filii sui: et audientes Rodulfum, filium Rodulfi de Gangliaco, quasi ad invadendam terram patris eorum advenisse, agressi eidem interemerunt. Quo audito, rex Ludovicus valde tristis efficitur." The *Annals* furnished four additional names: Wedon and Herbert, sons of Herbert, Bernard of Rethel, and Ernaut of Douai. The epic was composed in the vicinity of the collegial church of Saint-Géri, close to Cambrai. A fair was celebrated there twice a year, on August 11 and November 18, in honor of Saint-Géri. Our jongleur who was responsible for the earliest version of *Raoul de Cambrai* must have frequented this district and have known the two oldest documents of donation belonging to the church. In them a

Countess Aalis appears as benefactress, giving property for the soul of her son, Raoul of Gouy. The jongleur knew of the existence of two tombs, both of men with the name Raoul, in this very same church. With such material at his disposal he added his imagination thereto and the result was *Raoul de Cambrai*. But we must not forget the abbeys of Waulsort, Homblières, and Saint-Michel-en-Tierache. They, likewise, had some connection, not wholly clear, with this jongleur. Without them, Bédier declares, there would be no character known as Ybert de Ribemont in this *chanson de geste*. F. Lot *(loc. cit.)* says, in contradiction, that this *chanson·*could not have been composed at either Saint-Géri de Cambrai or at Waulsort. The theme of the poem is decidedly "anti-Ribemont" and the Ybert de Ribemont whom Raoul opposes is obviously Eilbertus of Ribemont, a tenth-century count who held the territory just mentioned. No jongleur attached to Ribemont or its dependencies would have written thus about Eilbertus or Ybert. Lot believes the original of the poem was a lament composed by Bertolai to bemoan the death of a historical Raoul.[1] Here again it is difficult to decide for Bédier or for Lot in our final judgment. Each is citing material which it is not easy to check. The statement that the *chanson* is "anti-Ribemont" should not carry much weight.

*Doön de la Roche* is another feudal epic of the close of the twelfth century. The meter is unusual: twelve-syllable verse in assonance with caesura after the sixth syllable. It has been preserved chiefly in a single MS, Harley 4404 of the British Museum, which contains a number of brief *lacunae*. In addition to this MS there are some odd sheets, containing vss. 1146-1325 and vss. 3110-3289, which belong to M. Eugène Lelong. As shown by Paul Meyer, it is very possible that these are fragments of the original from which the Harley MS was copied (ed. Meyer and Huet, Introduction). The poem is in the Lorrain dialect. There are 4,638 verses intact. There was doubtless a slightly earlier version than this one which we now possess. The jongleur was no master of his art: several times he confuses the condition of his characters, and the final vengeance is somewhat anticlimaxed. An amusing, though not surprising, error is the confusion of *dromedary* with *horse*.

Count Doön de la Roche has married Olive, the sister of Pepin. Their son is named Landri. The mother's ruin is plotted by Tomiles, uncle of Ganelon. He persuades a page to lie beside her, without her knowledge, and the husband believes her unfaithful. She is cast aside and Doön marries Audigour, Tomiles' daughter. Pepin is heartbroken. Eventually Olive is driven into exile and Landri is made to flee for his life, by the malice of Tomiles. Pepin does not aid Landri but he attacks Doön in

---

[1] Lot turns to the *cantilena* theory of epic origins, in this one instance. On the *Raoul de Cambrai*, see further A. Longnon in *Rom* XXXVII, 193-208; J. Acher, *Rlr* LIII, 101-60.

La Roche, as retaliation for his sister's disgrace, and forces him, too, into exile. Doön and Landri, father and son, meet years later at Constantinople. Landri is one of the chief followers of the Emperor of Constantinople. In the meantime Olive has recaptured La Roche with the help of the Bishop of Hungary. Doön and Landri arrive with an army from Constantinople. The traitor, Tomiles, and his adherents are all captured and slain with exquisite tortures. Landri first scorns his uncle for his refusal of aid, but later saves his life. All set out for Constantinople where Landri is yielded the throne by Emperor Alexander. Landri's marriage with Salmandrin, the Emperor's daughter, is celebrated.

As Ferdinand Lot has pointed out (*Rom* XXXII, 12), this whole poem is pure fantasy, save for the name of Pepin. Except for the epic setting it resembles a romance of adventure based upon folk themes (Mt. 883 A, B, *FFC*, 74, 78, 81). The prototype cannot be set very early in the century.

## EDITIONS

*Gormont et Isembart*, ed. A. Bayot (2nd ed.; Paris: *Cfmâ*, 1921).—*Girart de Roussillon*, ed. C. Hofmann (Berlin, 1855-1857); translated into French prose by Paul Meyer (Paris: Champion, 1884); a fifteenth-century version of this same poem was edited by L. de Montille (Paris, 1880). R. Louis has in preparation a new edition of the twelfth-century text and Dr. E. B. Ham of Yale University is preparing a fourteenth-century version for the press.—*Les Quatre Fils Aymon*, ed. F. Castets (Montpellier, 1909); also *Rlr* XLIX, 97 ff., 369 ff.—*Chevalerie Ogier de Danemarche*, ed. J. Barrois (Paris: *Rdp*, 1842); a new critical edition, prepared by R. W. Linker as a doctoral dissertation, is still unpublished, but may be consulted in MS in the University of North Carolina Library.—*Raoul de Cambrai*, ed. P. Meyer-A. Longnon (Paris: *SATF*, 1882).—*Doön de la Roche*, ed. P. Meyer-G. Huet (Paris: *SATF*, 1921).

# CHAPTER X

## THE *GESTE* OF GARIN DE MONGLANE

In the year 782, one Witiza of Maguelonne withdrew from the world, assuming the name Benoît. He founded a monastery in the diocese of Lodève, at Aniane, a few miles north of Montpellier (department of Hérault). His influence was immediate and he became the reformer of the Benedictine order in France. (His rule was the one adopted at the new Abbey of Cluny, founded in 910, destined to unparalleled greatness.) In 804 William, Count of Toulouse (since 790), who had fought the Saracens near Narbonne and in Catalonia, retired to this monastery of Aniane. In 806 he withdrew a few leagues to the north and built a monastery of his own, Gellone, now known as Saint-Guilhem-le-Desert. Not long after this he died.

Concerning this Count William there are two documents which belonged to Aniane and two to Gellone. Aniane possessed a donation, dictated by William on December 15, 804, in which he left certain lands to Gellone—on condition it remain forever subordinate to Aniane. It is here that his wife, Guibourc, is mentioned. A second document was an authentic life of St. Benoît of Aniane, composed in 823 by a monk, Ardon; it contained a chapter devoted to William. Gellone's documents corresponded to these. There was a donation dictated by William on December 15, 804, in which he granted the same land but did not mention Aniane; secondly, there was a *Vita Sancti Wilhelmi* which corresponded, point for point, with the chapter on William in Aniane's *Vita Sancti Benedicti*. Our concern is only that these documents were in the possession of the two monasteries in the eleventh and twelfth centuries, *treated as authentic.*

The popular pilgrimage of the eleventh century was the journey to the tomb of St. James at Compostella in Galicia. There were four routes open to travellers from northern France:

1. through Saint-Gilles, Montpellier, Toulouse, and Port-d'Aspre, known as the *via Tolosana;*
2. through Le Puy, Conques (Aveyron), Moissac;
3. through Vézelay, Saint-Léonard (Haute-Vienne), and Périgueux;
4. through Tours, Poitiers, Saint-Jean-d'Angely, Bordeaux. (*"Codex de Saint-Jacques de Compostella,"* in *Liber de miraculis S. Jacobi,* ed. Fita and Vinson, p. 62 ff.*)

The various shrines and monasteries which lined these routes, or were adjacent to them, sought as much patronage as possible. As has been said before, they indulged in what might be called advertising, accomplished with the aid of the jongleur. The chief detour recommended to the pilgrim along the *via Tolosana* was a visit to the shrine of Saint-Guilhem-le-Desert. This was brought about by *chansons de geste* dealing with the valorous exploits of William against the Saracens. To these were added later the adventures of his brothers, his father, and his great-grandfather, the whole forming a complete history of the family of Garin de Monglane (the great-grandfather). The family history was largely imaginary. What historical data there was in it concerning Count William of Toulouse, the Saint William in question, was furnished by the monks of Aniane and Gellone from their documents. This can be reduced to a few meager facts: William, a powerful noble of the south of France, fought with honor the Saracens of Spain, beyond the Pyrenees and perhaps before Barcelona. His wife was named Guibourc. After a long career he took monastic vows at Aniane, and later founded Gellone. The Church venerates him under the name Saint William. This was the historical information furnished the jongleurs by the monks whose abbeys were materially benefited from the fame of Count William. He was referred to as William of Orange posterior to the *chanson* which first narrated the capture of that city.

There are twenty-four epics which served to develop this theme, and, as we have observed, they form a closely knit family. They are preserved in cyclic thirteenth-century MSS with one exception, the *Chanson de Guillaume*.[1a] In this way the men of the thirteenth and fourteenth centuries regarded them as one continuous story. Such was not the case in the twelfth. At that time only a few had been written, dealing mostly with William himself and containing mere suggestions of his *parenté*. That some of these poems were among the earliest epics to be composed, if they were not the very earliest, is shown by the Hague fragment (early eleventh century) which is to be attached to this cycle. The completed cycle of twenty-four extant poems is subdivided into three groups:

1. The group of Garin de Monglane
2. The group of Aymeri (father of William)
3. The group of William of Orange

All but one of the *chansons* attached to the third group existed in the twelfth century. Of the other two, only three are twelfth-century, which indicates plainly how these were grafted upon the original legend of William of Orange in order to complete the family history. In naming the cycle Bertrand de Bar-sur-Aube baptized it with the name of the

[1a] F. Lot (*Rom* LIII, 454-73) believes that this epic has nothing to do with the pilgrim routes, that it is based upon oral tradition from the eighth and ninth centuries.

family's ancestor, but modern scholars often refer to the whole cycle by the name of the chief and original hero, calling it the cycle of William of Orange. In this chapter we shall retain the point of view of the twelfth century, conscious of the existence of a few episodical poems with no unity as yet, and we shall discuss them in chronological order.

The oldest of these *chansons de geste* was perhaps contemporary with the *Chanson de Roland*. It belongs, in all events, in the early years of the twelfth century, or perhaps as far back as 1070-80 (F. M. Warren in *MPhil* XXIX, 385-9). This is the *Chanson de Guillaume*. The unique thirteenth century MS containing the poem was not discovered till 1903 and was first published by the owner (*Cf.* R. Weeks in *MPhil* II, 1-16). The MS passed to the British Museum in 1912. The dialect is Anglo-Norman and the poem contains 3,553 ten-syllable lines in assonance. A number of the *laisses* have such a refrain as *Lunsdi al vespre*. This, like the *Aoi* of the *Chanson de Roland*, may be one of the signs of antiquity. The style of the *Chanson de Guillaume* is cruder than that of the *Roland;* its psychology is more primitive and it has some spirit of parody.

King Deramed of Cordova has landed at Archamp with a huge Saracen force. He is met by Count Vivian, William's nephew, who takes command of the Christians after Count Tedbalt of Bourges has fled in shame. Vivian has sworn never to flee one step before the Saracens. His men are slain, and he nearly so, but he succeeds in sending a messenger for his uncle William. William comes, but loses all his men in battle. He returns to Orange and comes back once more with thirty thousand men whom his wife has gathered for him. These, too, are slain, but he finds the dying Vivian and administers to him the last communion. Deramed is killed. William appears once more before the walls of Orange but his wife does not recognize him and will not let him in: for William, she says, would never flee before the Saracens. He at length establishes his identity. He departs for Louis's court at Laon where he demands the aid that is due him according to his feudal pact. The miserable king begins by refusing this aid but recoils before William's wrath. He agrees to send twenty thousand men. At this point begins the second division of the poem, which is generally supposed to be an independent addition. It is the so-called Reneward episode.

De la quisine al rei issit un bacheler (vs. 2650).

William now takes second place and Renewal, the giant kitchen-knave with club on shoulder, becomes the protagonist. When the Christians come to quarters again with the Saracens, he is invaluable; he slays rank after rank of the enemy and avenges completely the previous defeats and the death of Vivian. When the victors return to Orange, Renewal, through an oversight, is not invited to dinner. His wrath knows no bounds and he sets out for Spain to collect an army and destroy his erstwhile friends. But he is appeased by William's wife, Guibourc, who, on learning his history, informs him that she is his sister.

Bédier's estimate of this second portion of the poem is excellent:

> . . . l'épopée, jusque-là si belle du pathétique de la défaite, s'achève en une sorte de bouffonnerie héroïque, et sainte crestienté est sauvée par la massue d'une sorte de butor, Rainouart. . . . Ce qu'il choque en nous, ce n'est pas tant notre instinct classique de l'unité de ton et de la distinction des genres, c'est un sentiment plus profond: on eût aimé que celui qui a communié Vivien mourant fût aussi son vengeur, et que Guillaume dès qu'apparaît le bon géant Rainouart, ne fût pas rejeté tout à fait à l'arrière-plan (*op. cit.,* pp. 196-7).

As A. H. Krappe has indicated, Renreward or Rainouart is a folklore character as found in the tales of Bear's Son and Strong John (*Neuph Mitteil* XXIV, 1-10).[1]

William is here named not only William of Orange, but also *Williame, le marchiz od le curb nes* (vs. 2313)—"William with the aquiline nose." This was understood as *Williame od le court nes,* "William Shortnose," in subsequent poems.

The *Couronnement de Louis*[2] is among the finer poems of the cycle, and it has been preserved in a large number of MSS, a good gauge of popularity. There are 2,695 verses in ten-syllable assonance. The dialect is that of the region between Picardy and the Ile-de-France. This poem may be dated shortly after 1130. Professor I. C. Lecompte of the University of Minnesota, in a paper delivered before the Modern Language Association of America, in 1928, fixes the date definitely as 1131. He believes that the *Couronnement* was composed as a reflexion upon the crowning of the young Louis VII at the age of eleven years. There may be something to this theory, but it cannot be proved. Hitherto it has been assumed that this epic was a fusion of five independent poems. These are referred to as branches. Bédier, preceded by Salzman, has opposed this division strongly and argued for the unity of the whole. Their arguments should be accepted.

(So-called first branch, vss. 1-271)—Charles, worn out by many years as emperor, is crowning his fifteen year old son, Louis, at Aix-la-Chapelle. The youth is timid and hesitates before lifting the crown from the altar. This weakness strikes fury into the father's heart. It is then that a traitor, Anseïs of Orléans, offers himself as regent for a period of three years.

[1] I. N. Raamsdonk believes that the Old Testament, notably Chap. V of *Macchabees,* was a source for the *Chanson de Guillaume* as a whole (*Neoph* XIV, 168-70). This is unlikely.

[2] See D. Scheludko in *ZfrSL* LIV, 448-52.

The King is inclined to accept, but William, returning late from the hunt, penetrates the traitor's real purpose and strikes him dead with his fist. He himself crowns Louis and is appointed protector of the young king. Some five years later, Charles, not yet dead, gives him reluctant permission to make a pilgrimage to Rome. (So-called second branch, vss. 272-1429.) Once at Rome, William learns that the Saracens under Galafre have landed in Italy. He takes command of the Pope's army. It is agreed that a combat between William and the pagan giant Corsolt shall decide the war. William kills Corsolt but loses the tip of his nose—hence the appellative *od le curt nes!* The pagans do not keep their promise and proceed to a general engagement, in which they are thoroughly defeated. Galafre, their leader, turns Christian. King Guaifier of Spoleto is one of the captives freed and out of gratitude he offers his daughter and one half of his kingdom to William. The wedding is under way when two messengers arrive. Breathless, they announce the formation of a conspiracy against Louis: rebellious barons desire to crown king the son of Richard of Normandy. William then abandons his betrothed and sets out once more for France. (So-called third branch, vss. 1430-2224.) William is joined by certain of his nephews with 140 additional knights. He has a thousand of his own. Louis has taken refuge with the abbot of St. Martin's of Tours, but the enemy are in possession of this city and betrayal of the King is imminent. William lays four ambuscades before the town and enters with forty men. He summons the men in ambush to his aid when necessary, and punishes those inclined to betray the King. He slays Acelin, the usurper, with a vineyard pole. He trims Richard of Normandy's hair as a badge of servitude, and a patched-up peace is made between them. Several more years are required to quell the other rebels. Richard breaks their peace and attempts to ambush William. He is defeated and dies in jail. No more rebellions. (So-called fourth part, vss. 2225-2562)—Messengers arrive and summon both Louis and William to Rome. The Pope and Guaifier are dead and Guy of Germany has seized the Eternal City. Louis shows his cowardice but William slays Guy in single combat and flings the body into the Tiber. The miserable Louis is crowned King of Italy by William. (So-called fifth branch, vss. 2641-2688)—New rebellions against the King. William quells them and unites his sister to Louis.

In addition to the material utilized for the cycle in general, two other historical facts were known to the composer of this poem: that Charlemagne crowned his son Louis in 813, and, possibly, that Guaifier III of Salerno (871-873) was besieged by the Saracens. These facts were doubtless suggested to him by clerics. It is very unlikely that this jongleur consulted the chronicles. F. M. Warren traced the name of the Saracen Corsolt from the town of Corseult (MPhil XXVIII, 467-8).

In his mention of the detour to the tomb of St. William, Aimeri Picaud, author of the *Codex of St. James of Compostella* (*ca.* 1150) mentions that William

". . . urbem Nemausessem, ut fertur, et Aurasicam, aliosque multos, christiano imperio sua virtuti potenti subiugavit" (*op. cit.,* p. 27).

This is unquestionably a reference to the *Charroi de Nîmes* and to the *Prise d'Orange,* which have survived intact. The *Charroi de Nîmes,* which necessarily follows the *Couronnement de Louis,* may be dated some time after 1140. It is short, containing but 1,450 decasyllables in assonance.

As William returns from the chase he meets his nephew Bertrand. Bertrand tells him that Louis has just finished the distribution of fiefs among his vassals. William has not been remembered. Infuriated, the Count rides on into the palace and reproaches Louis for his ingratitude. This reproach contains a résumé of the events in the *Couronnement de Louis* (vs. 134 ff.). Louis seeks to make amends, but uselessly. He goes so far as to offer a fourth of France. William refuses to be appeased. On the advice of Bertrand, William finally demands as fiefs the kingdom of Spain and the cities of Nîmes and Orange. The King grants these, but the land must first be conquered from the Saracens. Thirty thousand men flock to William's standard. They begin with Nîmes. The men are hidden in wine casks and brought to town in carts. William is the wine merchant, and his nephews are the carters. Thus the city of Nîmes is conquered and William's life work has begun (*Cf.* Mt. 954, *FFC,* 74). This poem is ironic at times, resembling a parody. Such comic element makes for occasional obscurity.

The *Prise d'Orange* is apparently a continuation of the *Charroi de Nîmes,* in which event we should place it before 1150. There is a problem connected with it. This is the poem which narrates the capture of the city of Orange and consequently explains the future title to be borne by William. As we should expect, the *Couronnement de Louis* and *Charroi de Nîmes* refer to William as Guillelme *al cort nes,* Guillelme Fierebrace, Guillelme Brachefier, Guillelme de Narbonne, or simply Guillelme, but never as Guillelme d'Orange. However, the *Chanson de Guillaume,* which is the oldest extant poem of the cycle, and which antedates all these mentioned, shows William already in possession of Orange. Furthermore, it is in accordance with the promise of feudal aid, made by Louis when he assigns the fiefs of Spain and Orange to William, that William comes for help in the *Chanson de Guillaume*. There are three possible explanations for these discrepancies:

1. That prototypes of the *Couronnement de Louis, Charroi de Nîmes*, and *Prise d'Orange*, antedate the *Chanson de Guillaume;* 2. That a prototype of the *Prise d'Orange* alone antedates the *Chanson de Guillaume*, and that the *Charroi de Nîmes* was later made to order as introduction to the new *Prise d'Orange*. In this case the author of the *Couronnement de Louis* did not happen, by chance, to make use of the *Prise d'Orange*. 3. That the *Chanson de Guillaume* is not as old as we have placed it.

In view of the age of the *Hague fragment*, and other points considered, I am in favor of the first solution.

The *Prise d'Orange* contains 1,888 decasyllable verses in assonance. William, tired of inactivity in his town of Nîmes, desires to win Orange and its pagan princess, Orable. She is the virgin wife of the Saracen king, Tiebaut d'Arabie. Dressed as a Saracen, William, with two companions, enters Orange. The Christians are recognized and cast into prison whence they are rescued by Orable. They defend themselves with arms furnished by her until their comrades from Nîmes come to the rescue. The town is captured, Orable is christened Guibourc and wedded to William. (*Cf.* Mt. 516 I b, II, *FFC*, 74; Mt. 516, *FFC*, 81, 78). Guibourc, as we have seen, was the real name of Count William of Toulouse's first wife. The name was obtained, beyond a doubt, from the donation in the possession of Aniane. Both Orange and Nîmes were two principal stops on the *via Tolosana* preceding Montpellier and the detour to Saint-Guilhem-le-Desert. Perhaps these towns were first associated with the William legend by jongleurs who were natives of Nîmes and Orange.

Towards 1165 *Aliscans*, a rehandling of the theme of the *Chanson de Guillaume*, was written. There are 8,435 verses, in the usual ten-syllable assonance. At the close of each *laisse* there is a six-syllable line, as in the case of the *Chanson de Guillaume*. This may be conscious imitation of the older model. We shall cite only the main variations from the theme of the *Chanson de Guillaume*. William is fighting with Vivian beside him on the field of Aliscans (not Archamp)[8] and Vivian does not, therefore, send for William. When his men are destroyed William flees towards Orange upon his horse Baucent. He does not escape far and, when forced to return, he administers to the dying Vivian. Twice more William attempts to flee but is forced back by the enemy. He finally escapes in the armor of a pagan, Aerofle des Puis de Valfondée. He is not recognized in this disguise and is refused admittance into Orange. The Saracens under Tiebaut, Guibourc's former husband, lay siege to the town, but William escapes before dawn to seek help from King Louis

---

[8] Aliscans is the name of a cemetery near Arles.

at Saint-Denis. He is received with hostility at Orleans and forced to slay more than fifty citizens. He rides on and meets his brother, Hernaut de Gironde, who promises aid. Louis's court shows indifference and open contempt, as in the older poem. The King repents first and later Queen Blancheflor, who is William's own sister. They send two hundred thousand men, though the King does not go himself.

"De la quisine vait Rainoart torner" (vs. 3148) and the second part begins as in the *Chanson de Guillaume*. When the southbound army reaches Orange, they find the city burned and the women locked in the donjon, or main-keep. William must again show his face before his wife will recognize him. In the remaining portion the poem is much the same as its model.

Paulin Paris and others argued that this poem was a fusion of two independent parts—the Aliscans and the Rainoart eposides. But since we find this fusion in the *Chanson de Guillaume*, it is likely that *Aliscans* was imitated entire.

The *Chevalerie Vivien* or *Covenant Vivien*, composed between 1150 and 1175, is another later treatment of this theme of the *Chanson de Guillaume*. Jeanroy has suggested that it was based upon the *Enfances Vivien* and *Aliscans*, with some material from a more primitive *Chevalerie Vivien* (*Rom* XXVI, 175-207). He even sees resemblances in style to the *Roland*. The versification of the *Chevalerie Vivien* is the same as that of *Aliscans* with a six-syllable line closing the *laisses*. The *Chevalerie* is much shorter, comprising only 1,918 verses. It does not begin with the battle of *Aliscans*, but with the knighting of Vivian by his uncle William. Vivian sets out for Spain with ten thousand men. The next four years are spent in the capture of Barcelona and Balaguet. Tortosa is also taken. At Portpaillart, the Christians mutilate horribly some of the men of King Deramed of Cordova. The Saracens seek revenge and meet Vivian at Aliscans. After a cruel battle Vivian, wounded, gathers the remnant of his army into a deserted castle. It is from there that he sends for William, who comes with all speed. In the meantime Vivian has once more begun battle. The relief is in good stead, but Vivian is frightfully wounded. He and William do not recognize each other and they fight. When they do discover each other's identity, Vivian is once more placed upon a horse and enters the press, to meet his death. Thus ends one of the shortest epics of the cycle.

There are two existing versions, or redactions, of a theme treating William as a monk and known as the *Moniage Guillaume*, which utilized those legends current locally at Gellone and Aniane. The first of these belongs between 1139 and 1170, probably in 1160. It shows knowledge of the *Prise d'Orange*, the *Charroi de Nîmes*, and the *Chanson de Guil-*

*laume.* There remains but a fragment of it, 934 decasyllables with a six-syllable refrain at the close of each *laisse.* There is much casual rhyme mixed with the assonances. The second version is complete, comprising 6,629 lines in the familiar epic meter. The six-syllable end line occurs only twenty-two times in this case, after the *laisses* which form the Sinagon episode. These twenty-two *laisses* are dated 1170 and the rest between 1180 and 1190.

The first version begins in this way: After a hundred years of married life Guibourc dies. William cannot be consoled, but an angel visits him in a dream and bids him go to Genoa. He goes and enters a monastery there. He is soon detested by both his fellow monks and the abbot, for he beats them and eats more than his share. They send him to the sea-coast to buy fish, directing him to pass through a wood which they know to be infested with dangerous robbers. To insure his untimely end, the abbot forbids him to strike a blow in self defense unless he be robbed of his *braies* ("linen drawers"). In order to make sure of his defense, William purchases a valuable belt, or *braiel;* but he reaches the sea in safety. On his return journey he begins to sing the *Prise d'Orange* in too loud a voice and is heard by the robbers. He turns the other cheek till they disturb his *braies* and then he well-nigh annihilates all fifteen of them. The monastery is closed when he arrives there, but he secures admission by force. That night the angel appears once more and tells him to become a hermit near Montpellier. The following day he leaves, to the monks' great joy. He repairs an ancient hermitage at Gellone, but for protection from the Saracens he dwells in a castle situated upon a nearby mountain. There follows what is known as the Ysoré episode. Louis is living in Paris, in the lowest depths of meanness and distrust. To cap the climax he is besieged there by Ysoré, son of Brehier whom Ogier had killed. Louis has no longer a worthy champion: he can only weep and lament. The version breaks off here.

In the second redaction, Guibourc has already died; William goes at once to Aniane, and not to Genoa. He is hated by the monks at this abbey and sent upon the journey to the seacoast. On his return through the wood his servant sings an unspecified song which attracts fifteen robbers. William kills all but one of the thieves; the episode of his arrival at the monastery tallies with that in the previous poem. He himself decides to move on, there being here no angel messenger in his dreams. He stops with a hermit who proves to be a cousin. They defeat twelve robbers and William's fame spreads. He at length reaches a spot near Montpellier (Gellone). He wishes to establish his hermitage on a high hill, but there are too many reptiles. Like a French St. Patrick he prays God for their destruction, and with a terrible thunderclap they are hurled into the nearby ravine. An angel appears that night and bids him build a hermitage there; but he is prevented by a giant fourteen feet high. After a long struggle he hurls this giant into the same gorge, and the people of the countryside come to aid him in his labors. At this point begins the Sinagon portion (vss. 2944-4612). The Saracen king of Palermo, Sinagon, captures William and retains him in a horrible prison for seven years. He is finally rescued by King Louis and his Franks. William returns to Gellone. Next comes the Ysoré episode. Ysoré, who is a nephew of Sinagon, besieges Paris for a long time. Anseïs is sent in quest of William, since there is no other champion capable of delivering the city. William goes for his horse and armor where he had left them, at Aniane, and then rides on to Paris. He is refused admittance late at night and takes refuge with a woodcutter who lives in the moat. He kills Ysoré in single combat the next morning and orders the woodcutter to present the Saracen's head to the king. William returns immediately to Gellone. He attempts to build a bridge, but is prevented by the devil who destroys his work each night. He wrestles with the fiend and throws him into the ravine, where he still is! The old warrior now dwells in peace until his life's end.

The episode of the fight with the devil is still current because of the horrible appearance of a certain ravine at Gellone. The castle upon the hill in which William sought refuge is the castle of Verdus. And so it is possible to trace many of the details incorporated in this poem back to local legends around Gellone and Aniane.

The *Enfances Vivien* has been dated by Gaston Paris and Cloëtta between 1165 and 1170. Alfred Nordfelt believes it belongs in the first quarter of the thirteenth century. There are 3,200 ten-syllable lines in assonance. This is the only poem which occurs in the cyclic MSS between the *Prise d'Orange,* where William is beginning his career, and the *Aliscans,* in which William is a mature man. Was this gap ever filled by the jongleurs who wished to render the career of William of Orange complete? Were epics ever written dealing with his conquests of Tortolosa and Portpaillart, which he possessed in his later days? There is no necessity for assuming their existence. Below is a rapid sketch of the plot of the *Enfances Vivien:*

The Saracens have captured Garin d'Anseüne and are torturing him at Luiserne-sur-Mer in Spain. They offer to free him if Garin's wife, Wistace, will offer their son Vivian in exchange. She goes to Paris for the advice of her kinsfolk. William insists that the boy be given in exchange for the father, though he promises to avenge his death many times over. The change is made and Vivian is miraculously rescued just as his torture is about to begin. The remainder of the poem narrates Vivian's early deeds of knighthood till the day he captures Luiserne, in which he had so nearly met his fate.

*Guibert d'Andrenas* belongs to the group of Aimeri de Narbonne. Densusianu in the Introduction to his edition of the *Prise de Cordres et de Sebille* places it in the first quarter of the thirteenth century because of a supposed reference to the *Siege of Narbonne* and because of certain linguistic traits. The latter may be dismissed at once and the first is not sure. In all events, Densusianu himself admits that there must have been an earlier version of this poem by 1185; the *Prise de Cordres et de Sebille,* dated in the last years of the twelfth century, is a continuation of the *Guibert d'Andrenas.* While we are assuming prototypes in order to systematize chronology, why not assume one for the *Siege of Narbonne* as easily as for the *Guibert d'Andrenas?* This would remove the last argument for placing the *Andrenas* in the thirteenth century. In view of a generally accepted belief that a form of the *Guibert d'Andrenas* existed by 1185, we are treating it in this chapter. There are 2,406 verses in assonance with much casual rhyme. The verses are decasyllabic with the now familiar six-syllable refrain to each *laisse.* This will appear to have been a general convention for the *geste* of Garin de Monglane.

The narrative of *Guibert d'Andrenas* tells how Aymeri, seeing his six oldest sons well endowed with fiefs, determines to leave Narbonne to his godson Aymeri. For his youngest and remaining son, Guibert, he has destined the Saracen city of Andrenas and also the daughter of its king as his wife. The old man assembles an army to aid Guibert in the capture. They first take Balaguer; at Andrenas there is intense opposition, but they capture it too. King Judas is killed and Guibert marries his daughter Augaiete. He is established as lord of the city, while Aymeri returns to Narbonne to confirm his godson in his succession.

In the *Siège de Barbastre,* second half of twelfth century, written in twelve-syllable assonance (7,392 verses), Bueves of Commarcis and his sons are captured and led prisoners to Barbastre (Balbastro?) in Spain. Girart falls in love with the emir's daughter; she aids them. King Louis with Aymeri and Guillaume come to their help just in time.

In one cyclic MS there follows directly after the *Andrenas,* the *Prise de Cordres et de Sebille,* which is a continuation. Some later poet placed between the two a transition *laisse* of eight alexandrines followed by a line of six syllables, making them a continuous whole. These transition verses sum up the essential facts of the *Guibert d'Andrenas.* This unique MS (unique as the *Prise de Cordres et de Sebille* is not preserved elsewhere), is B.N. 1448 (dating 1270-1280).

The *Prise de Cordres et de Sebille,* also of the group of Aymeri, has 2,948 verses preserved, lacking about 325 of being complete. The ten-syllable line is the meter of the first seventy-eight *laisses;* the last two are in alexandrines. The usual closing refrain of six syllables is here also.

The *chanson* opens with the wedding of Guibert and Agaie (or Augaiete) at Salerie. The Saracen king, Judas, through some inconsistency, has come to life again. He takes advantage of the festivities and makes an attack. He leads away as prisoners Hernaut de Gironde, Bertrand, William of Orange, and Guibert himself; the Christians capture Butor. Guibert is taken to Sebille and the remainder are entrusted to a nameless *aumaçor* at Cordres (Cordova). Nubie, the *aumaçor's* daughter, falls in love with Bertrand; she drugs the whole town and escapes with the prisoners. She then aids in the capture of her own father and they finally reach Salerie. Cordres surrenders later on the plea of the *aumaçor* who has turned Christian. A compact is made with Judas that Butor and Guibert shall engage in single combat. The winner shall have Agaie and the towns of Salerie and Andrenas; and if Butor loses, Judas will be converted. The combat takes place, and Butor, of course, is slain. The poem breaks off here but the ending is easily surmised: Judas must turn Christian and Guibert is left in possession of his wife and lands.

The versification and the language have caused the *Mort Aymeri de Narbonne* to be dated in the last years of the twelfth century. This is very uncertain evidence, but we have no arguments to the contrary; accordingly, this *chanson* will be discussed here. It has 4,176 decasyllabic lines in assonance with the usual six-syllable refrain.

The poem as we have it shows the effects of much retouching, which was frequently inconsistent. King Louis at Paris is harassed by his enemy, Hugh Capet, and he sends for the aid of Aymeri. The messenger finds Aymeri ill abed; a Jew, Saolin, has foretold his approaching end. Aymeri desires the presence of King Louis and of his own sons to bid them a last farewell.

When Corsolt the Saracen hears of Aymeri's last illness he determines to regain Narbonne. But Aymeri is not yet dead: he rises from his bed to defend the city. He is captured by treachery and saved from the stake by the promise of his wife, Hermenjart, that she will surrender the city. This is done, but the treacherous Saracens do not keep their promise: they handle the burghers vilely and Aymeri is sent to Spain under escort. Fortunately, the main-keep, into which Hermenjart and her women have been driven, holds out, though short of food. Corsolt sends Auquaire d'Aumarie to fetch his lady fair, Clarissant, with fourteen thousand attendant maidens. These damsels are captured by Franks who are on their way to the relief of Narbonne. Aymeri is rescued by his sons, and the emperor, Louis, arrives on the scene. Auquaire has been converted and he turns against his former master, aiding the Christians to retake Narbonne. He dresses up Aymeri as Clarissant(!) and French knights as the attendant maidens. In this way they enter Narbonne where they seize the city. Corsolt is slain. In the meantime the fourteen thousand girls are carried off by the Sajetaires (pagan centaurs) who live close at hand. They are thrown into a horrible prison. When this is reported to Aymeri, he and Louis lead their men to the rescue. The Sajetaires are destroyed, but one of them wounds Aymeri fatally with an arrow. The same happens to two of his sons. They are buried with great solemnity in the Church of St. Paul, at Narbonne. Hermenjart dies shortly after. Auquaire marries Clarissant and the godson, Aymeri (Aymeriet, as he is frequently called), inherits Narbonne.

Gaston Paris thought to recognize the various strata in this epic:

1. the primitive poem, which ends with Aymeri dying in his bed surrounded by his sons and Louis;
2. a second part added by a later jongleur: the Saracen attack, to enable Aymeri to die with his boots on;
3. a third poet added the maidens, the Sajetaires, and other adventurous episodes;
4. a final reviser introduced Aymeriet, the godson. (See Bédier, *op. cit.*, I, 62, note 2.)

These divisions are very possible but will always remain conjectural. Note the resemblance to the death of Hercules.

This ends our treatment of the cycle of Garin de Monglane for the twelfth century. Under the thirteenth century something will be said of the *Enfances Garin, Garin de Monglane, Girart de Vienne, Aymeri of Narbonne*, the *Narbonnais, Bueve de Commarchis*, the *Enfances Guillaume*, the *Bataille Loquifer*, and the *Moniage Rainouart*.[4]

## EDITIONS

*Chançun de Willame*, ed. E. S. Tyler (New York: Oxford Press, 1919); ed. H. Suchier (Halle: *BN*, 1911).—*Le Couronnement de Louis*, ed. E. Langlois (2nd ed.; Paris: *Cfmâ*, 1923); by the same editor, in the *SATF* (Paris, 1888).—*Charroi de Nîmes* and *Prise d'Orange*, ed. Jonckbloet in *Guillaume d'Orange* (Hague, 1859), II; *Charroi de Nîmes*, ed. J.-L. Perrier (*Cfmâ*, 1931); MS-D of the same, ed. E. Lange-Kowal (Berlin, 1934).—*Aliscans*, ed. E. Wienbeck-W. Hartnacke-P. Rasch (Halle: Niemeyer, 1913).—*La Chevalerie Vivien*, ed. A. L. Terracher (Paris: Champion, 1909, 2 vols.)—*Enfances Vivien*, ed. C. Wahlund-H. von Feilitzen (Upsala, 1892).—*Deux Rédactions du Moniage Guillaume*, ed. W. Cloetta (Paris: *SATF*, 1911, 2 vols.).—*Guibert d'Andrenas*, ed. Jesse Croslands (Longmans, Green, 1923); also by J. Mélander (Paris: Champion, 1922).—*Le Siège de Barbastre*, ed. J. L. Perrier (Paris: *Cfmâ*, 1926); also excerpts by R. Weeks in *R Rev* X, 287-321; XI, 349-69; XII, 155-67).—*La Prise de Cordres et de Sebille*, ed. O. Densusianu (Paris: *SATF*, 1896).—*Mort Aymeri de Narbonne*, ed. J. Couraye du Parc (Paris: *SATF*, 1884).

[4] Consult J. Runeberg, *Etudes sur la geste Rainouart* (diss., Helsingfors, 1905).

# CHAPTER XI

## MISCELLANEOUS *CHANSONS DE GESTE*

There are a number of poems in the epic form which do not fit exactly into the three cycles we have discussed. These are apt to be translations or adaptations from a foreign epic source; sometimes they may be a conscious effort to advertise an individual feudal family through connivance between jongleur and family; more often they are independent compositions, not attached to any shrine or pilgrimage, introducing a new set of characters, and free from all propaganda. It is true that eventually, after 1200, these independent *chansons* were often made to conform: their chief heroes were attached in some way to the three major *gestes,* but this was not always the case. In one instance a pious Christian legend which had taken on the epic form along the pilgrim route to Rome was reworked to suit a special purpose and then continued by an imitation of a late Latin romance. Despite their varied nature, these poems are all *chansons de geste* because of their literary form and because of their settings. Unceasing warfare, Charlemagne's court, the protection of *Sainte Chrestienté,* are present to some degree in all of them, and none of them can be confused with the later type of the romance.

The *geste de Blaye* is a term often applied to two epic poems, the *Amis et Amiles* and the *Jourdains de Blaivies.* The first of these, in its surviving form, is a composition of the closing years of the twelfth century. It has 3,504 verses in assonanced decasyllables with a large percentage of casual rhyme. There is only one MS (B.N. fr. 860), of beautiful execution. We assume that there was an earlier version of this epic which took form in the eleventh century and which has since been lost. Perhaps it was never written down. Joseph Bédier has explained that there was a Church of Saint Albin, near Mortara in Lombardy, along the pilgrim route from France to Rome, which possessed two ancient sarcophagi lying side by side. He suggests that one of these bore the name *Aemilius,* a name of ultimate Semitic origin. The local clergy knew of a Christian legend which told of two devoted friends and how one of them was stricken with leprosy because of some ethical sin. He could be cured only by a bath in the blood of his friend's children. In keeping with the prevalent practice of exploiting local legends the clergy of Saint Albin's allowed a jongleur to elaborate this legend into a *chanson de geste,* associating the two sarcophagi with the famous friends who now became Aemilius and Amicus (a commonplace name).

The Old French poet of the surviving epic version was the first to designate Amis as lord of Blaye. He is the exact double of Amiles, though no blood relation. He substitutes for him in a judicial combat at Charlemagne's court, and then marries for Amiles, in Amiles' name, the daughter of Charlemagne. As Amis is already married to Lubias, niece of the traitor Hardre, God inflicts him with leprosy for his technical bigamy. He is abandoned and driven forth by his false wife. After many wanderings he is cured by Amiles in the manner already narrated; and, as a happy sequel, God restores the children to life. The two set out for a pilgrimage to the Holy Land, and on their return they both meet death, from sickness, at Mortara.[1]

It is certainly probable that the poet of the existing version called Amis, Lord of Blaye at the suggestion of the family of Blaye. This family already had some claim to literary fame in the Provençal poet, Jaufre Rudel. In the surviving, or perhaps in the lost primitive version. there was first introduced a combination with the folktale of the two brothers (Mt. 303, *FFC*, 74, 78, 81). There are other possible folk motifs such as those of the Jealous Seneschal and the Wooing Princess.

The Latin prose *Vita Sanctorum Amici et Amelii* was made in the twelfth century. In the thirteenth century this was adapted into Old French prose as *Li Amitiez de Ami et Amile*. In the twelfth century there was also composed an Anglo-Norman *Amis et Amilun* in short rhymed couplets. There are later versions in Norse and Middle English. *Der arme Heinrich* (*ca.* 1200), of Hartmann von Aue, was based upon the original Christian folk legend, with no influence from France or Italy. The Middle English *Amis e Amilun* (late thirteenth century) is closest to the Anglo-Norman form.

The second *chanson* of the *geste de Blaye* is a continuation of the *Amis et Amiles*. It dates from the first decades of the thirteenth century but for convenience we shall discuss it here. This *chanson*, the *Jourdains de Blaivies* (4,245 decasyllables) was based upon a folk theme which had two early literary elaborations: the *Apollonius of Tyre* and the legend of Saint Eustachius. In both of these a family is divided by accident, and after many individual wanderings the members are reunited. In the *Eustachius* there is a particular variant in which the newly born twins are borne off by robber beasts. In the *Jourdains de Blaivies* the protagonist is the grandson of Amis. His land is seized by the traitor Fromont, his father and mother are slain, and he is forced to flee with his godfather and godmother. They are captured by Saracens and separated; Jourdains marries the princess Oriabel who bears him a daughter;

[1] In the *Chevalerie Ogier*, verses 5772-5850, they are slain by Ogier and buried by Charlemagne.

wife and child also become lost, and the tale ends when they all find each
other again. Jourdains succeeds to his father-in-law's kingdom and his
daughter, Gaudisce, is empress of Constantinople. Blaye, which had been
won back from the traitor Fromont, is given to the godfather, Renier.

From the close of the twelfth century we have two poems of the
geste de Nanteuil: Aye d'Avignon and Gui de Nanteuil. The Doön de
Nanteuil belonged to the same period of composition but has been lost;
we have a fragment of a dozen lines of the thirteenth century redaction
of this chanson by Huon de Villeneuve, preserved by Claude Fauchet.
The geste was continued in the thirteenth century by Parise la duchesse
and in the fourteenth by Tristan de Nanteuil. This Nanteuil may be
Nanteuil-le-Doon or Nanteuil l'Audouin (Oise). The geste may have
had no purpose at all, other than amusement.

Aye d'Avignon as it has been conserved in a unique MS (B. N. fr.
2170) consists of the original poem (vss. 1-2283) and a continuation (vss.
2284-4136). The first is in rhymed alexandrines and the second in twelve
syllable assonance. Claude Fauchet believed that Huon de Villeneuve was
the author of the original geste de Nanteuil as well as of Renaus de Mon
tauban.[2] Modern scholars deny this. Perhaps Huon was a remanieur;
at any rate, Aye d'Avignon remains for us an anonymous work. Al
though the setting begins at Charlemagne's court, the characters are new,
with few exceptions, and the plot, pure fiction. The ultimate origins of
the poem cannot antedate 1160; it was doubtless composed for amuse
ment only. It is interesting to observe that certain of the new charac
ters receive brief mention in Renaus de Montauban; perhaps Fauchet
was not altogether wrong in seeing a relationship between that chanson
and the geste de Nanteuil.

Charlemagne gives Aye, the heiress of the fief of Avignon, in mar
riage to Garnier of Nanteuil. This match is opposed by Berengier, a
son of Ganelon, who desires the heiress and her fief for himself. He
makes several fruitless attempts to ruin Garnier. After two sieges, he
succeeds in capturing Aye, during the absence of her husband. He flees
and takes refuge at Aigremore. Aye is taken from him by the Saracen
king Ganor, who has fallen in love with her, and he (Berengier) is sent
to his father's friend, Marsilies, in Spain. Garnier learns where he may
find his wife. He goes there in disguise, takes service with Ganor, and
kills Berengier in a fight between the forces of Ganor and Marsilies.
He returns to Avignon, carrying with him Aye, who has been captive
for three years. Gui is born to them. The second part now begins.
Ganor dresses as a pilgrim and comes to Avignon, where he succeeds

¹ Recueil de l'origine de la langue et poésie française (Mamert Patisson, 1581), p. iii.
² Op. cit., pp. 109-110.

n stealing Gui. Garnier continues to be a victim of the race of Ganelon
nd Berengier. His own two brothers-in-law are on the side of his
nemies. He captures them and is escorting them to Charlemagne's
ourt when he falls victim to another attack and is slain. Ganor comes
vith an army to avenge Garnier, provided he may have the fair Aye in
ecompense. The traitors are punished and Ganor, after becoming a
Christian, marries Aye.

The second part of this poem could not have been composed long
fter the first.

*Gui de Nanteuil*, the continuation of *Aye d'Avignon*, is mentioned by
he Provençal poet, Raimbaut de Vaqueiras, who died in 1207. We must
late it also in the last years of the twelfth century. It has 3,019 alexandrine
erses in rhymed *laisses*, a style of versification just winning popularity
n the epics at the close of the twelfth century. The poet, who knew
oth parts of the *Aye d'Avignon*, began with a brief résumé of that poem.
Gui, who is lord of Avignon as well as of his father's fief, Nanteuil (of
nknown location), sets out for Paris. Charlemagne makes him his
tandard bearer, to the great grief of the relatives of Ganelon. One of
hese traitors, Hervieu de Lyon, accuses Gui before Charlemagne, espe-
ially of being a descendant of Doön de Nanteuil, the second of the
welve sons of the rebel Doön de Mayence. By this genealogy the poet
onnects this minor *geste* with one of the three major cycles. Hervieu
s conquered in a trial by combat with Gui. Charlemagne, however, is
orced to support him against Gui in his pretensions for the hand of
Aiglentine, daughter of Yon of Gascony. Charles has received a bribe
rom Hervieu. The two of them pursue Gui to the walls of Nanteuil;
ut Ganor comes to the help of his stepson. Hervieu is slain by Gui
nd Charlemagne is forced to consent to and to be present at the wed-
ling of Gui and Aiglentine. He returns to Paris in shame and anger
against the traitors who surround him.

This *chanson* was particularly popular in the south of France as it
s mentioned by the troubadours, Aimeric de Peguilhan, Raimon Vidal,
nd Lanfranc Cigala et Lantelm, as well as by Raimbaut de Vaqueiras
nd the unknown author of the *Flamenca* romance. In northern France
he poem is referred to in the *Guillaume de Dôle* and by Philippe
Mouskés.

Two poems, composed in the twelfth century, were made over in the
hirteenth, possibly by the same jongleur, and thereafter referred to as
he *Geste de Saint Gilles*. They were then partially connected with the
cycle of Doön de Mayence, and, in the case of the *Elie*, also with the
cycle of Garin de Monglane. *Aiol et Mirabel*, the better known of the
two, is attested by the Provençal troubadours, Guiraut de Cabreira and

Raimbaut d'Aurenga as existing in the twelfth century. We know noth
ing of the form of this lost version although we assume that it was i
decasyllables, to judge from the mixed meter of the surviving poem
(122 alexandrines + 4,847 decasyllables + another 6,014 alexandrines
all in assonanced *laisses*). These indicate a revamping into alexandrine
from decasyllables. The plot can be briefly told: Elie de Saint Gilles an
his wife, Avisse, are exiled from King Louis's court because of the machi
nations of a traitor, Macaire de Lauzanne. They have a son whom the
name Aiol (<*anguillolus*) because of an infant escapade in which h
slays a serpent *à la Héraclès*. When grown, the young Aiol goes, un
known, to the King's service where he wins renown and a restoratio
of his father's fiefs. Aiol steals the pagan princess Mirabel from he
father, Mibrien of Pampeluna. But the loving pair are now capture
by the traitor Macaire. Eventually they are freed, and the traitor i
drawn by horses. This epic combines the Eustachius and the Crescenti
(persecuted wife) motifs. *Elie de Saint-Gilles,* the second epic of th
*geste,* narrates the adventures of the father. The poet of the *Raoul d
Cambrai* (twelfth-century) doubtless knew this second epic in an earl
form as he refers to the birth of the father of Elie, namely Julien, th
son of Bernier and Béatrice of Saint-Gilles. The existing version of th
*Elie de Saint-Gilles* is told in 2,761 alexandrines. Elie is reproached b
his father because he has not proved his prowess. Elie leaves in anger
He attempts to save William of Orange from pagan captors; William
escapes but Elie is taken prisoner. Elie also escapes and enters the paga
town of Sorbrie with a newly-acquired companion, Galopin. Th
Saracen princess Rosemonde falls in love with Elie and aids them. The
are besieged by the true lord of Sorbrie, Macabré, but Julien de Saint
Gilles and William of Orange raise the siege. Rosemonde is converte
and, in the original poem, certainly married Elie. In this later version th
poet was anxious to make the poem conform with the *Aiol,* in whic
Elie's wife is Avisse, sister of Louis of France. Accordingly the poe
imagines an accident whereby Elie becomes "consanguineous" with Rose
monde and marries Avisse instead. Rosemonde takes Galopin.

The town of Saint-Gilles, of which there is question in these *chansons,* has not been identified.

The *Bevis of Hampton* was a popular tale and is preserved in Anglo
Norman, continental French, Norse, Welsh, Middle English, Irish, and
Italian dress. C. Boje (*Beihefte, ZfrPh* XIX, 145) believes that these
all go back to a continental French original composed after 1200. He
denies the various theories of German, Anglo-Saxon, Persian, Armenian,
Viking, or Celtic origin, and sees the poem as the work of a cultivated
Frenchman who was influenced only indirectly by the epics and ro-

mances of his day. The Provençal *Daurel e Beton* shows clear influence from this original *Bevis* and as the *Daurel e Beton* is dated in the last quarter of the twelfth century, possibly as early as 1170, this should throw the dating of the original *Bevis* a little earlier than Boje wishes. Matzke was inclined to believe that this first version was an Anglo-Norman poem (*MPhil* X, 19-54). Pio Rajna suggested (in 1872) that Hantone might originally have been continental Hunstein or Hammerstein on the Rhine, rather than Southampton in England. Zenker's somewhat elaborate discussion (*Boeve-Amlethus,* Berlin and Leipzig, 1905) in which he connects the story with the ancient Bellerophon tale and with the Brutus story in Livy (I, 56), as well as with the Hamlet tale in *Saxo Grammaticus.* may have some truth in it.

There are extant two long fragments of an Anglo-Norman *Boeve de Haumtone* (3850 mixed decasyllables and alexandrines) dating from the early thirteenth century. The original of this is lost; but from it were derived also three continental variants of the story preserved in nine MSS; of these the best MSS are in Rome and Paris. Variant I (10,614 vss.) was made near Rheims, *ca.* 1200; II (19,127 vss.) belongs to Beauvaisis, *ca.* 1225; III (16,391 vss.) is Picard, written around 1220. Briefly, the plot tells how Gui of Hampton was murdered by Doön de Mayence, on the suggestion of Gui's wife. They intend also to kill the boy Bevis but he is saved by his tutor and is later sold into slavery, to a potentate of Asia Minor. Bevis falls in love with his master's daughter and defeats her cruel suitor. They are falsely accused of intimacy and Bevis is sent with his death warrant to a heathen king. He escapes and runs away with his beloved princess, Josiane, whom a magic potion has saved from the consequences of a forced marriage. There are more adventures in which Josiane undergoes another forced marriage and is made a widow a second time. Finally, she returns to Hampton with her true husband, Bevis, and he wins back his lands from the usurper. But he is again forced into exile, and here once more is the Apollonius motif. The wedded pair and their twin sons are separated. Josiane eventually reunites them all. Bevis grows old, receives an angelic warning, and dies. There is a crusading *chanson de geste* flavor to the French versions of this story; and so we have included them here rather than with the romances.

*Horn et Rimel* is another tale of romantic plot composed in the spirit of a *chanson de geste* (*Rom* XV, 575-96). This French poem belonged in the last years of the twelfth century and was the work of an Anglo-Norman poet, Mestre Thomas. There are 5,250 alexandrine verses. The source of the material is very difficult to establish. Norse saga, Anglo-Saxon, Danish, and Anglo-Norman tradition have all been suggested.

Suchier and Deutschbein (*Studien zur Sagengeschichte Englands,* Cöthen 1906) saw the hero, Horn, as an echo of a Danish Horm who went to Ireland in 851 and fought against the Vikings. Schofield (*PML* XVIII, 1-83) traced the tale to a Viking saga of the tenth century. In any case the surviving Anglo-Norman poem shows influence from the *Tristan* of Thomas. A. H. Krappe indicates some relation between the *Horn* and *Amis et Amiles.* (The Middle English *Horn Childe* was adapted from this French poem. The Middle English *King Horne* shows more independent traits.) Horn's father was Aaluf, a foundling at the court of King Silaf. Aaluf married the Princess Samburc and became king, in the face of difficulties. He was later killed in a fight with invaders. His son Horn is exposed in a rudderless boat, and eventually arrives at the court of Hunlaf, in Brittany. He is educated there and loves Rimel the king's daughter. He is falsely accused and goes into a second exile. He returns in disguise to rescue his love from unwelcome marriage, on two occasions. In the end he wins his lady and his heritage. An interesting folk element in the Old French *chanson* is the many riddles and parables of which Horn is fond. Horn's son is Hadermod. It would appear from a statement by Mestre Thomas (vs. 192) that he had written a *Chanson d'Aaluf* which is now lost. As to whether he ever wrote a *Chanson de Hadermod,* also lost, we cannot say.

In his *Estorie des Engleis* (vss. 41-818) Gaimar told the story of Havelok the Dane, as though the episodes had taken place in the period 495-556. This account was elaborated into the *Lai d'Havelok* in the latter part of the twelfth century (E. Fahnestock, *A Study of the Sources and Composition of the Old French Lai d'Havelok,* Bryn Mawr, 1915). Havelok's father, the king of Denmark, is slain and his kingdom alienated by King Arthur. The boy is reared by the faithful Grim as one of his own sons. They flee to a place later called Grimsby. Havelok takes service as a scullion with the King of Lincoln. The young prince is distinguished by a flame that comes from his mouth while he sleeps and by his ability to blow a horn; he also has great strength. The King of Lincoln forces his niece, Argentille, to make what he considers a cruel marriage with this churl, Havelok coheran (and *coheran* we are told means "cook"). The girl learns of the true character of her husband from a dream. Eventually, Havelok recovers Argentille's heritage from her cruel uncle, wins back his own kingdom, and finally succeeds to the kingdom of Lincoln. There is a Middle English *Havelok the Dane* (1280-1290) which may go back to a lost French source. It has no connection with the surviving French versions. The ultimate source of all these versions was probably a legend current in Lincolnshire. Was the Scandinavian Olaf Sictricson, also known as Anlaf Cuaran, the his orical prototype of Havelok? We cannot say. We can see possible resemblances in the story with episodes in the *Aliscans,* in *Ogier li Danois,* and with *Boeve de Haumtone.*

Next to be discussed is the vast Lotharingian cycle. There are five poems preserved in one complete cyclic MS (Arsenal 181, Belles Lettres), and variously in other MSS. Only two of the cycle belong to the last years of the twelfth century: the *Mort de Garin le Loherenc* and the *Girbert de Mes.* The *Hervis de Mes, Anseïs fils de Gerbert,* and *Yon* are thirteenth century continuations. Both the *Mort de Garin le Loherenc* and *Girbert de Mes* were composed in the usual ten-syllable *laisses* with frequent casual rhyme.

The origins of this cycle are unknown. Paulin Paris, F. Lot, Leonhard Gleich, and A. Eckhardt (*Mél. Baldensperger,* I, 215-224) have all demonstrated that two poems at least, *Mort de Garin le Loherenc* and *Hervis de Mes,* are filled with learned historical allusions. One episode, that of Charles Martel forcing the clergy to give money for his wars, with his subsequent damnation, has been traced by Bédier to a fable in the *Vita sancti Eucherii* (*op. cit.,* IV, 374 ff.) This is all we know of the sources. The entire cycle has been retold as a continuous whole by Paul Meyer in the *Histoire littéraire de la France.* It is the story of strife to the bitter end between the Lotharingians and the Bordelais. Miss Ruth Parmly has made a study of the geographic names in the first poem (*The Geographical References in the Chanson de Garin le Loherain,* New York: IFS, 1935).

The *Mort de Garin le Loherenc* is made up of three distinct parts. The first tells of the war with the Vandres (Vandals), the death of Charles Martel, the crowning of Pepin, and the death of Hervis of Metz. The second part narrates the beginning of hostilities between the Lotharingians and the Bordelais over the proposed marriage of Garin with Blancheflor, daughter of Thierri of Arles. There are three truces and three renewals of conflict. The warfare is particularly savage, a fact which caused the older literary historians to believe that this epic represented a rather primitive stage of society. There is the scene in which Bègue removes the entrails of Ysoré and strikes Guillaume de Monclin in the face with them. The most blood-thirsty accounts in fiction are frequently written by men who have seen the least action. There are many Jules Vernes in literature. There is little to be drawn from these gruesome episodes save that the poet was a man who possessed a vivid imagination. The third division tells of the death of Bègue and Garin. The entire poem is supposed to be the work of one Jean de Flagy who is mentioned in some of the MSS. This is doubted by many critics. Flagy is presumably a village in Artois, which would render our poet a Picard.

In the *Girbert de Mes* we are introduced to the next generation of Lotharingians and Bordelais. Girbert seeks vengeance for his father's death; Fromont of Lens, the leader of the Bordelais, flees to Spain. Ludie, the daughter of Fromont, marries the Lotharingian Hernaut le Poitevin, son of Bègue. She aids the Lotharingians in their struggle against Fromondin, her brother. A rather brutal touch is the use of Fromont's skull as a drinking cup after he has been slain by Girbert. Fromondin unknowingly drinks from this skull of his father. Girbert finally slays Fromondin and then meets his own end in the deadly feud.

The complete cycle was turned into prose by Philippe de Vigneulles, a citizen of Metz, at the beginning of the sixteenth century. There has been recent activity in the discovery of new MS fragments of *chansons* of this Lotharingian group. Eugénie Droz has published a new version of 128 verses of the *Mort de Garin le Loherenc* found in an early binding (*Rom* LVII, 570-573). Mme Pamfilova has reproduced a new fragment of the same, some forty lines long, from a binding in the Vatican (*ibid.*, pp. 546-547) and also another version of two hundred lines of the *Hervis de Mes* from a fragment in the Archives of Moselle (*ibid.*, pp. 538-546).

## EDITIONS

*Amis et Amiles u. Jourdains de Blaivies*, ed. K. Hofmann (2nd ed.; Erlangen: A. Deichert, 1882); E. Kölbing, in his *Amis e Amilun* (Heilbronn: *Altengl. Bibl.*, 1884) publishes the Anglo-Norman and Latin texts.—*Aye d'Avignon et Gui de Nanteuil*, ed. M.-F. Guessard (Paris: *APF*, 1861).—*Aiol*, ed. J. Normand-G.Raynaud (Paris: *SATF*, 1877).—*Elie de Saint-Gilles*, ed. G. Raynaud (Paris: *SATF*, 1879); *Aiol et Mirabel und Elie de Saint-Gilles*, ed. W. Foerster (Heilbronn, 1878-1882).—*Der anglonorm. Boeve de Haumtone*, ed. A. Stimming (Halle: *BN*, 1889); *Der festländische Bueve de Hantone*, ed. A. Stimming (Dresden: *GrL*, 1911-1920); *Die franko-italienische Version des B. de H.*, ed. J. Reinhold in *ZfrPh* XXXV, 555, 607.—*Horn*, ed. Brede-Stengel (*Ausg. u. Abhandl.*, 1883).—*Lai d'Haveloc*, ed. Alexander Bell (Manchester Univ. Press, 1925).—*Garin le Loherenc* was edited partially by Paulin Paris (Paris: *Rdp*, 1833-1835) and by E. du Méril in *La Mort de Garin le Loherenc* (Paris, 1846); also by Stengel in the *Festschrift W. Vietor* (Marburg, 1919).— The *Girbert* awaits an editor.—The publication of these Lotharingian epics is being undertaken by students at Columbia University, under the direction of Professors H. F. Muller and Pauline Taylor.

# CHAPTER XII

## CRUSADE EPICS AND RHYMED CHRONICLES

A. Hatem, *Les poèmes épiques des Croisades* (Paris: Geuthner, 1932).

"For us, history is fixed; we are trying minutely to observe it. For the medieval scholar, history is plastic; he refashions it to suit the needs of his day." We see history through a magnifying glass; the man of the twelfth century through a mirror. (*Spec* I, 262). These words by that learned medievalist Professor E. K. Rand phrase succinctly what should be kept in mind throughout this chapter. They will account for the frequent flights of imagination indulged in by even the most serious of medieval chroniclers. Men of that time were not incapable of accuracy; somehow they did not care, so long as the broad facts were present. Let us note, in passing, three grades of history: legend, chronicle, and history proper. Legend is accumulated imagination surrounding a detail or so of fact; chronicle is a bare statement of events; history is chronicle with an attempt to analyze, interpret, and show cause and effect. History in the Old French vernacular begins in the first few years of the thirteenth century with Villehardouin. Legend was enjoyed especially by the lay folk in the form of the *chanson de geste*. The clerics were responsible for the bare statements of the past; so Latin is the common language of the chronicles. When, however, an event or series of events was of first magnitude it interested the people also and there was likely to be a poet who would make of it a rhymed chronicle in the vulgar tongue. Such a poet was often a member of the clerical class for his sources were necessarily in Latin. Events of national importance also accumulated about them a certain amount of legend; *e.g.,* the First Crusade (1096-1099). There came into existence a cycle of poems treating this event, half legend and half chronicle, which is commonly called the epic cycle of the First Crusade. The poems are known as Crusade epics. Why was it that the First Crusade occupied a greater place in the minds of the people than any of the subsequent ones? It was because the First Crusade was the only one to be successful. It accomplished its purpose with the capture of Jerusalem (1098). The others were abortive attempts.

We know that a Limousin knight, Gregory Bechada, wrote a poem on the events of the First Crusade, because of a statement by Geoffroi de Vigeois in his Latin chronicle. This narrative by Bechada was composed for Bishop Eustorgius (1106-1137) of Limoges. It has disappeared. Another chronicler, Ordericus Vitalis, is our authority that the Provençal troubadour William of Poitiers wrote a narrative poem dealing with this Crusade; but this too has been lost. Still another Provençal poem on the First Crusade is mentioned by Guilhem de Tudela in his *Canso* on the Albigensian Crusade, a poem of 1210-1213:

> Senhors, esta canso es faita d'aital guia
> Com sela d'Antiocha et ayssi· s versifia (vss. 1-2)

Gaston Paris thought that such a Provençal *Canso* was incorporated into the Spanish *Gran Conquista de Ultramar* (*ca.* 1300). To-day we possess a *Canso d'Antiocha,* a fragment of seven hundred lines, which may be all that remains of any one of the four works we mention above. Gaston Paris was convinced that the poem by Gregory Bechada, the narrative incorporated into the *Gran Conquista,* and the extant fragment were one and the same. This may be true. Paul Meyer has dated the existing fragment, because of its language, in the last years of the twelfth century.

A northern French poet from Artois, Richard the Pilgrim, is reputed to have composed at the beginning of the twelfth century two Crusade poems: a *Chanson d'Antioche* and a *Chanson de Jerusalem.* The originals of these have been lost; they survive in revisions made by Graindor de Douai between 1180 and 1200. Paulin Paris was inclined to believe that Graindor's revising was limited to polishing and improvement of repetitions and obscurities. Graindor also wrote a Crusade poem of pure imagination, showing influence of the romance, the *Chetifs* (4,164 vss.). Paulin Paris wished to attribute the original of these to William VII of Poitiers. All three of the poems, in the form Graindor gave them, are in monorhymed alexandrine *laïsses.* The *Chanson d'Antioche* (9,000 verses odd) narrates the ill-fated expedition of Peter the Hermit (1097) and the activity of Godfrey of Bouillon, including the capture of the city of Antioch, until the entrance of his army into Palestine. The *Chanson de Jerusalem* (9,135 vss.), less historical than the *Antioche,* tells of the capture of Jerusalem and of the election of Godfrey of Bouillon as king of Jerusalem. The *Chetifs* relates how five knights, captured after the defeat of Peter the Hermit at Nicaea, were led to the pagan city Oliferne. Like the Jews of the Old Testament they were set to building. Corbarant of Oliferne desired to prove the superiority of the Franks over the Persians, in order to excuse the fall of Antioch. Richard of Caumont, one of the *chetifs* (captives), was victorious over the pagans Golias and Sorgalés. The Christians were freed as recompense and made their way to Jerusalem, after certain adventures, including a combat between one of the captives, Baldwin of Beauvaisis, and a monstrous serpent which had eaten Baldwin's brother. Graindor is our authority that this serpent episode was first composed by a canon of Saint Peter's on the request of Raymond of Poitiers, in the Holy Land. (This Raymond will be familiar to many as the uncle, by marriage, of Eleanor of Aquitaine, with whom she became somewhat involved as a prelude to her divorce from Louis VII of France.) Whether the other chief episodes of the *Chetifs* were original with Graindor we cannot say, although there is little cause to doubt it. These three poems which we call the *Chanson d'Antioche,* the *Chanson de Jerusalem,* and the *Chetifs,* are so closely joined in the nine extant manuscripts that it is extremely difficult to separate them.

A jongleur named Renaut went a step further into the realms of fiction when he grafted upon the cycle of the First Crusade certain poems to explain the fairy origin of Godfrey of Bouillon. It is common to divide this material into two poems which we call the *Naissance du Chevalier au Cygne* (or *Elioxe*) and the *Chevalier au Cygne et Enfances Godefroi.* The late Professor H. A. Todd, in his edition of the *Naissance,* dated this poem in the twelfth century; to-day a number of the critics place both of the swan-knight poems in the thirteenth century and consider the *Naissance* the younger of the two. In any case, there is no doubt Godfrey of Bouillon and the tale of the swan brothers were associated before the middle of the twelfth century and perhaps even earlier, for the chronicler William of Tyre sees fit to deny the association in his *Historia rerum in partibus transmarinis gestarum* (IX, 6). Gui de Bazoches (Letter XXIII) admits it and claims both the swan knight and Godfrey in his own genealogical tree.

The *Naissance du Chevalier au Cygne,* as published by Todd, has 3,500 alexandrine verses in rhymed *laisses.* A King Lothair of Hungary finds a beautiful woman, Elioxe, beside a fountain, with a gold fairy chain in her hand. He takes her home and marries her despite the opposition of his wicked mother, Matrasilie. He is called away by war and during his absence Elioxe fulfils a prophecy which she had previously made: she gives birth to six sons and a daughter at one birth, and dies. The wicked grandmother sends the children into the woods to be killed, but the servant, Monicier, leaves them with a hermit instead. Lothair on his return, is told that the children were serpents and that they have flown away. Many years later the grandmother recognizes the children as they bathe, each having a gold chain around his neck. She sends a man to steal the chains, which he does, except for the chain belonging to the daughter. The brothers are forced to remain as swans; the girl alone retains her shape. The swan brothers take up their abode in a pond near their father's castle. The wicked grandmother uses one of the chains for the repair of a broken gold basin. When, through the efforts of the sister, the king finally learns the truth, the wicked woman gives up the chains, enabling all but one of the swans to resume his natural shape. This poor swan is henceforth accompanied by one of his brothers who is then known as the swan knight. There is another version of this *chanson* which has been published by Hippeau. Here the names are changed: Lothair becoming King Oriant and Elioxe being replaced by Beatrice. The swan knight is given the name of Helyas or Elias. Another folk motif is there added—a motif still common in present-day Scotland—that a woman cannot give birth to more than one child at a single birth, unless she has been adulterous. Beatrice criticizes a mother of twins and is punished by herself giving birth to seven.[1]

The source of this swan legend has been a much discussed question. There are undeniable folk motifs: Mt. 313, 451 in *FFC* 74, 78, 81. Another literary version is the tale *Cygnus* in the *Dolopathos*. G. Poisson (*Rev Celt*, XXXIV, 182, 184) and others have stated that the legend was first current in the lower Rhine region. F. Lot has developed its connection with the Celtic tale of the *Children of Lír* (*Rom* XXI, 62-65), and this is a likely suggestion. G. Poisson (*loc. cit.*) identified the legend with a solar myth.

The *Chevalier au Cygne et Enfances Godefroi*[2] is also preserved in two slightly differing versions. The swan knight sets sail in a boat, with his swan brother as the motive power, and arrives at Bouillon in time to champion the Duchess of Bouillon in combat with Renier, the Saxon Duke. He is successful and marries Beatrice, the daughter of the duchess, bidding them not ask concerning his origins. For seven years they ask no questions, but at last the temptation becomes too strong. Sorrowfully the knight climbs into his boat and disappears forever. His daughter Ida, seven years later, marries Eustace of Boulogne, by whom she has three sons, Godfrey, Eustace, and Baldwin. A Saracen who has been informed of the future downfall of Islam through Godfrey seeks to assassinate the future champion. He is, of course, unsuccessful. There are folk motifs here also: Mt. 931 in *FFC*, 74, 78, 81 and 425 in *FFC* 74, 425A in 78, 81. First suggested by J. Grimm and elaborated by Olrik is the theory that the *Chevalier au Cygne* was derived from the legend of the Danish hero Scyld, or Skéaf (*JEGP* XIX, 190 ff., 413 ff.). Historically, Godfrey of Bouillon was the second son of Eustace of Bologne and of Ida, sister of Godfrey *le bossu* of Brabant. He was reared by his uncle and fell heir to his possessions, including the castle of Bouillon. His brothers were Eustace of Boulogne and Baudouin who accompanied him on the Crusade in 1096. It is obvious from these historical facts that the author of the *Chevalier au Cygne* was not ignorant of Godfrey's history.

[1] Cf. A. H. Krappe in *Mythologie universelle* (Paris, 1930), 57 ff.
[2] Some critics consider this as two separate poems: the *Chevalier au Cygne* and the *Enfances Godefroi*.

From chapters 47-68 of the Spanish *Gran Conquista de Ultramar*
Gaston Paris assumed the existence of a lost twelfth century French poem
called *Isomberte*. At the close of the *Parzival* of Wolfram von Eschen
bach there is a short narrative concerning *Loherangrin* (<*Loherenc
Garin*) which connects the swan knight with the Grail legend. Wolfram
gives as his source one Kiot or Guiot, a Provençal Perhaps this is Guiot
de Provins. The German epic *Lohengrin* (1276-1290) is based upon
Wolfram.

Aside from the Crusade epics and their legendary continuations, the
continental French (omitting Normandy) left the recording of contemporary events and the near past to the clerics. At a time when the land
was disunited, when county warred upon county and province upon
province, these people found their common patriotism in the legends of
a king who had lived four hundred years before—Charlemagne.

The exact contrary was true of the Norman subjects of the Plan-
tagenets. They might also claim an interest in Charlemagne, but in addition they were making history of their own. There was the invasion of
England, the colonization of Sicily, and the gradual expansion on the
Continent at the expense of the Capetian. Surely these were sufficient
to arouse racial pride in the present. In accordance with this we observe
the Normans and Anglo-Normans of the first half of the twelfth century
developing the vernacular rhymed chronicle, which differed from the
*chansons de geste* in every essential detail. The rhymed chronicle was
composed usually in rhymed octosyllables, the heroes were more or less
contemporary historical characters, and the emphasis was upon events or
genealogies, not upon descriptions of battles, exaltation of the Christian
religion as opposed to the pagan, or the prowess of the individual hero.
In other words, the rhymed chronicles were vernacular chronicles and not
fiction with a thesis, as were the *chansons de geste*. But there was one
marked resemblance between the two: they both admitted large doses of
legend and imagination, though the rhymed chronicles used more freely
the Latin chronicles and the testimony of eyewitnesses. The difference
was in degree and proportion. That the Anglo-Normans and Normans
were not happy in the exploitation of Charlemagne—the hero of their
enemies, the French—will help account for the spread of the rhymed
chronicle among the people, and it was perhaps responsible for the resur-
recting of another hero in the early years of the twelfth century, King
Arthur. They could then claim a hero who was the equal, if not the
superior, of Charlemagne.

The first rhymed chronicle of which we have mention is the life of
Henry I of England (d. 1135) which was commanded by Aaliz de Lou-

vain, the King's young wife, of one David, a jongleur. This has been lost.

Between 1138 and 1140 Geoffrey Gaimar composed an *Estoire des Engleis* at the request of Constance, wife of Robert Fiz-Gislebert of Scrampton, (Lincs.). He mentions as his sources *le livere Walter Espoc,* a *bon livere de Oxford, de Wassinburc un livere engleis,* and *l'estoire de Wincestre* (vs. 6468). This last is unquestionably a version of the *Anglo-Saxon Chronicle,* probably a MS related to the surviving Laud MS of the *Chronicle.* The MSS of the *Estoire des Engleis* preserve two differing epilogues, a longer and a shorter. The longer is the authentic work of Gaimar (A. Bell in *MLR* XXV, 52-59). Gaimar was also the author of an *Estoire des Bretuns,* adapted in part from the work of Geoffrey of Monmouth. This second *Estoire* has been lost.

A Norman, Jordan Fantosme, Chancellor of the Cathedral Chapter at Winchester (from 1160), wrote a history of the war between Henry II, his son the Young King, the King of Scotland, and Louis VII in 1173-1174. He had been an eyewitness of part of it. This must have been written before 1183.

Of the Third Crusade (1190-1192) there exists a chronicle which is a monument of the first order. This is the *Estoire de la Guerre Sainte,* the work of Ambroise, a Norman jongleur from Evreux. He was a follower of Richard the Lion-Hearted and witnessed much that he tells. The date of composition is prior to 1196. The poem is long, 12,332 octosyllables in monorhymed *laisses;* it is preserved in a single MS of the Vatican Library. There is a strong accent of truth and reality throughout this account: it is very close to genuine history in its treatment. The author was not a noble who had personal access to the councils of war, so his narrative presents the viewpoint of the "little men," the common soldiers.

The *Roman du Mont-Saint-Michel,* by Guillaume de Paier, is an account of the famous monastery at this place. It was composed between 1130 and 1180 in an interesting Norman dialect, probably that of the present-day department of the Orne.

This brings us to the greatest vernacular chronicler of the century, Wace (1100?-1174?),[3] whom we have already mentioned as the author of several saints' lives. He was born on the island of Jersey and studied at Paris and at Caen; in the latter place he held the title of *clerc lisant*

---

[3] These dates were conjectured by Gaston Paris on the basis of three points: (a) Mention by Wace that he had served under the three Henrys (Henry I, Henry II, and the Young King), (b) the date of the siege of Rouen (1174), (c) three mentions of Wace in the charters of Bayeux (1169-1172, and 1174).

after 1135. It was at this time that he began to write, from his own admission. Before 1155 he may have crossed into England. At all events he had composed by that date his *Brut,* which is a history of the Britons, dedicated to Queen Eleanor. This appears to have met with instant success, and he was commanded by Henry II, in 1160, to begin a history of the Normans, his *Roman de Rou.* He did so and had composed the first 751 verses in octosyllabic rhymed couplets before he changed to monorhymed *laisses.* After 4,424 verses of these he stopped. He gives as his reason that the King was neglecting him financially and he was not working for love. To remind Henry and Eleanor of his task and their obligations he addressed to them a short poem of 315 monorhymed alexandrines, in which he states his purpose and adds, by way of flattery, that Henry is descended from Mathilda, Henry I, William the Conqueror, Robert the Devil, Richard, Richard the Elder, William Long Sword, and Rou (Rollo). He narrates the deeds of those leaders again, though some had already been set forth in his main poem.

The purpose of these 315 lines, usually termed the *Chronique ascendante,* is evident. In modern parlance we should call it a prospectus of the vast compilation in the process of making, intended to secure funds. There was some effect, for Wace speedily received a canonicate at Bayeux and resumed his labors. He reverted to his original verse scheme, octosyllabic rhymed couplets. He composed 11,500 of these, consuming apparently eight or nine years in the task. This pace did not suit the King; he may have doubted whether Wace could complete it, for the poet had doubtless grown old. Before 1174, Henry turned to Maistre Beneëit (Beneëit de Sainte-More?), a younger and more enterprising writer whom he asked to write the work anew. Wace had brought the chronicle down to the battle of Tinchebray (1106).

Wace's *Roman de Rou,* as we possess it, consists, then, of the three parts:

1. 751 octosyllables and 4,424 alexandrines,
2. 315 alexandrines (the *Chronique ascendante*),
3. 11,502 octosyllables.

Note that the *Chronique ascendante* was inserted by Wace into the main poem. There are 16,992 verses in the entire work.

In the first division Wace begins with the fall of Troy. The Danes are descended from a king called Danaüs. The deeds of the sea-robber Hasting are recounted in full. With the alexandrine verse begins the story of Rou (or Rollo) who has given his name to the poem. The chronicle then proceeds through Dukes William Long Sword, Richard the Elder, and Richard. The *Chronique ascendante,* which has been outlined above, was added here. The third division is concerned with Duke Richard, Robert the Devil, William the Conqueror, William Rufus, and Henry I. The poet enters into great detail when he narrates the invasion of England (1066).

The sources for the *Roman de Rou* were the chronicles of Dudo of St. Quentin, William of Jumièges, William of Malmesbury, much legendary material, and the poet's imagination. A. H. Krappe believes Wace used the *De consolatione philosophiae* of Boethius (*Leuvensche Bijdragen,* XVIII, 1-6).

The *Brut,* Wace's earlier work, is even more interesting than the *Rou:* it has some passages of lyric beauty, and it includes the legends of Arthur and Lear. There are 15,300 octosyllabic rhymed couplets. This poem also begins with the fall of Troy. The son of Aeneas, Ascanius, has a son, Silvius, who engenders Brutus (or Brut). Brut is forced to leave Italy, followed by many companions. He goes first to Greece but eventually lands in Britain, having reinforced his company with the descendants of Trojans in Spain. We wade with difficulty through the list of a hundred legendary kings which follow. They are: Locrimos, Madan, Malins, Ebrac, Hudibras, Baldad, *Lear,* Cordelia, Cunedages, Rival, Gurgustius, Lisilius, Lago, Rimas, Corbodiabo, Porreus, Stater, Piguer, Rudac, Clotan, Donvalo, Belin, Gurgint, Guineclin, Sisillius, Rommarus, Damus, Morpidus, Gorbonian, Agar, Elidur, Gorbonian, Margan, Eumanus, Juvalon, Runo, Geronces, Catullus, Caüllus, Porreus, Cerin, Fulgentius, Eldadus, Andrigeus, Urian, Eliu, Cledantius, Cloten, Gurgustius, Merian, Bledudo, Cap, Oenus, Sillius, Blegabres, Achinal, Eldol, Region, Aredrec, Phanupenisel, Pir, Caporus, *Nennius,* Ely, *Lud,* Cassibelan, Androgeus, *Caesar,* Arivargus, Marius, Coïl, Lucius (first Christian king), Sever, Basian, Carausius, Asclepiodar, Hoël, Constantin, Octave, Trahen, Maximinian, Clionas, Constantin, Constant, Vortigern, and the coming of the Saxons, Vortimer, Vortigern, Aurelius, Ambrosius, Uter, Artur (vss. 9239-13,706), Costentin, Conan, Notaporus, Malgo, Caris, Gurmon (and the Saxons once more), Cadwalon, Cavalance, and last of all, Cadwalander.

Lear, Vortigern, and Arthur, through their literary associations, interest us the most. The whole work is merely a free translation of Geoffrey of Monmouth's *Historia regum Brittaniae* with some original additions. Wace omitted the famous *Prophecies of Merlin;* he expanded greatly all the conversational material in Geoffrey. In 1204 the Middle English poet, Layamon, rehandled, in turn, the poem of Wace with still further additions. Layamon's English poem has 32,250 lines as opposed to the

15,300 of Wace's *Brut*. This Layamon, or Lawman, was a priest of Ernley-on-Saxon who knew Anglo-Saxon and admits that he travelled far and wide to obtain copies of Bede and Wace. Tatlock has demonstrated that Layamon had personal knowledge of Ireland (*SPhil* XXVIII, 55-61). Wace introduced the Round Table, which is not found in Geoffrey, presumably from Pan-Celtic tradition; Layamon redeveloped this in greater detail and narrated how the table was first adopted by Arthur: that there might be none seated high at his board and none low.

We have yet to speak of Beneëit de Sainte-More's *Estoire des dus de Normandie*, composed on the request of Henry II to replace that of Wace. For the first part Beneëit reworked his predecessor's material; he continued from various Latin chronicles of the times. Critics seldom do justice to this history, because it is so dimmed by the fame of Wace's chronicle, and because its length has an unpleasant suggestion of tedium. The poem has its merits, none the less. Beneëit gives more detail on Norman customs and, though he lacks Wace's joviality, his verse is clear and effective. On sober comparison the *Rou* and the *Estoire* are on a par. F. Michel, the editor, insisted that this Beneëit was not the same as Beneëit de Sainte-More who composed the *Roman de Troie*. His arguments are not convincing. The *Estoire* and the *Roman de Troie* are contemporary and all indications would show that they were composed at the same court, for the same public. G. Paris, De la Rue, and Duval were convinced that the two Beneëits were the same. The *Estoire* ends with Henry I; it comprises 42,310 octosyllables in rhymed couplets. Neither Wace nor Beneëit could bring their narrative as far as their patron, Henry II.

## EDITIONS

*La Gran conquista de Ultramar*, ed. Pascual de Gayangos (Madrid: *Bibl. Aut. Esp.*, 1926); but better still for the Spanish *Isomberte* is *La Leyenda del Cavallero del Cisne*, ed. Emeterio Mazorriaga (Madrid: V. Suárez, 1924).— Guilhem de Tudela, *La Chanson de la Croisade Albigeoise*, ed. E. Martin-Chabot (Paris: *CHFmâ*, 1931).—*Canso d'Antiocha* in Carl Appel's *Provenzalische Chrestomathie* (6th ed.; Leipzig, 1930); *Fragment d'une chanson d'Antioche en provençal*, ed. P. Meyer (Paris, 1883).—*La Chanson d'Antioche*, ed. Paulin Paris (Paris, 1848, 2 vols.).—*La Conquête de Jérusalem*, ed. C. Hippeau (Paris, 1868).—*Les Aventures du Chevalier au Cygne et les Enfances de Godefroi*, ed. C. Hippeau (Paris, 1874-1877, 2 vols.) contains one version of both Swan epics, also selections, amounting to 2,539 lines, of the *Chetifs*, as an appendix. The entire *Chetifs* has been edited as a dissertation by Mrs. Lucy Wenhold, but this remains unpublished, in the Library of the University of North Carolina; another complete edition of the *Chetifs* has been announced by A. Hatem.—*Elioxe,* ed. H. A. Todd in *PMLA,* IV.—Geoffrei Gaimar, *Estorie des Engleis,* ed. T. D. Hardy; C. T. Martin (2 vols., London, 1888-89).—Jordan Fantosme, *Chronique,* ed. F. Michel in his edition of the *Chronique des ducs de Normandie* by Beneëit (Paris: *CdiHF,* 1836-1844), III. —*Roman du Mont-Saint-Michel,* ed. Paul Redlich (Marburg, 1894).—Ambroise, *Estoire de la Guerre Sainte,* ed. G. Paris (Paris: *CdiHF,* 1897).—Wace, *Roman de Rou,* ed. H. Andresen (Heilbronn: Henninger, 1877-1879, 2 vols.); *Brut,* ed. Le Roux de Lincy (Rouen, 1836, 2 vols.) and ed. Ivor Arnold (Paris: *SATF,* 1938—), I.—Beneëit, *La Chronique des ducs de Normandie,* ed. F. Michel (Paris: *CdiHF,* 1836-1844, 3 vols.).

# CHAPTER XIII

## THE ORIGINS OF THE ROMANCE; ITS STYLE

Edmond Faral, *Recherches sur les sources latines des contes et romans courtois du moyen âge* (Paris: Champion, 1913).

Maurice Wilmotte, *De l'origine du roman en France (La Tradition antique et les éléments chrétiens du roman)* (Brussels, 1923).

Edmond Faral, *Les arts poétiques du XII^e et du XIII^e siècle* (Paris: Champion, 1923).

W. W. Comfort in *PMLA*, XIX, 64-74 [distinction between romance and epic].[1]

Since the period of the Carolingian Renaissance (790-877), at least, the adverb *romanice* was in use to express 'in the vulgar tongue,' as opposed to *latine*. By the time it had completed its phonetic transition into the form *romanz* it was a noun used to designate a translation from Latin into the vulgar tongue. This meaning, though it must have existed much earlier, is first attested in 1140. Wace extended this to include any work in the vernacular, whether a translation or not. From the thirteenth century on, the sense 'fictitious narrative,' which the word has today, predominated. In this chapter we are restricting the term to that type of fictitious narrative which Faral defines as follows:

Nous avons conservé, du XII^e siècle, un certain nombre d'œuvres écrites en vers de huit syllabes, généralement assez développées (leur longueur varie de 8,000 à 30,000 vers), et qui ont pour sujet des histoires de chevalerie et d'amour: elles portent le titre de romans. (*Recherches, etc.*, p. 391).

Just as we have in contemporary literature the novel and the short story, there is a shorter form of the romance with the same broad characteristics, called in the twelfth century the *lai* (Celtic *láed*, "a song"), or *conte courtois*, and sometimes *dit*. The *lai* or *conte* differs from the romance in three ways: it is much shorter (commonly under a thousand lines); all its details converge towards one main scene, which is the climax of the theme; the poetic style is strictly subordinate to the action which speeds on towards its climax. Apropos of the *conte* and romance Faral says:

Aussi bien voyons-nous que l'histoire des deux genres, au moins en ses débuts, a été la même, qu'ils ont suivi des voies parallèles ou communes, et qu'une obligation s'impose, quand on les étudie, qui est de les considérer comme formant un bloc indissoluble (*ibid.*, p. 392).

[1] Nathaniel E. Griffin has also defined the romance in *PMLA* XXXVIII, 50-70.

At the close of the twelfth century, Jean Bodel, in his *Chanson des Saisnes,* divided the subject matter of vernacular literature into three *matières:* the *matière de Rome,* the *matière de Bretagne,* and the *matière de Charlemagne.* The last refers to the *chansons de geste,* which have already received discussion; the other two apply to the romance. Modern scholars are more systematic and classify the romance into three dominant types, according to content:

1. *romans antiques,* or *matière de Rome,*
2. adventure and Graeco-Byzantine romances,
3. Breton romances *(matière de Bretagne),*
   a. Arthurian romances,
   b. The Tristan story.

This division is not absolute, but, as classification is essential to serve as a framework upon which to drape further information, we shall adopt it. The *conte* or *lai* may also be classified into three groups:

1. *conte* adapted from Ovid, etc.,
2. *conte d'aventure,*
3. Breton *lai.*

There are no *contes* of Graeco-Byzantine origin.

This brings us to the problem of origin of this type of literature. In a preceding chapter we have discussed the second medieval renaissance, that of the twelfth century; it was this second reawakening which saw the birth of the romance. The main centers in which letters flourished were the schools at Orleans and at Paris. The twelfth century clerics possessed nearly all the Latin poets which are now known to us. As M. Gilson, the eminent historian of medieval philosophy, has said:

Dès qu'on ouvre les œuvres d'Abélard par exemple, on constate que ce dialecticien cite couramment Cicéron, Sénèque, Virgile, Horace, Ovide, et que ce ne sont pas là des citations artificielles, introduites en vertu d'un procédé mécanique (E. Gilson, *La Philosophie au moyen âge,* Payot, 1922, I, 91).

While using the term *renaissance* for this movement the student must bear in mind how it differs from that greater renaissance of the sixteenth century. This medieval renaissance was for the clerics, the Latin speakers only. The great mass of laïcs shared in it only indirectly. Then again, the twelfth-century "humanist" was a "modernist." His chronological sense had not been developed, and he saw in antiquity only those things which could still be of benefit to him in his own life and time. He modernized the ancients, as we sometimes stage *Hamlet* in evening clothes! It is quite possible that John of Salisbury and Thierri of Chartres would be thoroughly disgusted if they could return today and see the antiquarian zeal with which we delve into their period. They might be the first to raise the utilitarian cry.

With such a host of admirers for Vergil, Statius, etc., from the "modern" point of view, it was natural that many sought to write like them. Many also tried their hands at hexameters after the Ovidian style; but few of these Latin imitations have survived till the present day in buried and forgotten MSS. To quote Faral once more:

Il faut cultiver les anciens, nos poètes doivent imiter les leurs: voilà ce qu'on répétait depuis Bernard de Chartres; et on imagine quelles importantes conséquences eut cette doctrine pour la littérature, le jour où l'imitation, cessant de se faire en latin, se rendit accessible au grand public en revêtant la forme romane, le jour où, sortant de l'école, tel clerc s'avisa, laissant le vers latin aux orties, de faire servir son érudition à la confection d'un poème en français. Ce jour-là, le roman antique était né (*op. cit.,* p. 399).

That is to say, the first French romance was an imitation of a Latin epic.

The *roman antique* is the oldest form of the romance; it was a conscious imitation in the vulgar tongue of such classic writers as Vergil and Statius. Of the imitation of episodes in Ovid's *Metamorphoses* we shall speak later, for those were, perhaps, the beginnings of the *conte*.

This imitation of the ancients did not remain slavish. Once established, the material was embellished and brought thoroughly up to date for the twelfth-century reader. The love element was increased, marvels were introduced from many written sources, from traditions, and from the imagination. The medieval man loved marvels and could conceive of anything. Indeed, to him the world was filled with fascinating mystery. He believed in unicorns because he had seen a narwhale's tusk and had been told it was a unicorn's horn; griffins inspired implicit faith on the strength of the ibex horn (the griffin's claw!) and a few ostrich eggs. In fact, the twelfth-century man would not be astounded at our aeroplanes and electric lights. The first were actually attempted (gliders) in the eleventh century, and the second were anticipated in those remarkable *charboncles*, or gleaming precious stones, which used to light the Saracen ships and secret chambers. Need it be said that for the twelfth-century cleric these stones were mere conceits of the imagination? Automatons also fascinated him, but these he had seen in the East while crusading. We shall quote from a passage in the *Arabian Nights*, translated by Burton, in which the narrator speaks of a Greek monastery in Asia Minor.

About the saloon were figures carved in human form, and fashioned on such wise that the air passed through them and set in motion musical instruments within, so that the beholder would fancy they spoke.

Such Eastern marvels as these are attested elsewhere beyond dispute. (See Margaret Schlauch's "The Palace of Hugon de Constantinople" in *Spec* VII, 500-14). The romance began to conform also to the twelfth-century's favorite style in psychological analysis. This style was cultivated from the reading of Ovid, especially from the *Amores* and the *Tristia,* from Horace's *Ars poetica* or *Epistola ad Pisones,* from Cicero's *De inventione* and the *Rhetoric* of Corneficius, and from many similar works. There came into existence by the close of the century several *artes poeticae* or arts of poetic rhetoric. These were written in Latin but the rules and suggestions which they gave seem to have been followed also by the composers of romances in the vulgar tongue; indeed, many of the writers of vernacular romances were educated clerics. The two surviving twelfth-century *artes poeticae* are the *Ars versificatoria* (1175) of Matthieu Vendome and the *Poetria nova* (1199) of Galfredus de Vinosalvo, an Englishman.

The doctrine promulgated by these poetic arts is most interesting. For instance, one should begin a composition with a proverb or a moral tale; at the end should come a proverb or a general idea, which expresses the *intentio* of the poem. Much space was devoted in these rhetorics to two devices known as amplification and abbreviation of ideas. The first was very popular in the vernacular romance, which explains why the poet was often prolix to the disgust of modern readers. The rhetorics also say much about the three styles of composition: simple, moderate and sublime. Vergil is the model *par excellence;* his *Bucolics* are in the simple style, his *Georgics* in the moderate, and his *Aeneid* is typical of the sublime. Needless to say, the poets of the vernacular romances preferred the sublime. The differences involved were primarily choice of words and of subjects.

Maurice Wilmotte has made it clear that many of the elements which we consider as developed in the romance form existed already in the Church literature, being found in the writings of Sulpicius Severus (363-406), Paulinus of Nola (353-431), Ausonius (310-394), and Gregory of Tours (538-594). This is doubtless true. There are not an infinite number of ways to tell a good story, whether it be a hagiographic legend or an amorous adventure. Then again, according to Faral's account, the romance is an imitation of the Latin epic plus other elements which were popular to the hearers of the twelfth century. It takes many years to form tastes; surely the writings of Gregory of Tours, and of the others, had had a share in the formation of what was desired by the public in the period that saw the birth of the Old French romance. As Mario Roques had occasion to remark, this work of Wilmotte's should have for sub-title "the romantic elements in the Christian literature".

# CHAPTER XIV

## THE *MATIÈRE DE ROME* OR THE *ROMAN ANTIQUE;* THE *ROMAN D'ALEXANDRE*

Edmond Faral, *Les sources latines, etc.*
Paul Meyer, *Alexandre le grand dans la littérature française du moyen âge* (2 vols.; Paris: Vieweg, 1886).
F. P. Magoun, *The Gests of King Alexander of Macedon* (Harvard Univ. Press, 1929), Introduction.

The earliest example of the romance form which is extant is the fragmentary Alexander poem of Alberich de Pisançon, which was written before 1130. We shall discuss this and its content later in the chapter, passing on now to the oldest romance which has survived complete, the *Roman de Thèbes,* composed by an unknown Norman soon after 1150. It is an adaptation of the *Thebaïs* of P. Papinius Statius (61-96 A.D.) which had great vogue in the schools of the Middle Ages. Statius composed his work around 90 A.D.. As explained in the preceding chapter, the anonymous French poet was not slavish in his imitation; he eliminated from the theme all details that would be uninteresting to his contemporaries, and added some things which were more likely to please them. This meant a suppression of pagan mythology and the addition of the medieval conception of the "marvellous." He also copied the *chansons de geste* in their fondness for embassies, scenes of councils, battles, etc., as well as the Crusade epics for certain episodes. He made use of minute descriptions of objects and animals, after the fashion of Catullus, Vergil, Ovid, Lucan, Silius Italicus, and the *Ilias Latina;* to be sure there were some similar descriptions in his sober original, the *Thebaïs* of Statius. The resulting heterogeneous mixture of the medieval and the ancient formed a new type—the romance—minus one capital element which was brought to perfection in the succeeding efforts, a well developed love element.

Love and womankind had very little place in the *chansons de geste.* In the *Roland* there is brief mention of the *belle Aude* who dies from grief when she hears of Roland's death; in some of the others we are told, in a few lines, that the Saracen king's daughter or betrothed has fallen in love with one of the Christians. This is manifested by her supplying the beloved with arms and aiding him in his escape, along with his companions. She receives baptism and usually marries her heart's desire. There is no description here of love for its own sake; there is a bare statement of facts which aids the intrigue; the poet is primarily concerned with combats and the exaltation of Christianity. Now the *Roman de Thèbes*, the first romance, is not very much ahead of the *chanson de geste* in this portrayal of love. Amorous intrigue is still in its infancy in literature! The *Thèbes* has two intrigues, such as they are: the love of Partonopeus and Antigone, and that of Aton and Ismène. The first was invented by the Norman poet; the second is found in its elements in Statius. The lamentations of Ismène over the body of Aton (vs. 6381 ff.), inspired doubtless by Ovid, are perhaps the only marked improvement of this first romance over the *chansons de geste* in the treatment of love.

The *Roman de Thèbes* narrates the story of Oedipus and ends with the War of the Seven against Thebes. There are 10,230 verses in eight-syllable rhymed couplets. This verse scheme was to be the standard versification for the romance.

Also in Normandy, about 1160,[1] was composed an imitation of Vergil's *Aeneid*, known as the *Roman d'Enéas*. It is more faithful to Vergil in its plot than the *Roman de Thèbes* is to Statius. This second romance also contains the marvellous and the paraphernalia of medieval combat; but, in addition, the love motif is developed further. The composer was a more cultured man than the author of the *Thèbes*. He utilized bestiaries, tales of the seven marvels of the ancient world, and certain legends of a marvellous nature current at Rome, in addition to material that had been previously exploited by the author of the *Thèbes* (largely distortions of classic mythology.)

The *Aeneid* of Vergil already contained the love affair of Aeneas and Dido, but the unknown author of the *Enéas* developed this further, and transformed the sober account of the relations of Aeneas and Lavinia into a love story of great passion. This he spun out to great length, 1,600 verses. The desperation of the young girl, her long monologues in which she analyzes her feelings, the lengthy, drawn-out groanings of Aeneas, all were to be in vogue in future romances as an essential feature of all love episodes. They can be traced in part to Ovid's *Amores* and to his *Ex-Pontine Letters*. With the love motif receiving emphasis in this peculiar way, and with the exploitation of the marvellous, the medieval romance was born. It remained to future poets only to vary the plots and settings. The romance was completely and fully defined in the first two examples of its kind. A remarkable discussion of the transformations suffered by the Vergilian original, in this Old

---

[1] Miss Edna C. Frederick (*PMLA* L, 984-96) argues for a date as early as 1150. Hoepffner would place this poem between 1165 and 1170.

French *Enéas,* and of the theory that was behind it, is given by A. Pauphilet in *Rom* LV, 195-213.

The *Enéas* has 10,156 verses in octosyllabic rhymed couplets. Besides Vergil's *Aeneid,* the bestiaries, and other material already mentioned, the poet must have known the *conte* of Pyramus and Thisbe (which will be discussed later), and his predecessor's poem, the *Roman de Thèbes.* E. Hoepffner insists that he made extensive use of Wace's *Brut* (*Archiv Rom* XV, 248-69; XVI, 162-66).

The next in this chain of development, so far as we can judge from extant works, is the *Roman de Troie,* a vast compilation of 30,316 verses in octosyllabic rhymed couplets. It was written by one Beneëit de Sainte-More, presumably the same Beneëit who was ordered to relieve Wace of his history of the dukes of Normandy. The date of the poem is 1154-1173 (MPhil XXVII, 379-382). Beneëit did not know, of course, the Greek original of Homer's *Iliad* and the *Ilias Latina,* that debased and abridged version of the great bard, was seemingly unworthy of the poet's credence. Beneëit remarks concerning the Homer of the *Ilias Latina:*

> Ne dist pas ses livres veir
> Quar bien savons senz nul espeir
> Qu'il ne fu puis de cent anz nez
> . . . . . . . . .
> Quar anc n'i fu ne riens n'en vit (vs. 1 ff.).

Indeed, Guido di Colonna, who adapted Beneëit's poem into Latin in the thirteenth century, also assures us that Homer was a liar, and this was believed by all men of the ime. Beneëit's sources were the *Historia de excidio Trojae* of the supposed Phrygian, Dares, and the *Ephemeris belli Trojani* of the pseudo-Cretan eyewitness, Dictys. Dares was reputed to have fought on the Trojan side and Dictys on the Greek. Unfortunately, the former account was faked around 550 A.D. and the latter, somewhat earlier, in 300 A.D. Did these false Latin chronicles have Greek originals? It is thought that a part of the Greek original of Dictys has been found in a papyrus fragment dating from 250 A.D.[2] Both these works are Christian in point of view in that they suppress most of the pagan mythology. Beneëit de Sainte-More used Dares as his main source as far as vs. 24,424; from there to the end he utilized Dictys. Other sources were the *Roman de Thèbes,* the *Roman d'Enéas,* the *Chronicle of Fredegarius,* some account of the Argonaut expedition, and a description of the world by Aethicus.

Beneëit did not add much to the recently developed romance, save length! He did, however, solidify the type and stress the love element still more. There are the loves of Jason and Medea, of Diomedes, Troilus and Cressida (*Briseis* or *Briseida*), and of Achilles and Polyxena. The Troilus and Cressida episode was destined to become famous. Guido della Colonna wrote in Latin prose, after Beneëit's romance, his *Historia destructionis Trojae,* in the last third of the thirteenth century. It is probably from this source that Boccaccio took the episode of Troilus and Cressida for his *Filostrato;* thence it passed to Chaucer, and from there to Shakespeare.

Beneëit's poem begins with the Argonaut expedition and the previous destruction of Troy by Jason and Hercules. The city is rebuilt by Priam. The Trojans seek revenge for this destruction, and that is the cause for the theft of Helen! The Greeks assemble and eventually set out to retrieve her. There are more than twenty battles, which are described in detail, before the walls of Troy, particularly the capture of Penthesilea. All of these battles are narrated in good twelfth-century *chanson de geste* fashion. Troy is finally captured and we are then treated to the wanderings of Odysseus, the death of Telegonus, Circe's son, the death of Agamemnon, the story of Orestes, that of Andromache, and finally the end of Pyrrhus. The medieval man, acquainted with this romance, knew most of the legendary history of Greece, though Aeschylus and Sophocles were to him not even names. The love affair of Troilus and Briseïda (in Shakespeare, Cressida), occurs at vs. 13,261 ff. Briseïda, the daughter of Calcas, is a prisoner at Troy. She and Troilus, son of Priam, are in love. She is ransomed, but when she returns to the Greek camp she forgets Troilus and accepts the attentions of Diomedes. Troilus does not forget; later he is killed by Achilles in battle. (On the *Roman de Troie* in medieval art see G. L. Hamilton in *Rom* XLII, 584-86.)

Nowhere are the words of *Ecclesiastes* truer than in medieval scholarship, when it says that all is vanity! This relative order of *Thèbes, Enéas,* and *Troie,* which explains the evolution of the romance so nicely in point of doctrine and content, is beginning to be questioned by certain authorities. One has the feeling that the logicalness of the order is so neat that one must take a shot at it! All levity aside, it is quite possible that in the near future there may be some change in our relative discussion of these three *antique* romances, but to date there has been no evidence strong enough for us to make the change. I might note here that I myself have been surprised by the presence of the word *genouillère* in the *Roman de Troie.* This occurs also in the *Guillaume d'Angleterre,* supposedly by Chrétien de Troyes. The *genouillère* is generally understood to have come into use in the thirteenth century. I have no doubt an expert in armor can explain this away.

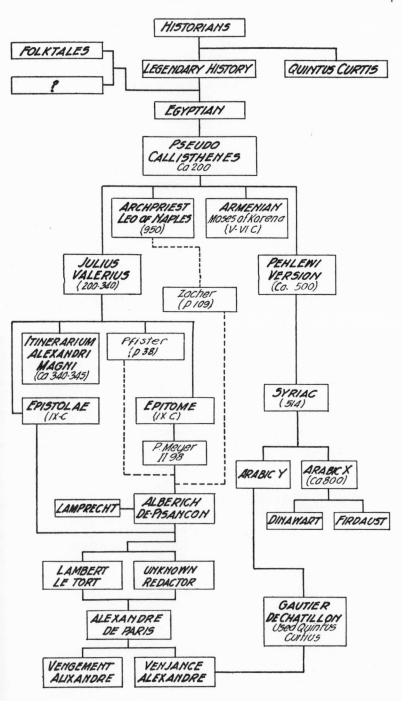

These three romances which we have discussed form what is generally termed the *matière de Rome*. There is another theme which the medieval critic would certainly have included within this group, although it is often treated separately by modern literary historians. We refer to the legend of Alexander. The origins of this theme and the stages through which it passed before reaching twelfth-century France can best be perceived in the accompanying diagram. The first we hear of this material in France is in the Franco-Provençal fragment of Alberich de Pisançon. The name of this minstrel is recorded by the priest Lamprecht who turned Alberich's poem into Middle High German. Lamprecht calls him Elberich von Bisenzûn. Some have identified this placename with Besançon, others with Briançon (because of the dialect), and now Jules Ronjat suggests that we prefer Pisançon, near Valence (*Rom* LIII, 222-3). Only a hundred and five lines of Alberich's original are extant, discovered by Paul Heyse on two folios, left empty by a previous scribe, of a twelfth-century codex in the Laurentian Library at Florence. The number is 35, Plut. LXIV, fols. 115 and 116 r. The fragment breaks off while describing Alexander's boyhood education. The *laisses* contain from six to eight verses, and, in one case, ten. Strangely enough the eight-syllable lines have a caesura in the middle.

How far Alberich carried his poem into the legendary career of Alexander cannot be estimated with certainty. Lamprecht's German version ends with the marvels seen by Alexander and with his voyage to Paradise. As Lamprecht made this adaptation by 1130 Alberich's original was older. The German poem has 7,302 verses which gives an idea of the length of the Franco-Provençal form. Another redactor, perhaps a Poitevin, turned Alberich's version into ten-syllable *laisses,* during the first half of the century. He stopped with Alexander's war against Nicholas of Caesaria.

A glance at the diagram on page 141 will show that leading authorities are not in accord over the chief source used by Alberich. Friedrich Pfister (*Der Alexanderroman des Archipresbyters Leo,* Heidelberg: *SmlT*, 1913) prefers the *Res gestae Alexandri Macedonis* of Julius Valerius as the immediate source. Paul Meyer *(op. cit.)* indicates as source the *Epitome* to Julius Valerius. Zacher (*Pseudokallisthenes,* Halle, 1867) prefers the *Nativitas et victoria Alexandri Magni regis* of the Archpriest Leo of Naples as the *point de départ.* I should assume the first two as sources and omit the Archpriest Leo.

The *Pseudo-Callisthenes* was a forgery, made at Alexandria, which traded on the name of one of Alexander's generals, purporting to be of his composition. A. H. Krappe (*AJP* XLVIII, 359-66) believes it to be certain that there were Greek versions of this forgery as early as the

Christian Era. E. A. W. Budge held that the *Pseudo-Callisthenes* was written originally in Egyptian (*The History of Alexander the Great . . . the Syriac version,* Cambridge, 1888, p. xxxvi). The ninth-century *epistolae* which we have marked on the diagram are entitled *Epistola de situ Indiae* and *Epistola de moribus Bragamanorum.* Note that Julius Valerius made an adaptation of the *Pseudo-Callisthenes* into Latin in the third or fourth century A.D.

We have now come to the composite twelve-syllable version, in Old French, which is known currently as the *Roman d'Alexandre* (15,000 vss.). It has given the name *alexandrine* to the twelve-syllable verse. It was of composite authorship, pieced together into its existing form before 1177, by an unknown arranger. How did he make up his romance?

First of all there was the anonymous ten-syllable line adaptation of Alberich, which we have mentioned in a previous paragraph. This was continued by a poet named Lambert le Tort, in twelve-syllable verse, in which he told of the death of Darius, Alexander's vengeance upon the murderers, his expeditions into India and to the Pillars of Hercules, the Queen Candace episode, Alexander's trip in an airship, his taking of Babylon, the victory over the Amazons, and finally the plot of Antipater and Divinuspater against Alexander. Possibly Lambert also told of the death of Alexander; if so, this portion has been lost. The arranger began by making a redaction into twelve-syllable verse of the anonymous ten-syllable version. He added to this a poem on Alexander known as the *Foraging of Gaza,* by a certain Eustache. With a few lines of transition he prefixed this newly made whole to the vast poem of Lambert le Tort which we have just described. The conclusion he composed himself, narrating in detail the circumstances of Alexander's death. It is not clear whether a certain Pierre de Saint-Cloud had a hand in the manufacture of the conclusion. Several of the MSS mention him; but Albert Henry has strong arguments for opposing this collaboration (*Rom* LXII, 102-6). The resulting composite version was later revised by Alexandre de Paris (or de Bernai). This is the poem as we have it.

Lambert's sources (see diagram) were the *Epitome,* the *Iter ad Paradisum,* and the *Epistolae,* notably those of Alexander to his preceptor, Aristotle. The anonymous arranger for the parts that were original with him, made use of Quintus Curtius, the *Epitome,* and the Archpriest Leo.

We shall repeat and tabulate for the sake of clarity the divisions of this composite work:

1. The twelve-syllable version of the anonymous ten-syllable poem. It narrates the birth and childhood of Alexander, and his youth up to the war with Darius (pp. 1-92 of Michelant edition).

2. The episode of the *Foraging of Gaza*, probably by Eustache (pp. 93-249).

3. The longest portion, by Lambert le Tort, narrating many marvels which we have listed in a preceding paragraph (pp. 249-505).

4. The death of Alexander and the division of the empire among his twelve peers.

Gautier de Châtillon, or de l'Isle, who was secretary to Archbishop Guillaume-aux-Blanches-Mains, composed in the third quarter of the century a Latin *Alexandreïs* (5,400 verses) based largely upon the historical *De rebus gestis Alexandri Magni* of Quintus Curtius and upon certain sources which it is difficult to trace. He received much inspiration from Vergil. Knowledge of this *Alexandreïs* may have inspired Jean le Névelon, second son of the Royal Marshal and *bailli* of Arras, to write his *Venjance Alixandre* which continues the *Roman d'Alexandre* of Alexandre de Bernai. Jean dedicated this to Count Henry of Champagne, who died in 1181. Jean was archdeacon of Arras. Nearly contemporary with this Jean le Névelon was Gui de Cambrai who composed a poem on the same theme, which we shall entitle the *Vengement Alixandre*. This Gui was in all probability a monk at Saint-Nicholas d'Arrouaise and he is identical with the author of the French version of *Barlaam and Josephat* (E. C. Armstrong, *The Authorship of the Vengement Alixandre and of the Venjance Alixandre*, Princeton: EM, 1926).

In England, at the close of the twelfth century, a poet who was either Thomas or Eustache of Kent, wrote another complete Alexander romance, the *Roman de toute chevalerie* (more than 12,000 verses). His principal source was Julius Valerius.

In conclusion, we must mention the work which has been going forward at Princeton University under the direction of Professor Edward C. Armstrong. A group of scholars have been preparing a new and authoritative edition of the Alexander poems and among these will appear very shortly the romance by Alexandre de Bernai and Lambert le Tort. In connection with this Princeton institute, Dr. Alfred Foulet is making a new survey of the sources of the legend and of the interrelations of the various versions.

## EDITIONS

*Roman de Thèbes*, ed. L. Constans (Paris: *SATF*, 1890, 2 vols.).—*Eneas*, ed. J. Salverda de Grave (Paris: *Cfmá*, 1925-1929, 2 vols.); there is an earlier edition by the same editor (Halle: *BN*, 1892).—Benoît de Sainte-More, *Roman de Troie*, ed. L. Constans (Paris: *SATF*, 1904-1912, 5 vols.).—For minor Alexander texts consult the second volume of Paul Meyer's *Alexandre le Grand*, etc.; *v. supra.* The Alberich fragment and corresponding portions of the

German translation by Lamprecht are published in the Foerster-Koschwitz, *Uebungsbuch, etc.,* pp. 238-246.—Lambert li Tors and Alexandre de Bernai, *Li Romans d'Alixandre,* ed. H. Michelant (Stuttgart: *LV,* 1846); *Alexandriade de Lambert le Court et Alexandre de Bernay,* ed. F. Le Court de la Ville-thassetz et E. Talbot (Dinan, 1861).—Gui de Cambrai, *Vengement Alixandre,* ed. Bateman Edwards (Princeton: *EM,* 1930); B. Edwards, "An unpublished fragment of G. de C.'s *Vengement*" in *MLN* XLIX, 366-9.—Jean le Névelon, *Venjance Alexandre,* ed. E. B. Ham (Princeton: *EM,* 1931).—Eustache or Thomas of Kent, *Roman de toute chevalerie,* extracts in P. Meyer's *Alexandre le Grand, etc.—Juli Valeri res gestae Alexandri Macedonis,* ed. B. Kübler (Leipzig: Teubner, 1888).—*Der Alexanderroman des Archipresbyters Leo,* ed. F. Pfister (Heidelberg: *SmlT,* 1913).—*Kleine Texte zum Alexanderroman,* ed. F. Pfister (Heidelberg: *SmlT,* 1910).—This contains the *Commonitorium Palladii,* the letters between Alexander and Dindimus, the letter of Alexander to Aristotle on the wonders of India.—*Epitome rerum gestarum Alexandri Magni,* ed. O. Wagner (Leipzig, 1900).—*Pseudokallisthenes,* ed. Zacher (Halle, 1867). —The edition of the *aljamiado Rrekontamiento del Rrey Alixand^ere* by A. R. Nykl in *Revue Hispanique,* LXXVII, 1-207, contains much valuable information, particularly on the Oriental versions.—Gautier de Châtillon, *Alexandreïs,* ed. Müldener (Leipzig: Teubner, 1863).—*Der altfranzösische Prosa-Alexanderroman,* ed. A. Hilka (Halle: Niemeyer, 1921).—Dares Phrygius, *De Excidio Troiae historia,* ed. Meister (Leipzig: Teubner, 1873).—Dictys Cretensis, *Ephemeridos Belli Troiani,* ed. Meister (Leipzig: Teubner, 1872).

# CHAPTER XV

# THE GRAECO-BYZANTINE AND ADVENTURE ROMANCES

*Histoire littéraire de la France,* vols. XIX, XXIII.
E. Freymond in Vollmöller's *Jahresberichte,* I (1892-1895), 382-388 [a study of possible Byzantine sources].
Laura A. Hibbard (Mrs. Loomis), *Mediaeval Romance in England* (New York: Oxford Press, 1924).

The newly developed romance soon spread from direct imitation of the ancients, which we call *matière de Rome,* to subjects of a more general nature. It is a question whether the spread to newer themes included the exploitation of oral Byzantine stories which could have been carried from southern Italy or directly from Constantinople by the Crusaders. It is true that a number of the twelfth-century adventure romances in France had their main settings in southern Italy, Constantinople, or Rome, and that the names of some of their characters are distortions from the Greek. I am tempted, with Freymond and others, to see some Greek influence, although most of the surviving evidence points to more influence running the other way: that is, we have numerous Byzantine Greek romances which are obvious adaptations from the French, and which are far easier to trace than the French romances taken from the Greek.

In the Graeco-Byzantine class I should place the *Eracle* of Gautier d'Arras, the *Florimont* of Aimon de Varenne, the *Ipomedon* of the Englishman Hue de Roteland, the *Athis et Prophilias* by an unknown poet Alexander, and the *Floire et Blancheflor.* Chrétien de Troyes's *Cligés* might be placed in this group also, but it will be discussed in a later chapter because of its Arthurian content.

There are still other adventure romances belonging to twelfth-century France, where there is virtually no evidence of a Greek influence. These are based upon current folk-themes, recent events, other literary predecessors, and upon the imagination of the poets. Under this heading we should include the *Guillaume d'Angleterre* of Chrétien de Troyes, the *Partonopeus de Blois, Robert le Diable, Guillaume de Palerne, Amadas et Ydoine, Gilles de Chin* by Gautier le Cordier, the *Ille et Galeron* of Gautier d'Arras, and the *Prothesilaus* of Hue de Roteland.

We noted, in connection with the *Jourdains de Blaivies,* the theme of the divided family, where husband, wife, and child or children are separated by shipwreck òr pirates and finally reunited after many wanderings. We also spoke of the two literary variants found in the eighth-century Latin prose version of the *Apollonius of Tyre*, which goes back to a third-century original, and the Placidus-Eustachius legend. The Eustachius contains the special motif of the newly born twin sons carried off by wild beasts. Several of the romances in this present chapter show these motifs. I have hesitation in deciding whether these literary sources were used, or whether the same motifs were not common folk-tales (Mt. 938, *FFC*, 74), popular in France as well as in *Graeca minora*. Discussion on the sources of all the adventure, or so-called non-cyclic romances has been very keen, although not often profitable. An analysis of theories proposed between 1900 and 1923 inclusive has been made by Mrs. Loomis for ten of the romances and for certain epics and lays. She was primarily concerned with the Middle English material, but where these have French analogues she has been very generous in her treatment. She discounts the Byzantine influence more than some of us, and, apparently, she takes the *Aucassin et Nicolette* more seriously. As it is quite probable that the *Aucassin* was a recitation of a dramatic nature, intended to parody certain epic formulae and stock situations of the romance and lyric poetry, we have not included it in the present chapter.

Prominent among the twelfth-century writers of romance was Gautier d'Arras. F. A. G. Cowper has investigated thoroughly the charters of Arras and he concludes very plausibly that this poet was none other than the powerful noble Gautier d'Arras who is mentioned in a number of documents between 1160 and 1202. This noble was active in the service of Philippe d'Alsace, Count of Flanders, and he was also in close association with Baudouin V of Hainaut, one of the patrons to whom the romance *Eracle* is dedicated. This Gautier was also one of the members of the order of *Notre Dame des Ardents* which was an association of minstrels at Arras. To us this identification seems certain. (Cowper has not yet published his conclusions.) Gautier's two romances belong to his earlier years. He wrote the *Eracle* after 1164; Marie, the Countess of Champagne, is mentioned and her marriage took place at that date. It is dedicated to Thibaut V of Blois (Count in 1152-1191), the husband of Aaliz, Marie's sister, and to Baudouin V of Hainaut. The romance is divided into three main episodes.

1. The first recalls the life of Saint Alexis. Eracle is the only son of an old nobleman. He is endowed from birth with three precious gifts: the power to judge precious stones, a knowledge of women, and the ability to judge horses. His mother sells him, after the father's death, to the seneschal of Rome for one thousand *besanz*. This is to secure the

wherewithal to pray for the father's soul. Eracle displays his gifts at the court and chooses for the emperor a wife, Athenaïs (vss. 1-2758).

2. "Huimais cumencera li contes." War breaks out and the emperor is called away. Contrary to Eracle's advice the young Empress Athenaïs is locked in a tower for sake keeping (Mt. 310, FFC, 74; Mt. 310 I, FFC, 78). She strives at once to justify her husband's suspicions. She contrives a love affair with Paridis. On the emperor's return he renounces his wife, on Eracle's urging, and the guilty pair are wedded (vss. 2759-5117).

3. Cosdres has invaded Jerusalem and carried away the True Cross to Persia. Foucar, the Emperor of Constantinople, has been treacherously murdered. Eracle is chosen emperor of Constantinople and soon puts an end to all strife.

This is one of the Graeco-Byzantine romances where a genuine Byzantine source is very likely. There is extant to-day, in three varying versions, a Greek romance known as the *Story of Ptocholeon,* or as περὶ τοῦ γέροντος τοῦ Φρονίμου μουτζοκουρεμένου. The plot is very close to the first episode of Gautier's romance, the main difference being that the protagonist sells himself into slavery. It is probable that Gautier d'Arras and the unknown author of the Greek *Ptocholeon* derived their accounts from a common source, although Gautier may have heard the story orally. The common source, in turn, must have been ultimately indebted to India. The *Chronicle of Fredegarius* is also a source for the third part of this poem. This *Chronicle* narrates (IV, 63-66) that Chosru II of Persia was defeated by Emperor Heraclius of Constantinople in 628. Chosru is the Cosdres of Gautier d'Arras. The historical Chosru mounted the imperial throne in 610 after a revolt against Phokas. Chrétien de Troyes's *Cligés* is usually named as having employed the *Eracle* for a source; but if the *Cligés* can be dated 1162, and the *Eracle* after 1164, the influence would be the other way.

Hue de Roteland was a native of Creden hill (Hereford), or perhaps of Flintshire; the patron whom he served was Gilbert Fitz-Baderon of Monmouth (See *Prothesilaus* vs. 12700 ff.). Between 1174 and 1191 Hue composed his *Ipomedon,* a love romance of possible Byzantine origin, although many doubt this, and the *Prothesilaus.* An examination of these romances in search of source material (cf. H. F. Carter in *Kritisches Jahrbuch,* XII and Kluckow's Introduction to his edition of *Prothesilaus*) shows that Hue was well versed in the French literature of his day. He used Marie's *Lais,* some version of the Tristan theme, *Le Bel Inconnu* of Renaut de Beaujeu, the Thebes, Troy, and Eneas romances, at least the *Cligés* of Chrétien de Troyes, and possibly the Latin fables of Hyginus.

In case the *Bel Inconnu* is to be dated 1190, which is only a hypothesis, it is excluded as a source.

In the *Ipomedon* (10,578 octosyllables) the hero, Prince of Apulia, woos the Princess Fiere of Calabria. He shows his prowess on various occasions and finally in a three day tourney (Mt. 314 VIb, *FFC,* 74). In the other romance (12,471 octosyllables) Prothesilaus and Daunus are the sons of Ipomedon. After the death of their father they are betrayed into strife. Prothesilaus must defend his heritage of Calabria against his brother Daunus of Apulia. These two romances contain numerous folk and literary motifs which have considerable interest for the student of comparative literature. There are three English versions of the *Ipomedon*.

The *Florimont* of Aimon de Varenne, composed in 1188, may show genuine Byzantine influence—from ultimate oriental or Albanian sources. Perhaps the Varennes is that near Châlon-sur-Saone (*Rom* LXI, 369). Alfred Risop in the *Abhandl. Herrn Prof. Dr. Tobler* (Halle, 1895, pp. 430-463) supports vigorously the belief that Aimon knew Greek sources. J. Psichari (*Mélanges G. Paris,* p. 507) contends the opposite, that what Aimon knew of Greek came through Latin. In any case Aimon wrote the romance in France in the Francian dialect. Florimont is named as the grandfather of Alexander the Great, and the poem narrates his youthful adventures. He aids Philippus Macemus in a fight against the Bulgars and eventually wins the king's daughter, Romadanople. In the course of his adventures Florimont kills a monster and falls in love —temporarily—with a fairy.

There are two versions of *Athis et Prophilias,* a longer and a shorter. The first part of the romance is usually traced to Exemplum II of the *Disciplina clericalis* of Petrus Alfonsi in which a man relinquishes his intended wife to a friend who is likewise in love with her. In this romance the Athenian, Athis, gives his wedded wife to the friend, Prophilias, consoling himself with the sister, Gaïte. This last brings on an expedition against Athens by King Bilas of Bile. The rest of the romance is devoted to Athenian wars, caused by the women. The poet seems to wish to give to his poem the color of a history of Athens. We know nothing further concerning him except that his name was Alexander. (Students of later literature will recognize in this the same plot as in Alexandre Hardy's *Gésippe ou les deux amis.*)

*Floire et Blancheflor* is one of the oldest of the twelfth-century adventure romances, belonging in the third quarter of the century. There is Byzantine, and perhaps Oriental, influence (mention of harem, etc.) The possible use of the *Apollonius of Tyre* as a source has already been mentioned. The popularity of the *Floire et Blancheflor* was widespread.

It is cited by the German minnesinger Ulrich von Gutenburg and was translated into Middle High German by Kuonrat Fleck in the first half of the thirteenth century. There is a second French version dating from the last years of the twelfth century, and written in more heroic style. Boccaccio's prose *Filocolo* is one of the later descendants. Felis, a pagan king of Spain, has a son, Floire, who was born on the same day as Blancheflor, a Christian maiden, whose mother he holds in captivity. The two young people fall in love. Felis, in anger, sends his son away and sells Blancheflor to a merchant ship. When the boy returns he is told that Blancheflor has died. When he (Floire) suspects the truth and threatens to kill himself his parents confess all and allow him to go in search of the girl. She has been sold to the emir of Babylon for seven times her weight in gold and is kept in the *tor as pucelles*, a sort of harem (Mt. 310, *FFC*, 74). After many wanderings Floire reaches Babylon, discovers where his love is kept, and tries to gain admittance hidden in a flower basket (Mt. 1360 C, *FFC*, 74). He is discovered and for a time all is lost. The sultan is softened in heart and celebrates the marriage of the lovers. They learn of the death of Felis and return to their kingdom. There are 2,974 verses to the older version of the poem. The later twelfth-century version is incomplete at 3,470 lines. It is certain that this romance was known to the author of *Aucassin et Nicolette*.

*Guillaume de Palerne* is a lengthy romance (9,663 verses) belonging to the very close of the twelfth century. As the poet tells us, at the end, it was adapted from the Latin for the Countess Yolanda of Hainaut. This Latin original may have furnished a few meager details; most of the romance is imagination and legend. Miss Irene McKeehan has examined the poem in its relation to sources and to the Celtic werewolf themes (*PMLA* XLI, 785-809). She concludes that the poet was concerned only with the writing of a best seller and that it is impossible to study the source strata. It is probable that this romance contains folk material: Mt. 428, *FFC*, 74; Mt. 931, *FFC*, 74, 78, 81. Ebron, King of Apuleia, has married Felise, daughter of the Emperor of Constantinople. They have a son, Guillaume, whose uncle seeks to destroy him that he (the uncle) may inherit the kingdom. Guillaume is saved by a werewolf, the enchanted son of the King of Spain, who carries him off to the woods under the very eyes of Ebron and Felise. After many adventures Guillaume arrives at Constantinople where the young Princess Melior falls in love with him. They flee to avoid the projected marriage of Melior with the son of the Emperor of Greece. They are aided in their flight by the werewolf and arrive at the palace of the widowed Felise. Guillaume helps her against her enemy, the King of Spain. When the latter is captured, reconciliation takes place all around. The werewolf is disenchanted on the instance of his father, the King of Spain. Melior and Guillaume are married. This romance is preserved in a single MS, Arsenal B. L. F. 174, along with the thirteenth-century *Escoufle*.

The *Cligés* of Chrétien will be discussed in the next chapter; although it is a so-called Graeco-Byzantine adventure romance it contains mention of King Arthur. Not so the *Guillaume d'Angleterre*, which is commonly ascribed to Chrétien de Troyes. There are some scholars who doubt this attribution. The *Guillaume d'Angleterre* is an ordinary adventure romance, with family division and wanderings, possibly due to imitation of the *Apollonius of Tyre*. The hero, a King William of England, is an imaginary person and has no historical prototype. He and his queen, Graciene, are resident in Bristol. After seven years of marriage the Queen is with child. On three successive nights a voice from heaven bids the King flee. He does so and the Queen accompanies him. On the way she gives birth to twin boys. The Queen, the two infants, and the King all are separated. After various adventures the King becomes steward in the household of a burgher of Galveide; the Queen, without breaking faith with her husband, becomes the lady of Sorlinc, sole ruler of the fief; the twins are baptized Lovel and Marin and are brought up first by peasants, then by the King of Quatenasse. Twenty-one years have passed since the flight of the royal pair. William, the king, is sent by his master on a merchant voyage to Bristol. On his leaving that town his ship is cast ashore at Sorlinc. His wife recognizes him and they are united. He goes hunting and is threatened with death by two knights of the neighboring but hostile King of Quatenasse. He tells his story to them and they recognize him as their father. They did not know until that time that they were brothers. The family, completely united, return to England where the crown is surrendered to them. There are 3,310 verses in the usual rhymed couplets. The date of composition was probably shortly after 1170. It is worthy of special note that here there is no love motif, save the mutual devotion of a wedded pair. This is so unlike the usual romance where there are told the amorous adventures of two unwedded lovers, or, in the case of the courtly romance, the love of a married woman and her lover. It was Maurice Wilmotte (*Moyen âge*, 1889) who first sought to demonstrate the connection with the *Apollonius* legend; Angelo Monteverdi (*Studi medievali* (1909-1910), pp. 169 ff., 392 ff.) indicated analogies with the life of Saint Eustachius. The author of the *Guillaume d'Angleterre* says (vs. 3308 ff.) that the material for the story was narrated to him by a friend, "Roger the well-informed"; elsewhere (vss. 11, 46) the author refers to the *estoires d'Engleterre*, and to his original which one can hear at Bury St. Edmund's. Professor Haxo (*MPhil* XII, 345-66) is inclined to the belief that this Roger was Roger of Hingham, cellarer of Saint Edmund's, who went with his abbot to Rome in 1159-1162. Mr. Haxo infers that Roger could have told the tale to Chrétien somewhere along the route. It is probable that this identification is correct; but it is more likely that Chrétien visited Saint Edmund's or that Roger may have made a later voyage into Normandy around 1170, when he could have met Chrétien at a town such as Beauvais. There is no valid reason for assuming that Chrétien was never in England; such an assumption in the affirmative would aid us in the problem of Arthurian origins, if it could be seriously established. Gröber (*Grundriss,* II, 524) identified this Roger as Rogier de Lisaïs. Monteverdi believed (*op. cit.,* p. 28) that the ultimate source of the *Guillaume d'Angleterre* started on Greek soil and was told in the Greek language. I can feel no justification for this: for me the poem of Chrétien has a decided western flavor. Wilmotte, after Foerster, has established quite conclusively that the Chrétien who wrote the *Guillaume d'Angleterre* and Chrétien de Troyes were one and the same (*Rom* XLVI, 1-38.)

The *Partonopeus de Blois* was composed before the *Florimont,* that is, before 1188, according to Gröber. (*Grundriss,* p. 589). It is a queer mixture of material. Partonopeus is the nephew of Clovis. He is led by a mysterious boar to a ship which carries him to the fairy castle of Chief d'Oire. Here he wins the love, by night, of the fairy mistress, Melior. She makes with him a compact that he must not gaze upon her till she marries him publicly. After a year's stay on these terms Partonopeus returns to France and frees the land from the Danes. He is affianced to his cousin but he returns to his fairy mistress. He violates his promise not to look, on his mother's persuasion, and causes Melior, who is the daughter of the Emperor of Constantinople, to lose her magic powers and renounce him forever. He returns to France and wanders in the woods, a madman. He is found by Urake, Melior's sister, who seeks to reconcile him with his mistress. He is taken prisoner by Armant on the island of Thenedon but he succeeds in reaching the tourney where knights, among them the Sultan of Persia, are competing for the hand of Melior. Partonopeus is declared the best knight on three successive days and wins once more his lady's favor. Urake marries King Lohier of France. There are about eleven thousand lines. Some of the sources are quite apparent. The poet has used Chrétien de Troyes's *Cligés, Lancelot* and *Yvain*—certain of the *lais,* principally *Guingamor* and *Guigemar,* and some version of the Cupid and Psyche story, perhaps that of Apuleius. The motif of the combat with the Danes is borrowed from the *chansons de geste.* Folk motifs employed are Mt. 400 II a, b,

III d, IV b, V, VI, *FFC,* 74 and Mt. 314 VI b, *FFC,* 74. Denis Piramus mentions the *Partonopeus* in his *Life of Saint Edmund* (vss. 32-34), an allusion which has long been wrongly interpreted by some scholars: they believe that Piramus was the author of this romance (cf. Ward, *Catalogue of Romances in B.M.,* I, 700 ff.). Today everyone considers the *Partonopeus* as anonymous. Kawczynski thinks the author was attached to the Count of Blois (*Rom* XXX, 475). The name *Partonopeus* was suggested by the *Roman de Thèbes.*

*Robert le Diable* is a romance of exceeding interest, 5,078 verses in length. A certain duchess of Normandy, who has had no children, asks the devil to send her one, as God has failed to do so. A child with the most evil instincts is born. (His birth is extremely painful for the mother.) He is willfully cruel to all around him; by the time he has reached the age of twenty he is extraordinarily large and strong. The pope excommunicates him and his father banishes him. He becomes an inhuman bandit. Finally, struck with wonder at his own wickedness, he forces his mother, sword in hand, to tell him the circumstances of his birth. He is overcome with sorrow at the facts and goes as a pilgrim to Rome. Neither the pope nor a certain holy hermit can give him penance for such a life of fiendishness; a note from heaven informs the hermit what the sinner must do. To save his soul he must simulate madness, not utter a word, must take his food only from the mouth of a dog, and must cause himself to be chased by the populace about the streets every day. Robert accepts this penance and receives absolution from the hermit. After ten years of this life the lands of his patron, the Emperor of Rome, are invaded by the Turks. He secretly arms himself and saves the day for the Romans. This is repeated on two later occasions, though he is wounded on the last. The Emperor promises his daughter to the conquering knight if he can be found. The seneschal pretends that it is he. The Emperor's daughter, who is dumb, knows that the knight is Robert, recovers her speech, and tells all. Robert refuses her hand in marriage and an offer to return to Normandy. He wishes to save his soul as a hermit (Mt. 307 I a, b, son, III, *FFC,* 74). Some time after his death his bones are transported to Le Puy in Normandy, where he becomes known as Saint Robert.

The theme of this romance exists today as a folktale in northern Spain (Mt. Sp. 756 B as I, *FFC,* 90). The prayer to the devil and the birth of a diabolical child are two widespread folk motifs, C 751 and T 554 respectively, according to Thompson's classification (*FFC,* 74, p. 49; also in *FFC,* 106, 107).

An ecclesiastical version (colored from the medieval churchman's point of view), exists in the eleventh-century Irish *Immram Hui Corra,* an account of the careers of the Irish saints, Lochan, Enne, and Sylvester. This parallel was pointed out by Professor Ronald S. Crane (*RRev* V, 55-67). The question is, are the French romance and the Irish *Immram* intimately connected or do they go back to a common folklore source? As there are other instances of Irish hagiographic literature influencing French literature of the twelfth century, the former supposition is not impossible. There is absolutely no historical material in the French romance of *Robert le Diable,* unless we except the fact that Robert was a common name among the dukes of Normandy and that there was an eleventh-century duke called Robert the Devil. This aided in localizing the folklore (or Irish?) legend in Normandy. The story is also told by Etienne de Bourbon in his *Exempla* of the first half of the thirteenth century. It occurs also in a miracle play of the fourteenth century. It has some resemblance to the Merlin theme.

*Amadas et Ydoine* is a romance intended to exalt "fine et loyal amour."[1] Amadas, son of the seneschal of the duke of Burgundy, wins the love of the daughter of the Duke, Ydoine. She sends him away to roam the world and acquire fame and prowess. He goes mad on learning that Ydoine is to marry the Count of Nevers. The marriage takes place but is not consummated. Ydoine insists on making a pilgrimage to Rome. She finds the mad Amadas at Lucca; he recovers his senses. She is carried off by a discourteous knight. When Amadas recovers her she dies, seemingly, at Rome, making Amadas promise to live and have masses said for her soul. The discourteous knight reappears and confesses all. Ydoine is not dead but enchanted by a fairy ring he had placed upon her finger (Mt. 706*B, *FFC,* 90). The lovers return to Burgundy, the Count of Nevers divorces Ydoine, and the two are joined in happiness. It would seem that the unknown author of this poem knew *Floire et Blancheflor;* the abduction theme may go back to a Celtic source. See also Mt. 400 V a, VI, *FFC,* 74; Mt. 400, *FFC,* 78, 81. Reinhard dates this romance about 1220. We have retained the traditional dating of F. M. Warren and Gaston Paris.

*Gilles de Chin,* by Gautier le Cordier de Tournai, is unique. The hero is an historical personage who died on August 12, 1137, but the adventures which are here attributed to him are legendary or imaginary. The chronicler, Gislebert de Mons, speaks highly of the real Gilles de Chin, naming him one of the most valiant knights of the century. M. Félix Lajard (*HLF* XXIII, 407) informs us that one of Gilles' legendary exploits, his victory over the dragon which devastated Wasmes, is still

---

[1] F. M. Warren (*MLN* XIII, 339-51), once made a striking comparison of the love theme here with its treatment in the *Tristan* and in Chrétien's *Cligés.* In the *Tristan,* love is unrestrained by morality or opinion; in the *Cligés,* public opinion is more prominent; in the *Amadas et Ydoine,* both personal morality and public opinion are considered.

celebrated in Hainaut. In this romance, Gilles de Chin and his close comrade, Gerart de Saint-Aubert, follow many tourneys. Gilles falls in love with the Countess of Duras, a young matron of eighteen years. He goes on a crusade, but before his departure promises faith to his lady. He performs marvellous deeds in the Holy Land. The Queen of Jerusalem loses her heart to him, but he has not forgotten his true "amie." He learns of the Countess's death before his return to France. His grief seems consolable for he marries Domison de Chievres (this marriage is a historical fact) and follows once more the tourneys. He aids the Count of Hainaut against the Duke of Brabant. Finally, he returns to Berlaimont where he lives for years in peace and conjugal happiness. He dies of a lance thrust at the battle of Rollecourt. The chronicler, Gislebert de Mons, affirms that he was slain in a war between the Count of Namur and the Duke of Louvain. This poem was turned into prose at the close of the fourteenth or the beginning of the fifteenth century. It is usually termed the first historico-biographical romance.

The *Ille et Galeron* of Gautier d'Arras (also author of the *Eracle*) was dedicated to Baudouin V of Hainaut and to Beatrice, the second wife of Frederick Barbarossa, a fact which enables us to fix the date of composition with some precision between 1167 and 1170 (cf. Cowper in *MPhil* XVIII, 601-8; XX, 35-44). F. E. Guyer has sought to place the date after 1170 (*MPhil* XXVI, 277). This adventure romance shows an acquaintance with two *lais* of Marie de France, the *Eliduc* and *Le Fraisne,* but Gautier claims that his main source was an *estoire* which F. Lot (*Rom* XXV, 585-588) identifies with the *Chronique de Nantes* (dating between 1050 and 1056). Lot believes that the first fifteen hundred lines of this poem have a historical basis. F. A. G. Cowper has suggested that the *estoire* was a *Chronique de Blois,* now lost, which in turn went back to the *Chronique de Nantes.*

Ille is the son of Eliduc, a Breton noble. After the death of his father he is dispossessed by Hoël and his nephews; Duke Conan is too weak to interfere. Ille receives his training and is armed knight at the court of France. Ille returns to Brittany and wins the love of Duke Conan's sister, Galeron. They marry. Alas, he loses the sight of his left eye in a battle (Wollaton MS). He flees from Galeron, afraid of her finding him an imperfect lover, despite all evidence to the contrary. He takes service with the Emperor of Rome and she wanders about in search of him. She, too, finally arrives at Rome and dwells there as a penitent. Ille is to wed Ganor, daughter of the Emperor. Galeron presents herself at the wedding, discloses herself, and wins back her husband. They return to Brittany. After the birth of three children Galeron takes the veil, and Ille goes once more to Rome, where he marries Ganor. There are 6,700 verses. In the judgment of many this poem is inferior to Gautier's other work, the *Eracle*. One of the children of Galeron is named Ydoine. The influence of this poem upon the *Amadas et Ydoine* is extremely probable.

## EDITIONS

Gautier d'Arras, *Eracle*, ed. E. Löseth (Paris: Bouillon, 1890).—Hue de Rotelande, *Ipomedon*, ed. Kölbing-Koschwitz (Breslaus, 1889); *Protheselaus*, ed. F. Kluckow (Halle: *GrL*, 1924).—*Athis et Prophilias*, ed. A. Hilka (Halle: *GrL*, 1912-1916, 2 vols.).—*Floire et Blancheflor*, ed. E. du Méril (Paris: *BElz*, 1856).—*Guillaume de Palerne*, ed. H. Micheland (Paris: *SATF*, 1876).—*Partenopeus de Blois*, ed. Paris: Robert Crapelet, 1834, 2 vols.). Dr. Leon Smith has a new edition of this in preparation.—*Robert le Diable*, ed. E. Löseth (Paris: *SATF*, 1903).—*Amadas et Ydoine*, ed. J. R. Reinhard (Paris: *Cfmâ*, 1926).—Gautier le Cordier, *Gilles de Chin*, ed. Reiffenberg in *Mon. pour servir à l'histoire des provinces de Namur*, VII (1847), 1 ff. A new edition is being prepared by E. B. Place and John Keith.—Gautier d'Arras, *Ille et Galeron*, ed. W. Foerster (Halle: *RomB*, 1891); ed. E. Löseth (Paris: Bouillon, 1890).—Aimon von Varennes, *Florimont*, ed. A. Hilka-A.Risop (Göttingen: *GrL*, 1933).—Chrétien de Troyes, *Guillaume d'Angleterre*, ed. Maurice Wilmotte (Paris: *Cfmâ*, 1927).

# CHAPTER XVI

## THE MATIÈRE DE BRETAGNE

E. Faral, *La Légende arthurienne*, 3 vols. (Paris: Champion, 1929).

J. D. Bruce, *The Evolution of Arthurian Romance* (2nd ed.; 2 vols., Göttingen: Hesperia series, 1928).

E. K. Chambers, *Arthur of Britain* (London: Sidgewick, 1927).

*A Bibliography of Critical Arthurian Literature for the Years 1922-1935*, prepared by John J. Parry and Margaret Schlauch (Modern Language Association, 1931, 1936, 2 numbers).

"An Index of Abbreviations in Miss Alma Blount's Unpublished *Onomasticon Arthurianum*," in *Spec* I, 190-216.

R. Thurneysen, *Die irische Helden- und Königssage bis zum 17. Jh.* (Halle, 1921).

R. S. Loomis, *Celtic Myth and Arthurian Romance* (Columbia University Press, 1927).[1]

Annette B. Hopkins, *The Influence of Wace on the Arthurian Romances of Crestien de Troies* (University of Chicago Press, 1913).

Margaret Pelan, *L'Influence du Brut de Wace sur les romanciers français de son temps* (Paris: E. Droz, 1931).

Gustave Cohen, *Chrétien de Troyes et son œuvre* (Paris: Boivin, 1931).[2]

W. W. Comfort, tr. *Arthurian Romances by Chrétien de Troyes* (Everyman series, 1928). There is a selective bibliography for Chrétien de Troyes (pp. 373-77).

Reinhard, J. R., "Chrétien de Troyes: A Bibliographical Essay," *EUM* (Ann Arbor, 1932), pp. 195-231.

Philip A. Becker in *ZfrPh* LV, 257-92, 385-445, 513-60.

The *matière de Bretagne* represents a decided step forward in the history of the romance; it developed around a king called Arthur (in Old French *Artu(r)*). No medieval subject has aroused more interest among scholars than the attempt to understand this material, and for that reason the bibliography has become formidable. In this chapter we can only hope to introduce the reader to the main problems, while well aware that their aspect may be altered at any time by subsequent research. Such scholars as Jessie L. Weston, W. Foerster, E. Brugger, J. D. Bruce, A. C. L. Brown, W. A. Nitze, R. S. Loomis, J. J. Parry are devoting, or have devoted their lives to Arthurian investigation. In the following pages we shall consider, in order, the identity of Arthur, the early legend concerning

---

[1] Also *MPhil* XXXIII, 225-38.

[2] See further *Annales Univ. de Paris* (1931), pp. 128-39.

him found in saints' lives and chronicles, his introduction into the newly developed romance form, the development of new themes concerning Arthur's court and his knights—probably from Celtic sources—and last, the extant romances which belong to this *matière de Bretagne*.

Heinrich Zimmer, and after him Bruce, believed that Arthur may be traced to a Romanized Celt, Arturus, who directed and won the battle of Badon Hill, in the first part of the sixth century. This fact and the name *Arturus* are mentioned by Nennius in his *Historia Britonum* (early ninth century), and again in the anonymous *Annales Cambriae* (*ca.* 976). Gildas in the *De Excidio et Conquestu Britanniae* (540) mentions the battle but not Arthur. As several scholars have made clear, Gildas was writing a lament and not a chronicle; he knew only southwestern Britain and had no acquaintance with his country's past (F. Lot in *Schoepperle Loomis Med. St.,* pp. 229-64). A still earlier occurrence of the name *Arturus,* although it has nothing to do with the hero of Badon Hill, is in Adamnan's *Life of Saint Columba* (*ca.* 692-97).

Those who do not accept this historical figure who fought at Badon Hill as the prototype of the legendary king are apt to see in King Arthur a mythical, folklore personification, as though he were a composite of the Celtic ideal, of pan-Celtic hero worship. E. W. B. Nicholson (*The Academy,* Oct. 12, 1895) regarded the name as a composite of *artos,* 'bear,' and *viros,* 'man' meaning 'bear-male,' with folk-significance. S. Singer (*Die Artussage,* Berne and Leipzig: P. Haupt, 1926), following the lead of Rhys, derives *Arthur* from *Artaios,* the Celtic god equated with *Mercurius cultor.* Singer adds that this myth was crossed with the myth of Tarmis, the god of hell.

Kemp Malone believes that the Arthurian legend grew primarily in Cornwall and that it was a combination of a primitive belief and of an historical character. He believes that the Welsh expression *aruthr,* meaning 'terrible,' passed into use in Cornwall and from there back into Wales, undergoing regular phonologic syncope to *arthur.* It was applied to a primitive Celtic hero who was thereafter known as Arthur, or 'the terrible.' This hero was occasionally referred to as *mab uthr,* 'terrible son,' and later narrators misunderstood this, inferring that it meant 'son of Uter' (*JEGP* XXIII, 463-91). This primitive hero of folk origin became crossed in the minds of the people with the memory, or rather legend, of one L. Artorius Castus, prefect of the VI Victrix Legion stationed at York, in Britain, in the third century. During an insurrection in Armorica this Artorius was appointed *dux* of the punitive expedition, thus giving cause for the tale that King Arthur made an overseas' expedition into Britanny. When L. Artorius Castus was incapacitated for military service he was withdrawn and given a post in civil life in his native Dalmatia. Malone intimates that his sudden departure from Britain may have given rise to the legend concerning the "Passing of Arthur," particularly if he were sadly missed (*MPhil* XXII, 367-374). Although we incline to the identification proposed by Zimmer, it is quite possible that Malone and the others are right in thinking of the legend of Arthur as a growth with its roots in Celtic mythology. Perhaps, as Rhys once suggested, the Britons conceived of Arthur as successor to the Roman Count of Britain, after the withdrawal of the Romans. Until some new discovery is brought to light it will be difficult to state the case with more certainty.

The earliest occurrence of a King Arthur in legend is in a life of Saint Goeznovius, presumably of the year 1019, where it speaks of the Saxons "Quorum superbia postmodum per magnum Arturum Britonum regem fuit ad tempus repressa, eis pro parte maxima ab insula repulsis et servire coactis." It is probable that the Arthurian legend received its first wide growth in the eleventh century. Arthur is referred to again in the *Vita Cadoci* (*ca.* 1075) at some length; also in the *Vita Carantoci* (*ca.* 1100?). Two other saints' lives, the *Vita Iltuti* (*ca.* 1100) and the *Vita Paterni* (early twelfth) also give notice to this legendary king. The *De Miraculis Sanctae Mariae Laudunensis* of Hermann of Tournai, which is dated as late as 1146, tells how the monks of Laon sent to England in the interest of their cathedral building fund in the year 1113. Their servants disputed with Cornishmen over the question whether Arthur was still alive "sicut Britone solent iurgari cum Francis pro rege Arturo" (Migne, *PL* vol. 156, col. 973). In the *Vita Carantoci* (see above) Arthur is referred to as still reigning in Cornwall where he hunts a dragon which devastates his dominions. The difficulty with all these scattered references in the saints' lives is that the lives themselves are difficult to date within fifty years. William of Malmesbury, in his *De Rebus gestis regum Anglorum* (*ca.* 1125) is severe for the legends saying "Hic est Artur de quo Britonum nugae hodieque delirant." William deems the true Arthur of Badon Hill to be worthy of honest chronicles rather than of this fictitious prattling. William of Malmesbury also speaks of Walwen or Gawain (the first occurrence of the name) as a "non degener Arturis ex sorore nepos" who was buried in Wales. Henry of Huntingdon in his *Historia Anglorum* (*ca.* 1129) takes his account of Arthur from Nennius. Our only detailed pictures of Arthur as he was conceived by the Welsh, uncontaminated by French influence, are in the *Kilhwch and Olwen* and in the *Dream of Rhonabwy*, two tales which are preserved in the *Red Book of Hergest* (*ca.* 1380) and in the *White Book* (close of thirteenth century). These tales must go back in some form to early tradition.

There are mentions of a non-literary character which have been assigned to the early part of the twelfth century. Pio Rajna discovered in the Italian archives some Arthurian names and among them was *Artusius* (*Rom* XVII, 161 ff., 355 ff.). Faral is not wrong in arguing that this *Artusius* is not the same as *Arturus* or even *Artorius*. It should be noted that *Arturus* is the Latin form of the king's name in the proved references. The other names found by Rajna apparently are later in date than Geoffrey of Monmouth's chronicle. There is something else of major importance. Above the Porta della Pescheria of the cathedral at Modena, a town to the northwest of Bologna, there figures a siege of a castle, in relief. The knights are marked with Arthurian names, Arthur, Kay, etc. Leonardo Olschki (*Arch Rom* XIX, 145-182) declares definitively that the carvings belong to the period 1150-1184. R. S. Loomis and others believe they can be assigned to 1099-1106 and Faral says that they are not earlier than shortly before 1200. Probably the castle scene is a primitive version of the abduction of Guenevere, a tale which forms the theme of Chrétien's *Lancelot*. There are also animal figures in this Arthurian relief which resemble somewhat the figures on the lower border of the Bayeux Tapestry (early twelfth century). At any rate these Modena animals do not seem to refer to the *Roman de Renart* which would prove beyond question a later date in the twelfth century.

None of these citations, literary or otherwise, gives the detail which is found in the *Historia regum Brittaniae* (1137) of Geoffrey of Monmouth. This clerk was at Oxford after 1129 and it is possible that he was a master there. Presumably, in 1134-1135, he composed the *Libellus Merlini*, or *Prophecies of Merlin*, where, in language so obscure that it could be read in many ways, he foisted upon a prophet Merlin readings of the future which he, Geoffrey, professed to have found in old Breton or Welsh material. This Merlin was probably the sixth-century Welsh poet Myrddin, whose existence Faral is disposed to doubt. The name *Merlinus* is certainly older than the *Libellus Merlini* of Geoffrey; Faral, following D'Arbois de Jubainville, suggests that it was originally the name of a town. I tend to agree with Gaston Paris that *Merlinus* is the Latinization of *Myrddin,* with a change of *d* to *l* to avoid the suggestion of *merda,* an obscene term (*Rom* XII, 367-76). The *Libellus Merlini* was dedicated to Bishop Alexander of Lincoln, who had urged its publication. It was immensely successful; one of the prophecies was applied to Henry I of England, by both Suger and Ordericus Vitalis. It was then that Geoffrey either continued or began his *Historia regum Brittaniae,* in which he sketched the reigns of all the British kings from Brutus, three generations after the fall of Troy, to Cadwallader (d. 689 A.D.) We give the year 1137 as the date of completion for this history and as the date of its first dedication, but there may be an error of a

year or more. The book was rededicated three times, according to political exigencies, possibly in 1138, 1139, and 1141-1142. In 1148 Geoffrey
issued it again with no dedication. We can discern in this *Historia regum
Brittaniae* the influence of Bede, Nennius, and Livy, but there is other
material which has no apparent prototype. Geoffrey names as his
source a "librum . . . britanici sermonis, quem Walterus, Oxenefordensis
archidiaconus, ex Britannia advexit." Dr. V. Burch, lecturer in theology
at Liverpool Cathedral, believes he has found this book, written in
Latin, and is preparing it for publication. Archdeacon Walter is a historical personage, whatever we may decide about his famous *libellum*.
Faral believes that this *libellum* did not exist and that Geoffrey's chief
sources were his imagination and an anonymous *Historia Britonum*
(ninth century?). I can see no valid reason for doubting Geoffrey's statement about the *libellum*, although this may have been written in Latin
and not in Breton. Geoffrey could have known also oral Celtic tradition.

Geoffrey repeated in his *Historia* the legend of Ambrosius told by
Nennius (§§40 ff.) while identifying this Ambrosius with Merlin, and
he then proceeded to repeat his famous "Prophecies of Merlin" (Bk. VII,
chap. 110-119). King Vortigern, fleeing from the Saxon invaders, sought
to build himself a castle exceedingly strong, but the work of each day
was swallowed up by the ground on the next, and Vortigern asked his
wizards for advice. They advised him to sprinkle the foundations with
the blood of a boy who had no father. In the town, later called Carmar-
then, a boy was found whose father was an incubus demon who had
visited the boy's mother, daughter of the King of Demetia. This boy,
Merlin Ambrosius, then showed King Vortigern that his wizards had
erred: that the tower fell because of a pool and two dragons which lay
beneath. When the two dragons were found they engaged each other
in combat, and it was at this point in the story that Geoffrey of Monmouth added his prophecies of Merlin. This account of the finding of
Merlin Ambrosius, for the preservation of which we must first thank
Nennius, contains important folk motifs and has many analogues in
literature.

The *Historia* was the first work to introduce into general literature
the tales of Lear, Cymbeline, and Locris, and, most important, the legend
of Arthur. According to its account Arthur was the son of Utherpen-
dragon; he won many victories over the Saxons, Norwegians, Gauls, and
Romans. While away on the continent his kingdom was left in the hands
of his nephew Modred. This nephew turned traitor and seized not only
the kingdom but Queen Guanhumara (Guenevere) as well. Arthur
returned and there was a terrible battle in which Modred was slain and
Arthur mortally wounded. The dying king was carried to Avalon (which

was later identified with Glastonbury). Louis Cons and Clark Slover have argued (*MPhil* XXVIII, 385-399) that Avallon is a derivative of *avallo,* the Celtic form for "apple," and that the "Land of Apples" was another term for the Celtic underworld, the Land of the Blessed. Faral and the school of Bédier would see in most of this the facile mind of Geoffrey; other scholars continue to search in the legends of Wales, Cornwall, and Brittany for traces of the folk legends upon which Archdeacon Walter's book might rest.

According to the Gwentian *Brut,* an unreliable Welsh version of Geoffrey's material, Geoffrey was archdeacon of Llandaff (in 1146?). This may be true, although J. J. Parry writes me that he doubts it. In 1148 or thereafter, Geoffrey completed a third work called the *Vita Merlini,* in which the character of Merlin is so different from that of Merlinus Ambrosius that Giraldus Cambrensis (*Itinerarium Cambriae,* II, 8) assures us that there were two Merlins: Merlin Ambrosius, the prophet, and Merlin Sylvestris. This same Giraldus, who is often referred to as Giraut de Barri and who flourished in the last quarter of the twelfth century, is also our authority that Geoffrey was a great liar. This may have been a general opinion among Geoffrey's immediate successors, but J. J. Parry sees in this remark an effort made by Giraldus to be clever, as is often the case in modern book reviews! Geoffrey was named Bishop of Asaph in 1152 but he never dwelt in his See. He died in 1154.

Under influence from the *Historia* of Geoffrey, Gaimar incorporated into his vernacular *Estoire des Engleis* (1147-1151) the Arthur story, and certain other accounts. But the true fortune of Geoffrey lay in the adaptation made by Wace which we commonly call the *Brut.* Wace added to the Arthur story the possession of the Round Table. Whence did Wace get it? Was it a Celtic legend, as A. C. L. Brown believes (*HSN,* VII, 183-205)? The Irish sagas are filled with quarrelsome heroes; and Layamon, in his adaptation of Wace, informs us that the purpose of the table was to remove all distinction between those who were "seated high" and those who were "seated low." Consider the Irish quarrels over prestige as in the *Scél Mucce mic Datho* or in the *Fled Bricrenn* ('Feast of Bricriu'). Most tantalizing is the suggestion by Mrs. Laura Hibbard Loomis (*PMLA* XLI, 771-784 and *MLN* XLIV, 511-519) that the Round Table was taken from iconography, representations in stained-glass windows and MS illuminations, of the Last Supper, suggesting "the exalted loyalty and equality of the first apostolic twelve." An examination of some of these medieval representations of the Last Supper will show that the table pictured was usually round. Still another suggestion was made by George Y. Wardle in 1903 (*Y Cymmrodor,* XVI, 127 ff.) He reminds us that formal Roman meals were eaten on couches and that informal meals were consumed on a circular bolster, a *sigma,* on the floor or ground, with the food in the center. The Round Table might be reminiscent of the Roman meal customs in Britain. Giraldus Cambrensis indicates that something like this was still current in twelfth-century Wales. The Round Table would be a normal officer's mess, before the introduction of the long wooden table supported by trestles. This is possible, particularly if we view Arthur more as a normal Romanized Briton than as a folk character.

These histories all speak enthusiastically of Arthur but there is still a considerable gap before we reach Arthurian romance. The points to be considered in the bridging of this gap are: (1) a motive for the popularity of Arthur; (2) creation of the romance form; (3) the presence of certain Celtic or folk motifs to be centered about this legendary king; (4) the identity of the poet who took the first step and united all these necessary elements. If we are to believe Faral and the prevailing theory, the literary form of the romance came into being with the *matière de Rome,* or imitation of the Latin epics. This has been discussed in a previous chapter. The date would not be long before 1150. Why did literary interest in Arthur and his court suddenly grow in the course of the twelfth century? There is an old theory that the legends of Arthur were deliberately fostered by Henry I of England to furnish a "Charlemagne" for his subjects (*Spec* II, 317-21). The Charlemagne of the epics was essentially a continental monarch; he was King of the Franks (which no twelfth century man would have associated with Germany). The British peoples were called upon to furnish their Norman lord with a hero who would encourage loyalty to his throne. Geoffrey wrote his *Historia* as a political contribution for Henry I. Faral disagrees with this explanation of the rise in Arthurian popularity. He believes that the Normans had been hard upon their Celtic subjects and more lenient with the Saxons. Geoffrey wished to recall the British folk favorably to the Normans, in opposition to the Saxons. This was the cause, says Faral, of Geoffrey's wholly fictitious chronicle. A. C. L. Brown (*Spec* II, 449-455) assures us that the early Arthurian legends were only fairy legends at the beginning of the twelfth century. Geoffrey chanced to dignify them by giving the main legend of Arthur's existence a semi-historical background. From then on men of letters considered the Arthurian legend sufficiently orthodox for exploitation. R. S. Loomis (*Spec* III, 16-33) thinks that the Celtic *fabulae* about Arthur did not leave Welsh, Cornish, and Breton territory till the close of the eleventh century, and that they grew into popularity just as quickly as their own charm and the ability of the Celtic minstrels would allow. As A. C. L. Brown indicated before him, Loomis adds that Geoffrey's part was to raise the legendary Arthur to a place of respectability in learned circles.

How about the primitive Celtic *fabulae* which were to furnish the plots for so many of the later Arthurian romances? To Faral and his group these did not exist. Others believe that they spread from western Wales where the people were of the same extraction as the Irish. Myths and folklore motifs of these people soon passed into currency among the Welsh and the Cornish: from there to the Bretons and thence to the French. Loomis goes further than most of the other Arthurian scholars and endeavors to explain the myths themselves among the Gaelic folk (*Celtic Myth and Arthurian Romance,* Columbia University Press, 1927). Cuchulinn is the young sun god and Curoi is the old sun god. Morgan the Fairy is a water divinity, while the original of Gawain also has sun traits, etc. The arguments of Loomis on this mythical origin seem plausible; it is possible, however, to point out certain objections which time and further research may remove. Loomis tends to believe that these *fabulae* were of Irish origin, spreading from Ireland to Wales or Cornwall and then to Brittany. It is more probable that the tales were a common Celtic heritage preserved best in Ireland, which was farther from Anglo-Saxon influence. In these tales, as they appear in the romance, Arthur himself falls into the background and the protagonists are other newly created characters. This may well be traced to influence from the French epics where Charlemagne is a dominating genius and no longer an active hero.

Was Chrétien the first poet to combine all these elements and create the Arthurian romance proper? This does not seem likely, for Chrétien was a native of Champagne and an ultimate vassal of Louis VII of France. We should expect Arthurian romance to arise first in the territory of the English king. Chrétien visited Normandy (he refers to his stay at Beauvais in the *Cligés*) and perhaps even England.[3] Being a poet of great ability he may have been attracted by the possibilities in the crude Arthurian romances which he found there. After his own compositions came to enjoy a great vogue, the more primitive attempts would tend to disappear; they may never have been written down. Certainly, Chrétien does not refer to his earliest extant romance as an unusual undertaking and it is obvious that he was inspired by no other motive in his choice of themes than a desire to compose a worthwhile tale. He had no propaganda (W. Kücheler in *ZfrPh* XL, 83-99) unless it were to instruct in courtly conversation and grace (*ibid.,* LV, 673-681).

We have been referring to Chrétien de Troyes as to the author of our earliest extant, and best, Arthurian romances. We know nothing of his

[3] A visit to England might be inferred from what is said in the *Guillaume d'Angleterre.*

life and circumstances save what is apparent from his poems. He gives a list of his early works at the beginning of his *Cligés*. From his dialect we should judge that he was reared in eastern Champagne, but we know that he spent the better part of his career at the court of Henri I, Count of Champagne, at Troyes, and that he was probably a cleric. This last does not mean necessarily that he was an ordained priest. There were five possibilities of social status in the twelfth century: noble or administrator, cleric or professional man, burgher or tradesman, free peasant, and finally the peasant bound to an estate—the serf. Chrétien's reference to Latin sources indicate that he had had a clerical training. It is not likely that he was a member of the noble class. It is true that knights and men of high degree served as jongleurs, but such a practice was far more frequent among clerics of the lower orders. The preacher Jacques de Vitry, of whom more anon, gives a picture of three young student clerics making plans for the future. One wished to become a teacher at Paris, another a Cistercian monk, and the third, "Volo esse organizator, hystrio, et joculator." If Chrétien had been a man of high standing socially at the court of Henry I, Count of Champagne, we should expect some definite record of his existence. The name Chrétien or *Christianus* has been found twice in legal documents; first in a document dated 1172, where the fief is probably that of Aiguizy (Aisne), and secondly in a charter dated 1173 of the Abbey of La Chapelle-aux-Planches where the individual is named as a canon of Saint-Loup. On the first of these mentions see P. A. Becker (*ZfrPh* LV, 385-455); for the second consult L. A. Vigneras (*MPhil* XXXII, 341-2). Aside from the bare name Chrétien, in neither of these instances is there any evidence that the man was our poet. These possibilities should be kept in mind, however, while awaiting further discoveries.

There was never any valid reason for believing that Chrétien was a herald. Gaston Paris made this suggestion (*JS* (1902), p. 296 ) because of verse 5591 of the *Lancelot*:

> Or est venuz qui aunera

which Chrétien goes on to explain by

> Nostre mestre en fu li livre
> Qui a dire le nos aprist.

According to Gaston Paris the poet was citing his master in heraldry. But *nostre mestre* is a common way of referring to an adage or familiar saying and this is doubtless what Chrétien had in mind.

In the opening lines of the *Cligés* Chrétien lists his earlier works; three were adaptations from Ovid:

1.  A translation of Ovid's *Ars amatoria*.
2.  A version of Ovid's *Remedia Amoris* (?)
3.  The episode of Procne and Philomela (*Metamorphoses*, VI, 424-674).
4.  The story of Pelops, from another Latin source, as the tale receives but brief mention in *Metamorphoses*, IV, 403-411.
5.  A poem on King Marc and Yseult the Blond.
6.  The romance of *Erec and Enid*.

The last of these has been preserved and may be called our oldest surviving Arthurian romance. The other five are lost with possibly one exception, the *Procne and Philomena*. In a fourteenth-century *Ovide moralisé* there is an inserted poem on this subject which may be as early as the twelfth century and the compiler attributes it to a *Crestiens li Gois*. Is *Crestiens li Gois* the same as Chrétien de Troyes? There is considerable difference of opinion on this among scholars. P. A. Becker (*ZfrPh* LV, 423) denies it, affirming that *Crestiens li Gois* was a poet of the thirteenth century who wrote both this *Philomena* and the *Guillaume d'Angleterre*, also ascribed to Chrétien de Troyes; but that he was not Chrétien de Troyes. Raphael Levy (*PMLA* XLVI, 312-320) also denies the identity of the two Chrétiens; he interprets *Gois* by Judaeo-Romance *goç* 'small dog' or 'dwarf.' O. Schultz-Gora (*ZfrPh* XXXVIII, 232-43) thought that *li Gois* was for *ligeois*. E. Gamillscheg suggests *Gois* < *coxus* (*ZfrSL* XLVI, 183-4). R. Pachnio, in a Königsberg dissertation of 1909, derived *Gois* from *\*gubium*. Personally I agree with E. Hoepffner who rehandled the whole question recently (*Rom* LVII, 13-75) and came to the conclusion that the two poets were the same. C. de Boer, who published the text of the *Philomena*, explains *Crestiens li Gois* by the Anglo-Saxon word *got* 'goat'—'Chrétien the Goat', or *La Chievre* (*Rom* LV, 116-8). He says in support of this that Chrétien de Troyes wrote a Tristan poem (no. 5 above) and that we are told elsewhere there was a Tristan romance by a La Chievre. This etymology can only be accepted with extreme reserve.

The relative order of the remaining works of Chrétien de Troyes has been established by critical investigation:

7.  The *Cligés*.
8.  The *Lancelot* or *Knight of the Cart*.
9.  The *Yvain* or *Knight of the Lion*.
10. The adventure romance of *Guillaume d'Angleterre* (?)
11. The *Perceval*, or *Romance of the Grail*.

Concerning the exact dates of these romances we have little information that is certain. The *Lancelot* was written at the behest of Marie de Champagne; so its date is posterior to 1164, when she married the

Count of Champagne. There is no reason for assuming that it was not written shortly after that date. The argument that the theme was too immoral and not likely to have been encouraged by a young bride has no value, granted the period and the conventions of Provençal courtly love. The *Cligés* might be placed in or near 1162. I base this dating upon the activity of Count Henry of Champagne in the interest of Frederick Barbarossa, an activity which was strong at that date. It is natural to suppose that the German leanings of his suzerain would be reflected in the imagination of Chrétien, the court poet. This German interest can be found in *Cligés*.

Chrétien left Troyes and Henry's court for some reason unknown to us. He composed his *Perceval* for Philippe d'Alsace, Count of Flanders (b. 1143, count in 1168, crusader in 1190, and d. 1191 at Acre). This Philippe reached the height of his power in 1180 when he supported the young King Philip Augustus against the Queen-mother, Adèle, and her Champenois family. As Henry I of Champagne, Chrétien's former patron, died on March 17, 1181, it is not improbable that Chrétien turned to this powerful new protector just a few years previous to 1180. Indeed, if he quarreled with Henry it is not unlikely that he went to Philippe in the year Philippe was opposed to Henry (1180).

Why was Chrétien so unproductive between the *Yvain* (*ca.* 1169) and the *Perceval*, dedicated to Philippe d'Alsace, a good ten years? The *Guillaume d'Angleterre* may be placed there. Again, Chrétien may have been advanced in years during that decade (fifty was old in the twelfth century), and he would have worked more slowly. Is it not possible that he was composing the lengthy *Perceval* while still at Troyes and that he rededicated it later to Philippe, for he claimed to have received the subject from Philippe? He left this poem unfinished and one of the continuators tells us that he was stopped by death. As Chrétien does not mention Philippe's departure for the Crusade (1190) he must have died before that date, possibly around 1185.

Foster E. Guyer (*MPhil* XXVI, 257-277) published an article which, if it could be accepted, would revolutionize the theory on Chrétien's place in the history of the romance. He believes that Chrétien preceded the *Roman de Thèbes*, the *Roman d'Enéas*, and the *Roman de Troie*. According to Guyer, Chrétien's *Erec and Enid* belongs as early as 1148-50, or earlier, and the *Guillaume d'Angleterre* must be placed around 1150. We shall list certain other dates which Guyer gives:

The translation of Ovid's *Ars amatoria*............before 1152
The other early works mentioned in *Cligés*........1152-1162
*Cligés* .........................................before 1164
*Lancelot* ......................................1164-65

*Yvain* ........................................ 1166-67
*Thèbes* ....................................... 1167-70
*Enéas* ........................................ before 1174
*Troie* ........................................ after 1184

It is quite conceivable that the traditional datings of *Thèbes, Enéas,* and *Troie* are incorrect by five or ten years and that the origins of the romance, from imitations of the Latin epic, did not arise so smoothly and regularly as is generally accepted. But the dating of all romances from internal evidence is a dangerous practice. Mr. Guyer believes (*ibid.*, p. 259) that the evolution of the romance, its "remarkable development in style and technique can more logically be ascribed to the famous poet Chrétien de Troyes than to the unknown authors of *Thèbes* and *Enéas.*" Guyer says that the *Erec and Enid* shows none of the Ovidian conception of love and therefore must have been composed before the Ovid imitations. He criticises his opponents (pp. 258-259) for allowing themselves to be influenced by "logic" in studying the evolution of the romance; and yet he lays himself open to that same "fault" throughout his discussion. Personally, I can see no evidence that Chrétien evolved the type of the romance. Seldom do we find it true that the individual who had the genius to put into play the original idea has the genius to develop that idea to the high plane that was achieved by Chrétien. For the time being we may continue to say that the *Thèbes* and the *Enéas* preceded the *Cligés,* although we are not so sure about the *Troie.*

E. Hoepffner (*Rom* LV, 1-16) has remarked again upon the dependence of the *Cligés* and the *Lancelot* on the Tristan story. The form of the legend which Chrétien utilized, doubtless his own and the so-called primitive French version (1154?), differed in details from the extant fragments of Thomas and Béroul, and from the adaptations of their imitators. Hoepffner is convinced that the *Cligés* shows a marked influence from the *Enéas:* this last poem, says Hoepffner, was not known to Chrétien at the time he wrote the earlier *Erec and Enid.* The episode of the "feigning of death" in the *Cligés* was drawn by Chrétien from an Oriental legend, or from a folktale. The precise nature of the source accessible to Chrétien is unknown but the same tale, with variations, is found in the *Marques de Rome* (Tale no. XI), a collection of tales with frame-story dating from the late thirteenth century. Chrétien was certainly a well-read man of his time; it is a queer irony of fate that withholds from us all exact knowledge of his life and associations. Beside the classics and contemporary written literature, he was familiar with the primitive contributions of the Celtic minstrel. These Breton singers may have made a regular stopping place of Troyes and Champagne; it is more likely that Chrétien went out of his way to hear them at Beauvais and other Norman fiefs of his lord, Henry of Champagne.

*Erec and Enid* is the oldest of the extant romances; it shows no influence from either the Ovidian type of love or from the doctrine of courtly love, which last was soon to spread north from Provence. Erec, son of King Lac, is a knight at Arthur's court. In the pursuit of a dwarf who has struck one of the queen's maidens he first meets Enid. He brings her to Arthur's court where they are wedded; they then set out for his father's kingdom. There Erec spends all of his time in contemplation of his new wife and forgets his knightly duties. People begin to talk. He hears his bride one morning lamenting over his fallen prowess. Chagrined and determined to test her love, he orders her roughly to follow him and not speak to him on any account. They set off unaccompanied. At each danger which they meet along the road her love brings her to warn him, though he upbraids her vigorously for so doing. In the course of this journey he is badly wounded, but she is loving and faithful to the last. He forgives her; they return once more to Arthur's court. When he hears of his father's death he is crowned king at Nantes with great festivities (6,958 verses). It is plain that Arthur is in the background here.

Note how well this poem is constructed. The first motif is that of the wife conquest (ending v. 1844), then there is the main theme, the travels of the pair in which her love is tested, which draws considerably upon materials in Wace's *Brut;* finally there is an episode known as *Joie de la Cort,* which resembles somewhat the first motif.

Arthur plays a very similar rôle in *Cligés.* The Byzantine prince, Alexander, comes to Arthur's court seeking knighthood and distinction. While there he marries Soredamors, Gawain's sister, and they have a son, Cligés. They return to Constantinople on the news of the death of Alexander's father, to find the brother established on the throne. He is allowed to remain there provided he will not marry and provided the crown shall pass eventually to Cligés. Alexander and his wife die. Here begins the second part, which is really a Graeco-Byzantine romance of adventure. Cligés's uncle, the reigning emperor, is resolved to break his oath and marry. He goes to Germany, personally, to secure the hand of Fenice, the Emperor of Germany's daughter. Some 1500 lines are devoted to his stay there, with his suite. Cligés and Fenice fall in love. Thessala, nurse and confidant of Fenice, gives the Emperor a draught so that he will possess his wife only in imagination. Later Thessala enables Fenice to feign death that she may go to Cligés for good. Fenice and Cligés live for a while in a secret subterranean chamber. When this artifice is discovered the two flee to Arthur's court and ask for aid. Arthur prepares to help them when news arrives of the insanity of the Greek emperor. The guilty couple return and take the crown at Constantinople. As a parting remark Chrétien states that Cligés instituted the system of the Oriental harem: that future emperors might not be deceived as was Cligés's uncle. There are 6,784 verses. This romance shows progress over *Erec and Enid*. The Ovidian conception that love is a sickness, with symptoms of weakness and aberration, and that it must be treated as such, is here enthroned. Borrowings from the *Thèbes* and *Enéas* romances complete the transition to full-fledged literary romance with due attention to style and to the "marvellous."

The *Lancelot,* or *Chevalier de la Charrette,* is the first French romance to make use of the theory of courtly love. If Ovid conceived love as a malady, it was at least a sickness that attacked man and woman equally. The girl was the first to declare as often as the man; the twelfth-century variety of Ovidian love had marriage as its end.[4] There was little secrecy when passion began to manifest itself: it was written all over both parties, in paleness of color, sighings, and wasting away. Each one would analyze his or her feelings at length, namely, the fears, the uncertainty, and the desire engendered by unrequited love. This strictly equal basis is not present in the courtly variety of love. This second type centers about the cult of woman. The lady is always married, and honorable marriage cannot be the goal of her lover. His affection must take the form of a service of secret and eternal devotion. There are certain well-defined grades or stages through which the lover is supposed to pass before he can be solaced by his lady: (1) the receiving of hope, (2) a kiss, (3) the enjoyment of an embrace, (4) the possession of the whole person. Once the lover has been admitted through all these grades, the lady must perforce grant the *solatia amoris* when requested.

Andreas Capellanus, or the Chaplain, drew up the official treatise on this courtly love for Marie de Champagne, entitled *De arte honeste amandi* (1174-1186). The correct dating is established through two Hungarian references (Steiner in *Spec* IV, 92-95). Andreas addresses his remarks ostensibly to a certain Walter. After defining love, its effects, those subject to it, and how it may be acquired, he presents eight model dialogues between man and woman, comprising all possible social conditions: bourgeois man and bourgeois woman, bourgeois man to noblewoman, bourgeois to very noble woman (countess or duchess), nobleman to bourgeoise, noble to noble, more noble man (count, duke) to bourgeoise, more noble to noble, more noble to more noble. For me

---

[4] In the *Cligés* the German princess's marriage with the Emperor has not been consummated.

the most interesting is number three, which was doubtless the mod\
used by a troubadour in addressing his lord's wife. Andreas continue\
by saying that the clerics make the best lovers of all, although they cannot claim as lovers a higher rank than that which they had before they
were ordained. The clergy should not love, but of course they will.
He also advises that nuns should have naught to do with love, that
true love cannot be purchased, and that peasants and *filles de joie* are
incapable of the true sort. His advice to a man who falls in love with
a peasant girl is to take what he desires by force; this is of interest in
view of the *pastourelles*. Here closes the First Book (twelve chapters).
The Second Book (eight chapters) discusses the conserving of love, its
end, the breaking of faith, and certain famous decisions of courts of love
which were presided over by the Countess of Champagne, the Countess
of Narbonne, Queen Eleanor of England, and the Countess of Flanders.
The question which comes to all of us is whether these courts ever had
genuine existence or whether they were conceits of Andreas's imagination. It is quite probable that they existed, in a half playful spirit, and
doubtless under the active inspiration of Marie de Champagne or of her
mother, Queen Eleanor. This Second Book also closes with a charming
little tale of how a Breton knight acquired the rules of love from Arthur's castle. The Third, and last, Book (one chapter) is entitled *De
reprobatione amoris*. Of the thirty-one rules which the Breton knight
brings home from Arthur's castle we should note (no. 1) *Causa coniugii
ab amore non est excusatio recta;* (no. 10) *Amor semper consuevit ab
avaritiae domiciliis exsulare;* (no. 30) *Verus amans assidua sine inter-
missione coamantis imaginatione detinetur.* Twelve general rules for
love are also cited in the dialogue of the nobleman with noblewoman of
which we cite (no. 6) *Amoris tui secretarios noli plures habere;* (no. 7)
*Dominarum praeceptis in omnibus obediens semper studeas amoris
aggregari militiae.* The famous decision of the Countess of Champagne
on married love is to be found in the dialogue of the more noble man
with the noblewoman. Marie answers in a letter: *Dicimus enim et
stabilito tenore firmamus, amorem non posse suas inter duos ingales
extendere vires.* As her reasons she states that man and wife are bound
to deny nothing to each other, and true jealousy cannot exist between them. These are requisites of genuine love: denial and jealousy.

Nearly every scholar is convinced that the kernel of courtly love,
the subjection of the lover to the lady's will, came north from Provence,
where it can first be remarked in the verse of Bernart de Ventadorn.
The troubadours before Bernart were either satirical or content with
a coarser concept of womanhood. Our ultimate problem is to determine the source from which this arose in Provence, and, if possible,

to establish how it was developed still further in northern France. The following suggestions have been made:

1. Cult of the Virgin.

2. Fairy mistress plot in Celtic legend, or in general folklore, where the fairy is necessarily the superior of her lover.

3. The respect due to the wife of the poet's feudal lord, which would cause him to address her in conventional love poems of flattery.

4. The crusades. Abandonment of their wives caused the absent knights to place them upon a higher plane and to long for them passionately (G. Cohen, *loc. cit.*).

5. The Platonic conception of *paiderastia,* which was a veil for sodomy, acquired in Byzantium a parallel which was a veil for adultery. This new ideal love of woman passed through the Bulgar region, along the Danube route, into Bavarian and Austrian cloisters, and thence into France (P. S. Allen in *The Romanesque Lyric,* University of North Carolina Press, 1928).

6. The idea of the subjection of the lover to the lady's will may have been an artificial construction conceived at the court of the Viscount of Ventadorn, in the border region between France and Provence, either under Ebles II or Ebles III. This idea was carried to the court of Count Henry of Champagne where his wife, Marie de Champagne, presided over its elaboration into a formal doctrine—doubtless under Celtic influence (Nitze and T. P. Cross in *Lancelot and Guenevere,* Chicago, 1930).

7. An earthly mysticism, an insatiable groping for the infinite, culminating in two directions—in the *dolce stil nuovo* and in courtly love—according as the *donna angelica,* a symbol, or the emotion itself were stressed. (Mme Lot-Borodine in *Mél. Jeanroy,* pp. 223-242, and Karl Vossler in *Die philosophischen Grundlagen des "süssen neuen Stil,"* Heidelberg, 1904).

8. M. Huet believes that something of the Cupid and Psyche myth may have passed through Apuleius to the Middle Ages (*Moyen âge,* vols. XXII and XXIX).

9. M. Eugène Anitchkof thinks that the *Commentary on the Song of Songs,* of Bernard de Clairvaux, which, in turn, was influenced by the *Pseudo-Dionysius* and certain Montanist doctrine, was the source drawn upon by the "clericising" troubadours of Provence (*Joachim de Flore et les milieux courtois,* Rome, 1931). The growing Albigensian heresy probably contributed to the development, for the Albigensians sanctioned illegitimate liaisons. See also J. W. Thompson in *RRev* XXVII, 99-104.

10. Alois Nykl seeks to prove that Arabic poetic conventions, spreading from Arabic colonies in Spain and southern France, are responsible. (*The Dove's Neck Ring,* Paris: Geuthner, 1931.) These Arabic conventions, in turn, go back to Plato.

The special cult of the Virgin does not begin in the south of France till after the Albigensian Crusade (1209-1228); so this removes theory number one. The theory by Mr. Cohen is an interesting one, coming from a Frenchman and not from an American. The statement that American husbands spoil their wives is usually backed by the theory that it is tradition from the pioneer days when women were scarce. Such was not the case with the crusaders. There were too many camp-followers on those expeditions; indeed, some of the knights took their wives along. Besides, the courtly lover does not yearn for his own wife but for somebody else's. The sixth suggestion is most worthy of attention because it is the conclusion drawn from an extensive study of the subject; the other suggestions have been, for the most part, chance comments by their authors. Professor Nitze has defined with care the precise Provençal contribution; it is from an oral comment, which he made to me in 1929, that I draw his statement about the possible responsibility of Ebles de Ventadorn; this point is not developed in the book which Nitze has written with T. P. Cross. It may be that the Provençals had Celtic inspiration. It has recently been called to mind (J. Anglade in *Rlr* LXV, 195-303) that the Celtic minstrels *did* carry their wares into Provence. The Welsh minstrel Bleheri, mentioned by Giraldus Cambrensis as a *fabulator* in the *Descriptio Cambriae,* is supposed to have dwelt at Poitiers. M. F. Lot prefers to identify this Bleheri with no minstrel but with Bishop Bledhericus of Llandaff (983-1022) (see *Rom* LI, 397-408). If Celtic jongleurs travelled through the South, and of that there can be no doubt, the fairy mistress theme may well have had a share in the history of this courtly conception. As to whether any indirect Platonic sources were utilized we cannot be so precise. The monks in the vicinity of Poitiers and Limoges were learned and well read. It is doubtful that they would have obtained material through a German source. We cannot utterly disregard the explanation of courtly love as a feudal love. Provence, in its wider sense, abounded in troubadours in the twelfth century. These sweet singers were dependent upon favor if they wished a livelihood, and there was no surer road to a noble's purse than through his wife.

On the other hand more and more medievalists today are adhering to the theory that the Arabic lyricists were responsible for courtly love in southern France. Although the most active defender of this theory is Alois Nykl the suggestion is not a new one. It is probable that acceptance of this theory will grow more and more in the next decade of scholarly writing.

Of the poetic interests of Marie, Countess of Champagne, there is abundant proof. Chrétien de Troyes was living at her court, Andreas Capellanus wrote for her, and there are certain translations, such as the *Eructavit,* which were dedicated to her. It must be remembered that she was the daughter of a Provençal queen, Eleanor of Aquitaine, and

also that Celtic motifs flourished in a group which could develop a
Chrétien de Troyes. Amy Kelly has an excellent discussion of polite
society at the Court of Queen Eleanor in *Spec* XII, 3-19.

The *Lancelot,* or *Chevalier de la charrette,* was written for Marie de
Champagne, who had suggested the theme. Chrétien did not finish the
poem, but left it to one Godefroi de Laigny to add the ending, or epilogue. It is suggested that Chrétien was disgusted with this new style
of "amorous slavery." (Raoul Glaber, the northern French chronicler of
one hundred and fifty years previous, spoke in scorn of all things Provençal. He characterized the people as without faith and without shame,
whose contagious example would corrupt the French nation. Maybe
there was some of this resentment in Chrétien.) Love between southern and northern France was not enhanced at this time by the manner
in which their religious convictions were growing apart. The Church
lacked vigor in the South, and the Albigensian heresy was spreading, to
the dismay of northern Frenchmen. The theme of the *Lancelot,* aside
from the courtly love code, is woven from Celtic motifs: the abduction
by an other-world person, or previous lover; the lover asks a boon or
offers combat and as a result snatches away the queen or promises delay
in marriage; the queen's rescue by her husband or a follower, who crosses
a narrow passage, with or without an army; the rescuer redeems the
queen by trickery, a boon, or the help of a wise man. These are found in
the English *Sir Orfeo,* in *Durmart le Gallois,* in *Diu Krone,* in the German *Lanzelet,* in the Tristan theme, in the *Vita Gildae,* in the Welsh
*Pwyll* of the *Mabinogion,* in the Irish *Scél Mongain, Tochmarc Etaine,*
and in the *Aided Conroi Maic Dairi.* In the carving over the portal of
the Cathedral of Modena referred to earlier in this chapter there is portrayed still another version of this abduction, the abduction of the fairy
Winlogee, to be identified with Guenevere. On this abduction and rescue
theme consult Cross and Nitze, *op. cit.* What are its relations to the
Persephone myth of the Mediterranean regions?

Following is the plot of Chrétien's *Lancelot:* Meleaganz holds prisoner
many of Arthur's people. He comes to Arthur's court and flaunts this
fact in Arthur's face, wagering all his captives against Guenevere on single combat between himself and a selected champion. Sir Kay appoints
himself to defend the Queen; he fails and Meleaganz leads them both
away. Lancelot and Gawain set out to rescue them (cf. Mt. 465C, *FFC,*
74). They separate and Lancelot, after the loss of his horse, rides in a
peasant's cart in order to continue his journey. This is a disgrace which
he undergoes for his lady, because he loves Guenevere and will give up
all in her service. Both he and Gawain reach the river which separates
them from the land of Meleaganz. Gawain cannot cross the bridge that

is under water, but Lancelot passes over the sword bridge (Mt. 471 Ia, IIe, *FFC*, 74). King Bodemages, the father of Meleaganz, befriends Lancelot and allows him to fight Meleaganz for Guenevere's freedom. Lancelot wins and lies with Guenevere that night. Blood stains made by his wounds are noticed and Kay is accused. Guenevere returns, but Lancelot is secretly taken prisoner by Meleaganz. Arthur holds a tourney and Lancelot secures permission from his captor to go. The Queen recognizes him and to test his love she bids him be a coward the first and second days. He obeys, but distinguishes himself on the third. He returns and is walled up by Meleaganz in a tower cf. Mt. 310, *FFC*, 74; 310I, *FFC*, 78. (Here Chrétien breaks off and Geoffroi de Laigny continues the narrative.) Lancelot is eventually freed by Bodemages's daughter; he fights Meleaganz before Arthur's court and slays him.

In addition to expression of courtly love, Arthurian romance has advanced considerably in this *Lancelot*. The court plays a major rôle. Gorre, the kingdom of Bodemages and Meleaganz, is plainly a representation of the Celtic Other-world, the land of perpetual spring from which one cannot return (*Lancelot*, vs. 645 ff.) The underwater bridge may be what Professor K. G. T. Webster has suggested (*MLR XXVI*, 69-73), a memory of the *crånnog* causeway of Ireland.[5] The Irish used to fortify themselves on a natural or artificial island; for bridge they would construct a wooden causeway and submerge it in the stream which separated the island from the mainland; the initiated knew where to ford.

The character of Lancelot has passing mention in the *Erec and Enid,* which is the first occurrence of the name. Was it, as F. Lot has suggested with hesitation, a combination of the Welsh *Llanleawc* with the German-French name *Lancelin?* *Llanleawc* occurs in the Welsh Arthurian tale *Kilhwch and Olwen* (*Rom LI*, 423).

Ulrich von Zatzikoven composed a *Lanzelet* in Middle High German at the close of the twelfth century. It is biographical, being made up of episodes from Chrétien's *Lancelot*. Gaston Paris thought that Chrétien and Ulrich utilized the same source independently (*Rom X*, 465-96).

The *Yvain*, or *Chevalier au lion,* has two natural divisions. In the first, Yvain and King Arthur hear a tale of adventure from the knight Calogrenanz. While in quest of excitement Calogrenanz had stumbled upon a beautiful fountain in the forest of Broceliande. A huge giant of a peasant, who was herding bulls, had previously told him that if he desired adventure he should pour some of the fountain's water upon a stone and await results. Calogrenanz did so and there resulted a terrific storm. An unknown knight then came riding up, charged him

---

[5] My friend Robert V. Merrill, of the University of Chicago, had had this same solution in mind for some five years, independent of Webster.

without further ado, and worsted him completely. Calogrenanz was forced to give up his horse and return on foot, in disgrace. Arthur, highly entertained, vows he will be there and see for himself on St. John the Baptist's Eve. Yvain secretly vows to get there ahead of Arthur. He does so and slays the knight, guardian of the fountain; after some difficulties he marries the knight's widow, Laudine, with the help of her maid Lunete (Mt. 1510, *FFC*, 74). When Arthur arrives at the fountain Yvain is the new guardian, unknown to the King, and he unhorses Kay. He makes himself known and takes Arthur to his new castle to feast. Yvain secures permission from his new wife to follow the tourneys with Gawain, provided he will be absent only a year and a day. Yvain overstays his leave and his wife renounces him forever. *(Second Part)* He goes mad but is eventually cured by an ointment belonging to the fairy Morgue, sister of Arthur. He champions a lion in the beast's fight with a snake and out of gratitude the lion follows him as a companion. Hence the subtitle, *Chevalier au lion*. He fights for Lunete as her champion and saves her from the stake; he aids several other needy persons in distress. Eventually, he determines to win back his wife by force. He goes to the fountain with intent to make it storm till she forgives him. She finally does so. (6,818 verses.)

Professor A. C. L. Brown sees the source for the first part of this romance in a Celtic mistress theme such as the *Serglige Conchulaind* ('Sickbed of Cuchulinn'), an Old Irish saga (*HSN* VIII, 1-147). Here Cuchulinn goes to the Other-world, but is preceded there by his man, Loégaire, who makes report of it to him. Cuchulinn lives with Fann, the wife of Manánan mac Lir. Eventually he returns to the outer world and forgets Fann when her husband, Manánan, shakes his cloak between them. Similar fairy mistress material is in the *Echtra Loégaire* and the *Tochmarc Emere* (Brown in *MPhil* IX, 109-28). W. A. Nitze suggested that the ultimate origin of the Fountain episode was an Arician Diana myth localized in Gaul (*MPhil* VIII, 63-86). According to R. S. Loomis the character Calogrenanz is reminiscent of Sir Kay (*MLN* XLIII, 215-22). The motif of the Sudden Storm has been discussed by L. B. Morgan (*MPhil* VI, 331-41).

Wendelin Foerster opposed the Celtic origins theory very rigorously: he believed that the *Yvain* was mostly due to Chrétien's imagination. The fountain in the Forest of Broceliande was owed to Wace, according to Foerster. He believed that Yvain's marriage with the wife of the man whom he had murdered can be traced to the *Thèbes* romance; the thankful lion he traced to the story of Androcles; the invisibility ring given to Yvain by Lunete, and the healing salve, he derived from the *Roman de Troie*. Foerster's mature opinion on the sources of Chrétien is valuable, although extreme in its denial of Celtic sources.

It may be found in the Introduction to his *Wörterbuch zu Christian von Troyes* (Halle: Niemeyer, 1914). The dialect used by Chrétien was that of eastern Champagne, with an occasional Picard form. His versification was the usual one for the romance, the octosyllabic rhymed couplet. He introduced an innovation into this conventional meter: he was the first to break the unity of thought in the individual couplet. He would frequently end a sentence with the first line of the couplet and begin another with the second.

At this point we must mention the perplexing problem offered by three Welsh prose romances (of the twelfth century?), preserved in the fourteenth-century *Red Book of Hergest* and in the *White Book* (thirteenth century). These romances are *Geraint the son of Erbin*, the *Lady of the Fountain*, and the *Peredur;* they parallel Chrétien's *Erec, Yvain,* and *Perceval,* respectively. The discussion as to whether they represent a source for Chrétien, an adaptation of his romances, or whether they go back independently to the same traditions used by him, has been so lively that scholars refer to it generally as the *Mabinogion Controversy.* The first view was proposed by San Marte and H. de la Villemarqué, but this has long been discarded. Othmer, Philipot, Zenker, A. C. L. Brown, J. Loth, and Alfred Nutt have argued for the second view: that the Welsh and the Chrétien romances go back to some common source; G. Paris accepted this, although he later modified it (*Rom* XX, 145-66). W. Foerster, E. Brugger, P. A. Becker, Nitze, and J. D. Bruce have been inclined towards the belief that one or more of the Welsh romances was based upon Chrétien's French version. The controversy centers around the fact that the Welsh romances are occasionally better constructed and more logical than the French. How can this fact be interpreted? As new evidence is presented I find myself changing back and forth between the second and third suggestions. (See Mary R. Williams's *Essai sur la composition du roman gallois de Peredur,* Paris, 1909). Very recently Timothy Lewis has put into doubt our whole solution of the *Mabinogi* problem with his *Mabinogi Cymru* (Aberystwyth: Cwasg y Gwynant, 1931). This book, written in Welsh, argues that the Viking settlements in Wales are responsible for the background of the *Mabinogi* and that the Celtic mythology supposedly contained therein is an invention of Sir John Rhys. We are not ready to accept this yet, but it is possible that much of the discussion on the *Mabinogi* may some day be retracted. (Consult J. J. Parry's review in *JEGP* XXXII, 403-406).

There is a minor question to be considered: whether Chrétien was consciously anti-Tristan in his *Cligés* and in the *Lancelot.* W. Foerster was the first to see in the *Cligés* a polemic against the coarser view of love in the Tristan, and this has been accepted, with some reservation, by G. Paris, Van Hamel, and Golther. J. D. Bruce says of the *Lancelot* (*op.*

*cit.,* I, 205), "In framing this story there can be no doubt that the poet
or the countess, if it was really she that invented it, was consciously or-
dering it so that it might present a direct contrast to the loves of Tristan
and Iseult." In other words, if we combine this statement of Bruce with
the evolution of courtly love as expressed by Nitze and Cross, we might
say that courtly love came to full flower as an opposition to the crudity
of love in the *Tristan.* There is nothing positive to be said contrary to
this, but it seems to me to be an unnecessary exaltation of the influence of
the Tristan theme.

Chrétien's *Perceval,* or *Conte du Graal,* will be discussed in a later
chapter with the Grail cycle as a whole.

There remains another twelfth-century romance of Arthurian subject,
written by a younger contemporary of Chrétien. Renals de Biauju, or,
as we know him, Renaut de Beaujeu, professed to be an inexperienced
poet writing for his lady. His *Guinglain,* or *Li Biaus Descouneus,* referred to in modern French as *Le Bel Inconnu,* has been preserved in a
single MS, 472 of the Musée Condé, at Chantilly. The poem has 6,266
octosyllabic verses of which a dozen or more are illegible. It is the story
of a young knight of unproven ability who demands the first quest which
shall follow his arrival at Arthur's court, a common folk motif (Mt. 300,
*FFC,* 74, 78; Mt. 300 I, *FFC,* 81). A maiden comes demanding help for
her mistress, La Blonde Esmerée; the unknown knight is sent with her,
much to her disgust. But the young man, in a series of fights which becomes slightly monotonous to the reader, wins the respect of all concerned. When he finally frees La Blonde Esmerée by kissing her while
she is disguised as a dragon—*le fier baisier*—he finds that he does not want
her as much as *la Pucelle as blanches mains,* a fair enchantress who has
watched over him and from whom he had fled shamefully. Here the modern reader would like to have the story end; it is proper that he should
remain with the enchantress. But Renaut causes him to be lured back
to La Blonde Esmerée by the trickery of a tourney which he cannot resist. We usually date this romance around 1190. So far Renaut de Beaujeu has not been identified, unless the reader will accept my suggestion
that he was the Renaut de Decize who married the daughter of Count
Humbert de Beaujeu (*RRev* XVIII, 334 ff.) The Middle English romance
*Li Biaus Desconus* was based upon the same French original as Renaut's
poem. A. H. Krappe (*Rom* LVIII, 426-30) traces the episode of Guinglain's stay with the enchantress back to a Celtic source.

Arthur was frequently mentioned outside of the Arthurian romances.
Professor Critchlow collected a representative, though not exhaustive, list
of these allusions which was published in *MPhil* VI (1909), 477-86.

Geoffrey of Monmouth, *Historia regum Brittaniae, etc.*, ed. Acton Griscom (New York: Longmans, Green, 1929); this *Historia* is also published by Edmond Faral in his *La Légende arthurienne*, vol. III.—*The Vita Merlini*, ed. J. J. Parry (Urbana: *UIS*, 1925).—Chrétien de Troyes, *Cligés*, ed. W. Foerster—A. Hilka (4th ed.; Halle: *BRom*, 1921); also ed. Foerster (Halle: Niemeyer, 1884).—*Erec und Enide*, ed. W. Foerster (2nd ed.; Halle: *BRom*, 1911); also ed. W. Foerster (Halle: Niemeyer, 1890).—*Yvain (der Löwenritter)*, ed. W. Foerster-A. Hilka (2nd ed.; Halle: *BRom*, 1926); also ed. W. Foerster (Halle: Niemeyer, 1887).—*Der Karrenritter (Lancelot)*, ed. W. Foerster (Halle: Niemeyer, 1899).—*Andreae Capellani regii Francorum De Amore libre tres*, ed. E. Trojel (Copenhagen, 1892), also *De Amore libri tres*, ed. Amadeu Pagès (Castelló de la Plana, 1930).—Renaut de Beaujeu, *Le Bel Inconnu*, ed. G. Perrie Williams (Paris: Cfmâ, 1929).—*The Text of the Mabinogion* [the Welsh], ed. J. Rhys-Gwenogvryn Evans (Oxford, 1887); *Die Vier Zweige des Mabinogi*, ed. Ludwig Mühlhausen (Halle: Niemeyer, 1925). A good translation is that by Joseph Loth in his *Les Mabinogion traduits en entier* (2nd ed.; Paris, 1913, 2 vols.). There is a new English version by T. P. Ellis and J. Lloyd (New York: Oxford Press, 1929, 2 vols.). The English translation made by Lady Charlotte Guest, and first published in 1849, is available in the Everyman series. The Everyman series also publishes an English rendering of the *Historia* of Geoffrey, as well as translations of Chrétien's works and of the Arthurian portions of the Wace and Layamon *Bruts*.—The minor texts containing references to Arthur are reproduced in the original in the *Arthur of Britain* of E. K. Chambers, *q.v.supra*.—Chrétien de Troyes, *Philomena*, ed. C. de Boer (Paris: Geuthner, 1909).—Louis Cons and R. S. Loomis of Columbia University are preparing new editions of Chrétien's works, with the aid of students.

# CHAPTER XVII

## THE TRISTAN LEGEND

J. D. M. Bruce, *The Evolution of Arthurian Romance, etc.*

Gertrude Schoepperle, *Tristan and Isolt, A Study of the Sources of the Romance* (New York University Press, 1913, 2 vols.).

J. Kelemina, *Geschichte der Tristansage nach den Dichtungen des Mittelalters* (Vienna: Holzel, 1923).

R. Thurneysen in the *ZfrPh* XLIII, 386, 402; and J. van Dam in *Neoph* XV, 18-34.

The Tristan legend is second in importance only to the legend of Arthur, in the *matière de Bretagne*. It was the late Mrs. Loomis (Gertrude Schoepperle) who first pointed out the Celtic analogues in the Tristan story. The results of her investigations and those of various other scholars cause us to postulate the following:

1. The legend may have started among the Picts, where Drostan (the same as Tristan) is attested as a royal name since the eighth century. In Wales the name occurs as Drystan or Trystan in the eleventh century. From the Picts the story could have spread to Cornwall, receiving there much of its definitive form. Its next passage would be to Brittany, whence it was transmitted to the French-speaking world. The tale must have been exceedingly rude while confined to the Celts. The basic theme is the same as that of Deirdriu in the *Longes macc Uislenn,* and the saga of *Diarmaid and Greinne,* in both of which a young vassal or relative of the king steals a lady whom the king had destined for himself. Before the legend took on its surviving form elements from classical sources were added. Thurneysen saw a resemblance to the Irish *Scéla Cano meic Gartnain* also.

Still another suggestion, held by some, contrary to Miss Schoepperle, is that the Tristan legend is a reflection of the Viking kingdom at Dublin which levied tribute on the Irish coast. The proper names *Gormond* and *Iseult,* occurring in the O. French versions, are of Germanic origin.

The date at which this material found its way into French is not certain. Carl Appel thought he saw an allusion to it in a poem by Cercamon (*fl.* 1150-60), which would be the earliest reference (*ZfrPh* XLI, 219-27). There are undoubted allusions in two poems by Bernart de Ventadorn who was a slightly younger contemporary of Cercamon. See Bernart's lyrics which begin "Quant vey la lauzeta mover" and "Tant ai mo cor ple le ioya" (J. L. Deister in *MPhil* XIX, 287-96). Chrétien de Troyes, at the beginning of his *Cligés*, is our authority that he had written *Del roi Marc et d'Iseut la blonde*. It is particularly unfortunate that this poem is lost. Some scholars have thought that Chrétien treated only an episode of the story because he does not mention Tristan by name. This argument is not convincing and we have no reason to doubt that Chrétien was the author of a complete version of the tale. It is generally assumed, however, that his poem was not the *Ur-Tristan*, or first French version, which we should like so much to see.

A poet who called himself La Chievre, or Li Kievre, treated this same subject in a poem now lost. The first mention of this is in the second prologue to the *Roman de Renart*: "De Tristan que La Chievre fist" *BEcCh* ĈCXI, 38 ff.) Another mention which is often quoted is "Et li Kievres qui rimer volt, L'amor de Tristan et d'Isault" (consult *Foerster Festgabe*, Halle, 1902, p. 428). Who was this La Chievre? Gröber believed him to be the lyric poet Robert La Chievre of Rheims. Carl de Boer makes the rather bold suggestion that this La Chievre and Chrétien de Troyes could have been one and the same (*Rom* LV, 116-8). The author of the *Philomena*, usually attributed to Chrétien, is designated in that poem as *Crestiens li gois*. This word *gois*, says De Boer, might be an Anglicism, meaning "goat," which would agree with La Chievre. This is not impossible, but it is not likely.

The *Ur-Tristan*, or first version of the legend in the Old French language, is placed by most scholars around 1154. Kelemina thinks that there were two of these lost *Ur-Tristans*, both of them in verse. We assume that all the extant versions in O. French go back directly or indirectly to this early form. The surviving forms are:

1. The *Tristan* of an Anglo-Norman Thomas, composed between 1155 and 1178. He had for sources the *Ur-Tristan*, Wace's *Brut*, the *Disciplina Clericalis*, and perhaps Chrétien's *Cligés*. There is no reason for assuming that he knew the *Roman de Troie*. This poem is fragmentary: only 3,130 lines have survived, in five MSS. The fragments do not make continuity. Bédier has edited this text, supplying the missing episodes in modern French prose from versions in Norse, Middle High German, English, and Italian.

2. The *Tristan* of Béroul, a continental Norman, who wrote in a dialect close to that of the town of Amiens. His work was drawn possibly from a lost derivative of the *Ur-Tristan*. Only 4,485 lines have been preserved; the beginning and the end are lost. The tone is more gross than what we find in the version of Thomas. Perhaps Béroul was writing for a less cultivated audience. Some scholars would divide this *Tristan* into two parts, assuming two distinct poets. The first, they say, composed as

far as verse 3027 in the period 1165-70, and the second poet completed the
poem in 1190 or 1191. E. Muret favors this division; but Joseph Bédier is
much opposed to it. I agree with Bédier.

3. *La folie Tristan* (Oxford version), written by an Anglo-Norman
poet of the close of the twelfth century. This is a single episode, depend-
ing upon the work of Thomas and narrating how Tristan gained access to
Iseult, during his last exile, disguised as a madman. The source may
have been a folk tale (Mt. 885, *FFC, 74*).

4. *La folie Tristan* (Berne version) was the work of a poet from northeastern France, in the early thirteenth century. It tells essentially the same
story as the Oxford version, but it is closer to the *Tristan* of Béroul.
Bédier does not believe that this was directly dependent upon Béroul.

5. A *lai* by Marie de France entitled *Chievrefueil*. This, too, is an
episode referring to Tristan's first exile.

6. An episode in the *Donnei des amanz* (Vss. 453-662). This is commonly referred to as *Tristan rossignol*. The *Donnei* was a debate between
a lady and her lover, written in England towards the end of the twelfth
century.

7. The early prose *Tristan* (1215-30) based upon the *Ur-Tristan,* or a
lost derivative, and preserved in MSS fr. 104 and 1434 of the Bibliothèque
Nationale.

8. The cyclic prose *Tristan* as in MS fr. 757 of that same Library.

9. The episode of *Tristan menestrel* in Gerbert's continuation of Chrétien de Troyes' *Perceval* (Vss. 3309-4832).

The plot of the common Tristan theme does not vary greatly at the
hands of Thomas, Béroul, and those who adapted it into other languages
Joseph Bédier has attempted a reconstruction, in modern French prose,
of the plot of their lost original, the *Ur-Tristan.* (Do not confuse this with
his reconstruction of Thomas' *Tristan,* for which see the bibliography at
the close of this chapter). This he does in his *Le roman de Tristan et
d'Iseult* (Paris: Piazza, 1923). We will summarize the principal episodes
of the theme as he gives them, with an occasional variation.

Tristan, son of King Rivalen of Ermonie (Welsh Y *Manau* ?), or of
Loenois in South Wales, and nephew of King Mark of Cornwall through
his mother, is a great favorite at the Cornish court where he was reared.
He slays Morholt of Ireland who comes to exact tribute from the Cornishmen. In the combat, which takes place upon an island not named, Tristan
is wounded by Morholt's poisoned blade. Disguised as a minstrel Tristan
sets forth at random, in a small boat, hoping to find a cure; eventually he

arrives at Ireland. (Some authorities, including Bédier, believe that Tristan went directly to Ireland on the suggestion of the dying Morholt.) In Ireland, Tristan is healed by the Queen, Morholt's sister, and by Iseult her daughter, who do not recognize in him the slayer of Morholt.

King Mark had promised not to wed, and to make Tristan his heir; but his promise is forgotten when a lock of golden hair is brought by a bird to the coast of Cornwall. Tristan who has returned hale and hearty recognizes this hair as belonging to Iseult and agrees to set out again for Ireland, to ask for the princess. This time he goes as a knight, slays a dragon, and, after some trouble, wins the lady's hand—for King Mark (Mt. 300 IIIa, IVa, c, Va, b, *FFC,* 74; Mt. 300, *FFC,* 78, 81). The Queen knows that King Mark is old; so, in order to insure love between her daughter and the King of Cornwall, she brews a love potion which, when drunk by the wedded pair, will cause them to love each other for life. (Some authorities believe that the potion was to last only a limited length of time, three years.)

On the slow voyage across the Irish Sea, Tristan and Iseult become thirsty; they are given the love potion by mistake, and thus their loves begin. They are unfaithful to Mark, but Brangwen, Iseult's maid, substitutes for her on the wedding night and saves her mistress's reputation for the time being. This unfaithfulness continues in secret. There is the episode of the Irish minstrel who wins Iseult by a wager carelessly accepted, on his minstrelsy; Tristan wins her back—for Mark. Another nephew of Mark's, Audret, is an evil dwarf (Cf. A. H. Krappe in *RFor* XLV, 95-9). He becomes aware of the lovers' secret and warns the husband. Once King Mark is hidden in a tree above a fountain where he was told the two would meet in tryst. Iseult sees his reflection in the fountain and averts the danger by well chosen words. Another time Tristan is caught by blood stains between his bed and the King's; he is forced to flee into exile. This is his first exile and it is during this period, while supposedly in Ermonie, or Loenois, that he returns in disguise to see the Queen, as a fool or as a minstrel.

Iseult secures his return to the Cornish court when by means of a trick she exonerates herself of all suspicion of guilt with Tristan. (The trick is the *Bocca della Verità* motif.)[1] The guilty pair begin their love again; this time, when caught, they take to the forest and live there for two years. Finally, the King comes upon them by chance and finds them asleep, with a sword accidentally laid between them. The King, who is still gullible, is rather inclined to believe that they were not guilty after all. Tristan finds Mark's glove and other tokens of his presence

---

[1] See A. H. Krappe in *Nuovi studi medievali,* II, 119-24.

beside them as they slept; by a stupendous act of resignation or, as some would have it, because the potion had run its course, Tristan determines to send Iseult back to her husband. She is taken back and Tristan goes into exile in Brittany.

There he marries another Iseult, Iseult of the white hands. While aiding Kaherdin, her brother, Tristan is mortally wounded in battle. He sends to Cornwall, pleading that Iseult *la blonde* be allowed to come to him, as her presence only can give him cure. She agrees to go. By a previous arrangement the ship which is sent to fetch her shall fly a black sail if Iseult is not in it on the return voyage—a white sail if she is coming. (This is a motif occurring in the Theseus story.) In her jealousy Iseult of the white hands calls to Tristan that the ship bears a black sail. The shock is too much for him. When Iseult arrives she finds him dying. He dies and she expires soon after. By the generosity of Mark the lovers are buried in the same tomb.

The popularity of this story can scarcely be paralleled. L. Sudre has collected some of the allusions to it in literature (*Rom* XV, 534-57). In iconography, carved ivories, mirrors, tiles, etc., it was a favorite theme from the twelfth to the fifteenth centuries. The Chertsey tiles, the Strasbourg casket, the Basilewsky casket, the Hamburg mirror are outstanding examples. See R. S. Loomis's studies on this material, in *RRev* VIII, 196-209, and in *MLR* XIV, 38-43. E. Hoepffner has recently discussed the Strasbourg casket (*Rom* LIX, 548-56).

## EDITIONS

Thomas, *Le roman de Tristan,* ed. J. Bédier (Paris: *SATF,* 1902-5, 2 vols. J. Bédier, *Specimen d'un essai de reconstruction conjecturale du Tristan de Thomas* (Halle: Niemeyer, 1900).—Béroul, *Li roman de Tristan,* ed. E. Muret (3rd ed.; Paris: *Cfmâ,* 1922); earlier by the same editor, in the *SATF,* 1903.— Joseph Bédier, *Le roman de Tristan et d'Iseult* (Paris: Piazza, 1923).—*Les deux poèmes de la Folie Tristan,* ed. Joseph Bédier (Paris: *SATF,* 1907).— *Donnei des amanz,* ed. Gaston Paris in *Rom* XXV, 497-541.—Read the analysis of the prose *Tristans* in E. Löseth's *Le roman en prose de Tristan, le roman de Palamède et la compilation de Rusticien de Pise* (Paris: *BEcHE,* 1891).— The poems by Bernart de Ventadorn which mention the *Tristan* are conveniently found in Carl Appel's *Provenzalische Chrestomathie* (6th ed.; Leipzig: Reisland, 1930).

# CHAPTER XVIII

## THE *CONTES* AND THE *LAIS*

J. Bédier, "Les lais de Marie de France," in *Rev. Deux Mondes*, CVII, 838 ff.
The literary *conte* parallels the romance, in shorter form. A more complete definition will be found at the beginning of Chapter XIII. The first examples of the type were, according to Faral, adaptations from episodes of Ovid's *Metamorphoses*. The best known of these is the *Piramus et Tisbé*, the work of a Norman poet in the third quarter of the twelfth century. It is adapted from *Metamorphoses* IV, 55-166. Another is the *Narcissus* from the same source, III, 341-510. The *Orpheus* has been lost, but it is mentioned in the *Lai de l'espine*. A *Hero and Leander* is referred to in the *Roman de Troie* (vss. 22, 121-22, 127) and a *Conte de Tantale* is named in Chrétien's *Guillaume d'Angleterre* (vs. 903). The *Piramus et Tisbé* and the *Narcissus* are the only *contes* of this *matière de Rome* which have survived.[1] These shorter imitations from the ancients are contemporary with the spirit of innovation that brought about the formation of the romance. They belong to the same age of enthusiasm for vulgar adaptations of Latin originals. An excellent catalogue of such translations is to be found in the Provençal *Flamenca* (vs. 650 ff.).

The *Narcissus* (1,010 vss.) does not follow too closely its Ovidian source. When Narcissus is born, a Theban sage warns that the boy must never behold his own reflection. Narcissus grows to manhood and Danés, daughter of the king, falls in love with him. He repulses her. This is occasion for a most elaborate description of the pangs of love, told from the so-called Ovidian standpoint. Danés veritably wastes away. On one occasion, after repulsing her vigorously, Narcissus goes into a wood and gazes upon his own face in a fountain; he is followed by Danés who arrives just in time to catch his expiring form in her arms. The prophecy of the Theban sage has been fulfilled. Danés also dies, over the body of her love.

The mentions of Narcissus in the *Roman de Troie* and in the *Cligés* are probably references to the tale as told by Ovid. There is a reference to the Old French *lai*, however, in the *Verbum abbreviatum* of Pierre le Chantre (last quarter of the twelfth century) which enables us to date the *Narcissus* in that period. The *Piramus et Tisbé* is older (ca. 1150). This has 921 lines and the meter is decidedly unusual. Although the narrative proper is in octosyllabic rhymed couplets there are five monologues —Ovidian love laments—in strophes of three or four lines each, where a

[1] Unless we add the *Philomena* of Chrétien.

line of two syllables is followed by two or three octosyllabic lines of the same rhyme.

The *lai* was originally a *conte* with a Celtic motif, though the term soon came to be used more generally. The word *lai* is presumably derived from some equivalent of the Irish *laed*, 'song'; it was also used to denote a lyric verse type. It is assumed that Breton and other Celtic bards carried about many short tales, singing them in the language of their hearers, usually French, with occasional Celtic words interspersed. Such tales were crude, but fascinating. Some scholars have suggested that these minstrels sang in their own language with prose summaries in French. This is hardly likely. Our problem is to determine when these Celtic tales were first polished and retold by cultivated French speakers in the newly developed form of the *conte*. Was Marie de France the first to start this new vogue? In the prologue of her *Lais* she says as much. She had thought of translating from the Latin, but since so many were engaged in that task she resolved instead to retell some *lais* which she had heard—presumably from Breton bards, in her youth.

Although she may have heard them from the Bretons, all of Marie's *lais* do not have Celtic themes. The *Milon* is a literary tale that seemingly spread from the Orient. It is the familiar father and son combat which occurs also in the *Shahnama* of Firdusi, in the Old High German *Hildebrandslied*, and in the Ulster cycle of Irish sagas. In spite of such wide diffusion this theme is not present as a folktale in those countries where folkthemes have been classified according to the Finnish method. The *Deus amanz* is a local tradition in Normandy; the *Le Fresne* is generally cited as a folktheme (Mt. 887, *FFC*, 74) related to the Clerk's tale in Chaucer, and to the ballad of Poor Annie (*English and Scottish Popular Ballads*, Cambridge Press, p. 117 ff.) *Chaitivel* and *Equitan* have no traceable predecessors. On the other hand, seven or eight of Marie's *lais* are accepted as Celtic: *Guigemar, Lanval, Chievrefueil* (a Tristan tale), *Laostic, Bisclavret, Yonec, Eliduc,* and the *Tydorel.* This last has not been universally accepted as the work of Marie. Friedrich Hiller (*Tydorel, ein Lai der Marie de France*, Rostock, 1927) argues quite plausibly for this attribution. M. B. Ogle says that it has no Celtic themes (*TAPA* LIX, 179-204), but A. H. Krappe refutes this successfully (*MLR* XXIV, 200-04).

In *Guigemar* (886 vss.) a knight wounds a hind who is *fée;* the arrow bounds back and strikes him in the thigh. He cannot be cured till he shall undergo the sufferings of love. He is borne off, by chance, in a ship which lands him at a seaside castle where a lovely lady is confined by her elderly husband. The two soon love and are eventually discovered. Meanwhile they had pledged mutual constancy: she that she would marry no man who could not undo a certain belt, and he that he would marry no woman who could not untie a knot in his shirt. The knight is forced to enter again the ship and is conveyed home, in the same mysterious way. The lady escapes at a later date and is carried away in the same ship, landing in the domain of one Meriaduc. Guigemar helps Meriaduc in a private war and meets his ladylove again. The knot and belt are unfastened but Meriaduc refuses to part with the lady. Guigemar shifts his alliance and wars against his erstwhile friend. Meriaduc is slain and the lovers are reunited.

*Lanval* (664 vss.) is the story of a knight who has a fairy mistress. Arthur's queen also loves him but he rebuffs her with the assertion that he already has a lady whose handmaids are fairer than she, the queen. The Phaedra or Hippolytus motif now enters the story and the queen accuses Lanval before the king. Things are turning out ill for Lanval when the fairy mistress arrives and carries him off to Avalon. The *Chievrefueil* (118 vss.) is merely an account of how Tristan once visited Iseult during his first exile, writing a message to her, as in ogham, on a honeysuckle stick. *Laostic* (160 vss.) narrates how a jealous husband slew a nightingale (*eostik* in Breton) which furnished innocent entertainment to his wife and to her lover.

*Bisclavret* (318 vss.) is a werewolf story. The *Deus amanz* (254 vss.) tells how a lover undertook to carry a maiden to the summit of a mountain in contest for her hand. Although he had a specially prepared strength-giving potion, in his ecstasy he refused to drink it and died thereby of fatigue. *Chaitivel* (240 vss.) narrates how a lady loved four knights collectively but could not bring herself to marry the one of them who survived a combat. *Equitan* (320 vss.) is the tale of a lover killed in the trap prepared for the husband. *Eliduc* (1,184 vss.) is the most ambitious and at the same time the best constructed of these *lais*. It presents the problem of a married knight who gradually finds himself in love with another woman. The entanglement is cleared by the first wife who generously withdraws to a nunnery. There are place names in this *lai* which cause me to believe that Marie knew something of the locale in Devonshire.

The plot of *Le Fresne* (536 vss.) must be familiar to many of our readers: a mother abandons one of her twin daughters to avoid an accusation of adultery which she has foolishly brought upon herself. As in *Elioxe*, the lady has suggested, concerning a neighbor, that twin children meant two fathers. This is certainly a folk motif (Mt. 884, *FFC*, 72). The abandoned child is left in the fork of an ash tree in a nunnery garden. The girl is reared by the abbess, and christened Le Fresne but she ill repays the kindness when she runs away to become the mistress of a knight. The knight is persuaded by his men to marry the girl's sister. Fortunately the mother identifies her lost child at the crucial moment and it is Le Fresne who finally weds her lover. *Yonec* (562 vss.) presents the old motif (Mt. 432, *FFC*, 74) of a supernatural lover appearing before an incarcerated lady in the disguise of a bird in order to obtain ingress. The husband discovers the ruse and successfully sets a trap. The lady is left with child, and her son, once grown, avenges his slain father. *Milon* (534 vss.), as mentioned above, combines the motif of father and son combat with that of two lovers communicating with the aid of a swan (which is found, among other places, in the Nala story of the Sanskrit *Mahabharata*). The *Tydorel* has some resemblance to the legend of Merlin Ambrosius—of a young man who does not know his father and who is taunted because of a supernatural abnormality.

Mystery shrouds the identity of Marie. All that we can state with some surety is that she lived in England; that she composed her *Lais* between 1167 and 1184, the *Espurgatoire Saint Patriz* between 1180 and 1190; that she adapted a collection of fables from the English; that she dedicated her *Lais* to a king (probably Henry II of England) and her *Fables* to a Count William; and that she was of noble birth. Lucien Foulet doubts this last fact (*Rom* XLVII, 156-57), but nearly every one else is disposed to accept it. Denis Piramus, in his *Vie de Saint Edmunt* (vss. 35-65), calls her *dame Marie*, and, in addition, the spirit of her work and the source material suggest a cultivated mind such as one would expect to find only in the noble class. G. Paris and Julian Harris believe that the relative order of *Lais*, *Fables*, and *Espurgatoire*, in date of composition, was F, L, E; Mall, Gustave Cohen, and T. A. Jenkins have placed them E, F, L; Warnke, Suchier, and Voretzsch arrange them L, F, E, and I agree with this. Ezio Levi is alone in the arrangement L, E, F.

Claude Fauchet was the first to call this Marie by the full appellation *Marie de France,* on the strength of her statement in the *Fables* (Epilogus, vs. 4),

Marie ai num, si sui de France.

It is useless, therefore, to argue that she was of royal birth because of the designation *de France*. Emil Winkler, preceded by De La Rue, Robert, Méon, and Von Reiffenberg, was deceived by this, and sought to identify her with Marie de Champagne, daughter of Louis VII of France and of Eleanor of Aquitaine (*Sitzungsberichte der Wiener Akademie,* vol. 188, Abh. 3, Vienna, 1918). As Marie de Champagne never lived in England, this suggestion is very doubtful. Constans attempted to prove that a certain Marie de Compiègne, mentioned in an amplified version of the *Evangile aux femmes,* was the same as our Marie, but he himself renounced this after a penetrating criticism by Mall (*ZfrPh* VIII, 24). A recent theory is by Ezio Levi who seeks to demonstrate that Marie was a nun at Reading and that the William to whom she dedicated her *Fables,* and whom she flattered by naming him *le plus vaillant de cest reialme,* was none other than Guillaume le Maréchal (*Archiv Rom* V, 448-93; *Nuovi studi medievali* I, 41-72). The king to whom the *Lais* are dedicated was, he says, Henry the Young King. Of course, the proofs for this theory of Levi's are purely subjective—they can be neither proved nor disproved. J. C. Fox is the author of still another theory which has been accepted quite widely (*Engl. Hist. Rev.* XXV, 303-06 and XXVI, 317-26). He believes that Marie was abbess of the Abbey of Shaftesbury, which position she held between 1181 and 1216. This Marie of Shaftesbury was an illegitimate daughter of Geoffrey Plantagenet (d. 1151) and was therefore a half sister of Henry II of England. The "valiant William" would be Guillaume Longespee who was Count of Salisbury, beyond question, in 1198. Mr. Fox's proofs are as follows: King Alfred restored this abbey of Shaftesbury in 888 and it would have been a logical act for Marie to translate her *Fables* from the fable collection of a founder of the abbey (Marie refers to Alfred as her source); that a fragment of a French *Espurgatoire Saint Patriz,* although not Marie's version, once belonged to this abbey; that Guillaume Longespee, if he be the William in question, was a patron of the abbey. Here again, it is difficult to either prove or disprove, for all the evidence is pure conjecture.

I myself have made still another conjecture concerning the identity of Marie de France (*SPhil* XXIX, 1-10). Starting with the premises that Marie was of noble birth, that she lived and wrote in England between 1167 and 1190, and that she was born and reared in France, which are facts admitted by the majority of scholars, I have hazarded an identification. *France* in the second half of the twelfth century meant usually the Ile de France—the district around Paris confined by the rivers Seine, Marne, Oise, Nonette, and Thérouanne—the French Vexin, and French Gâtinais.[1] If this be true, we have Marie's word for it that she came from this region, and, if we may postulate that she was of noble birth and that she later moved to England, we should expect to find some reference to her in the genealogical records of the Ile de France, a district which did not comprise many noble families. There is a Marie who fits the above requirements quite exactly, namely Marie the daughter of Count Waleran de Meulan, who married a Hue Talbot and presumably went to live in Herefordshire and Devon. Since we have no reference

---

[1] Marie distinguishes *France* from *Normandie* in *Chaitivel,* vs. 77.

at all to this lady as a *poetissa* we are again confronted with a lack of proof other than the process of logical elimination, but it is my hope to be able to find some additional evidence in the future. It should be remembered that Herefordshire was the scene of a renaissance of letters at the close of the twelfth century and that it was at that time a district in Wales.

Leo Spitzer (*ZfrPh* L, 29-67) has suggested that Marie's *Lais* are full of symbolic meaning and are not simple tales. Much the same stand is assumed by Friedrich Schürr (*ZfrPh* L, 556-82). S. Foster Damon (*PMLA* XLIV, 968-96) demonstrates that she understood fully the psychology of love. A detailed investigation of the conditions under which she wrote, as well as an effort to determine the chronology of Marie's craftmanship from an examination of the rhymes was undertaken by Erich Nagel (*RFor* XLIV, 1-102). E. Hoepffner (*Rom* LIX, 351-70; LX, 36-66) has also made an effort to date some of the individual *lais*. He believes that the *Lanval* was composed around 1160, using as important sources Wace's *Brut,* the *Roman de Thèbes,* and a version of the *Tristan.* The *Yonec* would be contemporaneous with this. *Guigemar* and *Eliduc,* however, show definite influence from the *Enéas:* they must have been written some years later. These arguments are, of course, not conclusive if we admit, as I am disposed to do, an early dating for the *Enéas.* Hoepffner has demonstrated (*Rom* LVI, 1-32) that the geographic references in Marie were owed to Wace's *Brut* and to an early *Tristan.*

( In a preceding paragraph we mentioned the problem of Marie's originality. Was she the first to contrive the narrative *lai*—a *conte* based upon Celtic material and not upon the Classics? An answer to this must be a guess. It is entirely possible that the narrative *lai* was introduced into French literature by two or more poets, independently, when the time was ripe for it. Some scholars, notably M. B. Ogle and Lucien Foulet (*ZfrPh* XXIX, 19-56, 293-322), have rigorously opposed serious Celtic influence in this *genre.* This is in keeping with the general attitude expressed by the school of Bédier and Faral, in which most of Old French literature is viewed as owed to clerical inspiration with a minimum of tradition and of folkthemes. The Celts themselves were great borrowers. They too may have adapted and recolored classical material into a form which we consider Celtic tradition. In the fifth and sixth centuries their scholars knew not only Latin but also Greek, and from scholars it is not difficult for legends to pass to the popular poet. It is not impossible, therefore, to reconcile some of the opinions of the Classicists with the "Celticists"; but, to deny the presence of Celtic lore—as we know it—in certain of the *Lais* of Marie de France is for me incomprehensible.

Gaston Paris in his *Manuel* (p. 98), as well as Foulet and Bruce, have assigned to Marie the *lai* entitled *Guingamor* (687 vss.). I doubt this attribution but the *lai* shows undoubted influence from Marie's *Guigemar* and resembles somewhat the *Lanval*. A rejected queen provokes Guingamor to slay a boar, he crosses into fairy land where he lives with a fairy for three hundred years, which seem to him only three days. The fairy permits him to return on a visit, warning him not to eat. He partakes of some wild apples, is shrivelled into extreme age, is recalled into fairy land, and returns no more. The *Lai del désiré* (764 vss.) also shows resemblance to the Lanval theme, but it is treated from a more Christian aspect. Still another variant of the Lanval story is the *Graelent* (732 vss.) which may be dated before 1200 because of allusions to it by Gottfried von Strassburg and in the *Aspremont*. On these *lais* which are similar to the *Lanval* consult W. H. Schofield in *PMLA* XV, 121-80.

In the *Doön* (288 vss.), which may be dated at the very close of the twelfth century, or in the early part of the thirteenth, there is a contest for a lady's hand in which the lovers must ride from Southampton to Daneborc *(Castellum puellarum)* in a single day. All but one of the riders sleep in the beds provided for them and are slain by the girl; Doön alone does not enter the trap. There is another test which he must undergo, but eventually he wins the lady. The *lai* closes with the father and son combat theme. In the *Lai de l'espine* (514 vss. but incomplete) a prince and a princess love each other. His father and her mother are united in second marriage. When the boy and girl are seen embracing too fondly, in all innocence, they are separated and the girl is confined. Years later the young prince seeks to prove his knighthood by watching at the *Gué de l'espine* where difficult adventures are known to happen eight days before the festival of Saint John. The maiden learns of this and sleeps at the ford, where her lover finds her. He succeeds in worsting, before her eyes, a series of knights and he wins a noble horse. On their return to court the lovers are united in marriage.

The *Lai du cor* by Robert Biket, an Englishman, and the *Lai du mantel mautaillié* are really *fabliaux*. They are versions of the chastity-testing theme which is found also in the *Vengeance Raguidel*, in the *Renart le contrefait*, in the earliest continuation of Chrétien's *Perceval* and in the prose *Tristan* (consult T. P. Cross in *MPhil* X, 289-99, E. K. Heller in *Spec* IX, 38-50).

The *Lai d'Ignaurés* (671 vss.), which is mentioned by the Provençal Arnaut Guillem de Marsan, should be dated in the closing years of the twelfth century. The author, an unidentified Renaut, may have had satire in mind. Ignaurés, a Breton knight, visits regularly the Castle of Wriol where twelve knights live with their beautiful wives. He becomes the secret lover of each of the twelve women. They play the game of "confess" one day and the truth comes out that Ignaurés is the preferred lover of each of them. They give him a collective rendezvous and try to slay him, but his eloquence touches their hearts. They decide that he must choose only one among them, which he does. When the husbands learn this, through a traitor, they are furious, particularly the one whose wife was preferred. They kill Ignaurés secretly and serve up a dish of his heart and genitals to the wives. When the women learn the nature of this food they refuse to eat any inferior dish and perish from hunger. The resemblance of this tale to the Eaten Heart motif is worthy of attention. The *Lai de Guiron* (8 vss.) which Iseult sings in the Thomas *Tristan* (ed. Bédier, I, 295) is a version of the Eaten Heart theme.

Before or after 1200 the use of the word *lai* had broadened to include a tale of any type.

## EDITIONS

*Narcisuslai*, ed. A. Hilka in *ZfrPh* XLIX, 633-75.—*Piramus et Tisbé*, ed. C. de Boer (Paris: *Cfmâ*, 1921).—Marie de France, *Die Lais*, ed. K. Warnke (3rd ed.; Halle: *BN*, 1925); by the same editor *Vier Lais* (Halle: *SrT*, 1925); ed. E. Hoepffner (*Brom*, 1921, 2 small volumes). R. W. Linker has an edition in preparation.—*The Lays of Désiré, Graelent*, and *Melion*, ed. E. M. Grimes (New York: *IFS*, 1928)—*Le lai du cor*, ed. H. Dörner (Strassburg diss., 1907).—*Lais inédits des XIIe et XIIIe siècles*, ed. F. Michel (Paris and London, 1826).—*Lai de l'espine*, ed. R. Zenker in *ZfrPh* XVII, 283-55. —*Le lai de Guingamor; le lai de Tydorel*, ed. E. Lommatzsch (Berlin: *RT*, 1922).—G. Paris published the *Guingamor, Doön*, and *Tydorel* in *Rom* VIII, 29 ff.—The *Lai du mantel mautaillié*, ed. F. A. Wulff, is in *Rom* XIV, 343-80.—The *Lai d'Ignaurés*, ed. Monmerqué-Michel (1832), or in Bartsch's *Langue et littérature française* (Paris, 1887), p. 553 ff.

# CHAPTER XIX

## THE LYRIC POETRY

Alfred Jeanroy, *Les origines de la poésie lyrique en France* (2nd ed.; Paris, 1904).

Gaston Raynaud, *Bibliographie des chansonniers français des XIIIᵉ et XIVᵉ siècles* (Paris, 1884).

Alfred Jeanroy, *Bibliographie sommaire des chansonniers français du moyen âge* (Paris: Cfmâ, 1918).

Gaston Paris, review of Jeanroy's *Origines de la poésie lyrique* in *JS* (1891), pp. 674-88; 729-42; and (1892), pp. 155-67; 407-30.

Paul Meyer in *Rom* XIX, 1-62.

E. Faral, "La pastourelle" in *Rom* XLIX, 204-59.

W. P. Jones, *The Pastourelle* (Harvard University Press, 1931).

Joseph Bédier in *Rev. Deux Mondes*, CXXXV (1896), 146-172.

Friedrich Gennrich, *Grundriss einer Formenlehre des mittelalterlichen Liedes* (Halle: Niemeyer, 1932).

For the Music:

T. Gérold, *La musique du moyen âge* (Paris: Cfmâ, 1933).

J. B. Beck, *Die Melodien des Troubadours* (Strassburg, 1908).

J. B. Beck, *Les chansonniers des troubadours . . . transcrits en notation moderne*, vol. I (Philadelphia, 1927).

A. Möhler, *Geschichte der alten u. mittelalterlichen Musik* (*Samml. Göschen*, 1900).

In ancient times lyric verse was sung to the accompaniment of the lyre, as opposed to the dithyramb which was accompanied by the flute. In modern literature lyric verse is poetry, generally in stanzaïc form, expressive of the poet's feeling rather than of incident or event. (Note that this definition does not include the ballad.) Neither of these definitions fits exactly what we call lyric poetry in the study of Medieval French literature. This was a type of verse, brief in length, usually in stanzaïc form, with or without refrains, allowing considerable freedom in its versification. It could be sung with or without accompaniment, and it could be *narrative*.

Old French lyric poetry is ordinarily divided into two groups: those types which were borrowed directly from the Provençal troubadours, and those which were either native to northern France or which spread to it from the border territory where the French and Provençal speakers came together. This classification is based upon the theory that this border region was the original center for dance poetry—pertaining to the May Festival—whence it spread south and north. It is a remarkable fact that many of the oldest known lyric poets on French territory, such as William of Poitiers (1071-1127), Jaufre Rudel (before 1147), Viscount Ebles II of Ventadorn, and Bernart de Ventadorn (1150?-1170?), belonged to the border district.

F. M. Warren (*PMLA* XXVI, 280-314) examined in detail all the evidence for the existence of popular dance poetry prior to the earliest surviving Provençal lyrics. The decisions of local Church councils offer the best evidence for this. These councils inveighed against the *cantica turpia* of the populace, forbidding their performance within a given distance of churches. Obviously such *cantica* must have been of a coarse, erotic nature. The Council of Troyes (909) was the last to denounce such poetry. From then until the time of Bernard d'Angers, in the early eleventh century, there is complete silence on the subject of vernacular poetry, save for a few surviving specimens. It would be during this silent tenth century that these *cantica* took on a more respectable nature along the border of France and Provence. May day dance verse was elevated there to forms which Bernard d'Angers could note as *cantilenae rusticae* and even permit within the walls of churches. His observations of this popular poetry were made in 1010-15 at Sainte-Foi de Conques, in Aveyron; it was, therefore, popular Provençal verse. which had originated along the border, that he noted.

We will admit then, that rustic verse was first improved in the region of Poitou and in the border territory between French and Provençal speakers. The peasants sang and danced at the May festival to a singing accompaniment. The upper classes became interested and imitated the peasants in these forms of entertainment. Poetry improved in this way spread north and south in two waves: popular poetry and aristocratic verse. The popular did not survive the eleventh century in Provence; the aristocratic was there adopted by the populace. In the French-speaking territory the popular forms were the first to gain foothold. Later on the northern poets borrowed the courtly types from Provence. The rôle played along the border by Ebles II of Ventadorn, in the first half of the twelfth century, in the development of courtly verse, has never been fully estimated. None of his poems has survived, but it is quite probable that he was the inspiration in a school of verse where clerical elements were combined with those of aristo-popular origin. Be it noted that we have defined this improved border poetry as beginning with May day dance songs, expressing joy at the coming of spring. Some scholars have countered with the argument that spring is earlier than this in the southern half of France, appearing quite fully in March.

Granted that the May festival itself was a traditional time for celebration and that spring was very much in evidence at that period, such an argument should not be taken seriously.

Slightly opposed to all this is the view of Friedrich Gennrich that this vernacular poetry in France grew out of the religious lyric. Gennrich opposes various other theories such as the opinion of Burdach that French and Provençal lyric poets got their first influence from the Arabic, the suggestion of Ribera that inspiration came from the Arabs in Andalusia,[1] and the attempt of Brinkmann to see in this verse a development from learned Latin lyrics (F. Gennrich in *Zur Ursprungsfrage des Minnesangs, ein literarhistorisch-musikwissenschaftlicher Beitrag,* Halle: Niemeyer, 1929).

The lyric forms which northern France inherited from the border region were probably:

1. Dance songs: *rotrouenges, reverdies, mal mariee* songs.
2. *Pastourelles.*
3. Political and general types: *estrabot, serventois, débat.*
4. Crusade songs.

The *chansons-à-toile* or romances (to be distinguished from the larger non-lyric type commonly called romance) are generally accepted as a type indigenous to northern France.

Those lyric forms which were borrowed later from the Provençal troubadours are:

1. The *chanson,* from the Provençal *canso.*
2. The *aube,* from the *alba.*
3. *Jeux partis,* from the *juocs partitz.*
4. *Tençons,* from *tensos.*
5. Motets, *lais,* and *descorts.*

The Provençal influence had ready access to the courtly circles of northern France through Eleanor of Aquitaine, wife of Louis VII of France from 1136 to 1152, and through her daughters, the Countesses of Champagne and of Blois. Such influence was not strongly entrenched, however, until the thirteenth century.

For the *chanson-à-toile* consult C. B. Lewis in *PMLA* XXXVII, 141-181. It was a work song, chanted by women working at the loom, and hence the name.[2] It usually contained a short narrative concerning a young, unmarried woman and her lover. The heroine plays the more important part in the narrative, as we should expect in a song by women.

---

[1] The best argument for Andalusian-Arabic influence is by A. R. Nykl. See his *Cancionero de Abén Guzmán* (Madrid, 1933). He believes this inspiration is first seen in the later poems of William of Poitiers.

[2] A variant type of work song has its action beside a fountain.

There are no extant lyrics that we can definitely identify as *rotrouenges* and the source of the name is not clear. Suchier thought the proper name Rotrou, designating the inventor of this type, might be at the root of it. It has been suggested also that the term comes from *retro* ('back and forth'), and also that it might be derived from *rote,* a musical instrument. None of these etymologies is satisfactory. Gaston Paris suggested that all dance lyrics, not of Provençal origin, were *rotrouenges.*

The *reverdie* was a poem of rejoicing that spring has come and that the fields and woods are green again. In later poems of this type allegorical figures were sometimes introduced. In the *mal mariee* poems, a wife complains of her marital unhappiness. A variant, not so common, is where a nun laments her vocation and her spiritual husband, the Church. About forty of these have survived.

We possess today some one hundred and fifty *pastourelles* in the Old French language. The type is well defined. A knight goes riding through the country and meets a lovely shepherdess to whom he makes advances. Sometimes she accepts, sometimes she refuses, and often she calls for the help of her peasant lover, Robin or Perrin. There is a possibility that this type of lyric should be classified as a borrowing from the Provençal. Such is the opinion of Jeanroy and others, but Gaston Paris did not agree. Faral claims that the *pastourelle* was not of popular origin at all. He believes that it was first devised among the upper classes as a reflection of the pastoral literature of antiquity. From there it was carried to the people. E. Piguet in his *L'évolution de la pastourelle du XIIᵉ siècle à nos jours* (Bâle, 1927) has much the same idea. M. Delbouille (*Les origines de la pastourelle,* Brussels, 1926) suggests that the type spread from erotic poetry localized in Lorraine. W. P. Jones (*Spec* V, 207-15) demonstrates that none of these scholars has effectively proved his point with regard to the origins of the *pastourelle.* In his book *(cit. supra)* he admits the responsibility of both popular and clerical material, with emphasis on the popular.

The *débat* is an imaginary dialogue, often between inanimate objects. Jeanroy believes this type was borrowed from the Provençal, but this view was opposed by Gaston Paris whose opinion we have accepted. The *serventois,* first mentioned in Wace's *Rou,* is a common type of political poem in which the poet praises or denounces an outstanding character, or it may take a more general turn and become an observation upon some important event. It could be humorous, although it tended to be more and more serious in content during the thirteenth century. The name is derived from *serventensis* 'a poem sung by a *servitor.*'

The *estrabot* was of a satirical and injurious nature. Joseph Brüch derives the name from Germanic *strapa,—Strafe* in modern German;

Gaston Paris traced it back to Latin *strabus* 'crooked, squint-eyed,' which is also the origin of Italian *strambotto*. This second etymology is to be preferred. The word is mentioned by Beneëit de Sainte-More in his *Estoire des dus de Normandie* (chapts. VII, VIII). Probably the *derisoriae cantiones* which the Norman noble Luc de la Barre wrote against Henry I in 1124 were *estrabot*. Ordericus Vitalis is our authority that these were sung publicly and that Luc, condemned to be blinded, preferred death instead (*Hist. eccles.* XII, 39). The Crusade songs were popular calls for volunteers; or they could be the lament of a departing crusader, or of his lady, regretting the separation. Sometimes they took the form of a prayer.

The *chanson* was a love poem of the Provençal type. The lady addressed is apt to be married and she is served by her lover as a lord is served by his vassal. Occasionally the Blessed Virgin is so addressed in these *chansons*. The form usually consists of five or six stanzas with an *envoi*, in monorhyme or in rhymed couplets. In the *aube* a lady and her lover are visiting before the dawn. They voice their emotions as the watchman blows upon his horn to announce the approach of day, or they may be roused from their reverie by the warning of the nightingale who sings in the tree above them.

The *jeux partis* and the *tençons* were debates of a more genuine type than was the case with the *débat*. They were actually written by two or more poets. The *jeu parti* was a game, the subject for debate being named in the first stanza by one of the contestants who gives the other a choice of the side that pleases him better. The proposer takes what is left. (Consult Franz Fiset in *RFor* XIX, 407-544.) We find such a *jeu* in Chrétien's *Lancelot* (vs. 689 ff.) between Lancelot and Gawain. Some one hundred and eighty-two of these have survived. There was more of a genuine argument to the *tençon*, of which about twenty are extant. Most interesting is the one between Conon de Béthune and Raimbaut de Vaqueiras, each speaking in his native tongue.

The *motets,* of which there are about five hundred extant, flourished best in the thirteenth century. The name was first applied to a certain variety of music for two or more voices. When the term passed into the vernacular it denoted short compositions with popular refrains. The lyric *lai,* to be distinguished from the narrative *lai,* was a love song or religious song written to an older—perhaps Celtic(?)—popular tune. The *descort* had strophes of varying construction. There are some thirty *lais* and *descorts* surviving. The oldest are by Gautier de Dargies, who went on the Crusade of 1201.

The earliest lyric poet in France who has come to our notice is William VII of Poitiers, or the IX of Aquitaine, who lived 1071-1127. Al-

though a Frenchman he composed his verse in Provençal. Doubtless
there were other troubadours who preceded him but their work has been
lost, while his was certain to survive because of his high rank. Our oldest lyric poem in the French language is a crusade poem of the Second
Crusade (1146-7) written in England and beginning *Chevalier mult estes
guariz*. We have two lyrics that are generally ascribed to Chrétien de
Troyes. They begin *Amors, tançon et bataille* and *D'Amors, qui m'a
tolu a moi*. Aside from Chrétien no *trouvère*, or lyric poet of northern
France, is known to us by name before the period 1180-1200. At this
date we find Hue d'Oisy, Gace Brulé, Conon (or Quesnes) de Béthune,
Jean Bodel, Gui le Châtelain de Coucy, Gautier d'Epinal, Renaut de
Beaujeu, Gautier de Dargies, Richart de Semilli, Guiot de Provins, Hue
de Berzé, and Blondel de Nesle. Note how many of these were distinguished in other forms of literature. Blondel de Nesle is usually
identified with that Blondel who, as the *Ménestrel de Reims* relates,
found his master, Richard the Lion-hearted, in the Austrian prison in
1191.

This lyric verse of northern France is preserved to us in some fifty
or more collections, or *chansonniers*, of which twenty-five are very extensive. These were put together in the fourteenth and late thirteenth
centuries for certain wealthy amateurs. These men realized that the
lyric vein had grown thin in their own time and they sought to preserve
the more inspired verse of the twelfth and thirteenth centuries. The
first attempt to publish such medieval lyrics was made by René d'Argen-
çon in 1742. Some of the more prominent *chansonnier* MSS are B.N.fr.
847, 1109, 1591, n.a.1050, and those referred to as the Vatican, the Bern, and
the Oxford *chansonniers*.

It is now fitting to say a few words about the Goliards who wrote
certain types of Latin lyric verse in the eleventh and twelfth centuries.
We have stressed the importance of distinguishing between the Latin
speakers and those who used the vernacular, in the Middle Ages. The
clerics' world was an international one, and it comprised not only ordained priests but a vast number of men in lower orders, with simple
tonsure, who fulfilled such necessary functions as those of secretary,
schoolmaster, accountant, etc. All university students were Latin speakers, and this fact has survived today in the term Latin Quarter of Paris.
The clergy had their minstrels who traveled about from one ecclesiastical
community to another. These were apt to be needy students and de-
bauched clergy. But men of a much higher type were often the *trouvères*
or composers of the Latin songs. Such a one was Hue of Orleans
(b. 1090), known as *Primas*, who was a teacher of rhetoric in the schools
of Orleans.

Many of the writers of these Latin songs professed to be the followers of one Bishop Golias and they are referred to as Goliards. The name *gens Goliae* is supposedly as old as the ninth century and Walafrid Strabo, Sedulius Scottus, Archbishop Walter of Sens, and the author of the anonymous *Carmina Scottorum* all indicate that Golias and his satirical Latin crew were present in an undercurrent from the Carolingian age on (Jarcho in *Spec* III, 523-79). These Goliards flourished best in England. Scholars are agreed that the name *Golias* is a fictitious one, suggested by the Biblical Goliath or Golias. A twelfth-century Archpoet of Cologne wrote a *Confessio Golias* which many of his contemporaries ascribed to Golias himself. This archpoet was a minstrel attached to the court of Frederick Barbarossa. It is possible this minstrel was confused with Primas Hue of Orleans and that the writings of these two were all considered the work of Golias.

The best collection of the Goliardic lyrics is preserved in a thirteenth-century MS from a Benedictine abbey at Munich; these are the *Carmina Burana*. The MS has about one hundred and fifty Latin songs, as well as some fifty in German.

## EDITIONS

The two lyrics by Chrétien de Troyes are published by Foerster in his *Kristian von Troyes, Wörterbuch* (Halle: Niemeyer, 1914), pp. 202-9).—*Les chansons de Gace Brulé*, ed. G. Huet (Paris: *SATF*, 1902).—*Die Lieder des Blondel de Nesle*, ed. L. Wiese (Halle: *GrL*, 1904).—Conon de Béthune, *Chansons*, ed. A. Wallensköld (Paris: *Cfmâ*, 1921).—Jean Bodel, *Congés*, ed. G. Raynaud in *Rom* IX, 216-47.—*Recueil de motets français des XIIᵉ et XIIIᵉ siècles*, ed. G. Raynaud (Paris, 1881).—*Altfranzösische Romanzen und Pastourellen*, ed. Karl Bartsch (Leipzig, 1870).—F. Gennrich, *Die altfr. Rotrouange* (Halle, 1925).—The well-known lyric by Renaut de Beaujeu is included in the *Guillaume de Dôle*, ed. Servois (Paris: *SATF*, 1893), vs. 1449 ff.—The earliest surviving lyric in the French language is in *Les chansons de croisade*, ed. Joseph Bédier (Paris: Champion, 1909).—For Hue d'Oisy consult Jeanroy in *Rom* XXVIII, 238 ff.—Richart de Semilli, ed. G. Steffens in *Beiträge zur rom. und engl. Philologie, Festgabe für Wendelin Foerster* (Halle: Niemeyer, 1902), 331 ff.—Gautier de Dargies, *Chansons inédites*, ed. G. Huet (Paris: *SATF*, 1912).—*Die Lieder des Castellan von Coucy*, ed. F. Faith (Heidelberg diss., 1883).—Gautier d'Epinal, ed. Lindelöf-Wallensköld (Helsingfors, 1901).—Hue de Berzé, ed. Karl Engelcke in Herrig's *Archiv* LXXV, 147-76.—A facsimile edition of the *Carmina Burana* has been issued (Leipzig, 1927). The standard edition today is by A. Hilka and O. Schumann (Heidelberg: Carl Winter, 1930, 2 vols.).—Some of the Goliardic lyrics can be found also in Thomas Wright's *Political Songs of England* (Camden Society, 1839), and in his *Latin Poems Commonly Attributed to Walter Mapes* (Camden Society, 1841). A few of the best are reproduced by Stephen Gaselee in his *Oxford Book of Medieval Latin Verse* (Oxford Press, 1928).— *Poésies des Goliards*, ed. and tr. by Olga Dobiache-Rosdjestwensky (Paris: Rieder, 1931).

CHAPTER XX

THE *FABLIAU* AND THE TALE

J. Bédier, *Les fabliaux* (4th ed.; Paris, 1925).
E. Faral, "Le fabliau latin au moyen âge," *Rom L*, 321-85.
M. D. Comparetti, *Richerche intorno al libro di Sindibad* (2nd ed.; Florence, 1896).
A. H. Krappe, "The Seven Sages," in *Arch Rom* VIII, 386-407; IX, 345-65; XI, 163-76; XVI, 271-82; XIX, 213-26.

*Fabliau* is the Picard form of *fableau* (<*fabulellum*<*fabula*). This dialect form is in more common use than the Francian *fablel* because of the popularity of the type in Picardy. Obviously there is no reason for replacing the commonly accepted word *fabliau* with a Francian variant seldom encountered in the Middle Ages. The *fabliau* did not flourish till the thirteenth century; but the first one was a work of the twelfth, to judge from *Richeut*, the oldest survivor of the *genre*, which belongs to the third quarter of that century.

The *fabliau* was a droll story, a *conte-à-rire*, treating of adultery, wantonness, corruption of the clergy, and other *fabellae ignobilium;* at times it was a good-natured farce (in the general sense of the word). There are one hundred and fifty-two of these medieval stories which have been preserved; all but eleven of them are published in the collection of Montaiglon and Raynaud. They are brief, averaging three hundred or four hundred octosyllabic verses each, though one is as much as twelve hundred lines in length; the shortest has only eighteen lines.

The average *fabliau* was a versified folktale, so we need look no farther for the sources. It is amazing how the great torrent of popular tales has flowed through the centuries, in all countries, tapped at intervals to furnish literary plots for *fabliaux, nouvelles,* and farces. Whence came these tales and how did they spread so quickly throughout Europe? There are four theories:

1. That the folktales are disintegrations of Indo-European myths (Grimm brothers in *Kinder- und Hausmärchen*, 1812-1815; also in *Deutsche Mythologie*, 1854-1875; Max Müller in *Science and Language*, 1867).

2. That the tales are of Oriental, Indian, and Persian origin (Benfey in his *Pantschatantra*, vol. I, 1859).

3. That they are of polygenetic origin: there is not an infinite number of plots; people of similar cultural level widely separated can put together

the same motifs to make like stories (Andrew Lang in *Custom and Myth*, 1885; also in *Myth, Ritual, and Religion*, 1887).

4. That each folktale was originally the creation of one man, in a definite time and place; that such oral creations later spread widely just as written literature; a certain amount of polygenesis, and a certain amount of spread from India are also true (A. H. Krappe in *Science of Folklore* (New York: The Dial Press, 1930)). Such tales disintegrate frequently, leaving only detached motifs to circulate currently. Thus Krappe believes that tales precede motifs, rather than *vice versa*.

Theories one, two, and three stress collective or community composition of these oral themes, whereas Krappe stresses individual composition. Bédier's view is not unlike that of Krappe, although he admits some collective authorship. Folklorists are careful to distinguish between the terms myth, folktale, tradition, and legend. These are not synonymous. A *folktale* is a story, not essentially devoted to a given place or individual, (for which see *tradition* and *legend* respectively), possibly of collective authorship, which has circulated orally long before being written down, and which has circulated over a wide extent of territory, varying slightly according to the viewpoint of each cultural group which shares it.

Granted the folk origin of the *fabliau* themes or plots we must examine the literary, or recitation form which marks the medieval French *fabliau*. Surely there was a reason why the popular jokes which had been with the people for ages were suddenly put into a poetic form at the close of the twelfth and the beginning of the thirteenth century. Faral says that the poetic *fabliau* owed its existence to misconceptions of the ancient Latin comedy.[1] The man of the twelfth century had lost all idea of the true meaning of *comedia*. To him Terence and Plautus were the authors of humorous narrative poems. In the twelfth century, new Latin poems, of a humorous sort, were composed in imitation. We have sixteen of these extant to-day. They are the *Geta* and *Aulularia* of Vital de Blois, the *Alda* of Guillaume de Blois, the *Milo* of Matthieu de Vendome, the *Miles Gloriosus* and a *Lidia* by an anonymous poet, the *De nuntio sagaci*, *Babio, Baucis et Traso*, the *Pamphilus, Giscirum et Birria*, the *Pamphilus*, the *De clericis et rustico*, the *De tribus sociis*, the *De tribus puellis*, and the *De mercatore*. It is obvious, from the few authors whom we know, that these Latin comedies flourished in the vicinity of the schools at Orleans. Orleans, we must remember, continued to favor the literary classics rather than dialectic and theology. When it occurred to a poet to write a similar imitation of the ancient Latin comedy in the vulgar tongue—that was the first *fabliau*. Such is the theory of Faral

[1] On these misconceptions consult Cloetta, *Komödie und Tragödie im Mittelalter* (Halle, 1890).

(*Rom* L, 321-85). Gustave Cohen objects (*Mél. Jeanroy* pp. 255-263)[2] and says that these Latin comedies of the Middle Ages—especially the *Babio*—were played and were not looked upon as mere Latin *fabliaux* or narrative poems. He cites as evidence a *Ludus Prophetarum* of Riga (1204) which refers to the "ludus quem Latini comoediam vocant." The question is difficult to solve. Faral has a good case.

Richeut, the oldest surviving *fabliau*, does not necessarily belong to the year 1159 as Bédier once suggested. But the allusion which it contains to Henry II of England and the Count of Toulouse would certainly place it in the third quarter of the twelfth century. It is in stanzaïc form, 1,315 lines in length. Each stanza consists of three eight-syllable lines followed by a shorter verse of four. The three octosyllables are, in each case, in monorhyme, but the fourth line rhymes with the following group of octosyllables. This *fabliau* is most scurrilous throughout: it does not contain one respectable character. Richeut, a prostitute and apostate nun, has a son, Samson. She succeeds in persuading a priest, a knight, and a burgher, each of them in turn, that he is the father, and she draws revenue from them all. Samson grows up to be a famous seducer. His boasts of victory over womankind challenge his mother's pride. After an absence of twelve years he returns to his native town and does not recognize his mother. She dresses Hersent, her companion and a lady of the same ilk, like a fair young virgin. When Samson has been led on to win her and thinks he possesses a tender flower, he is grossly undeceived. To cap the climax he is beaten by a group of armed men whom Richeut has placed in hiding for that purpose.

This is the sole surviving *fabliau* of the twelfth century; the other one hundred and fifty belong to the thirteenth and fourteenth centuries.

Of a more learned nature are the collection of tales, usually held together by a frame story, which were derived from ultimate Oriental sources. Chief among these is the *Story of the Seven Sages;* another is the *Disciplina clericalis,* put together first in Spain. The *Barlaam et Josephat* and the occidental versions of the *Kalilah wa Dimnah* did not exist in France till the thirteenth century.

The *Story of the Seven Sages,* which is found in so many languages, is certainly of Indian origin in its frame story and in certain of the tales. At some time in its career it split into two traditions, the western and the eastern. The eastern version seems to have passed through Pahlavi (fl. 200-700 *A.D.*)—the ancestor of modern Persian—and from there to Arabic (ninth century), whence it spread broadly. The early Arabic version has been lost. Below are listed the more important survivals of this eastern group:

[2] Also in *Annales Univ. de Paris,* 1931, pp. 525-539; and in *Bull. G. Budé,* 1931, pp. 24-40.

1. The Greek *Syntipas,* second half of the eleventh century, from a Syriac original;
2. The Syriac *Sindban,* middle of eighth to end of the eleventh century, from an Arabic source;
3. The Persian *Sindabad-nâmeh* (1375), which rests upon a Persian prose version of the twelfth century now lost; another poetic form of the story, in Persian, was composed by Azraqî (d. 1132), but this has also been lost. Both of these go back ultimately to Arabic sources.
4. The Persian version by Nachschebi (d. 1329) in his *Tûtinâmeh*;
5. The medieval Hebrew *Mischle Sendabar,* from an Arabic original. This was translated into Latin and current in that language;
6. The sole surviving Arabic version, the episode of the Seven Wazirs in the *Thousand and One Nights* (fourteenth century);
7. This eastern tradition reached the Occident in the Spanish *Libro de los Engannos* (1253), a translation from the Arabic upon the order of the brother of Alfonso el Sabio.

It was presumably at Byzantium that the western tradition first arose. From there it spread westward through Crusaders, pilgrims, and perhaps merchant venturers. It spread in two waves: the *Story of the Seven Sages* proper and the *Dolopathos* variation. Krappe believes that the surviving western version of the *Seven Sages* was put together by a northern Frenchman *ca.* 1135, using folktales that had traveled to Europe after the First Crusade.

It is the *Dolopathos* form of the story which first appears in France in written form in the Latin prose *Dolopathos* of Johannis de Alta Silva (Haute-Seille), which was dedicated to Bishop Bertrand of Metz between 1179 and 1212, probably in the closing fifteen years of the twelfth century. This was translated into French, in 1210, by a jongleur named Herbert at the court of Philip Augustus. There are 12,901 octosyllabic verses; the full title is *Li Romans de Dolopathos.* The other western version, the *Seven Sages* proper, was represented by the *Estoire des sept sages*[1] (end of twelfth century) which was based upon a lost Latin original. (The Latin prose *Historia septem sapientum* is a work of the fifteenth century going back through intermediate stages to the Old French poem and to a lost *Liber de septem sapientibus.* This last is known only through a résumé made by the Dominican, Johannes Parvus, in the fourteenth century. It is certainly older than the early French version, though Gaston Paris does not identify it with the original of that poem.)

From the viewpoint of Old French literature the *Dolopathos* version is important. The frame story tells how Dolopathos, king of Sicily, confides his son, Lucinius, to the care of Vergil for instruction. The boy's mother dies and the King marries again. When he sends for Lucinius

[1] This survives in a derhymed form published by G. Paris and in two metrical variants edited by Mizrahi and H. A. Smith (*RRev* III, ɪ-68), respectively.

after some years, Vergil reads a dire prediction in the stars and warns the youth not to say a word at his father's court till he (Vergil) shall appear upon the scene. The boy obeys. His stepmother tries to seduce him, and when she receives no encouragement she accuses him before his father of making advances to her. Lucinius is condemned to death by fire. As the sentence is about to be carried out, a sage appears on the scene and tells a story, on condition the boy's life shall be spared for another day. Six other sages arrive thereafter on the six ensuing days and the same conditions are fulfilled. Vergil at last appears and tells his story; the boy is able to speak and defend himself, and the wicked queen is burned instead. On the death of his father, Lucinius is crowned and soon converted to Christianity. The story ends with his death. The ten stories narrated by the seven sages and Vergil are called by folklorists: *Canis, Gaza, Senex, Creditor, Viduae filius, Latronis filii, Polyphemus, Striges* (the last three all told by the sixth sage), *Cygnus* and *Puteus,* to which is affixed *Inclusa* in the French version. *Canis* is found in the Sanskrit *Hitopadeça* where it is a mongoose rather than a dog that saves the child and is killed in turn by the misguided parents. *Gaza* is the *Rhampsinitus* tale, found first in Herodotus, bk. ii. The story known as *Cygnus* is the same as the legend of *Elioxe. Creditor* is an ancestor of the pound of flesh episode in the *Merchant of Venice;* the *Viduae filius* is in Dante's *Purgatorio,* X, 73-93. The *Puteus* is found, in part, in Molière's *Georges Dandin,* having passed first through the *fabliaux.* The name *Dolopathos* is given as derived from Greek δόλος, 'deceit,' πάθος, 'suffering,' 'suffering in deceit.'

In the *Estoire des sept sages* (as distinct from the *Dolopathos*) Marcomeris, emperor of Rome and Constantinople, gives his son into the hands of seven sages, Bencilas, Lentulus, Cathon, Mauquidas, Gesse, Aussire, and Meros, for proper instruction. The Emperor marries again and his wicked second wife persuades the father to send for the boy that she may do him harm. The sages read in the heavens that he must not speak for seven days; they hasten with him to Rome. The boy is accused by his stepmother, as in the *Dolopathos,* and threatened with death. The stepmother tells the Emperor a story to induce him to hasten the sentence; one of the sages answers this story by another showing the deceitfulness of woman. This same procedure transpires every morning for seven days till the queen has told seven stories and each of the sages one. The boy, whose name is not given, can now speak and tells a story. The wicked queen is put to death. The fifteen tales vary with the version and frequently follow in different order. One order is: *Arbor, Canis, Aper, Medicus, Gaza, Puteus, Senescalcus, Tentamina, Virgilius, Avis, Sapientes, Vidua, Roma, Inclusa, Vaticinium.* There is no question of the son's conversion to Christianity.

Professor Krappe derives *Arbor*, which relates how the old tree must die and give way to the new, from a Byzantine gnomic saying. *Aper*, the tale of the man treed by a boar who lulls the animal by throwing down fruit, is connected by Krappe with the "Brave Tailor" folktale. The *Sapientes* has often been compared with the story of Merlin, and Krappe believes this tale was taken directly from Geoffrey of Monmouth. *Vaticinium* shows basic resemblance to the Joseph and Potiphar story in Genesis, and to the Ahikar legend. *Canis, Roma,* and *Inclusa*, are traced by Krappe ultimately to Sanskrit sources, the *Roma* to a lost Sanskrit tale which would be entitled "The Weaver who impersonated Vishnu." *Vidua* is the familiar "Widow of Ephesus" story. Krappe says *Virgilius* is an Oriental tale which may have been associated with the *Pharos* at Alexandria.

In the eastern tradition or group, the Queen is not put to death at the close. The following is a list of the stories, with their folklore names, as found in the *Mischle Sendabar: Leo, Avis, Lavator, Turtures, Catula, Striga* combined with *Fons, Canis, Pallium, Simia, Panes, Zuchara, Aper, Balenator, Gladius, Absalon rebellus, Absalon mortuus, Nomina, Juvenis femina, Gibbosi, Inclusa.* It is interesting to compare the survivals of the various stories. *Canis* and *Inclusa* seem to have followed the legend in all its forms.

Although the frame story and certain of the tales arose in India, many of the individual stories were additional folktales which the frame story collected as it traveled.

In a MS of Arras, which was copied in 1278, there is an elaboration upon the frame story of the *Sept sages*. It is the *Marques de Rome,* a prose compilation. Marques, son of the sage Cathon, is seneschal of Diocletian's son. The Queen, Diocletian's young wife, hates him because of a misadventure; she sends him to a powerful noble with a letter requesting that he, Marques, be put to death. Fortunately, the letter is not delivered. When Marques returns to Rome, he is freed by the intervention of the Seven Wise Men. He fights the Romans under the banner of the Emperor of Constantinople and marries the Emperor's daughter, Laurine. She dies and he returns to Rome. He is accused of relations with Diocletian's daughter. He is saved by twelve tales which are narrated under circumstances similar to those in the *Estoire des sept sages.* He brings about the discovery of the true culprit, Kanor, who is burned to death along with the wicked Queen. The tales are of miscellaneous origin. There are numerous MSS, but the Arras MS is the oldest.

The *Disciplina clericalis* was a popular collection of stories, with a prologue and an epilogue, but with no frame story, put together by the Spanish Jew, Petrus Alfonsi (1069-1110), who before his baptism on St.

Peter's Day in 1106, was Rabbi Moses Sephardi ('the Spaniard'). This Petrus received his Christian name in honor of the saint on whose feast he was christened and, as he was personal physician to Alfonsus VI of Castille, he was called "Alfonso's Peter" (M. Steinschneider, *Die Hebr. Übersetz. des Mittelalters*, Berlin, 1893, pp. 934-935). Although Petrus' illustrations are sometimes questionable, their purpose seems to have been to illustrate the principles of Christian morality. There are thirty-four *exempla* or tales. This important Latin collection, which was an inspiration for a fair amount of medieval literature, was translated into Old French verse at the close of the twelfth century, and the translation was commonly called the *Pierre Anfors* or *Castoiement d'un pere a son fils* (about 5,400 octosyllables). There are some twenty-seven tales in this French version. The translator was a Norman. Another verse translation was made at the close of the thirteenth century, and a prose version was adapted in the fifteenth.

The discussion of the tale must not be dropped without some mention of Cardinal Jacques de Vitry. This prelate wrote in Latin only, but the *exempla* which he used for illustration in his sermons are our best source of knowledge of medieval folklore. Jacques was born in Champagne, took an active part in preaching the Albigensian Crusade, and was named Bishop of Saint-Jean-d'Acre, in the Holy Land, in 1217. Pope Gregory IX made him a cardinal in 1229 and appointed him Bishop of Tusculum in 1230. From then on Jacques made frequent ecclesiastical and diplomatic visits to France and Germany. He was named Latin Patriarch of Jerusalem in 1239 but never occupied the post. He died at Rome in 1240.

## EDITIONS

*Richeut*, ed. I. C. Lecompte in *RRev* IV, 261-305.—The Latin comedies of the twelfth century have been newly edited by Gustave Cohen and a group of his students in *La Comédie latine en France au moyen âge* (Paris: Belles-Lettres, 1931, 2 vols.).—*Historia septem sapientum* (Johannes de Alta Silva's *Dolopathos* and the *Mischle Sendabar* in Latin translation), ed. Alfons Hilka (Heidelberg: *SmlT*, 1912-1913, 2 vols.).—*Li romans de Dolopathos*, ed. C. Brunet-Anatole de Montaiglon (Paris: *BElz*, 1856).—*Deux rédactions du roman des sept sages de Rome*, ed. G. Paris (Paris: *SATF*, 1876); *Sept Sages*, ed. J. Misrahi (Paris, 1933).—Petrus Alfonsi, *Disciplina clericalis*, ed. A. Hilka-W. Söderhjelm (Heidelberg: *SmlT*, 1911); also, by same editors, in *Acta Societatis Scientiarum Fennicae*, XXXVIII, 4 and 3, 1912, 1922; Part I, Latin text, II French prose text, III French verse translations.—*Die Exempla aus den Sermones feriales et communes des Jakob von Vitry*, ed. Joseph Greven (Heidelberg: *SmlT*, 1914); *The exempla . . . from the Sermones vulgares*, ed. T. F. Crane (Folklore Soc., 1890).—*Marques de Rome*, ed. J. Alton (Tübingen: *LV*, 1889).

# CHAPTER XXI

## THE FABLE

Léopold Hervieux, *Les fabulistes latins depuis le siècle d'Auguste jusqu'à la fin du moyen âge* (2nd ed.; 1893-1898, 5 vols.).

Georg Thiele, *Der lateinische Äsop des Romulus* (Heidelberg, 1910).

O. Keller, *Untersuchungen über die Geschichte der griechischen Fabel* (Leipzig: *Jahrb. für Class. Phil.* Supplementband, 1867).

A fable is an episode resulting in a moral, in which animals usually appear with the mental faculties of human beings but with their own physical characteristics. At times human beings are present with or without animals. This type of literature is as old as the dawn of history; it was particularly developed among the Greeks. Many of the most ancient fables have continued to be popular, in unbroken line, till the present day. The accompanying diagram will show the source relationships of the important fable collections from Aesop till approximately 1400.

The earliest known fabulist was Aesop, a slave from the Island of Samos, who flourished in the sixth century B.C. according to the testimony of Herodotus (II, 134). A large number of his fables were collected in verse some three centuries later by Demetrius Phaleron, and they served as a written source for all that followed. However, we cannot identify a single fable as being definitively the work of Aesop. A theory worth consideration is this, that Aesop never lived, that the so-called Aesop's fables were adapted by Ionian Greeks from a Babylonian original, known as the *Words of Ahikar*. A fragmentary version of the *Words of Ahikar* is extant in an Aramaïc papyrus. Clement of Alexandria mentions that one Democritus made a Greek version of the original (R. Smend in *Beiheft zur Zts. f. die alt-testamentliche Wiss.*, XIII, 1908). The collection we call Aesop at the present day is a prose version drawn from Demetrius, by Valerius Babrios of the third century *A.D.* The collection of the Latin poet Phaedrus, made in the time of Tiberius, is the direct ancestor of the western versions, through the important prose adaptation falsely ascribed to Romulus and known by that name (fifth century *A.D.*).

The correct text of Phaedrus seems to have been lost from the tenth century till 1596 when it was rediscovered by Pierre Pithou. This Phaedrus, a freedman of the Emperor Tiberius, composed five books

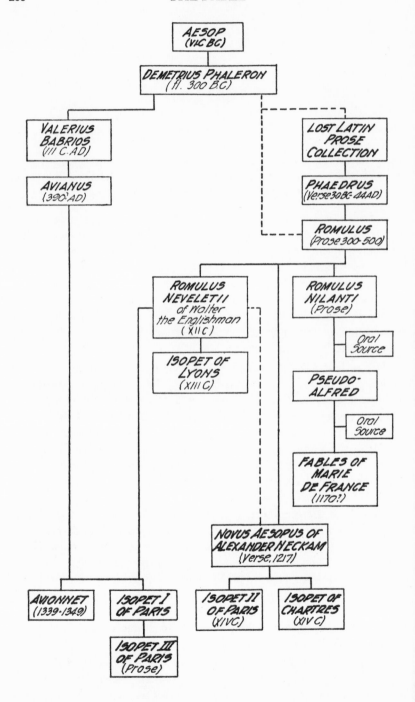

of fables, eighty-three tales in all. The collection was retold in prose between 300 and 550 *A.D.*, in a popular work that is known as the *Romulus:* because a prologue was added in which a certain Romulus pretends to have translated the fables from the Greek for his son Tiberinus. We pass quickly over two other prose adaptations of Phaedrus: the *Aesopus* of Adhemar and the *Aesopus* of Wissemburg, both of them made in the tenth century. From the first *Romulus* were derived six younger prose collections: the *Romulus ordinaire* (83 fables), the *Romulus* of Vienna and Berlin (82 fables), the *Romulus Nilantii* (52 fables), and three abridgements which we need not mention further. The *Nilantii* is so called because it was first published by J. Nilant in his *Fabulae antiquae* (Leyden, 1709). Its date cannot be established with accuracy.

A most important verse redaction of the early *Romulus* is the *Romulus Neveletii* (prologue and 62 fables) which derives its name from its publication by Isaac Nevelet in his *Mythologia Aesopica* (Frankfort, 1610). The probable author was Walter the Englishman, Bishop of Palermo and Chaplain of Henry II. The date of composition would be close to 1175. Another verse adaptation of the early prose *Romulus* was the work of Alexander Neckam and was entitled the *Novus Aesopus* (42 fables). This brings us to the French adaptations. The designations as *Isopet I* of Paris, *Isopet II,* were begun by A. C. M. Robert who made the first effort to publish these *Isopets,* in his *Fables inédites des XII<sup>e</sup>, XIII<sup>e</sup>, et XIV<sup>e</sup> siècles* (Paris, 1825, 2 vols.). The *Isopet* of Lyons has 61 fables with a prologue; the *Isopet* of Chartres and the *Isopet II* of Paris have forty apiece, in addition to prologue and epilogue. The *Isopet I* of Paris (68 fables with prol. and epil.) and the *Avionnet* (19 fables with prol. and epil.), which were originally placed together, were rearranged by a second cleric, probably a Burgundian, and dedicated to Jeanne of Burgundy between 1339 and 1348. The so-called York fragment, which we have not included in our diagram preserves nine fables, adapted from Avianus in the late twelfth century. The Latin prose collection of Odo of Cheriton contains only fifteen fables and the remainder of its seventy-five tales are bestiary stories or tales of Renart. This was adapted into French in the thirteenth century. (*Rom* XIV, 381-97).

The collection in which we are most interested is that by Marie de France (102 fables with prol. and epil.), with fables averaging twenty-five to seventy-five lines apiece. The meter is the common octosyllable in rhymed couplets. Each fable is given a Latin title. One of the gems of her collection is No. XV, the *De asino adulante*. The ass desires to compete with the little dog in the affection of their master; so he too runs out skipping, and paws the home-returning lord. The results can be surmised. The moral is one that makes me refuse to accept Marie as a lady of low degree; viz., one should not seek to rise to a position in life for which one was not intended.

Marie professed to be translating from a collection by Alfred the Great, but certain errors such as *sepande<sceppende* which she does not fully understand and treats as a feminine noun, caused Mall to believe that her chief source was a Middle English collection of the early twelfth century (*ZfrPh* IX, 161-203), possibly by an Alfred. Whether this supposed Middle English version made direct use of the *Romulus Nilantii* or used some related Latin version, for forty of the fables, is most difficult to determine. Either the Middle English author or Marie drew upon current oral stories, some of them Eastern in origin, for the remaining 62 fables. On the sources consult Warnke in the *Festgabe für Hermann Suchier* (Halle, 1900), pp. 161-284. Marie dedicated her *Fables* to a Count William, "le plus vaillant de cest reialme" (Epilogue), whom some would identify with William Longsword, natural son of Henry II and Rosamund Clifford.

Mlle. Hélène Chefneux (*Rom* LX, 1-35, 153-94) concludes that the nine fables represented on the border of the Bayeux tapestry go back to the same English source used by Marie—the lost *Romulus* of Alfred.

## EDITIONS

Marie de France, *Fabeln*, ed. Karl Warnke (Halle: *BN*, 1898); a few are selected by the same editor in his *Eine Auswahl von dreissig Stücken aus dem Esope der Marie de France* (Halle: *SrT*, 1926).—*Recueil général des Isopets*, ed. Julia Bastin (Paris: *SATF*, 1929-1930, 2 vols.). The *Isopet I-Avionnet* has been edited also by McKensie and Oldfather in *UIS*, V (1919), No. 4. The *Lyoner Yzopet*, ed. W. Foerster (Heilbronn: *AfrB* 1882) and the Isopet III of Paris, ed. M. P. Brush in *PMLA* XXIV, 494-546 are other independent publications.—For the Latin fable collections consult the works cited at the head of the chapter.—G. C. Keidel has studied the *Isopet* MSS in *PMLA* XXIV, 207-19. We should mention also his *Manual of Aesopic Fable Literature* (Baltimore: Friedewald, 1896).—A. Marshall Elliott was preparing an edition of Marie's *Fables* when he died in 1910. Consult G. C. Keidel, *Old French Fables, the interrupted work of the late Professor Elliott* (Baltimore: privately printed, 1910).

# CHAPTER XXII

## THE *ROMAN DE RENART*

Lucien Foulet, *Le roman de Renart* (Paris: Champion, 1914).
Léopold Sudre, *Les sources du roman de Renard* (Paris, 1893).

The composite collection of animal tales with stock characters, which is termed the *Roman de Renart,* is entirely distinct from the fable. There is no moral, nor genuine satire except in later branches; there is only mocking, good-natured, bourgeois humor. It was the introduction of much serious satire at the close of the thirteenth century which killed the appeal and consequently the popularity of these tales for the people at large.

Many of the tales, or branches, as they are usually called, show folklore motifs. This is particularly true of the earlier branches. Once the animal characters became fixed and named (as Renart the fox, Ysengrim the wolf, Tybert the cat, Dame Pinte the hen, Brichemer the deer, Roönel the mastiff, Bertrand the ass, Couart the hare, Chantecler the cock, Noble the lion, and Fiere the lioness) later poets felt free to indulge their imaginations. A glance at Thompson's translation of Aarne's folktale classification (*FFC* no. 74) will prove that a number of animal stories (similar to some in the *Roman de Renart*) are current folklore; other tales, found notably in Finland, have been rejected by Aarne as local enlargements upon earlier themes. The contents of the *Roman de Renart* have not been taken directly into account in his classification.

We must not ignore the early suggestion of Jacob Grimm (*Reinhart Fuchs,* Berlin, 1834), that such animal tales were in circulation far in the distant past and that they finally made their way into France through Germany: witness the Germanic proper names. This theory was improved upon by Paulin Paris, William Scherer, and others (the "Aesopians") who saw the first suggestion of the Renart tales as inspired directly from Aesop and Indian tale collections. They believed, on the other hand, that most of the individual plots had a collective, oral origin; it was only the form and such tales as the sick lion and the fox and the cheese which were learned. Léopold Sudre followed this lead. Although I agree with Foulet in noting the importance of the *Ysengrimus* and the *Ecbasis Captivi* in suggesting the form, I cannot see how we may deny the presence of popular animal tales that antedate these in the light of folklore evidence. Be it noted that our treatment, therefore, is slightly hybrid.

[1] See also J. W. Muller in *Nieuwe Taalgids,* X, 5.

The spirit is essentially that of the *fabliau;* the *Roman de Renart* is merely a specialized variety which soon acquired great literary possibilities. The relations of this collection to the Uncle Remus stories of Joel Chandler Harris have always bothered me. There has been little study of African folktales. Did Harris know the *Roman de Renart?* Had the Negroes of Louisiana and Georgia heard some of these branches, in rejuvenated form, from their former French masters, or are the Uncle Remus stories African folklore pure and simple? This problem must be approached by an examination of the spread of animal stories among the Negro and the American Indian, coupled with a classification of the purely African material. Until this has been done we can only indulge in conjecture. Many of the Uncle Remus stories are so very close to episodes in the *Roman de Renart* that it seems almost impossible to imagine anything but collusion. The publication by Méon (*Le Roman du Renard,* Paris, 1826) came too late to have much influence among French settlers along the Mississippi, but just as La Fontaine knew some of the medieval Isopet material it could have been possible for some of the Renart branches to circulate in the eighteenth century. Unfortunately, we cannot name the vehicle with any precision. The Tar Baby story (not found in *Renart*) has been identified by Espinosa as of Indian origin (*Journal of American Folklore,* XLIII, 129-209); my colleague, R. S. Boggs, believes he can prove it to be African. This would have some bearing upon our problem.

The *Roman de Renart,* forming a total of some thirty thousand lines, is composed of a series of independent episodical poems called branches. They are the work of many poets and jongleurs, whose names, for the most part, are lost. The branches have been numbered consecutively as they appear in the composite collections, but this order is not identical with the relative dates of composition; later jongleurs rearranged the branches to suit their own ideas of logical order. Below is a list, as established by Lucien Foulet, of the earlier branches with their dates:

| | |
|---|---|
| II, V | 1174-1177 |
| III, IV, XIV | *ca.* 1178 |
| I | *ca.* 1179 |
| X | 1180-1190 |
| VI, VIII, XII | *ca.* 1190 |
| VII, XI | 1195-1200 |
| IX | 1200 |
| XVII | 1205 |

The two oldest were by Pierre de Saint-Cloud, possibly the same priest who was reputed to have had a hand in the composite Alexander romance.

Branch IX was the work of a priest of Croix-en-Brie; XII was by Richard de Lison.

The suggestion for the literary form of these tales certainly reached France from two Latin works: the *Ecbasis Captivi* and the *Ysengrimus*. It would seem that Pierre de Saint-Cloud was delighted with his perusal of the *Ysengrimus*. In keeping with the great movement of translation and adaptation from the Latin which occurred in the third quarter of the twelfth century and which has accounted for the origins of the romance, and perhaps for the *fabliau*, Pierre decided to imitate the *Ysengrimus* in the vulgar tongue. Thus the *Roman de Renart* was born. To heighten the humor of his subject the poet mocked the feudal procedure of his time.

The *Ysengrimus* (3,287 distichs) was written in Flanders, around 1152, and it is filled with episodes of humorous conflict between the wolf, Ysengrimus, and the fox. There is considerable satire intended, particularly against the Church and the monastic orders. This *Ysengrimus* was probably inspired by the *Ecbasis Captivi* (1,175 verses). In this last, which was composed in a Lotharingian cloister (Saint-Eure of Toul), in the early tenth century, Aesop's fable of the sick lion, evil wolf, and sly fox, was elaborated. In the midst of mysticism and satire, the author made some borrowings from Prudentius, Horace, and Ovid. Personal experiences of the author were probably included under allegorical form. In the *Roman de Renart* all the moral remarks and allegory were abandoned by Pierre de Saint-Cloud, who sought only to amuse. Foulet has suggested with hesitancy that there might be some desire to parody the Tristan story in the first branches. Additional contributing sources are the *Disciplina clericalis*, the early *Romulus*, and possibly the fables of Marie de France. It is also possible that use was made of material from the saints' lives such as the Latin life of the Irish Saint Ciaran (*RRev* XVII, 143-148).

The popularity of the *Roman de Renart* is attested in many places. Scenes from the earlier branches figure in the decoration of religious edifices such as cathedrals at Strasbourg and at Amiens. The psychology of the use of material, highly profane, in the ornamentation of a religious monument is peculiarly medieval, on a par with the *Fête des Fous*. Further, there are many literary references to the *Renart*, of which we give a few examples:

Li dux Naymes parole, qi le cuer ot liart,
Valliant fu et prodon et de molt bone part,
Toz jorz ama le roi sanz branche de Renart
(*Chanson des Saisnes*, p. 33)

Ch'ert li confessions Renart (*Chev. au Barizel*, v. 134)

There are instances in the thirteenth century where, under the form of a branch of the *Roman de Renart,* a jongleur narrates a contemporary event, assigning to the actual participants the names of Renart, Ysengrim, Hersent, Roönel, etc. This was done sometimes through fear of displeasing the characters involved; but more often because the medieval man dearly loved an allegory and considered it the height of wit. So, in the memoirs of Philippe de Novare (Bk. II, Ch. 72), which were composed around 1258, we are told that Philippe composed a branch of the *Roman de Renart* as a veiled satire. The Lord of Beyrut was Ysengrim, Sire Anceau de Bries was Bruin the bear, Philippe himself Chantecler, and Sire Toringuel, Tinbert (that is Tibert) the cat. Sire Heimery was Renart; Aumariz, Grinbert the badger, and sire Hue, the monkey. The *chanson* began:

> Tant a esté Renart en guerre
> Qu'arce et destruite est la terre.

There is a similar case in the *Récits du ménestrel de Reims* (composed before 1263). Jehan d'Avesnes is Ysengrim, the Count of Anjou and the Count of Poitiers are Roönel and Taburel, respectively. Hersent and Renart also appear. Apparently there was no cause for bodily fear here; the *menestrel* was exercising the wit of which we have spoken. Efforts such as these, with genuine satire intended, became more and more frequent towards 1300; e.g., *Renart le Novel* (1288-92).[1] This last was by Jacquemart Gielée de Lille and is divided into two books of 2,630 vss. and 5,418 vss., respectively.

It would be too long a task to give a résumé of the older branches with which we are now immediately concerned. Faral has done this very charmingly in the Bédier and Hazard *Histoire de la littérature française* (pp. 29-31). Suffice it to say there is the branch where Chantecler is snatched by Renart through the cock's vanity over his voice; he escapes, in turn, through Renart's itching desire to revile his prisoners. There is also a primitive version of La Fontaine's "Maître corbeau sur un arbre perché." The branch commonly called *Renart Teinturier* is one of the most entertaining. Renart, who has to leave his old haunts due to "things being too hot for him," falls into a dyer's vat. Now, luckily, posing as an English jongleur, he is able to return home without danger of recognition. His broken English-French is of interest to modern English speakers. He persuades Ysengrim to fetch him a *vielle* from a villain's hut. Renart so arranges it that Ysengrim fails and suffers ignominy at the hands, or rather at the jaws, of the dog. Then there is the tale which appears to be the original for Uncle Remus's "How Brer Rabbit lost his great big bushy tail." This story becomes

[1] Consult J. G. Roberts in *Spec* XI, 472-7.

more meaningful when it is the wolf who sticks his tail through the ice-hole. The hare in the *Roman de Renart* is a very minor character, exceedingly timid, called *Couart* (*coda*>*coue* + *ward*). Is this the origin of our English *coward*? By 1270 was composed the branch known as *Le Couronnement de Renart*, in which Renart is elected to fill the position of the departed King Noble, the lion. This episode is very ill-constructed and was intended, apparently, as a satire against the mendicant orders; like the branch composed by Philippe de Novare (see above) this *Couronnement* was a *branche à clef*.

The name *Renart* (*Reinhardt*) was so popular that it replaced entirely the common noun *goupil*, meaning 'fox' in French. The name *Hersent* for the she-wolf occurs in the *fabliau* of *Richeut* to designate a woman of ill-fame. Is this imitated from the *Roman de Renart*, or was it from the *fabliau* that the she-wolf was named: a problem that cannot be definitely decided until we are positive of the relative chronology of *Richeut* and the *Roman de Renart*. The name *Richeut* is also found once in the *Renart* as the name of Renart's mate, the vixen; usually the vixen is called *Hermeline*.

## EDITIONS

*Ecbasis Captivi*, ed. E. Voigt (Strassburg 1875).—*Ysengrimus*, ed. E. Voigt (Halle, 1884).—*Le Roman de Renart*, ed. Ernest Martin (Strassburg: Trübner, 1882-1887, 3 vols.).—*Le Couronnement de Renard*, ed. Alfred Foulet (Princeton: EM, 1930).—*Roman de Renart* (*Einschliesslich der franco-italienischen Branche*), ed. H. Breuer (Halle: SrT, 1929).

# CHAPTER XXIII

# THE BACKGROUND OF THE THIRTEENTH CENTURY

Lavisse, *Histoire de France,* vol. III.
James J. Walsh, *The Thirteenth, Greatest of Centuries* (New York, 1920).
H. O. Taylor, *The Medieval Mind,* vol. II, etc.

As in our chapter on the background of the twelfth century, it is best to begin with a list of the sovereigns. They will be useful for ready reference and for appreciation of patrons and conditions.

KINGS OF FRANCE:

KINGS OF ENGLAND:

THE LATIN (FRENCH) EMPERORS OF CONSTANTINOPLE:

THE POPES:

The first act of importance in this century was the conquest of the English dominions in France. This was begun in 1203 (by the siege of Château-Gaillard) and confirmed in 1214 (by the battle of Bouvines). The English retained territory in only a small portion of Poitou; the rest of the Angevine empire built up by Henry II of England passed under the sovereignty of the energetic French king, Philip Augustus. From this time on England tended to develop a literature of her own and did not share quite so much in that of France. The first Middle English poem of importance was Layamon's *Brut* (1204). With one exception (a portion of Poitou), the French-speaking peoples were now subjects and vassals of the French king; this enabled the Englishmen of Anglo-Norman blood to concentrate upon their Middle English tongue and realize their nationality. England was for the English, and France for the French. To be sure, there were no political theorists of the time to point out the benefits of such a separation. Both the English and the French kings, throughout the medieval period, entertained high hopes of annexing the other's territory. The close of the Middle Ages (the fifteenth century) saw the near accomplishment of these hopes for the English.

Five crusades were led to the Holy Land during the thirteenth century; they lacked much of the enthusiasm found in the preceding period. The Fourth Crusade (1202-1204), conducted by Count Baldwin IX of Flanders, never reached the Saracens. Under urge from the Venetians, who transported the Crusaders in their ships, Constantinople was taken and a line of Latin (French) emperors was established. Baldwin was elected emperor. The Fifth Crusade did not concern France; it was a fruitless excursion into Egypt by the kings of Jerusalem and of Hungary. The Sixth Crusade was the work of Frederick II of Sicily who secured a most favorable treaty from the sultan of Egypt. The Seventh Crusade (1248-1252) was sponsored by Louis IX of France and it was important. Damietta was taken, though it had to be re-turned after the defeat of Mansourah. Joinville accompanied the king upon this expedition. The Eighth, and last, Crusade (1270) was also led by Louis and resulted in his death by pestilence before the walls of Tunis. Saint-Jean-d'Acre fell to the Saracens in 1291; this meant the withdrawal of the Crusaders from the Holy Land—forever, if we except the presence of the British and French in modern times.

A crusade of a more violent sort took place within the borders of France, the brutal expedition against the Albigensians (1209-1229). This was conducted first by Simon de Montfort and then by Prince Louis, who was, after his accession, Louis VIII. It was directed against the Cathars, or Albigensian heretics, though good Catholics perished with the rest in this bloody war of North against South. The heresy was checked almost completely but southern France never recovered her former glory. The troubadours, with their patrons gone, ceased to flourish, and the region became subservient to the North in both lit-erature and government.

In approaching the question of the cultural background of France in the thirteenth century, the first item of interest is the University, or "universal society of masters and students" welded into a corpora-tion. That year in which the multitude of schools clustered around the cathedral at Paris were placed under the authority of a single head, the Chancellor, was the date of birth of the University of Paris. Professor Haskins has remarked that such grouping may have taken place before the end of the twelfth century. The privilege issued by Philip Augustus in 1200, in which students were exempted from lay jurisdiction, is re-garded as the University's first charter. In 1215 the cardinal legate, Robert de Courçon, drew up its rules and regulations, with regard to the two degrees: *master in theology* and *master of arts;* he established the conduct of masters and scholars and the requirements to be fulfilled by those who gave instruction. The papal bull *Parens scientiarum* (1231) gave further rights and regulations. The *master of arts,* the more nu-merous group, were divided into four nations by 1222: the *French,* in-cluding the Italians, the *Norman* nation, the *Picard,* including the stu-dents from the Low Countries, and the *English,* comprising also Ger-mans and students from northern and eastern Europe. These four nations were to choose their principal—the rector, who superseded the chancellor of Notre-Dame as head. The University rapidly developed into an institution of papal control, under the direct authority of the pope and independent of the local ecclesiastical authorities.

The thirteenth century is apt to be neglected by the historian of medieval French literature because it was not a period of renaissance or originality; it followed upon the twelfth century and merely cultivated further the heritage which had been left it. What the preceding century had originated was then imitated and developed; and, in accord with the law of cycles, the people wore out their heritage. By the year 1300 the mind of the Frenchman was desirous of something new. This did not come immediately into the field of letters and the next two hundred years, the so-called Middle French period, were sterile ones indeed.

Before medieval civilization started upon the down-grade, the thirteenth century saw many masters and master works. St. Thomas Aquinas (1226-1274), a Neapolitan who taught at Cologne, Paris, and numerous Italian cities, brought scholastic philosophy to its greatest height. Among many writings, he composed the *Summa contra Gentiles* and the *Summa Theologica,* which were his masterpieces. We must not forget St. Bonaventure or Giovanni di Fidanza (1221-1274), who also taught at Paris and who brought the Augustinian philosophy of his predecessors to a perfection which could be surpassed only by St. Thomas and his Aristotelian system.[1] St. Bonaventure was a Franciscan and St. Thomas Aquinas was a Dominican. These two mendicant orders received papal approval in 1215 and 1216, respectively. St. Dominic founded his order at Toulouse for the express purpose of combatting the Albigensian heretics with preaching; St. Francis of Assisi was inspired by a desire for return to poverty. Both of these mendicant organizations were invited to Paris by Saint Louis. Because of their location on the rue Saint-Jacques the Dominicans, or Preachers, were later currently known as Jacobins; the Franciscans were called Minorites, or *Cordeliers.* These two orders of friars boasted among them other eminent scholars besides St. Thomas and St. Bonaventure. In 1255, the secular clergy of the University, led by Guillaume de Saint-Amour, objected strongly to mendicant teaching. The pope decided in favor of the monks, in 1257, but the University continued to feel aggrieved and feeling ran very high. The jongleurs were apt to be on the side of the University and this must be borne in mind when we see so many satires against the mendicants, from the thirteenth century on. While speaking of masters and masterpieces during this period we must not forget Albertus Magnus (1193-1280), the teacher of St. Thomas, and Roger Bacon (1214-1294), the Englishman. These two men were the first experimental scientists of modern civilization. Indeed Roger Bacon

[1] It is suggested that the *dolce stil nuovo* school of poetry in Italy owed much to the neo-Platonistic doctrine of St. Bernard. Leonard Olschki, *Struttura spirituale e linguistica del mondo neolatino* (Bari, 1935), p. 130.

has been named as the first to devise artificial lenses for deficient eyesight.[2] He suggested but did not construct the first telescope.

Gothic architecture, which began at Saint-Denis in 1150, reached inconceivable beauty in the Sainte-Chapelle (1242-1248) of Pierre Montereau. The rhymed chronicles of Wace, and similar twelfth-century writers, were followed in the thirteenth by the superior prose histories of Villehardouin and Joinville, in which cause and effect were handled with shrewdness. The *Roman de la Rose,* though not so interesting to the modern reader, was undoubtedly the most widely-read and long-lived medieval composition; it, too, was a production of the thirteenth century.

The floating population was on the increase and that meant larger crowds and more demand for the jongleur's wares. Serfs were freed with more and more frequency, and thousands of *hôtes,* or freedmen, were moving to the cities to increase the bourgeois population. This accounts somewhat for the decided growth of the *fabliaux,* satirical lyrics, and other forms of literature which appealed to the middle class. The times were more settled and peaceful under the reign of Saint Louis; both knight and burgher had more leisure for the enjoyment of vernacular literature. Such literature increased and multiplied, making up in quantity what a vast amount of it lacked in inspiration. As the center of the town population was in the North, the Picard and Walloon dialects enjoyed especial prominence.

The Latin classics which were popular in the twelfth century remained so in the thirteenth. Certain remarkable contemporary productions also came to be revered as classics: the *Doctrinale* (1199) of Alexander de Villa Dei, the *Graecismus* (1212) of Everard de Béthune, and the *Anticlaudianus* of Alain de l'Isle. But, unfortunately, the fondness for dialectic or logic now took supremacy with the majority of the reading public. The translations of Aristotle from the original Greek, by way of Sicily, and the adaptations made in Spain, from the Arabic, were becoming current in France. William of Moerbeke made a careful translation of Aristotle from the Greek, for St. Thomas Aquinas. The *Metaphysics* were banned or expurgated officially from 1215 on, but were read none the less. Eventually, in 1323, the papal authorities *required* Aristotle to be known entire. By the thirteenth century scholars had reached a point where they felt able to look back over past knowledge and to codify it. Encyclopedias, on the model of the *Etymologiae* of Isidore of Seville, came into being. There is the *Speculum maius* of Vincent de Beauvais (the librarian of Saint Louis), and the *De proprietatibus* of

---

[2] Salvino degli Armati, who died in Florence in 1318, had engraved upon his tomb the assertion that he was the inventor of eye lenses. This proves at least that spectacles were invented by that time.

Bartholomaeus Anglicus. The *Opus maius* of Roger Bacon indicated the possibilities of experimental science, but many centuries were to pass before these could be fully realized.

The conflict between interest in the classics, or Latin *belles lettres,* and studies in logic is represented in Henri d'Andeli's famous French poem, the *Battle of the Seven Arts* (after 1236). Grammar, with the ancient authors for her aïdes, is eventually defeated, but the poet prophesies that the next generation will prefer Grammar to Logic. He was not far wrong at that. A chief source for this work by D'Andeli was the *Wedding of Mercury and Philology,* of the fourth-century Latin poet, Martianus Capella. A poem similar to the *Battle of the Seven Arts,* but not so significant, is the *Mariage des sept arts,* by Jehan le Teinturier d'Arras, a contemporary of D'Andeli. Here the poet has a dream in which he beholds the weddings of Grammar with Faith, Logic with Penitence, Rhetoric with Alms, Music with Prayer, Astronomy with Love, Geometry with Abstinence, and Arithmetic with Confession. Theology seeks to dissuade them, but Physic decides their marriage is best. There are 310 octosyllables in rhymed couplets. There is an anonymous thirteenth-century poem with identical subject, composed in four-line stanzas of alexandrine verse. In these last two poems there is little to be gleaned concerning the relative status of the arts and the sciences; but they, too, drew upon Martianus Capella.

## EDITIONS

Alexander de Villa Dei, *Doctrinale,* ed. T. Reichling (*Mon. germ. paedogogica,* xii, Berlin, 1893).—Everard de Béthune, *Graecismus,* ed. J. Wrobel (1887).—Alain de l'Isle, *Anticlaudianus,* ed. Wright, in *Satirical Latin Poems of the XIIth and XIIIth Centuries* (London, 1877), vol. II, or in Migne, *P. L.,* vol. CCX.—Isidorus Hispalensis, *Etymologiae,* ed. W. M. Lindsay (Oxford Press, 1911, 2 vols.).—Bartholomew the Englishman can be consulted most conveniently in Robert Steele's *Medieval Lore . . . Classified Gleanings from Bartholomew the Englishman* (London: E. Stock, 1893).—Roger Bacon, *Opus maius,* ed. Bridges (Oxford Press, 1897).—The *Speculum maius* of Vincent of Beauvais has not been reëdited since the fifteenth century. There is great need for an offprint, at least, of this influential work.—Henri d'Andeli, *Battle of the Seven Arts,* ed. L. J. Paetow (Berkeley: *UCp,* 1927).—Jean le Teinturier d'Arras, *Le Mariage des sept arts,* ed. A. Långfors (Paris: *Cfmâ,* 1923). This includes the anonymous poem of the same subject.

# CHAPTER XXIV

## HAGIOGRAPHIC, BIBLICAL, AND MORAL LITERATURE OF THE THIRTEENTH CENTURY

Johan Vising, *Anglo-Norman Language and Literature* (Oxford Press, 1923). *Histoire littéraire de la France,* vols. XXXIII, XXXI, XXX.

Charles V. Langlois, *La vie en France au moyen âge* . . . *d'après des moralistes du temps* (Paris: Hachette, 1926), and *La vie spirituelle d'après des écrits en français à l'usage des laïcs.*

Gröber, *Grundriss,* vol. II, part 1.

E. Schwan, "La vie des anciens pères," in *Rom* XIII, 233-263.

J. C. Russell, *Dictionary of Writers of Thirteenth Century England* (London: Longmans, Green, 1936); and in *MPhil* XXVIII, 257-67.

H. Hatzfeld in *ZfrPh* LII, 693-727.

This chapter and chapter twenty-five are necessarily the most difficult portions of our book. Many of the thirteenth century saints' lives have not been published except in extract by Paul Meyer and others, and some of the scientific literature is either in MS only or is to be found in obscure editions long since grown scarce. This is an excellent territory for doctoral dissertations and for monographs. There is need for general studies on each of the didactic types. As early as in *Rom* XVIII (1889), 571-77, Paul Meyer stressed the importance of a complete survey of the Old French *materiae medicae* and of their herbalistic lore. An unusual proportion of the hagiographic and scientific writings of the thirteenth century was done in England in the Anglo-Norman, and occasionally in the Francian dialect, which should lead us to some generalizations on the superior patronage in England, because the scientist and the man of letters were apt to flourish where they could make the best living.

An examination of the career of Henry of Avranches (d. towards 1260) is interesting in this respect. It is quite possible that Henry was an envoy sent by Otto IV to the English King John. Apparently this Henry was first known as Henry of Cologne. John Lackland was a patron of letters: he had an efficient system for the lending and borrowing of books at his court; but there is no indication that he cared much for Henry in a material way. It is assumed that Henry taught grammar to the future Henry III of England and that he lost no time in seeking remuneration from great men such as Stephen Langton, the Archbishop of Canterbury, and Pandulph, the Papal legate. He also sought encouragement from lesser ecclesiasts, Bishop Richard Marsh of Durham—a rather shameless glutton—, Bishop Pierre des Roches of Winchester, Bishop Fulk Basset of London, and Abbot Henry of Croyland. (Nearly all the poems that Henry wrote for these notables were in Latin but the same patrons doubtless encouraged other clerics who made more frequent use of the vernacular.) Henry wrote a number of important saint's lives for monasteries such as Bury St. Edmunds, Peterborough, Christchurch at Canterbury, and Croyden. A little later he entered regularly into the employ of King Henry III, where he assumed duties which were similar to those of the poet laureate of later times. We have records of the salary then paid him, about twenty shillings a month, and occasional gifts such as two tuns of wine a year and clothing. As an indication of the price a poet was paid for separate works we find that Henry received ten marks (one hundred and fifty dollars) on March 7, 1245, for two poems, his lives of Saint Edward and of Saint George. An interesting sidelight is revealed from a quarrel which Henry had with a former pupil, Michael of Cornwall. It was the custom of the times for rival poets to hold poetic contests, with the judges to choose between or among them. Henry and Michael held such a contest at the Church of Saint Mary(?) of the Arches at London on Wednesday after the Purification, in a year between 1250 and 1254. We pass over briefly the attempts of Henry of Avranches to teach at Oxford and at Paris, an effort made by every cleric in those days, and the years which he spent in the service of Frederick II of Sicily.[1]

In the examination of the vernacular writings, of an ecclesiastical nature, composed during this period, we shall begin with two prominent source collections, then pass to the saints' lives in verse, to the pious tales and miracles, to the Barlaam and Josephat legend, to Biblical adaptations, and then to moral poems and those which professed to give doctrinal instruction.

The *Vita* or *Vitae Patrum* was the name which the Middle Ages gave collectively to the lives of early Christian saints who lived in the deserts of Upper Egypt near Thebes. The lives of these hermits were written by such authorities as Saint Jerome, Saint Athanasius, Paphnucius, Saint Ephraim, Amphilocus, Antonius, Leontius of Naplosa, Theophilus, Sergius, Hyginus, John Damascene, James the Deacon, Sophronius of Jerusalem, Rufinus of Aquileia, Sulpicius Severus, John Cassian, and Palladius of Helenopolis. In the middle of the sixth century these lives of the hermits were incorporated, in Latin translation, into collective MSS and from that date forward the *Vitae Patrum* was considered as a whole

---

[1] In making this survey we have had before us *The Shorter Latin Poems of Master Henry of Avranches Relating to England* (Med. Acad. Amer., 1935), edited by J. C. Russell and J. P. Heironimus. A work which can be easily consulted is K. J. Holzknecht, *Literary Patronage in the Middle Ages* (Philadelphia, 1923).

and furnished the source for many imitations. In imitation of the biography of Saint Paul, the first hermit, which the *Vitae Patrum* owed to Saint Jerome, Nicolas Bozon wrote at the very close of the thirteenth century a *Vie de Paul l'hermite*. In the early years of the century an unknown poet composed a *Vie de Saint-Jehan l'ausmonier* (7,700 octosyllables) after the life owed to Leontius of Naplosa in the *Vitae Patrum*. The jongleur Rutebeuf was the author of a *Life of Saint Mary the Egyptian:* there was another (406 verses) written in England after 1250, and still another, composed on the continent. Saint Ephraim wrote the original life, found in the *Vitae Patrum*. Saint Thaïs was another favorite subject. There is an Old French life of Sainte Marine, and others of Saint Jehan Bouche d'Or and of Saint John Paulus. There are at least six lives of Saint Margaret that have survived in fragments.

Another Latin source of considerable renown was the *Legenda aurea* of an Archbishop of Genoa, Jacobus de Voragine (d. 1298). This collection is familiar by name to many modern readers because of its mention by Anatole France in his *Crime de Silvestre Bonnard. Sic transit gloria!* Jacobus began narrating the legends of one hundred and eighty-one saints, following the order of the ecclesiastical calendar: Advent, Christmastide, Septuagesima, Easter, Pentecost. He added sixty-one additional lives later, and among these were a number of Virgin miracles. Because of its composition late in the century this collection did not influence many thirteenth-century poets. It was used by Nicolas Bozon, an Anglo-Norman, who wrote, in addition to a life of Saint Paul, a *Life of Saint Paphnucius* (214 verses), and lives of certain female saints —Agatha (208 verses), Agnes (303 verses), Christina (164 verses), Elisabeth of Hungary (414 verses), Juliana (175 verses), Lucy (177 verses), Margaret (330 verses), Martha (340 verses), and Mary Magdalene (504 verses). There are two other Anglo-Norman lives of Mary Magdalene, by anonymous poets, which survive in fragments. A *Vie de Saint Auban* (1,845 verses) is an Anglo-Norman poem which survives from the early thirteenth century. The chief source for this was an independent Latin life based, in turn, upon Bede. A *Vie Sainte Paule* exists in a single MS, Saint John's College (Cambridge). As the rhymes would show, it was written in the last part of the thirteenth century, after the Latin of Saint Jerome. There are 1,267 verses preserved. A Guillerme d'Oye composed a *Vie Saint Thibaut* in 1267, in four-line alexandrine strophes. There is a *Vie Saint Christofle* in octosyllables. A cleric named Renaut composed a *Vie Sainte Genevieve* for a lady of the house of Valois, who was possibly a wife of Charles of Valois, brother of Philip the Fair. There are three lives of Saint Francis of Assisi; one of them was written in England. There are two reworkings, in monorhymed *laisses*, of the eleventh century *Vie de Saint Alexis*.

Most of the thirteenth-century poets who were responsible for the saints' lives are not known by name. We have mentioned Nicolas Bozon and Henry of Avranches. Others were Chardri, Gautier de Coincy, Geoffroi de Paris, Rutebeuf, Henri d'Arci, Peter of Peckham, Huon le Roi de Cambrai, and several poets who are listed ambiguously as Guillaume le Clerc. That there were several such Guillaumes has been made certain by A. Schmidt in *Rom. Studien,* IV, 493. The most important of these Guillaumes we shall designate as Guillaume de Normandie.

Master Peter of Peckham (Surrey), who is the same as Pierre d'Abernum, wrote a *Life of Richard of Chichester* (1,696 verses) in 1267-1268. This Master Peter died in 1293. An unknown Master Gui wrote a *Life of Saint Catherine of Alexandria;* possibly he was a Poitevin. Three lives of King Edward the Confessor belong in this century; one of them, mentioned above, was written in 1245 by Henry of Avranches, for Queen Eleanor of England. Henri d'Arci, of Temple Bruer in Yorkshire, was the author of a *Life of Antichrist* (342 verses); there are three other lives of Antichrist, including one by Huon de Méri who was a monk at Saint-Germain-des-Prés, and who wrote his around 1223. Claude Fauchet was particularly fond of this poem by Huon de Méri. Four *Visions de Saint-Paul* date from this period, including one by Geoffroi de Paris, and another (273 verses) by Henri d'Arci.[2] There were three anonymous poems dealing with the same subject as the *Espurgatoire Saint Patriz,* of Marie de France. In addition, there was a similar work by Geoffroi of Paris inserted into his *Bible des set estaz du Monde,* and another in alexandrine verse by a poet named Béroul. The legend of Seth, the son of Adam, and of the tree from which the cross was made, was written in England about the middle of the century. Guillaume de Normandie composed a *Life of Tobias* for William, Prior of Kenilworth, in the first twenty years of the century. Gautier de Coincy wrote a poem in octosyllables dealing with the miraculous return of the lost bones of Sainte-Léocade. We have already mentioned the verse and prose versions of the Placidus-Eustachius legend which belong here. One of these was by Guillaume de Ferrières, in 896 lines. Another is extant in MS Dublin D. 4. 18; it has 1,250 verses. There is another from the second half of the century in MS.Br.Mus.add.1066. There is also a fragment of twelve six line stanzas in Oxford MS St. John's Coll. 183. For information on the other versions consult the reference by Holger Petersen. Huon le Roi de Cambrai wrote a *Life of Saint Quentin.* Rutebeuf was the author of a *Life of Saint Elizabeth,* written for Isabel of Champagne, the daughter of Saint Louis, between 1255 and 1271. An English monk, Benet of Saint Albans, composed a new *Life of Saint Thomas of Canter-*

[2] J. C. Russell (see above) suggests the possibility that Henri d'Arci wrote in the twelfth century.

*bury,* after a Latin source. It is in stanzas of six lines each, with verses of eight and four syllables. The first part is missing. Angier, a canon of Saint Frideswide in Oxford wrote a *Life of Saint Gregory* (2,954 vss.) and a version of the *Dialogues of Saint Gregory* (24,000 vss.). The *Life* dates from 1215 and the *Dialogues* are of 1212. In the *Dialogues* Gregory narrates the lives and the works of the Lombard monks.

There are certain anonymous pious tales which are not saints' lives: *Conte du Chevalier au Barisel,* the *Conte del Tumbeor Nostre Dame,* and the *Conte de l'hermite et del jongleour.* The first of these, about one thousand verses in length, narrates the conversion of a wicked atheistic knight who is forced to confession by a hermit. The sins of the knight are so appalling that the hermit promises absolution only when the knight shall fill a sieve with water. At first because of pride, and later because of sincere repentance, the knight wanders for a year. At last he returns in ragged state, fills the sieve with his tears, by a miracle, receives absolution and dies. Another version (1,262 verses) of this same *conte* was written by Jean de Blois, probably in 1216-7. This Jean went on the Crusade of 1226 and was attached to the court of Philip Augustus (Louise W. Stone in *Rom* LIX, 24-40). This version is commonly known as the *Conte du Barril* which distinguishes it from the anonymous version. R. C. Bates also ascribes to this poet a *Tournoiement d'Enfer* (2,048 vss.). See *Rom* LXII, 359-75. The *Tumbeor* (634 vv.) tells of a dancing jongleur who withdraws into a monastery. He can do nothing in praise of the Virgin save dance. He does this in secret; he is discovered, but receives the approbation of Our Lady.[3] In the third *conte* a holy hermit, waited upon by an angel, wishes to know who will be his companion in heaven. The angel replies that it will be a minstrel. The hermit in sinful pride revolts at this; he leaves his hermitage and goes to town. In the market place he sees a minstrel whom he at first reviles. The minstrel narrates his past life; he had been a thief (of the Robin Hood type) before becoming a jongleur. The hermit realizes that this sinner is better than he, and is overcome with remorse. The two return to the hermitage and, after due penance, the hermit is received into heaven along with the jongleur. There are 703 lines to this *conte.* Professor Louis Allen believed that these three tales were the work of one man, a monk of one of the Cistercian abbeys of Ponthieu, and that they were written in the third decade of the thirteenth century. All three go back ultimately to the Latin *Vita Patrum;* the *Tumbeor* also shows influence from the *Miracles Nostre Dame* of Gautier de Coincy (Louis Allen, *De l'Hermite et del jougleour,* diss., Paris: Solsone,

[3] This story has been retold in modern times by Anatole France and made into an opera, *Le jongleur de Notre Dame,* by Maurice Lena and Massenet.

1925.) The *Chevalier au Barisel* has its source in the vernacular *Vies des anciens Peres,* a collection of which we shall speak shortly.

Other independent pious tales, of the miracle type, are *Del prodome de Rome qui garda castee un an o sa femme* (540 verses), *Miracle de Sardenai* (522 verses), *De la tresoriere qui fu hors de s'abeie cinq ans et nostre Dame servi pour elle* (490 vss.), *Del clerc qui mist le crucifis en plege* (370 vss. in rich rhyme), and *Del diable qui se fist clerc et divin* (830 vss.).

Quite similar to the pious tales are the moral *dits.* A *dit* is a brief poem, often narrative, with a precept. Poems of this sort were apt to be written in Latin in the twelfth century, but the thirteenth century preferred them in the vernacular. It is difficult to classify the *dits.* Some of them are in jesting tone and might therefore be considered as *fabliaux;* others are sufficiently romantic to be grouped with the romances and *nouvelles.* Some are so satirical or lyric in quality, for example, the *dits* by Rutebeuf, that they must be discussed under lyric poetry. Others still are closely allied to the pious tale and we shall consider them here. The *Dit dou vrai aniel* (432 octosyllables) will strike a chord of remembrance in many a reader. Boccaccio used it in his *Decameron* (I, 3). It compares the relative truth of Christianity, Judaism, and Islam, with the story of the father who, according to custom, was to leave a certain ring to the son he loved best. He loved them all so well he caused two copies to be made and none of his sons ever knew which one was the true ring. *Le Dit l'empereur Constant* (630 octosyllables) might be treated as a *nouvelle.* Constant, the son of an astrologer, is declared, from the stars, to be the future son-in-law and successor of Emperor Floriien of Constantinople. The Emperor commands this child to be slain; but he is abandoned to die instead. He is reared by a physician and an abbot. When the Emperor learns of his existence much later he sends a letter, again commanding him to be slain. The Emperor's daughter reads this letter and substitutes another bidding him be united to her in marriage. This is done and all ends well. Still other moral *dits* are the *Dit de l'unicorne et del serpent,* the *Dit du hardi cheval* (58 octosyllables), *Dit du Cordouanier.* At the very close of the century Nicolas Bozon compiled a collection of one hundred and forty-five moral fables in prose. They are dull reading.

The Englishman Chardri composed, early in the century, the *Set dormanz,* a poem of 1,898 octosyllabic verses. Seven Christian youths, during the persecution of Emperor Decius (249-251), flee to a cave and are walled up. God miraculously preserves them in sleep till the reign of Emperor Theodosius (375-395). In a non-Christian form this *Story of the Seven Sleepers* was perhaps a folktale (Mt. 763,* FFC, 74).

An unexpected subject is found in the *Roman de Mahomet* which was written by Alexandre dou Pont in 1258, and which was adapted from a twelfth-century Latin poem, in distichs, by a certain Walterius. Alexandre adds considerable color to the account.

Having spoken of the individual saints' lives and pious tales we must now turn to the large vernacular collections. Two poets, the second writing after 1241, made two groupings of pious tales, based upon varied sources and including the *Historia monachorum* of Rufinus of Aquileia. These collections were joined together and known as the *Vies des Peres* or the *Vie des anciens Peres;* though the title was borrowed from the *Vita patrum,* the lives were drawn from miscellaneous material. The first poet included the life of Thaïs. The second poet was probably Ernoul de Langy. Henri d'Arci, whom we have mentioned and who was a Templar of the Bruer Temple in Yorkshire, made a free translation of the *Verba seniorum* (translated from the Greek by Deacon Pelagos and the Subdeacon John), which usually forms a portion of the *Vita patrum.* He also included a life of Thaïs. There are four partial translations into prose of the famous *Vita patrum* itself, three of them very free but the fourth scrupulous in its exactitude. The most interesting of these is a free translation by Wauchier de Denain which was undertaken for Philippe, Marshal of Namur (d. 1212).

We have remarked in a previous chapter upon the collections of miracles of the Virgin which were formed in the twelfth century, such as the famous Latin compilation of William of Malmesbury and the equally famous French collection by Adgar. These tales enjoyed immense popularity and we have also had occasion to mention isolated versions of single tales, such as the *Tumbeor Nostre Dame.* Paul Meyer made a bibliography of miracles, mostly Virgin miracles, which will be found in his *Notices et extraits des mss. de la Bibliothèque Nationale et autres bibliothèques* (Paris, 1895), XXXIV, 2, 32 ff. In the thirteenth century such collections became numerous. The most widely known is the *Miracles de la Sainte Vierge* of Gautier de Coincy[4] (1177-1236) which was made in 1223 or thereafter, while Gautier was prior of Vic-sur-Aisne (1214-1233). (At his death Gautier was prior of Saint-Médard at Soissons.) He grouped together fifty-four miracles, forming a compilation of some thirty thousand verses. His sources are not difficult to trace (A. Mussafia in *Denkschriften d. Kaiserl. Akad. d. Wissenschaften. Phil.-Hist. Classe,* Vienna, 1896). A similar collection was put together by Jean le Marchant, before 1262, which is known as the *Miracles de*

---

[4] The late Louis Allen thought that this Coincy was Conchy-les-Pots, in Picardy (*MPhil* XXXIII, 239-242). Gautier de Coincy was also a distinguished musician.

*Nostre Dame de Chartres.* Everard de Gateley, a monk of Bury Saint Edmund's, was responsible for still another group (*Rom* XXIX, 27-47). In a MS of the British Museum which bears the mark Old Royal 20 B XIV, there is an anonymous collection of fifty-eight Mary miracles written in Anglo-Norman dialect "After the scole of Stratford-atte-Bowe." These miracles show many similarities with those told by twelfth-century Adgar, and therefore with Albri and William of Malmesbury. The narrator refers to his task as though he were merely translating from the Latin. His direct source was doubtless the Latin MS Oxford, Balliol 240. A rather banal series of nine miracles is retold in the Picard dialect in B.N.MS.fr. 375. Although the work of Gautier de Coincy is best known and furnished the most material for the miracle plays of a later century, it is not the largest of the series. This honor is held by the vast collection of B.N.MS.fr. 818, formed in the vicinity of Lyons, in which there are more than a hundred tales. Some of these are reproduced from Gautier de Coincy and from the *Vies des anciens Peres.* There is one legend which occurs in several of the collections of which the Latin source has not been definitely traced. It is the story of the *soucretaine,* a nun, who is tempted by the devil to elope with a youth; while she is gone the Virgin fills her place. There are more than two hundred versions of this tale found in Europe and Asia in the period 1200-1900, which is a considerable sign of widespread popularity. R. Guiette, who has examined and classified these, could come to no definite decision concerning their history (*La légende de la Sacristine,* Paris: Champion, 1927). An independent version of this tale has been previously mentioned. It is a folktheme (Mt. 770, *FFC,* 74).

No mention as yet has been made of saints' lives in prose. These were addressed to a more cultivated lay audience than the lives in verse. The use of vernacular prose as a literary medium began almost with the birth of the thirteenth century. Most of the prose saints' lives were not intended to have an independent existence but formed part of hagiographic collections known as *légendiers.* The majority of prose lives were direct translations from the Latin, and not original compositions. Among the numerous MSS it is possible to recognize twenty-four *légendiers,* differing slightly but all arranged in the hierarchic order of the church litanies: Legends concerning Christ, concerning the Virgin, the Apostles, the martyrs, the simple confessors, and the virgins. In addition, there are a few *légendiers,* where the lives were arranged in the order of the saints' days, beginning with Advent. A collection of the latter type was a French translation of the Latin *Abbreviatio in gestis et miraculis sanctorum* or *Summa de vitis sanctorum* (after 1230), made in the diocese of Auxerre. (The Latin *abbreviationes,* after which the French *légendiers* were modelled, go back to lectionaries of the Carolingian epoch.) There are one hundred and sixty-eight lives in the above French translation and one hundred and fifty-six in its Latin original. Another *légendier* of the same type was that of Chartres, which contains only forty-five legends.

It is beyond our task here to list all the *Prière à la Vierge* poems, the various *Saluts à la Vierge,* and the *Joies de Nostre Dame.* Nearly all of these are noted in the Vising reference *(cit. supra)* or they have been analyzed by Paul Meyer. The Cult of the Virgin was particularly prominent after the early years of the thirteenth century. The Albigensian Crusade and the founding of the mendicant and preaching orders emphasize this. There are also numerous prayers, in verse, addressed to the saints, as well as vernacular Paternosters, Hours of the Cross, and *Miserere's.* It is occasionally difficult to distinguish between these and religious lyric verse. The chief difference lies in the emotional content. A poem which expresses pure exultation or emotional outpouring may rather be called lyric. Many of the *prières* were obvious accessories of worship. A commentary on the phrases of the *Ave Marie: Ave Maria gracia plena Dominus tecum Benedicta tu in mulieribus Et Benedictus fructus Ventris tui* was composed by Huon le Roi de Cambrai, in 312 lines. The lament of the Virgin at the Cross was another theme treated by him in *Li Regrés Nostre Dame. La Descrissions des religions,* also by Huon, bears some resemblance to the *Vers de la Mort* of the twelfth-century Hélinant of Froidmont; it discusses the various religious orders, in 228 lines. There is the *Nativité Nostre Dame,* ascribed to Gautier de Coincy. V. F. Koenig doubts that he wrote it, because its author states that he was converted from a worldly life, and there is no evidence that such conversion took place in the case of Gautier *(MLN LI, 335-37).*

Of the Barlaam and Josephat pious legend there were three metrical and three prose versions constructed in the thirteenth century. There is a poem by Gui de Cambrai composed not long after 1214, containing twelve thousand odd octosyllabic verses; there is an anonymous version of approximately the same length; lastly there is a poem 2,954 verses long, also in octosyllables composed in England by Chardri, at the beginning of the thirteenth century. Chardri's work is much shorter because he confined himself to the narrative only; in the others there are many digressions. It is probable that Gui wrote his poem at the behest of Gilles, Marquis de Vermandois, or of Gilles' wife Marie. Gui's digressions are largely condemnation of the upper classes and allusions to prominent figures of his day; in the anonymous work, which keeps fairly close to the theme of the Latin original, there are frequent classical allusions and epic accessories; Chardri's poem, as we have stated, is un-embellished. It appears that Gui did not complete his work; it was given a futile ending, possibly by a Cistercian monk living near Cambrai. Of the three prose versions of this legend, one is in the *Vies des anciens Peres,* one is a prose rendering of one of the above poems, and the other is independently based upon the common Latin source.

The origins of the Barlaam and Josephat material are to be sought in the legends surrounding Gautama (5th century B.C.), the Buddha. They came west from India and were put into Greek, with many addi-tions, in the seventh century A.D. The Greek version was abridged into Latin in the twelfth century, or a little later, as the *Historia de vitis et rebus gestis Sanctorum Barlaam Eremitae et Josaphat Regis Indorum.* The Latin was the source for the French material.

We come now to Bible translations in prose and to Biblical poems. Mention was made in Chapter IV of the attempt to put together the Old Testament, probably from scattered existing translations, for the use of Knights Templar. There are three manuscripts which include this collection, with some variation among them. We set the date as around 1220; in any case, the assembly was made before 1240. Berger speaks of a complete translation of the Bible (*ca.* 1235) which he refers to as the *Bible de Saint Louis.* Paul Meyer (*Rom* XVII, 121-44) is not aware of the existence of this translation. Geoffrey of Paris composed, in verse, *La Bible des set estaz du monde* (22,000 octosyllables) which, like the twelfth-century work of Herman de Valenciennes, contains a résumé of the narrative books of the Old and the New Testaments; but Geoffrey also included some extraneous material from the *Apocalypse Saint Paul,* or legend of Saint Patrick's descent into purgatory, from certain lyric debates, and from various poems on the Assumption of Our Lady. Jehan Malkeraume began a verse translation of the Old Testa ment, but the single MS breaks off after the account of Saul and David. Malkeraume included some extraneous and (alas!) profane material: the destruction of Troy, the story of Piramus and Thisbe, etc. A verse translation of the historical books of the Old and the New Testaments, plus the Song of Songs and the Apocalypse, was made by one Macé de la Charité, of Cencoins-sur-Loire, in 1299 or 1300. There are 42,650 octosyllabic verses. Gautier de Belleperche (Aisne) was the author of 23,615 octosyllables on the First Book of Judas Machabaeus, which he called the *Chevalerie de Judas Macabé.* He did not complete this, but Pierot du Ries added a conclusion of 1,600 verses around 1280. There are two anonymous prose translations of the Machabees which were com-posed in the thirteenth century. There is a well-known translation in prose of the *Apocalypse Saint Jehan,* with commentary; as proof of its popularity we cite the seventeen Anglo-Norman and ten Norman MSS. Despite this distribution the original was made on the Continent, in Normandy. The B.N.MS.fr. 403, one of those containing this text, has been issued in facsimile. It is so clear that it furnishes an admirable tool for beginners in paleography. The thirteenth century saw eight further translations of the Apocalypse, four of them with commentary and four without.

Among the many works of a moral nature we must mention the *Poème moral* (680 vss.) by an anonymous writer, in Walloon dialect. This poem emphasizes the futility of things of this world. Chardri was the author of the *Petit Plet* (1,780 vss.), a dialogue between an old and a young man on the futility of lament and the fear of death. An Anglo-Norman poem of the *Love of God* (780 vss.) of the middle of the century, is based largely on the *Vers de la mort* of Hélinant (twelfth century), and it, in turn, formed a source for the *Manuel des pechés* of Wilham de Wadington. Wilham was perhaps the priest of the Deanery of Rydal in York who paid five shillings to the Crusades in 1275. This *Manuel* (11,200 vss.) was written in 1275-9 and used, as further sources, the Bible, Gregory the Great, and the *Vitae patrum*. The *Trois ennemis* (3,328 verses) by a poet Simon of the early part of the century, deals with the world, the flesh, and the devil. Of the same part of the century is the *Chasteau d'amour* by Robert Grosseteste, bishop of Lincoln; it has 1,168 lines and gives an exposition of Christian doctrine. The allegory of God's daughters is first found here. He elaborated this further in another poem (310 vss.) which we call *The Four Daughters of God* (consult *Rom* XXXVII, 485). The four daughters are *Merci, Verite, Justise, Pes*. Of similar inspiration is the *Marriage of the Devil's Nine Daughters* (666 verses). The nine are *Symonye, Ypocrisye, Ravyne, Usure, Tricherie, Sacrilege, Fauce Servyse, Orguelle, Lecherye* (Paul Meyer in *Rom* XXIX, 61-72). Nicolas Bozon wrote a *Char d'orgueil* (560 vss. in four-line stanzas) in which he reproved the vanity of women. There is an allegorical poem called the *Battaile d'Anfer et de Paradis*, representing the conflict between Arras and the city of Paris. Let us not forget the *Vers sur la Mort* by Thibaut de Marly. The *Besant de Dieu* was composed by Guillaume de Normandie in 1226-1227; it discusses the miseries of the century, invokes the aid of God for the Church, and deplores the lack of a crusade. The *besant* is the unused talent which the unworthy servant in the Biblical parable renders to his Lord. Guillaume was a Norman married cleric who lived by writing. He was also author of *Les treiz moz*, dedicated to Bishop Alexander of Lichfield and Coventry (1224-1238), which was based largely upon the *De miseria humanae condicionis* of Innocent III. This Latin work of

Innocent III was translated in the thirteenth century by an anonymous poet as *Le livre de la misère de l'homme* (*Rom* XVI, 68-69). *Le Roman de Carité* (240 stanzas of twelve lines each) and the *Miserere* (273 stanzas) were the work of a recluse of Molliens-Vidame who was probably Bartholomew of the Abbey of Saint-Fuscien-au-bois (so called before he walled himself up in an isolated cell). The recluse doubtless wrote these poems towards the end of his life, in the first third of the century. Robert de Blois, who dedicated his work to Hue Tyrel and Jofroi de la Chapelle, and therefore wrote before 1260, has had the honor of being preserved to posterity in a magnificent manuscript, executed at the close of the thirteenth century (now Arsenal 5201). There are also a few minor manuscripts of some of his verses. He composed the *Chastoiement des dames* (755 verses), which is a handbook of female behavior, the *Enseignement des princes,* the *Onor des dames,* two romances, *Beaudous* and *Floris et Liriope,* and various minor moral poems. Philippe de Novare was the author of *Des quatre tenz d'aage d'ome* in 1265, at the age of seventy or more. It deals with the duties of man in the four ages of childhood, youth, middle age, and old age; docility, self control, wisdom, and repentance, respectively, appear to be the chief virtues of each age. A certain cleric, Master Mahieu, married a widow, after 1274, despite the fact that this made him a "bigamist," as the Middle Ages reckoned it. He was deprived of his privileges and his wife grew ugly and unpleasant. Sometime before 1301 this Mahieu wrote his *Lamenta Mattheoli,* in Latin, a brutal satire of marriage and womankind. This had the great fortune to receive a worthy translator in the person of Jehan le Fèvre in the following century (*ca.* 1370). There is a *Commentary on the Proverbs of Solomon* which may be Anglo-Norman and may be Continental. Lecompte has discussed the sources (*The Sources of the Anglo-French Commentary on the Proverbs of Solomon,* Collegeville, 1906). The work is in prose. Shortly before 1300, Nicolas Bozon, who wrote so much, compiled his *Proverbes de bon enseignement* (142 four- and six-line stanzas) from the Bible and from the *Florilegium* of Sedulius Scotus. Other proverb collections are the Anglo-Norman *Proverbes de Fraunce,* the *Proverbia Marie Magdalene,* and the *Enseignements Richart de Ho.*

The *Bible Guiot* was a moral satire by a Cluniac monk, Gui de Provins. This was written in 1206 and contains many valuable allusions to contemporary poets and protectors, for Guiot himself had been a jongleur. He frequented the court of Frederick Barbarossa and others; he had taken part in the Third Crusade. For some unspecified reason he entered the Abbey of Clairvaux. The rule of this monastery was too severe, so he transferred to Cluny after four months. Guiot composed another pious treatise, the *Armeure du chevalier,* which follows directly after the *Bible* in B.N. MS. fr. 25347. Guiot de Provins may be the Kiot referred to by Wolfram von Eschenbach in his *Parsifal.* The *Bible Guiot* has 2,691 octosyllables in which, after a series of regrets over departed patrons and lack of philosophers, there begins a diatribe against usurers, churchmen, canon-lawyers, and doctors; there is nothing against women. (Gui admits that he was a physical coward.)

Hugh III, lord of Berzé-le-Chatel, a veteran of the Fourth Crusade who seems to have returned to the Holy Land in 1220, whence he doubtless never returned, was the author of some lyric poems both in French and in bad Provençal. His chief claim to fame is a *Bible* (838 verses) which may have been a reply to that of Guiot. Hugh was residing not far from Cluny. In his *Bible* Hugh remarks on the suddenness of death and then lets himself go on the subject of the religious orders, to which group Guiot de Provins belonged. Hugh declares that he himself has seen much luxury and vice. *Li Contez dou monde,* composed by Renaut d'Andon (in the Gâtinais), is a similar satire, with emphasis upon the legal profession, although usurers, prideful folk, and others receive attention. The beginning is lost; there is only one MS. Ninety-four four-line strophes have been preserved.

There are three versions of a theme called the *Riote du monde,* a farcical dialogue, between a jongleur and the King of England, on how to behave oneself in life, in order to avoid evil tongues. Two of them are in verse, Anglo-Norman and Francian poems, respectively. The third, and best, is a Picard prose version.

There are works which aimed to give more definite religious instructions. The *Credo* of Jehan de Joinville, written in prose is a commentary on each phrase of the Nicene Creed. This was composed at Saint-Jean-d'Acre in 1250-1251, but planned, doubtless on the long voyage from Mansourah to Acre. It would seem that Joinville rehandled this commentary in 1287-1297; we possess only the second version in a single MS, BN. nouv. acq. fr. 4509.[5] Shortly before his death in 1270, Louis IX wrote out, with his own hand, a testament of instruction for his children, if we may believe the historian Geoffrey of Beaulieux (*HLF,* XX, 7). The original of this has been lost, but there remain a number of summaries, which, unfortunately, differ among themselves.

Of great importance is the verse *Lumiere as lais* (15,000 verses) of Peter of Peckham, or Pierre d'Abernum. This was based largely upon the *Elucidarium* of the twelfth-century Honorius (d'Autun?) and upon the *Sententiae* of Peter Lombard. It is a series of questions and answers on theology, and is rather entertaining today despite its curious style. There are six divisions: concerning God the Creator, concerning man

[5] See G. Lozinski in *NeuphMitteil* XXXI, 170-231.

and his sins, concerning the Incarnation, the Redemption, and the Passion, concerning the healing of the Seven Sacraments, concerning Hell and Paradise. This was composed in 1266-1267. There is a translation of the *Elucidarium* in BN. fr. 423, fol. 84 ff. The *Somme le roi* was written in 1279 for Philip III of France by his confessor, Laurent d'Orleans. This was based upon an anonymous *Miroir du monde* and upon the *Summa virtutum et vitiorum* of Guillaume Peraud. Laurent added something of his own. There is a resemblance in plan between a portion of this work and the *Manuel des pechés* of Wilham de Wadington; this is probably fortuitous. The *Somme* discusses the Ten Commandments, the Creed, the seven deadly sins, the sins of the tongue, the virtues, the Pater Noster, and the seven gifts of the Holy Ghost.

An Anglo-Norman, Robert de Gretham, wrote a sort of theological encyclopedia in more than 20,000 verses during the first half of the century. This is commonly referred to as the *Miroir* or *Evangiles des domnees*. The word *domnee* means Sunday and this work is an exposition of the gospels read on Sundays. It is dedicated to Dame Aline, the wife of Alain.

A vernacular sermon of a meditative type, by Thomas of Hales, has been published by Dominica Legge in *MLR* XXX, 212-18.

## EDITIONS

Bollandists, *Acta sanctorum* (Antwerp, 1643-1875). There are sixty-four volumes published to date.—*Jacobi a Voragine legenda aurea*, ed. T. Graesse (Dresden: Leipzig, 1846).—Nicolas Bozon, *Vie de Sainte Elisabeth*, ed. L. Karl in *ZfrPh* XXXIV, 305-14; *Vie de Sainte Agathe*, see Louis Brandin in *Mélanges Emile Picot*, I, 91.—*Pièce à refrains sur sainte Catherine*, ed. P. Meyer in *Recueil d'anciens textes*, p. 375; *Die franz. Bearbeitung der Legende der hl. Katharina von Alexandrien*, ed. Karl Manger (Zweibrücken, 1901); also H. Breuer in *ZfrPh, Beiheft* LIII (1919).—Rutebeuf, *Gedichte*, ed. R. Kressner (Wolfenbüttel, 1885); other versions of Mary the Egyptian's life are unpublished, to the best of my knowledge.— *Vie de Saint Auban*, ed. R. Atkinson (London, 1876).—*La Vie de Sainte Paule*, ed. K. Grass (Halle: Brom., 1908).—*Vie de Saint Thibaut*, ed. H. E. Manning (New York: IFS, 1927).—There are various fragments from lives of Saint Margaret published in *Rom* XXXII, 396, *Rom* XL, 541, *RFor* VI, 414-16, and in Scheler's *Deux rédactions diverses de la légende de Sainte Marguérite* (Antwerp, 1877).—On the thirteenth-century lives of Saint Alexis consult the Foerster-Koschwitz *Uebungsbuch*, pp. 98-162. —Pierre d'Abernum, *Richard de Chichestre*, ed. A. T. Baker in *Rlr*, LIII, 245-396.—Extracts from the lives of Edward the Confessor made by Luard in *Rolls Series* (1858), and by A. T. Baker in *MLR* III, 374-75 and *Rlr* LIV, 215-16. See also *Rom* XL, 45-62 and Fritz's *Ueber Verfasser und Quellen der altfr. Estoire de Saint Aedward* (Heidelberg, 1910).—Henri d'Arci,

*Antichriste*, ed. Kastner in *MLR* I, 267-82. On the same theme consult *Rom* XXIX, 78-82, and *Notices et Extraits*, etc., XXXIX, Iʳᵉ partie, 317. *Deux versions inédites de la légende de l'Antéchrist en vers français du XIIIᵉ siècle*, ed. E. Walberg (Lund, 1928).—On the *Descent* or *Vision of Saint Paul* see *Notices et Extraits*, etc., XXV, Iʳᵉ partie, 156 and *Rom* XXIV, 357-75.—On the metrical versions of Saint Patrick's *Purgatory* consult Mall, *RFor* VI, 139-97—The *Seth* is in Corp. Chr. Coll. MS no. 66. I know of no edition; it should certainly be published.—*Vie de Saint-François d'Assise*, ed. A. Schmidt (Leipzig, 1905).—Guillaume de Normandie, *Vie de Tobie*, ed. R. Reinsch in Herrig's *Archiv*, LXII, 375-96; see also Ruth J. Dean in *MPhil* XXXIII, 13-19.—*La Vie de Saint-Eustache*, ed. Holger Petersen (Paris: *Cfmå*, 1927); *La Vie de Saint-Eustache en prose*, ed. Jessie Murray (Paris: *Cfmå*, 1928)—Huon le Roi, *Life of Saint Quentin*, ed. A. Långfors-Söderhjelm (Helsingfors, 1909).—*Fragments d'une vie de Saint-Thomas de Cantorbéry*, ed. Paul Meyer (Paris: *SATF*, 1885).—Angier, *Vie Saint Grégoire*, see *Rom* XII, 114 ff.; *Li Dialoge Gregoire le Pape*, ed. W. Foerster (Halle: Niemeyer, 1876).—*Chevalier au barisel*, ed. Schultz-Gora in *Zwei altf. Dichtungen* (4th ed.; Halle: Niemeyer, 1919); *Le Conte du Barril*, ed. R. C. Bates (*Yale Rom St.*, 1931).—*Del Tumbeor Nostre Dame*, ed. Lommatzsch (Berlin *RT*, 1920); also in *RFor* XI, 223-88, ed. H. Wächter.—*De l'hermite et del jougleour*, ed. Louis Allen (Paris: Solsona, 1925).—*Les contes moralisés de Nicole Bozon*, ed. L. Toulmin Smity-Paul Meyer (Paris: *SATF*, 1889).—*Dit dou vrai aniel*, ed. A. Tobler (Leipzig, 1884).—*Le dit de l'empereur Coustant*, ed. A. Wesselofsky in *Rom* VI, 161-98.—*Dit de l'unicorne et del serpent*, ed. Jubinals in *Nouveau recueil de contes, dits, fabliaux, etc.* (Paris, 1839-1842, 2 vols.), II, 113 ff.—*Dit du cordouanier*, ed. A. H. Schutz in *RRev* XXII, 130-6.—*Dit du hardi cheval*, ed. Paul Meyer in *Rom* XLI, 90-04.—*Chardris Josaphaz, Set Dormanz, und Petit Plet*, ed. John Koch (Heilbronn *AfrB*, 1879).—*Alixandre dou Pont, Roman de Mahomet*, ed. B. Ziolecki (Oppeln, 1887).—The *Vies des anciens Pères* are now being edited. Until this edition appears the reader can find several of the individual tales in Méon's edition of Barbazan's *Fabliaux et contes des poètes français des XIᵉ, XIIᵉ siècles* (Paris, 1808), vol. II. The *Judenknabe*, ed. F. Wolter (Halle: *BN*, 1879), is one of the best known episodes.—The translation of the *Verba Seniorum* is unpublished, except for a few extracts in *Notices et Extraits, etc.*, XXXV, 140, 161.—Gautier de Coincy, *Miracles de Nostre Dame*, ed. Poquet (1859).—Jehan Marchant, *Le Livre des miracles de Nostre Dame de Chartres*, ed. G. Duplessis (Chartres, 1855).— Helding Kjellman, *La deuxième collection anglo-normande des miracles de la Sainte Vierge* (Paris: Champion, 1922).—Everard de Gateley, *Miracles de la Vierge*, ed. Paul Meyer in *Rom* XXIX, 27-47.—*Ein Marienmirakel*, ed. G. Gröber, in *Beitr. rom. u. eng. Ph.* (Halle: Niemeyer, 1902).—*Mariengebete*, ed. H. Suchier (Halle: Niemeyer, 1877).—*Marienlob*, ed. Hugo Andresen (Halle: Niemeyer, 1891).—*Salut à la Vierge*, ed. P. Meyer in *Rom.* XXXII, 111.—"Dame seynte Marie, mere de pietie," ed. R. Reinsch in Herrig's *Archiv*, LXIII, 66.—*Ave Marie*, ed. P. Meyer in *Rom* XV, 342-43.—*Les heures de la*

*Croix,* ed. P. Meyer in *Bull SATF,* XXVII, 65.—*Prière,* ed. Stengel in *ZfrSl.* XLIV, 146.—*Oraison,* ed. Holger Petersen in *NeuphMitteil,* 1911, p. 14.— A. Långfors, *Les traductions et paraphrases du Pater en vers français du m. â.* in *NeuphMitteil,* 1912, p. 35.—*Louange de la Vierge,* ed. Höpfner-Zacher in *Zfdeutsch. Phil.,* I, 178.—*Plainte de la Vierge auprès de la Croix,* ed. P. Meyer in *Bull SATF,* XXVII, 68.—*Prière à Saint Marc pour les Vénitiens,* ed. Martin da Canal in *Archivio storico ital,* VIII, 670.—*Prière abécédaire,* ed. A. Långfors in *Rom* XLI, 237-46.—Huon le Roi de Cambrai, *Oeuvres,* ed. A. Långfors (2nd ed.; Paris: *Cfmâ,* 1915), vol. I; *Li Regrés Nostre Dame,* ed. A. Långfors (Paris, 1907).—Guillaume le Clerc, *Les Joies Nostre Dame,* ed. R. Reinsch in *ZfrPh* III, 211-31.—There are some seven Anglo-Norman poems on the *Joies Nostre Dame,* mostly in prayer form. On these see T. Wright's *Specimens of Lyric Poetry* (1842), Paul Meyer in *Rom* XV, 307-08; XXXV, 571, 574, and R. Reinsch in Herrig's *Archiv* LXIII, 56, 93; also G. Priebsch, *MLR* IV, 73.—*Quatre Filles Dieu,* ed. Långfors in *Notices et Extraits des MSS* (1932).—Gui de Cambrai, *Barlam und Josaphas,* ed. C. Appel (Halle: Niemeyer, 1907); same, including an anonymous version of the legend, ed. P. Meyer-H. Zotenberg (Stuttgart, 1864); for the version by Chardri see reference above.—Geffroi de Paris, *Bible des set estaz du monde,* extracts by H. Andreson in *ZfrPh* XXII, 49-56.—Everlien, *Ueber Judas Macchabaeus von Gautier de Belleperche* (Halle: Niemeyer, 1897).—*Die beiden Bücher der Makkabäer,* ed. K. Goerlich (Halle: Brom, 1888).—E. Herzog, *Untersuchungen zu Macé de la Charité's afr. Uebersetzung des Alttestaments* (Vienna, 1900.—*Apocalypse en français au XIIIᵉ siècle,* ed. L. Delisle-P. Meyer (Paris: *SATF,* 1901).—*Poème moral,* ed. A. Bayot (Brussels: Acad. Roy. Lang. Lit. fr. de Belgique, 1929).—Chardri, *Petit Plet, etc.,* ed. J. Koch (Heilbronn: *AfrB,* 1879).—Hélinant, *Vers de la mort,* ed. F. Wulff-E. Walberg (Paris: *SATF,* 1905).—Wilham de Wadington, *Manuel des pechés,* extracts by Furnivall in *Roberd of Brunne's Handlynge Synne* (EETS, 1901-1903).—Robert Grosseteste, *Chasteau d'amour,* ed. J. Murray (Paris, 1918).—*L'Amour de Dieu,* ed. P. Meyer in *Rom* XXIX, 5-21.—Miss Hope Traver, *The Four Daughters of God* (Bryn Mawr Coll. monograph, 1907).—*Le mariage des neuf filles du diables* in *Rom* XXIX, 54-72.—Guillaume de Normandie, *Besant de Dieu,* ed. E. Martin (Halle, 1869).—*Les Treis moz,* see *ZfrPh* III, 225-31. —*Li reclus Molliens, Li romans Carité de Miserere,* ed. A.-G. van Hamel (Paris, *BEcHE,* 1885, 2 vols.).—Robert de Blois, *Sämtliche Werke,* ed. J. Ulrich (Berlin, 1889-1895, 3 vols.). *Deux poèmes de Nicolas Bozon,* ed. J. Vising, in *Göteborgs Högskolas Arsskrift,* 1919.—Philippe de Novare, *Quatre âges de l'homme,* ed. M. de Fréville (Paris: *SATF,* 1888).—*Les Lamentations de Matheolus, etc.,* ed. A.-G Van Hamel (Paris: E. Bouillon, 1892-1905).— *Comm. on Pr. of Solomon,* ed. Leroux de Lincy in *Livre des proverbes français,* II, 472 ff.—Nicole Bozon, *Proverbes de bon enseignment,* ed. A. C. Thorn in *Lunds Universitets Arsskrift,* vol. XVII.—Extracts from the *Proverbia Marie Magdalene* are in *Rom* XXXII, 40.—*Enseignments de Robert de Ho,* ed. Mary Vance Young (Paris, 1901).—Guiot de Provins, *Oeuvres,* ed. John

Orr (Manchester Univ. Press, 1915).—Renaut d'Andon, *Li Contenz dou monde*, ed. T. A. Jenkins in *Stud. M. Elliott*, I, 53-79.—*La Riote du monde*, ed. J. Ulrich in *ZfrPh* VIII, 275-289 and XXIV, 112-120.—Joinville, *Credo*, ed. Natalis de Wailly in *Jean, sire de Joinville* (Paris, 1874).—Extracts from the *Lumiere as lais* are given by Paul Meyer in *Rom* VIII, 328 and XV, 288. For this work and for the *Somme le roi* consult the paraphrase given by C.-V. Langlois in his *La Vie spirituelle d'après des écrits français à l'usage des laïcs* (Paris: Hachette, 1928).—The *Bible* of Hugh de Berzé has been edited as a Harvard doctoral dissertation. It can also be read in the Méon, *op. cit. supra.*—Robert de Gretham, *Evangiles des domnées*, extracts in *ZfrPh* I, 543; see also *Rom* XV, 298 and XXXII, 29, and M. Y. H. Aitken, *Etude sur le Miroir ou les Evangiles des Domnées* (Paris, 1922).—The newly formed Anglo-Norman Text Society is sponsoring an edition of the *Manuel des pechés* of Wilham de Wadington.

# CHAPTER XXV

# THE DIDACTIC AND SCIENTIFIC LITERATURE OF
# THE THIRTEENTH CENTURY

Charles-V. Langlois, *La connaissance de la nature et du monde* . . . (Paris: Hachette, 1927).

Johan Vising, *Anglo-Norman Language and Literature*, etc.

George Sarton, *Introduction to the History of Science*, vol. II, part 2 (Washington: Carnegie Institution, 1931).

We now turn to didactic works of a less religious nature. Huon le Roi de Cambrai wrote a *Dit de la senefiance de l'Abécés*, in which he names the letters of the alphabet in succession, telling what each one stands for, similar to the alphabet books which are given to little children to-day. There are four hundred and forty-six verses. (It is interesting to note how Huon pronounced the letters *x* and *y;* namely, as *ius,* and *ui,* respectively.) It is difficult to believe that this pious reflective Huon was also the author of two *fabliaux,* to be mentioned later.

Antoine Thomas discovered in 1919 and 1921 two anonymous adaptations of the *Consolatio philosophiae* of Boethius, both of which belong to the thirteenth century. The second is in MS 898 of the Bibliothèque de Troyes; the first is in MS lat. 2642 of the Stadtbibliothek of Vienna. Jean de Meun paraphrased a considerable portion of the *Consolatio* in his *Roman de la rose;* he made a complete adaptation in prose, dedicated to Philip the Fair, as the crowning work of his career (E. Langlois in *Rom* XLII, 331-336). Chaucer used this. There was another translation which enjoyed considerable popularity, to judge from the seventeen extant MSS, which was obviously intended to pass as the work of Jean de Meun; this was plagiarized from still another translation, of which we have two MSS, in which there is no mention of Jean de Meun. The *Consolatio* was translated five times more in the fourteenth century.

In England a courtesy book, intended for the young page and the budding knight, was known currently as *Urbain le courtois* (244 octosyllables) which varies slightly in eight extant MSS. The source on which the author drew most freely was the *Disticha Catonis,* but there is considerable originality. There were also similar treatises in Latin which used the name *Urbanus* but none of these appears to have been used as source for the Anglo-Norman text. Similar to this, but of a more restricted nature, are the *Edward* (332 verses), the *Bon enfant* (89 verses), the *Apprise* (238 verses) and the *Petit traitise de nature* (190 verses). It is difficult to date these but they are later than the *Urbain;* perhaps several are as late as the fifteenth century.

There was composed in Syriac (*ca.* 700) a book of moral and scientific content, ascribed to the great Aristotle. This was translated twice into Arabic, and one of these Arabic versions was put into Latin, in the first half of the thirteenth century, by an Italian of the Holy Land named Philip of Foligno. The translation was entitled the *Secreta secretorum.* Its popularity in the West was immense; Roger Bacon wrote a commentary on it in 1243. It was adapted very freely into French by the Anglo-Norman Peter of Peckham, in the second half of the century. There are 2,800 lines in this version. Jofroi de Watreford and Servais Copale (an Irishman?) made a French prose translation, with additions, at the close of the thirteenth century. There is another translation in MS B.N.fr. 571.

Guillaume de Normandie composed a *Bestiaire divin,* 4,200 verses in length. The date was 1211. He borrowed much from the *Liber de bestiis et aliis rebus,* supposedly by Hugh of Saint-Victor. A Norman named Gervaise wrote a *Livre des bestes.* Not a true bestiary, but of interest in this connection is the *Bestiaire d'Amour* of Richart de Fournival, an allegorical poem written first in prose. This Richart (*ca.* 1201-1260) was also a lyric poet and an expert on the theory of love. He was a son of Rogier de Fournival, physician of Philip Augustus, and of Elisabeth de la Pierre. Before 1240 Richart was a canon at Amiens, and later he was chancellor; he was also a surgeon. He died on March 1, 1260. This Richart had a splendid library and was a pioneer expert in library science with his *Biblionomia,* in which he proposed a cataloguing system. There are numerous minor scientific treatises composed by Anglo-Normans (for which consult the Vising reference). There are several prose treatises on diseases of hunting birds; there is an *Art de venerie* by Guillaume Twich, composed around 1300. Ralph or Rauf de Lenham (Kent) was the author of a metrical calendar (1,200 verses) for the year 1256. Quite numerous are minor Anglo-Norman writings on medicine and surgery, diseases of women, prescriptions, and formulas for exorcism. Let us mention also the surgical treatise of Roger of Parma in two prose translations (*Rom* XXXII, 91, 101), and the prose *Euperiston.* The *Régime du corps* of Aldobrandino of Siena was put together in 1256; it is an adaptation of extracts from the great medical works of Galen, Avicenna, Johannitius, and Hippocrates, combined with some personal experience by the author. Note that this is another Italian writing in French.

Next we seek for vernacular French herbals in the thirteenth century. There are a number of *materiae medicae* which have not received the attention they deserve. Paul Meyer published a list of them in *Bull SATF* (1906), 38 ff., and later he printed one of considerable interest in *Rom* XXXVII, 358-77. Quite recently (*Mél. A. Jeanroy,* 663-671) Leo Wiese has issued another from an Escurial MS (I. iii. 7). A large proportion of the herbs which these formularies discuss belong to the mint and mustard families. Typical of them all are *vetoine* (Stachys officinalis), *bugle* (creeping bugleweed), *matfelun* (brown knapweed), *senigle* (wood sanicle), *milfoille* (yarrow), *la mere des herbes* (mugwort), *aloine* (absinth), *celidonie* (great celandine), *cincfoille* (Potentilla reptans), *citerach* (scale fern), *fenoil* (fennel), *la petite consoude* (English daisy), *erbe alponin* or *alfenim* (sugar cane), *erbe salward* (saltwort or glasswort), *centaurea* (Blessed thistle), and such well-known herbs as plantain, peony, pimpernel, honesty, dittany, and mandrake (mandragora officinalis). This last should not be confused with the may apple, common in America.

There is a *Second Anglo-Norman prose lapidary* (for the first see treatment of twelfth-century) which enjoyed a great vogue. It circulated freely on the continent and was the source for the continental *Lapidaire chrétien*. An Englishman who had travelled on the continent wrote a stonebook now preserved in Cambridge MS O. There are several fragmentary verse and prose works of similar nature from the Anglo-Norman writers. There are two prose lapidaries of engraved gems in which the *intaglio* figures found on ancient cut stones are given magic significance.

In the *Chronicle* of Lambert d'Ardres the author mentions a French adaptation of the *De naturis rerum* of Simon de Boulogne. This has been lost. We possess a *Mappemonde* by Pierre de Beauvais composed around 1217 and dedicated to Philippe de Dreux. This Pierre had previously compiled a *Bestiaire* dedicated to the same prince. The sources for the *Mappemonde* were Solinus and the twelfth-century *Imago mundi* long ascribed to Honorius d'Autun. The *Imago mundi* soon found a more literal French adapter. It was done into 6,600 octosyllables, before 1246, by some cleric from Lorraine. It is possible to recognize three varying versions of this huge translation. Were they all by the same poet? One is dedicated to Bishop Jacques de Metz. The poet is called Gossouin in some MSS; elsewhere he is Gautier de Metz, and sometimes Omont! The adaptation is divided into three main subject headings; God and Man, the Earth, and the Heavens. Perot de Garbelei wrote an Anglo-Norman *Divisiones Mundi* in the first quarter of the thirteenth century (A. Bell in *PhilQ* X, 36-46).

Still another work of encyclopedic content was compiled in French by Brunetto Latini, a Florentine Guelph in exile in France between 1261 and 1268. This is the *Livre dou Tresor* (1262-1266), a detailed work which Brunetto had promised in his smaller but similar Italian poem the *Tesoretto*. There are three divisions to the *Livre dou Tresor*: Cosmography, Ethics, and Political Theory. Brunetto used French in preference to Italian "por ce que la parleure est plus delitable et plus commune a toutes gens." The dedication was to an anonymous protector. The author made a slightly revised version immediately after returning to Italy. An Italian translation was made almost immediately by Bono Giamboni.

*Le Livre de Sidrac* is a scientific work in prose dating from the last quarter of the thirteenth century, and, if we may believe Charles Langlois, by an anonymous cleric in the Holy Land. A prologue, which Langlois takes to be false, states that the author was one Jean Pierre de Lyons and that it was written in 1243. G. L. Hamilton (*RRev* III, 317 ff.) has investigated the sources and decided upon an *Elucidarium* (Migne, *P. L.*, CLXXII, IIII) and the works of Guillaume de Conches; another source was the *Introductorium in astronomiam* of Albumazar (*MPhil* IX, 342 ff). The name *Sidrac* is the same as Shadrach in Daniel I:7. The prologue tells us that his book is a report of the conversations of King Boctus of Bactriana and the sage Sidrach, grandson of Japheth, and that the book had many wanderings before being translated from Greek into Latin at Toledo in 1243. The questions which Boctus asks Sidrach comprise many subjects, including gynecology, geography, theology, medicine, dietetics, physical geography, zoölogy, ethics, lapidology, herbology, and astronomy. This *Livre de Sidrac* was expanded from time to time. The version found in B.N.fr. 1160 is perhaps the earliest and has some six hundred odd questions with answers; this number was later increased to 1,209; MS B.N.fr. 24395 appears to offer the most expanded version. We do not know who made these additions. There are also two MSS which offer an abridged selection.

The *Placidés et Timéo*, or *Livres des segrez aus philosophes*, was composed during the reign of Philip the Fair, prior to 1303, and survives in two versions. In the preface to one of these a Jehan Bonnet, doctor of theology, is named as author. The author shows very little acquaintance with theology; his chief sources were the writings of Guillaume de Conches, the *Secreta secretorum*, the *Imago mundi*, and the French *Image du monde*. The plan of his work is very similar to that of the *Sidrac*: Placidés asks his master, Timéo, many questions which the latter does not hesitate to solve. This medieval work of science was popular till about 1535. Its earlier form is found in B.N.fr. 212, if we agree with Charles Langlois. The last-named authority does not see much value in the work, except that it is superior to the *Sidrac*. Personally, I find in it a scientific spirit which is decidedly in advance over that which preceded, if we except the Latin writings of Albert the Great and Roger Bacon. Placidés, at least, had his doubts.

Mathematics is represented by two algorisms or treatises on elementary calculation. The earliest of these has 512 octosyllables and was composed early in the century from Latin sources, possibly from the *Algorismus* by John of Hollywood and from the so-called Salem *Algorismus*. It contains some novel rules for learning the multiplication table between 5-times-5 and 10-times-10. There is another algorism, in Picard dialect, from the second half of the century (*ca.* 1275) which is adapted from the *Carmen de algorismo* of Alexander of Villedieu.

An unknown astrologer of Baudouin II of Courtenay composed an *Introductoire d'astronomie* (*ca.* 1270) in the Francian dialect. It is preceded by an astrological poem of 394 lines in the same MS: B.N.fr. 1353. The astronomical doctrine there given is very obsolete, showing no dependence upon Ptolemy; apparently the sources were Macrobius, Chalcidius, and Martianus Capella.

Of legal works in the vernacular there were splendid examples in the *Coutumes du Beauvoisis* of Philippe de Rémi, sire de Beaumanoir, the *Livre de forme de plait* of Philippe de Novare, the *Coutume d'Amiens*, the *Livre des assises de Jerusalem* of Jean d'Ibelin, and the two Norman *coutumiers*: the *Tres ancien coutumier de Normandie* and the *Grand coutumier de Normandie*. These Norman compilations were translations from earlier Latin versions. The *Grand Coutumier* has had much influence and popularity. A considerable part of the Latin original was completed between 1254 and 1258. It was used by the Parlement of Paris in the winter of 1258 on the occasion of an inquest after the decease of certain persons suspected of usury. The French prose must date from after the death of Saint Louis in 1270. A verse translation also occurs. This was in octosyllables by a Guillaume Chapu at the close of the thirteenth or the beginning of the fourteenth century. Among other works of Norman jurisprudence let us mention the *Assises de Normandie* translated from a Latin original of 1237, or shortly after. The compiler has reviewed the practice resulting from judicial decisions of royal bailiffs at Caen, Bayeux, Falaise, Exmes, and Avranches—also from certain decisions rendered by the Court of Exchequer.[1]

The *Etablissements de Saint-Louis,* compiled before 1273, contain only nine chapters of ordinances by King Louis; the remainder of the two books deal with customs in Anjou, Maine, and Orléanais, influenced by

[1] Not in French, but of great importance for the study of medieval custom law are the *Assises de Romanie*, ed. Recoura (Paris, 1930).

a superficial knowledge of Justinian's *Corpus juris*. They were doubt-less put together in the schools at Orleans. The *Livre de justice et de plaid* (342 clauses) was also a work of the Orleans' jurists, being a mixture of Roman law with the *coutumes*. Pierre de Fontaines, bailiff of Vermandois, made a very poor compilation from the *Digest* and *Institutes* of Justinian in his *Conseil a un ami*. Richart Annebaut versified portions of the *Institutes* for a young Gascon noble, that he might be able to understand the Latin exposition more easily.

Among Anglo-Norman legal collections we mention the extract of laws commonly attributed to a jurist named Britton, but which was in reality adapted from the *De legibus* of Henry de Bracton or Bratton (d. 1268). *La Court de Baron* is a poem of some 500 verses, giving the procedure in court. The Coronation Act of William the First of England was translated into Anglo-Norman at the beginning of the thirteenth century.

## EDITIONS

Huon le Roi de Cambrai, *Oeuvres*, ed. A. Långfors (2nd ed.; *Cfmâ*, 1915), vol. I.—"Un fragment . . . de la Consolation de Boèce par Jean de Meun," ed. V. L. Dedeck-Héry, *RRev* XXVII, 110-24.—Two of the versions of *Urbain le courtois*, as well as the other four courtesy poems, are edited by H. Rosamond Parsons in *PMLA* XLIV, 383-455. Consult also P. Meyer in *Rom* XXXII, 68-73, and Stengel in *ZfrSL* XIV, 151.—*Three Prose Versions of the Secretum Secretorum*, ed. R. Steele (*EETS* LXXIV). Peter of Peckham, *Secreta Secretorum*, a new edition, is being prepared for the Anglo-Norman Text Society.—Guillaume de Normandie, *Bestiaire*, ed. R. Reinsch (Leipzig, 1890).—Richard de Fournival, *Bestiaire d'amour*, ed. Hippeau (Paris, 1860).—W. Twich, *Art de venerie*, extracts in *Rom* XIII, 505 and XXXVI, 531.—*Euperiston*, extracts by Paul Meyer in *Documents, manuscrits*, etc., p. 111.—Aldebrand de Florence, *Régime du corps*, ed. Landouzy-Pépin (Paris, 1911).—*The Cambridge Anglo-Norman Texts*, ed. O. H. Prior and others (Cambridge Univ. Press, 1924). This contains Perot de Garbelei's *Divisiones mundi*, a poem on the Day of Judgment and an Assumption.—Brunetto Latini, *Li Livres dou tresor*, ed. P. Chabaille (Paris: *CdiHF*, 1863).—*L'image du monde de maître Gossouin Rédaction en prose*, ed. O. H. Prior (Lausanne, 1913).—The *Sidrach* and the *Placidés et Timéo* can be best consulted in analyses by Charles Langlois, in his *Connaissance de la Nature etc.*; an edition of the *Sidrac* was printed by Galiot du Pré (Paris, 1531).—"A thirteenth century algorism in French verse," ed. E. G. R. Waters in *Isis* XI, 45-84; XIII, 160.—"Le plus ancien traité d'algorisme," ed. V. Mortet in *Bibliotheca mathematica*, IX, 55-64.—The astronomical works mentioned are unpublished.—Philippe de Beaumanoir, *Coutumes de Beauvaisis*, ed. A. Salmon (Paris, 1899-1900, 2 vols.).—P. de Novare, *Assises de Jerusalem*, ed. A. A. Beugnot (Paris, 1841-1843, 2 vols.). This edition contains also the *Livre de forme de*

*lait.—Nouveau coutumier général*, ed. Richebourg (1724).—Richart Anne-
*aut, Institutions de Justinien* awaits a modern editor.—Guillaume Chapu,
*e Coutumier Normant*, ed. Houard in *Dict. analytique du droit normand*
Rouen, 1782), IV, supplement, 49 ff.—*The Court Baron*, ed. F. W. Maitland
nd W. P. Baildon (Selden Society, 1891).—*Establissements de Saint-Louis*, ed.
*aul Viollet (Paris: ShF, 1881-1886, 4 vols.).—Le conseil de Pierre de Fon-
aines*, ed. A. I. Marnier (Paris, 1846).—*Li livres de jostice et de plet*, ed. P.
N. Rapetti (Paris, 1850).—Britton, *English Laws*, ed. F. M. Nichols (Oxford,
865).—*L'Antidotaire Nicolas*, ed. Dorveaux (Paris, 1896).—Dr. Raphael
evy is contemplating an edition of Ibn Ezra's *Le Commencement de
Sapience.*

# CHAPTER XXVI

## THE THIRTEENTH CENTURY DRAMA

See the references given for Chapter V.

Joseph Bédier, "Les commencements du théâtre comique en France," *Revue des Deux Mondes,* XCIX (1890), 865.

E. Faral, *Les mimes français du XIIIe siècle* (Paris, 1913).

Joachim Rolland, *Le théâtre comique en France avant le XVe siècle* (Paris 1926).

Joachim Rolland, *Origines latines du théâtre comique en France* (Paris, 1927)

G. Cohen, *Le théâtre en France au moyen âge,* vol. II, *Le théâtre profane* (Paris: Rieder, 1931).

Petit de Julleville, *Répertoire du théâtre comique au moyen âge* (Paris, 1887)

As representative of the liturgical drama in this century we have a fragment of three hundred and seventy-one verses in the *Resurrection of the Savior.* This *jeu* when complete may have comprised three or four thousand lines. Intercalated into the dialogue were short narrative pieces rhymed rubrics, which could have been added by a later hand. There are eighty-four such rubric verses in the existing fragment. Most important is the prologue which describes accurately the stage setting. The *décor simultané* appears to have shown, from left to right: Heaven, the Crucifix, the Tomb, a jail, Galilee, Emmaus, and Hell. Possibly Galilee and Emmaus were not represented on the *décor* but merely indicated in the center of the platform. The characters were all on the stage at the same time. They were arranged from left to right: Pilate and his men Caiphas with the Jews, Joseph of Arimathea, Nicodemus with his friends, the disciples of Christ, and the Three Marys. Joseph speaks first, asking Pilate with much flattery for the body of Christ. It is given him, after Pilate has sent knights to ascertain whether Christ is dead. These knights persuade Longinus, a blind man sitting by the wayside, to pierce the Savior with a lance. Longinus recovers his sight but is thrust into jail. On the advice of Caiphas, Pilate sends the knights to guard the tomb of Christ. It is here the fragment breaks off. This drama belonged to the first years of the thirteenth century; it is evident that the scriptural account was not followed closely.

At the beginning of the thirteenth century, or at the very close of the twelfth, there was composed a narrative poem on the Passion which is known as the *Passion des jongleurs;* but no one dramatized the Passion theme, the most pathetic of all dramas, till the close of the thirteenth entury. Perhaps there was a suggestion of impiety in a representation which would show the sufferings of the Lord. The cleric who finally undertook the dramatization made use of the Bible, certain *Complaintes de Marie,* and above all, of this early *Passion des jongleurs.* His work has been lost but we know of its existence from two *Passions* of the early fourteenth century which were based upon it. They are: the *Passion* preserved in the Vatican MS Palatinus Latinus 1969 (the *Passion du Palatinus*) and a fragment called the *Passion d'Autun.* The Passion subject became immensely popular in the fourteenth century. Various *confréries* who played this drama yearly at the Easter season were in existence after 1371.

Of miracle plays we had one specimen in the twelfth century, the *Jeu de Saint-Nicolas* of Jean Bodel. In the thirteenth century there was the *Miracle de Théophile,* a miracle of the Virgin, composed in or near 1265 by the jongleur Rutebeuf. This subject had been previously treated in non-dramatic verse by Adgar, Gautier de Coincy, and others, in their miracle collections. The legend, originally in Greek, told how Theophilus (d. 538), the administrator of a church in Cilicia, refused a bishopric and was dispossessed by the cleric who did accept the charge. In disgrace, Theophilus formed a compact with the devil. He was restored to his office; after seven years he repented and was saved by the intercession of the Virgin. This Greek legend was translated into Latin by Paul the Deacon of Naples in the ninth century, which translation forms the basis of all Occidental versions. In his treatment of this theme, Rutebeuf does not show much dramatic invention and his characters are superficial. There are 663 lines of varied meter. This legend had a part in the ultimate founding of the Faust story.

We have exhausted the subject of serious drama for the thirteenth century; we now turn to the secular farce. There was a comic element in the religious *jeux* of the twelfth century; *viz.,* the dialogue between Eve and Satan in the *Jeu d'Adam,* the tavern scenes in the *Jeu de Saint-Nicolas,* etc., and Petit de Julleville saw in these the origins of the thirteenth-century farce. Joseph Bédier, whose investigations have at one time or another embraced every phase of early French literature, suggested in 1890 that the profane jongleurs developed the farce among themselves, beginning with the comic monologue, then creating the comic dialogue, and at length passing to scenes with three or more characters. Until very recently I was inclined to accept this view without reservations, but the more general suggestions expressed lately by Gustave Cohen are very persuasive. He sees in the Old French comic drama, which had no independent existence until the early thirteenth century, a gradual evolution both from the humorous scenes of the preceding religious *jeux* and from profane folk traditions carried through the ages by the jongleurs, such as joyous celebrations at the summer solstice (June 24), representations of the totem, worship of the phallus. To these two sources Gustave Cohen adds his conviction that the comedies of Plautus, as well as Latin imitations of these made in the twelfth century, were sometimes played in character and were not regarded only as comic poems. (Chief among these would be the twelfth-century *Babio* whose influence Cohen thinks to have been considerable.) In sum, Cohen believes the medieval French comic theatre to have had a three-fold source: the religious drama, folk myths preserved by the profane jongleur, and the comedies of Plautus. (Terence was not well known at this time.) I agree with the first two sources, but in view of Faral's opposition (for which see our chapter on the *fabliaux*) must offer some reservation on the third. The suggestion made by J. F. Le Clerc, many years ago, (*HLF*, XXIII) that the medieval comedy was a mere drama-tization of the *fabliaux*, has long since been discarded. Consult also Salverda de Grave in *Neoph* XVII 205-10.

A view similar to that of Bédier is held by Grace Frank, only she em-phasizes that the first author of a secular comedy in the thirteenth cen-tury was simply a cleric with a good story to tell. He turned almost instinctively to the best way of telling it—a narrative poem *par per-sonnages*. One can easily see the force of this argument; but in the background of that cleric there might well have been present the ele-ments suggested by Cohen and others. Mrs. Frank's discussion is published in the *MLR* XXXI, 377-84.

Comedy, in its origins, is apt to be satirical. The Old Comedy of ancient Athens grew out of a combination of satire and religious celebra-tion. We should expect satire to flourish best in the bourgeois cen-ters, in flourishing towns, where the presence of a newly rich class, and the existence of hilarious mob spirit, is most conducive to such a develop-ment. This is precisely the case with medieval French Comedy which grew and flourished best at Arras and Tournai, the centers of the weav-ing industry in northeastern France. The chief exception is furnished by the Champenois poet Rutebeuf who was established at Paris; but it is true also that Paris offered many of the conditions found at Arras.

Rutebeuf has left us a comic harangue or monologue, the *Dit de l'herberie*, which, like most ancient *satyra*, is a mixture of verse and prose. It is an imitation of a quack medicine vendor and was written around 1260. The contents do not seem obsolete to us who are familiar with modern nostrums and their promises to cure anything from tooth-ache to tuberculosis.

The *Courtois d'Arras,* by an anonymous poet, was composed prior to 1228. It is a free dramatization, in characteristic medieval style, of the story of the prodigal son (Luke XV). There are eight characters but it is probable that these were all played by a single jongleur. The parts are: Courtois the Prodigal, his father, his brother, the tavern host, a boy, the women Pourette and Manchevaire, and a bourgeois who employs the Prodigal to tend his pigs. There are six hundred and sixty-four verses, of which only six are narrative (not included in the dialogue). The verses are in octosyllabic rhymed couplets. *Le Garçon et l'aveugle* is a farce which was doubtless played by a jongleur and his boy. It was composed around 1266. It is the first example of that type of comedy made so popular by the sixteenth-century *Lazarillo de Tormes,* where we meet a blind man and his rascally boy. There are two hundred and sixty-five lines in octosyllable.

On a higher plane are two farces by Adam le Bossu, or Adam de le Halle. He was born towards the middle of the century, of a good bourgeois family of Arras. He is mentioned for the first time in 1272, in a *Congé* of the poet Baude Fastoul. Adam left school in order to marry a young girl named Marie. After several years of married life he wished to leave Arras to continue his studies in Paris. This was in 1275 or 1276. He planned to leave his wife with his father for three or four years. We do not know whether these plans for study were successful. After 1282 he went with the Count of Artois, as poet and musician, to the south of Italy. This was the expedition in aid of Charles of Anjou. Adam died in Italy between 1285 and 1289, probably in 1288. He left two dramas: the *Jeu de la feuillée* and the *Jeu de Robin et de Marion,* as well as a *Congé,* or leave-taking poem, a fragment of *a chanson de geste* on the "Roi de Sezile," and numerous pieces of lyric verse. The *Jeu de la feuillée* and the *Congé* were composed on the occasion of his leaving Arras in 1275 and the *Jeu de Robin et de Marion* was composed in Italy on the suggestion of the Count of Artois.

The *Jeu de la feuillée* was acted by Adam himself and by a group of friends, perhaps under the trees, as the title would suggest. The subject is Adam's coming departure. The male characters were actual friends of Adam who carried their real names and were perhaps played by the individuals themselves. It is probable that the feminine roles, those of Dame Douche, an easy lady, and of the three fairies were enacted by men. Adam appears on the stage and announces his departure. His friends appear and there is much satire on each of them, as well as on women, in the course of the conversation. Rikier is a rake; maistre Henri, Adam's father, is a miser. A crazy man, his father, and a potter pass by. The fairies arrive and bestow three gifts apiece upon Rikier and Adam who have helped prepare for them. Rikier's gifts are calculated to make him more of a gallant than ever. The fairy Maglore will give nothing at first; then she wishes that Rikier may become baldheaded and that Adam in the arms of his wife shall forget his journey to Paris. The fairies depart. There is a dispute between a monk and the tavernkeeper over a piece of trickery played upon the monk. The crazy man and his parent furnish additional comedy. This little drama was very much after the spirit of Aristophanes and the Old Greek Comedy. There are 1,099 octosyllabic verses.

The *Jeu de Robin et de Marion* was a dramatized *pastourelle*, intended for a more elevated audience than the bourgeoisie who witnessed the other play. The knight approaches Marion on two occasions and seeks her favor, but she is true to Robin. The knight takes out his ill-humor by beating Robin whom he meets by chance. Robin forgets his blows at the sight of Marion and the play ends in dancing and singing by Robin, Marion, and their friends. There are 780 octosyllables. This *jeu* was played at Arras shortly after the death of Adam and it was there prefaced with a mediocre prologue, the *Jeu du pèlerin*. The pilgrim tells how he has wandered over southern Italy and heard everywhere the praise of Adam. Along with the Count of Artois he had visited Adam's tomb the previous year. He came to Arras because he heard that on that day they were reciting Adam's verses. The authorship of this prologue is unknown, but we are thankful for the information on Adam which it gives.

We close this survey of the thirteenth-century theatre with a surprise. Most readers think of the charming *Aucassin and Nicolette* as a delightful romance, as a *fabliau* or *conte;* but good authorities (Mario Roques, Aschner, Moland) are agreed that this *chantefable* was a dramatic recitation. (Gaston Paris considered the *Aucassin* as the only surviving specimen of a group of *chantefables,* a theory no longer held.) Grace Frank (*MLN* XLVII, 14-16) thinks that the prose portions were recited by one jongleur while the lyrics were sung by another. She explains this by the cues, *Or dient et content et fabloient* and *Or se cante.* The form is odd: alternating verse and prose sections, forty-one sections in all. The verse scheme is the seven-syllable line in assonance—a very unusual meter—each lyric ending in a four-syllable feminine line not in the assonance. The purpose of the author, who was unquestionably a professional familiar with the best literature of his time, was partly satire. Anyone who is familiar with the epic and romance literature of the twelfth and early thirteenth centuries will recognize that this jongleur was poking fun, slily and sometimes broadly, at the stock themes of his more serious predecessors. It is unlikely that he had any acquaintance with Byzantine material;[1] nor was he basing his story directly on the Old French *Floire et Blancheflor*. His sources were many, including the works of Chrétien de Troyes. In spite of the southern place-names, Beaucaire, Valence, Carthage, the author shows no personal acquaintance with such regions. His dialect is that of Picardy. The *conte* of *Piramus et Tisbé* and the epic *Boeve de Haumtone* were certainly known to him. Gustave Cohen is opposed to the suggestion that the *Aucassin et Nicolette* is in dramatic form.

The piece is beautifully constructed and well unified throughout. Aucassin is the son of the lord of Beaucaire, and Nicolette, a Saracen slave, is the adopted daughter of a petty vassal of Beaucaire. The parents of Aucassin will not permit a marriage between the two. Nicolette is forced to flee, and Aucassin rejoins her. They have several adventures: among them a visit to the kingdom of Torelore where the women fight and the men go to bed with child. (Is this reminiscent of the primitive custom of the *couvade?*) The women in their fighting use only rotten apples and cheeses. Aucassin is disgusted and makes the king promise to reform his practices. The two lovers are separated again. Nicolette is carried to Carthage where she discovers she is the daughter of the emir. She flees and disguises herself as a jongleur to find Aucassin. They meet at Beaucaire and when she learns that he still loves her she appears in her true character; they live happily ever after. The date of composition must be early in the thirteenth century, perhaps quite early. As Professor Reinhard has indicated, the mixture of prose and verse was not a unique type. The same form is present in the *De Consolatione philosophiae* of Boethius, and in other well-known models (*Spec* I, 157-169).

## EDITIONS

*La Résurrection du Sauveur* is reproduced in the Foerster-Koschwitz *Uebungsbuch*, pp. 214-223; also, in the *Théâtre français au moyen âge*, of L. J. N. Monmerqué and Fr. Michel (Paris, 1870), pp. 10-20, and most recently by Miss Jean Gray Wright (Paris: *Cfmâ*, 1931). A new MS of this play which contains more lines than the hitherto unique Paris MS has been discovered at Canterbury (Engl.) by John M. Manly. Publication of this discovery should appear shortly.—*Passion du Palatinus*, ed. Grace Frank (Paris: *Cfmâ*, 1922).—Rutebeuf, *Théophile*, ed. Grace Frank (Paris: *Cfmâ*, 1925).— The Latin comedies of the twelfth century have been reëdited by Gustave

---

[1] A. Nykl and others believe that the general construction was suggested by an Arabic model from Spain. Nykl has edited what he considers such a model, an edition which should appear shortly. Scholars who believe this theory propose *Alcasim* as the base for the name Aucassin.

Cohen and a group of his students (*La Comédie latine en France au XII^e siècle*, Paris: Aux Belles Lettres, 1931).—Rutebeuf, *Oeuvres*, ed. Adolf Kressner (Wolfenbüttel, 1885).—*Courtois d'Arras*, ed. E. Faral (2nd ed.; Paris: *Cfmâ*, 1922).—*Le Garçon et l'aveugle*, ed. M. Roques (2nd ed.; Paris: *Cfmâ*, 1921).—Adam le Bossu, *Jeu de la feuillée*, ed. E. Langlois (2nd ed.; Paris: *Cfmâ*, 1923).—*Jeu de Robin et Marion* [including the anonymous *Jeu du pèlerin*], ed. E. Langlois (Paris: *Cfmâ*, 1924).—*Aucassin et Nicolette*, ed. Mario Roques (2nd ed.; Paris: *Cfmâ*, 1929); also ed. Suchier (10th ed.; Paderborn, 1932); ed. R. W. Linker (Chapel Hill, 1937).—Several of the dramatic monologues, including the *Dit de l'herberie* of Rutebeuf, are published by E. Faral in his *Les mimes français* (Paris: *BEcHE*, 1910).

# CHAPTER XXVII

## CHRONICLE, HISTORY, AND TRAVEL

Auguste Molinier, *Les sources de l'histoire de France*, vol. I, p. cxxi.
Paul Meyer in *Annuaire-bulletin de la Société de l'Histoire de France* (1890).
Gaston Paris in *Histoire littéraire de la France*, XXXII, 291-459.
Colonel Sir Henry Yule, *Travels of Marco Polo* (London: John Murray, 1903 3 vols.).

There are no Crusade epics during the thirteenth century. The degenerate *Baudouin de Sebourc* and *Bastart de Bouillon*, the last of this genre, are classified as compositions of the fourteenth century. Rhymed chronicles such as were popular among the Normans and Anglo-Normans of the twelfth century still exist, and chief among them is the *Chronique rimée* of Philippe Mouskés of Tournai. It contains more than thirty-one thousand verses and narrates events from the fall of Troy to the France of 1241. Philippe sought to document his work, making use of the *Abreviatio gestorum*, or Latin chronicles of Saint-Denis, and of the works of Einhardt, the Astronomer, Guillaume de Jumièges, and Ordericus Vitalis, as well as of the pseudo-Turpin. The information concerning the Carolingian period is very curious: thousands of lines are devoted to Charlemagne which give material that is generally false. For the later period (1180-1241) the chronicle is more accurate; it has genuine historical value for the first forty years of the thirteenth century. Of little literary value is the *Chronique dite de Saint-Magloire*, composed by a bourgeois of Paris. It is concerned with the period between 1214 and 1304, becoming more accurate from 1270 on. A rhymed chronicle of some worth is the *Branche des royaux lignages* by Guillaume Guiard of Orleans. It is a history of the kings descended from Louis VIII, and thousands of lines are devoted to Saint Louis and to Philip III. The author, a soldier, gives original information from the accession of Philip IV on.

But the thirteenth century had something better to offer than rhymed chronicles, which in content as well as form were related to the *chansons de geste*. History, in its true sense of a reflective study of chronicled events, first appeared in French prose with the beginning of this century. A spirit of realism was under way.

Foremost among such prose historians was Geoffroi de Villehardouin, marshal of Champagne (b. 1150?—d. 1213?). He took part in the

Fourth Crusade (1202) and was made marshal of Romania after 1204. He never returned to France. His celebrated *Conquête de Constantinople* was dictated after 1207 in a sober, composed style. The information is excellent but it must be remembered that Villehardouin was not unprejudiced. He was striving in this history of the Fourth Crusade to justify the capture of Constantinople. Being a noble of high degree, his history represents the viewpoint of the leaders. The copyists later added to his work a continuation by Henri de Valenciennes. The work of Henri may have been originally in verse; here it is done over into prose.

The Fourth Crusade as it appeared to the rank and file of small knights is to be found in the *Estoire de chiaus qui conquisent Constantinople* of a Picard, Robert de Clari (1170?—1216). He returned to France in 1205, but he carried on his history as far as 1216. Although his historical pictures are often incomplete and he could not always resist the temptation to romance, Robert de Clari was a man of considerable talent and personality. He has been falsely accused of ignorance. He was conscious of the fact that he was writing a history and not a simple personal narrative. He omits all references to himself. He is interesting as a traveller, a historian, and a chronicler. For a penetrating study on Robert de Clari consult Albert Pauphilet in *Rom* LVI, 289-311.

The *Estoire des rois d'Angleterre et de Normandie* is a vivacious and amusing account of the wars between England and France at the beginning of the century. It was compiled by an anonymous writer of Béthune, in Picardy. The writer, doubtless a professional, had an excellent command of language. The *Estoire des rois de France* is a translation of the *Historia regum Francorum* (1185-1204) of the monks of Saint-Denis. This translation was also made at Béthune. Another French prose version of the same was made by a minstrel of Alfonse de Poitiers, in 1260; he continued the account as far as 1228.

Towards 1226 an anonymous cleric of Norman origin composed a *Life of Guillaume le Maréchal* for Count William of Pembroke, who was Guillaume le Maréchal's son. This was beautifully done and has great historical value. Among the historical writings of Anglo-Norman clerics we may mention the anonymous *Rei Dermot* or *Conqueste d'Irlande* (3,459 verses with beginning and end missing) and the *Livere de reis de Britannie et le livere de reis de Engletere* (in prose) of Peter of Ickham (d. 1289), a monk of Christchurch, Canterbury. There was a continuation to Wace's *Brut* of some 1,200 verses, made in the middle of the century by an unknown Anglo-Norman.

The *Récits d'un ménestrel de Reims* (*ca.* 1260) are owed to an itinerant minstrel, not to a historian. They are nothing more than a collection of anecdotes concerning France, England, and the Holy Land since the early twelfth century. They show just what knowledge of history of events, transpiring a hundred-odd years before, remained in the mind of the bourgeoisie. Louis VI is almost wholly forgotten. He is referred to as Raoul, father of Louis VII. On the other hand the minstrel is more accurate for the thirty-odd years preceding. These *récits* contain some valuable legends: the finding of Richard the Lion-hearted in an Austrian prison by the minstrel Blondel, for example. This tale may even be original with our minstrel of Reims, who could not have been averse to exalting the profession of the jongleur. His sources are virtually unknown. They must have been largely oral legends, though it is possible he utilized the anonymous chronicle of Béthune (see above).

Philippe de Novare (1195?-1265?) was an Italian who pursued his career in Cyprus. He was present at the siege of Damietta in 1218. He was an intimate of the Ibelins of Beirut. He wrote many things, among them the *Des quatre tenz d'aage d'ome* and the *Livre de forme de plait;* he collected his other works into a *recueil* and prefixed to them an autobiography. This collective MS has been lost. What we are concerned with here are his *Mémoires,* dealing with the period 1223-1243. They were a portion of his autobiography and his *Estoire de la guerre entre l'empereur Federic et Messire Jehan de Ybelin.* It is to be noted that this Philippe, an Italian, wrote always in French. Alfred Foulet (*Rom* LVI, 419-427) says that these *Mémoires* were a *plaidoyer* for the Ibelins.

Second only to the historical narrative of Villehardouin is the *Livre des saintes paroles et des bonnes actions de Saint Louis* of Jehan de Joinville (1224-1317), seneschal of Champagne and intimate friend of Louis IX. This intimacy dated from the Seventh Crusade (1248-1254). Joinville refused to accompany his royal master on the eighth and final expedition (1268-1270). He was one of the chief witnesses called for Louis's canonization in 1282. He began his history in 1304 at the behest of Jeanne de Navarre, Queen of France, but she died the following year. He completed the work in 1307 and dedicated it to the Queen's son, the future Louis X.

The best part of these memoirs of Joinville, for that is what they are, is the narrative of the Seventh Crusade, probably completed shortly after the events described and incorporated into the whole in 1304-7. Of the rest Langlois has remarked "plutôt une causerie qu'un livre." The latter part of the history was composed when the author was so old that he had to refresh his mind from secondary sources. Among these sources were the *Chronicle* of Primatus, and the *Gesta Ludovici noni* of Guillaume de Nangis. The portion dealing with the period 1248-1254 comprises 557 paragraphs and the account of the remaining sixteen years (to the death of King Louis in 1270) only 103. In the matter dealing with the Seventh Crusade, Joinville speaks frequently of himself. The other preserved writings of Joinville are a *Credo* (1251), a letter to Louis X (1315), and an epitaph for Geoffroi III of Joinville (1311). A *chanson* composed at Acre, between June 12 and June 19, 1250, was assigned to Joinville by Gaston Paris, but the attribution has never been proved. (Consult, however, A. Foulet in *MLN* XLIX, 464-8.).

While speaking of histories and prose memoirs we must not neglect the letters. The oldest preserved letter in the French language is that of Pons d'Aubon, Prior of the Temple, to Saint Louis concerning the progress of the Tartar invasion. It can be dated around 1238. There are ten others in continental French surviving from the thirteenth century. They are briefly (see Alfred Foulet, *Lettres françaises du XIIIe siècle*, Paris: *Cfmâ*, 1924):

1. Alphonse de Poitiers to Gérard Calains; January 5, 1242;
2-5. Four letters of Marie de Brienne, Empress of Constantinople, to Blanche of Castille; January-February 1249;
6. Simon de Montfort (?) to Henry III of England; April 3, 1249(?);
7. Jean Sarrasin, Chamberlain of Saint Louis, to Nicolas Arrode, Parisian, concerning the taking of Damietta, June 23, 1249;
8. Philippe, Treasurer of Saint-Hilaire of Poitiers, to Alphonse de Poitiers, April 20, 1250;
9. Jean, Count of Burgundy and Lord of Salins, to the Lord of Choiseul, March, 1260;
10. Blanche of Champagne, Duchess of Brittany, to Henry III of England, around 1260.

There are some Anglo-Norman letters in Oxford MS. All Souls, 182, of which I do not know the precise nature.

To return once more to chronicle and history proper: the first twenty-two books of the *Historia Hierosolymitana* of William of Tyre (1169-1184) were translated at the beginning of the thirteenth century, possibly by a Hugh Plagon, under the title of *Le Livre du conquest*, or *Le Livre d'Eracles* (from the name of the Byzantine emperor, Heraclius). This was continued to include 1229, with the title *Estoires d'oultremer et de la naissance de Sollehadin*, by Ernoul, possibly a servitor of Bailan d'Ibelin. The continuation was shortened and reworked by Bernard, Treasurer of the Abbey of Corbie. It, too, was continued to 1261 (the Rothelin continuation) and, independently of this, to 1275 (the Noailles continuation). The Rothelin continuation, named from a cleric of the eighteenth century who possessed one of its MSS, was perhaps the work of a monk of the Abbey of Saint-Médard at Soissons. It has preserved to us the Jean Sarrasin letter (number 7 above).

Since the time of Abbot Suger (1081-1151) the monks of the Abbey of Saint-Denis had considered themselves official chroniclers of France. The *Abbreviatio de gestis Francorum,* a chronicle of France from the origins to 1137, was one of their early compilations. In the middle of the thirteenth century they made a collection of existing Latin chronicles, forming a complete history of the French monarchy. This MS (B.N.lat. 5925) contained the *De gestis Francorum* of Aimoin as far as Bk. IV, 14, the *Gesta Dagoberti,* the *Annales Laurissenses,* Eginhard's *Vita Karoli,* the Astronomer for the years 840-1108, the continuation of Aimoin, Abbot Suger's *Vita Ludovici VI,* Rigord's *Gesta Philippi Augusti,* and Guillaume le Breton's *Gesta Philippi Regis.* By 1274 this mass of Latin chronicles was translated and adapted into French by Primatus, a monk of Saint-Denis, and presented to Philip III. Such is the beginning of the *Grandes chroniques de France,* which were soon accorded the title of the official chronicles of France and were continued till the close of the fifteenth century by the monks of Saint-Denis. After 1286 the *Gesta Ludovici IX* and the *Gesta Philippi III* of Guillaume de Nangis were adapted into French and added to the collection, bringing the *Grandes chroniques* down to the year 1300. Perhaps Guillaume de Nangis was responsible for this latest addition, as he was librarian of Saint-Denis from 1285 to 1300.

To the medieval man, history had two divisions; that prior to the conversion of Constantine (315), and the events thereafter. We mention this to show that the medieval man was as conscious of an ancient history and of a modern history as we are today! Caesar was the outstanding figure of his ancient history, if we except Adam and Eve and others of the vast multitude of biblical characters; universal chronicles always started with the father of man. The *Faits des Romains,* or *Livre de Cesar,* written 1213-14 by a cleric of Lille,[1] was based upon the works of Sallust, Suetonius, Lucan, and Caesar (Sneyders de Vogel in *Rom* LIX, 11-72). The author made of Julius Caesar an ideal knight. Another work, the *Livres des estoires,* composed in 1223-1230, begins with Creation and stops with Caesar's invasion of Gaul. This brings us to a composition by Jehan de Tuim, the *Hystoire de Julius Cesar,* based upon Lucan's *Pharsalia* and the *Bellum civile* of Caesar. The *Roman de Julius Cesar,* by Jacos Forest was a rendering into rhymed alexandrine *laisses* of the prose of Jehan de Tuim. Tuim is the modern Thouin in Belgium and that is all we know concerning this writer. (Consult V. L. Dedeck-Héry in his *Etude de . . . "Li Hystoire de Jean de Tuim"* Philadelphis: *UPRS,* 1925).

The first great narrative of authentic travel in the French language

[1] On this date consult Sneyders de Vogel in *Neoph* XVII, 271.

was the work of an Italian, Marco Polo (1254-1323). He was a Venetian who travelled to China through Mongolia, returning by way of Sumatra. He traversed many regions which were not to be visited again by Europeans till the nineteenth century. He saw Tibet, Burma, Siam, Cochin-China, Ceylon, Java, Sumatra, Madagascar, and Abyssinia, being in the East between the years 1271 and 1295. In 1298 he was captured in a sea fight by the Genoese and taken prisoner to their city. While there he dictated an account of his travels to a fellow prisoner, Rusticiano di Pisa. This work, the *Livre de Marco Polo*, did not excite much attention till the *Navagationi e viaggi* of Giovanni Battista Ramuşio (1485-1557) called attention to it. Strange to say, there is an Irish version of the voyage of Marco Polo preserved in the *Book of Lismore* (1400), adapted from a Latin translation of the French. A Spanish translation was made in 1385-1399 by Juan Fernández de Heredia, and an Italian translation was completed in the first years of the fourteenth century.

## EDITIONS

Philippe Mouskés, *Chronique rimée*, ed. Reiffenberg (Brussels, 1836-1838, 1845, 2 vols. with supplement).—*Chronique dite de Saint-Magloire*, ed. Buchon in his *Chroniques*, VII, 1-18.—Guillaume Guiard d'Orléans, *Branche des loyaux lignages*, ed. Buchon in *Chroniques*, vols. VII-VIII.—Geoffroi de Villehardouin, *Conquête de Constantinople*, ed. N. de Wailly (Paris: Firmin-Didot, 1882).—Robert de Clari, *Conquête de Constantinople*, ed. P. Lauer (Paris: Cfmâ, 1924).—*L'Histoire de Guillaume le Marechal*, ed. P. Meyer (Paris: ShF, 1891-1901, 3 vols.).—The two anonymous histories composed at Béthune are edited by Delisle in *Recueil des historiens des Gaulois* (Paris, 1905), vol. XXIV.—*Song of Dermot the Earl*, ed. Orpen (Oxford, 1892).— Peter of Ickham, *Livere des reis de Brittanie, etc.*, ed. Glover in *Rolls Series* (1865).—*Récits d'un ménestrel de Reims*, ed. N. de. Wailly (Paris: ShF, 1876).—Philippe de Novare, *Mémoires*, ed. C. Kohler (Paris, Cfmâ, 1913); *Gestes des Chiprois*, ed. R. Raynaud (Geneva, 1887); *Histoire de Chypre*, ed. Mas Latrie (Paris, 1852-1861, 3 vols.).—Joinville, *Histoire de Saint-Louis*, ed. Natalis de Wailly (Paris, 1874).—*Lettres françaises du XIII^e siècle*, ed. A. L. Foulet (Paris: Cfmâ, 1924). The Anglo-Norman letters of MS. All Souls, 182, are being published by the Anglo-Norman Text Society.—*Livre d'Eracles*, ed. Mas Latrie in *Chronique d'Ernoul et de Bernard le Trésorier* (Paris: ShF, 1871).—*Grandes chroniques de France*, ed. Jules Viard (Paris: ShF, 1920 —, 5 vols. have appeared).—Johann Loesch, *Die Abfassung der Faits des Romains* (Halle, 1907). K. Sneyders de Vogel and L.-F. Flutre have in preparation an edition of the *Faits des Romains.*—Jehan de Tuim, *Hystoire de Julius Cesar*, ed. F. Settegast (Halle, 1881).—Marco Polo, *Le Livre*, ed. M. G. Pauthier (Paris, 1865); a revised version of this with modern French translation is by A. J. H. Charignon (Peking, 1926); the first editing of this *Livre* was by J. B. G. Roux de Rochelle (Paris, 1824).

# CHAPTER XXVIII

## THE THIRTEENTH-CENTURY *CHANSONS DE GESTE*

Bédier, *Les légendes épiques,* etc.
Gröber, *Grundriss,* vol. II, Pt. I.
*Histoire littéraire de la France,* vol. XXX.

Nothing can be more uncertain than an attempt to determine definitely whether the surviving form of a *chanson de geste* was composed in the twelfth or the thirteenth century. These poems were constantly undergoing revision and nearly all the extant MSS were copied in the thirteenth century. The question of cycles is no longer an important one after the early years of the thirteenth century. It is true that a thirteenth-century poet, Bertrand de Bar-sur-Aube, was the first to tell us about these groupings of the epic, but his contemporaries and successors proceeded to mix the characters and combine the cycles where possible. The original purpose of the *chanson de geste,* as determined by Bédier, was now lost from sight and jongleurs continued to sing the deeds of William of Qrange and his brothers, or of the court of Charlemagne, only because the form was fixed and because they could still find hearers. At times we detect a hint that many people of the thirteenth century were no longer fond of this type of narrative; in fact, there is occasional scorn and burlesquing. Often a jongleur would combine his simple patriotic account with elements from a more aristocratic form, the romance. Rhyme, instead of assonance, became more common, and public taste even went so far as to prefer the twelve-syllable line, in place of the conventional ten-syllable, in imitation of the great *Roman d'Alexandre* of Alexandre de Bernai and Lambert le Tort. Many jongleurs, unable to make a satisfactory living with their wares in France, passed down into northern Italy and retold their narrative poems with slight Italianizations in a pseudo-dialect which we call Franco-Venetian, or Franco-Italian. We have eight epics in this altered Italian form: the *Roland, Renaut de Montauban, Gui de Nantueil, Aliscans, Macaire, Anseïs de Cartage, Fouque de Candie,* and *Aspremont.* King Haakon Magnusson of Norway, at the close of the century, caused a vast compilation in ten books, the *Karlamagnussaga,* to be composed in Norse prose from certain of the French epics and from the *Speculum* of Vincent of Beauvais.

Bertrand de Bar-sur-Aube, a native of Champagne, is given credit for two *chansons,* written between 1190 and 1217 (*MPhil* XVI, 151-158). They are *Aymeri de Narbonne* (4,708 verses, 10 syllables, rhymed) and *Girart de Vienne* (6,500 verses, 10 syllables, rhymed). The second of these, if not the other, was a reworking of an earlier poem. Bertrand was familiar with a multitude of existing epics; it is he who gives us our system of classification into three main cycles. In the first of the above epics, Aymeri, a youth, is returning with Charles after the sad defeat of Roncevaux. He is the only warrior who has the courage left to undertake the siege of Narbonne. He wins the town and receives it from Charles as a fief. He goes to seek the hand of Hermenjart of Pavia, wherein he is aided by Girart de Vienne. When he returns with his bride he is forced to reconquer his fief from the Saracens, but is successful. The descendants of Aymeri and Hermenjart are destined to be most daring; they shall cause the Saracens to suffer many a set-back. In the *Girart de Vienne,* which certainly had a prototype,[1] the Duchess of Burgundy had been promised to Girart, son of Garin de Monglane, but Charlemagne took her instead, recompensing the disappointed lover with the fief of Vienne. Girart wounded the lady by his insolence, so she made him kiss her toe, on the wedding night, in the place of the foot of Charlemagne. She boasted of this many years later to Girart's sons. Mortal war followed. Charlemagne besieged Vienne, where Girart was aided by his brother, Renier de Genes, and by Renier's son, Olivier. The hostilities were eventually halted when a single combat between the young Roland and Olivier was arranged on an island. The combat was ended by an angel whom God sent in a cloud to demand that they love each other and fight the pagans instead. Charles accepted Girart's homage and the *belle* Aude, Olivier's sister, was affianced to Roland. New wars against the pagans aroused all the warriors in France.

The *Narbonnais* was by an unknown poet who wrote in the same period as Bertrand de Bar-sur-Aube. The older sons of Aymeri, Guibert, Bernart, Guillaume, Garin, Hernaut, Beuve, Aymer, are told by their father that they must leave and seek their own fiefs. Narbonne shall be reserved for the youngest son, Guibelin. The old father is rather brutal about this decision and his sons are infuriated. Aymeri strikes their mother, Hermenjart. Fortunately, the sons are successful and win lands as their father had predicted. They return to aid him against the Saracens when he is in danger. Aymer swears that he will not rest under a roof until he has driven the Saracens from the land.

Garin de Monglane, the grandfather of Aymeri, is mentioned in

[1] Perhaps this prototype was identical with the lost *Girart de Frete.* See p. 93.

*Girart de Vienne, Doön de Mayence, Gaufrey,* the *Destruction de Rome,* and in the much earlier *Fierabras.* The epic entitled *Garin de Monglane* is a long laborious composition of the second half of the thirteenth century, consisting of some fourteen thousand alexandrine lines. Garin is told by an angel to abandon his heritage of Aquitaine to his brothers and to win Monglane. Monglane belongs to the Albigensian heretic, Gaufroi. Charlemagne gives Garin permission to acquire this fief after he is defeated by Garin in a game of chess. Garin also wins for his bride Mabile, who is betrothed to Hugo of Auvergne. There are adventures with robbers and other misfortunes. This *chanson* is a mixture of the old style epic and the romance. The *Enfances Garin* (5,000 verses, 12 syllables) might be dated into the early fourteenth century. Garin is the son of Savari d'Aquitaine and Floure.

In the *Bataille Loquifer* (4,180 verses, 10 syllables, rhymed), the characters of the William of Orange epics are mingled with giants, fairies, Arthurian knights, and a monster. Grandor de Brie, who has lived in Norman Sicily, names himself as the author.[2] Rainouart is the hero of this marvelous tale and Loquifer (Lucifer) is a son of hell with whom Rainouart engages in single combat. Rainouart is carried to Avalon by the fairies. This poem dates from the first part of the thirteenth century. The *Moniage Rainouart* (7,600 verses, 10 syllables), also by Grandor, shows indications of being a parody on the *chanson de geste,* with a plot similar to the *Moniage Guillaume* (twelfth century). Both these epics were remade by a poet named Guillaume de Bapaume.

Charles Samaran has discovered, and Mme. Pamfilova has published (*Rom* LVII, 504-517), 268 lines which formed the close of another *chanson* of the cycle of Garin de Monglane. The *Moniage Rainouart* and the *Moniage Guillaume* were immediate sources. In this fragment Count William is a prisoner at Loquiferne. Maillefer, the son of Renouart, goes to fetch his father, who is a monk at Bride, or Brioude. Accompanied by these two champions and by a large army, Charlemagne proceeds to the rescue. This is accomplished, thanks to the heroism of Maillefer who, like his father, is armed with a club. William returns to his hermitage, where he still has to fight with a dreadful giant. He slays this last adversary. After a long and saintly life, he dies and goes directly to heaven.

The *Enfances Guillaume* (3,400 verses, 10 syllables, assonanced) narrates how Guillaume first heard of the Saracen princess Orable and how he contended for her with Tibaut of Orange. Tibaut cannot consummate his marriage with Orable because of magic brought to bear

[2] In one MS the name is given as Jendeus.

upon him. He attacks Narbonne and is driven off by Guillaume and his brothers.

Adenet ('little Adam') was educated as a minstrel by Henry III of Brabant, himself a poet. In 1269 Adenet went to Flanders and became *roi des menestrels* at the court of Gui de Dampierre. He accompanied Gui into Italy where he became acquainted with many ancient landmarks. He returned through Switzerland and then spent some time at the royal court in Paris. Adenet was still a retainer of Gui in 1296; he was honored by the King of England in 1297, and presumably died not long thereafter. He also wrote at the behest of Marie, daughter of Henry of Brabant and queen of King Philip III of France, and for Blanche, the daughter of Saint Louis, who married Ferdinand of Castille in 1269. Adenet's active literary career began in the 1260's and probably did not continue after 1282. He fails to mention in his poetry which has survived any works later than that date. A notable task undertaken by Adenet was the renewal of interest in the *chansons de geste*. He himself reworked three of the old legends and called them the *Enfances Ogier*, the *Berthe aus grans piés,* and the *Bueve de Commarchis*. He admitted the authorship of these in the course of his long romance, the *Cléomadès*. The *Enfances Ogier* was based upon the first part of the *Chevalerie Ogier le Danois* (twelfth century); the second epic he took from an original now lost (existing in the twelfth century); the *Bueve de Commarchis* is a new version of the twelfth-century *Siège de Barbastre*. Adenet was no mean poet and an excellent psychologist. His *chansons* are beautifully put together and the original simplicity of character found in his source is transformed into a logical play of light and shade. The religious fervor is much reduced; the marvellous (except in *Cléomadès*) becomes non-existent.

In *Berthe aus grans piés,* Bertha (the actual name of Charlemagne's mother) is a princess of Hungary who is betrothed to Pepin of France. Her female attendant persuades Bertha that Pepin will be too much for her on her wedding night   Bertha consents for Aliste, the daughter of the attendant, to substitute for her. The next morning Aliste slips a knife into Bertha's hand, screams, and accuses Bertha of seeking to kill her—the true queen. Bertha is carried off into the wood near Le Mans to be slain, but her captors spare her and she takes refuge in the house of Simon, a well-to-do peasant. Bertha's mother, Queen Blancheflor of Hungary, comes to Paris to visit her daughter and discovers the deception. The evil attendant is burned, the false Bertha is sent to the Convent on Montmartre and all seek the real queen. Eventually Pepin comes upon her by chance, while hunting, and she mentions her identity to save herself from his attentions. She later retracts this, but her mother recognizes her and she is restored as queen. The earlier version of this *chanson*, belonging to the twelfth century, has been lost, but we know of its existence from a twelfth-century reference. The ultimate source of this plot must be a folktale (Mt. 403 IV c, V a in *FFC*, 74; also Mt. 403 A in *FFC*, 78, 81). There are later literary versions in Germany, Italy, Spain, and France. Note that the father and mother of Berthe are the Floire and Blancheflor whom we have met in a twelfth-century romance. Adenet's epic has 3,484 alexandrines; it was written in 1270-5.

*Galiens li restorés* and *Simon de Pouille* are, in a way, continuations of the *Pèlerinage de Charlemagne*. In the *Galiens* a son is born to Jacqueline, daughter of Hue the Strong, as a result of her liaison with Oliver. This boy, when grown, seeks his father and eventually finds him on the field at Roncesvalles where he and five other peers alone survive. In the *Simon de Pouille* (6,300 alex. preserved) Charles and his peers oppose Simon at Jerusalem. Again there is a question of *gabs*.

The *Doön de Mayence* (11,505 verses, 12 syllables, rhymed), written after the middle of the thirteenth century, links up all the heroes of the rebellious vassal cycle. Doön is reared in a forest with his hermit father. The father is bound to keep an oath to prepare his son to avenge the mother's death. Doön eventually slays the traitors. He has combat with the young Charlemagne. The two go to aid the Saracen Aubigant against the Danes. Doön desires Aubigant's daughter, Flandrine, for wife. After a considerable number of adventures all turns out well. The *Perceval* of Chrétien de Troyes, and the *Huon de Bordeaux* were conspicuous sources of this *chanson*.

*Gaufrey* (10,731 verses, 12 syllables, rhymed) is the story of the oldest son of Doön. It also tells of the adventures of Robastre and of Berart de Montdidier. The dwarf Oberon, of *Huon de Bordeaux*, has here an imitation in the elf Malabron. In the *Gui de Bourgogne* (4,304 verses, 12 syllables, rhymed) Charles has been in Spain for twenty-seven years. He is worn out; he needs reinforcements. Help comes from the youths of France under the leadership of Gui de Bourgogne. This Gui is a mysterious character. All that the mature army of Charlemagne could not win in Spain, the young men, under Gui, succeed in taking. Gui receives Spain as a fief and conquers Luiserne. God causes this rich city to disappear, swallowed up, because of the covetousness which it excites. There is a folk significance to the plot (Mt. 513, 514 II, III f. *FFC*, 74; 513A, *FFC*, 78, 81).

*Macaire* (3,615 verses, 10 syllables, rhymed) has survived in the Franco-Italian dialect. It is the story of a queen of France slandered by the traitor Macaire because she refused his wooing. The traitor accuses her before the king and she is forced into exile. She gives birth to a son in Hungary, marked with a white cross, the sign of his royal birth. Her father, the Emperor of Constantinople, declares war to avenge her. Eventually the truth is known and the traitor Macaire meets a horrible death. There are folk motifs here (Mt. 883A and B, *FFC,* 74, 78, 81). *Gaydon* (10,887 verses, 10 syllables, rhymed) is the story of Tierri d'Anjou, called Gaydon, who defeated Pinabel in the trial by combat at Aix-la-Chapelle (see the *Chanson de Roland*). The traitors accuse him before the weak-minded Charlemagne. There are many adventures in which Gaydon is victorious and finally saves Charles himself, whom the traitors are about to put to death. The date of composition may lie between 1218 and 1240. It was reworked from an earlier *chanson* in assonance. *Otinel* (2,133 verses, 10 syllables, rhymed) was written in the first quarter of the century. Otinel, a young pagan champion, fights Roland but God suddenly sends the Holy Ghost, in the form of a dove, to convert him. Otinel now joins the Christians, wins a bride, Belissant, daughter of Charles, and receives the marches of Italy as a fief. He besieges Garsile (or Marsile) and is killed. Dante Bianchi (*La Leggenda di Otinel,* Aquila: Verchioni, 1926) is persuaded that this chanson echoes a tradition of the Ospinelli family of Tortona.

The *Anseïs de Cartage* (11,607 verses, 10 syllables) also belongs in the first half of the thirteenth century. Anseïs becomes the King of Spain, under Charlemagne. Because of his treatment of the Saracen Ysoré's daughter there is a new invasion of Spain. Charles comes with help and Anseïs marries Gaudisse, Marsilie's daughter.

The *Orson de Beauvais* (3,745 verses, 12 syllables, rhymed) was dated by Gaston Paris between 1180 and 1188, but Suchier has shown with more reason that it belongs in the early part of the thirteenth century. Orson is a close friend of a traitor, Hugo de Berri. Hugo leads him on a supposed pilgrimage to the Holy Land and sells him into slavery to the Saracens. Hugo returns and pretends that Orson has died. He forces Orson's widow to marry him, but she possesses a magic herb which protects her chastity. The son of Orson, Miles, escapes, and eventually discovers his father to be a prisoner of the Saracen Ysoré. The son frees the father and they return home. In the meantime, Hugo has tried to burn his unwilling wife but she is rescued by Doön de Clermont. When Orson appears to confront Hugo, the traitor tells a wonderful lie about Orson's treachery, which Charlemagne believes! Miles defeats Hugo in a trial by combat and Hugo is hanged in full armor. Miles had fallen in love with the beautiful Oriente while among the Saracens. There must have existed a continuation telling of his adventures in the winning of this princess.

In *Jean de Lanson* (6,000 odd alexandrines) Charlemagne besieges

Jean, the nephew of Guenelon. This *chanson* makes free use of *Renaus de Montauban*. It contains a good deal of supernatural material. As it is still unpublished it was not accessible to Professor A.-J. Dickman in his *Le Rôle du surnaturel dans les chansons de geste* (Paris: Champion, 1926). Another epic in which the marvellous plays a predominant role is *Fouque de Candie*, by Herbert le Duc de Dammartin, a poem of tedious length (16,000 odd verses in both decasyllables and alexandrine verse, rhymed). It is a continuation of *Aliscans*. Gaston Paris thought the lost original of this mid-thirteenth century poem should be dated about 1170. Fouque is the grandnephew of Guillaume Fierabras; he accompanies Vivien and Gui to the rescue of Guillaume, who is besieged by Tibaut d'Orange. Fouque is a sort of Rainouart who wins the love of Anfelise de Candie (Gandía). She delivers Candie to Fouque and the fighting shifts to that scene. The Christians besiege Arrablai. Another Saracen maiden, Fausette, delivers the town of Montire to Gui.

The last 2,444 verses, in alexandrines, are by a later poet and this portion is referred to as the *Chançon nouvele*.

*Octavian* (5,371 octosyllables) might be classed as a romance but in its spirit it resembles a *chanson de geste*. The poem is in Anglo-Norman dialect and was composed between 1229-1244, as it refers to Jerusalem in the hands of the Crusaders. G. Paris did not accept this dating (*Rom* XI, 609-14). The plot is a mixture of the divided family motif, familiar in the *Apollonius* and in the Placidus-Eustachius legend, the motif of the persecuted wife (Crescentia), and the motif of the faithful lion. It begins with the birth of twin sons to the Empress of Rome. She is accused of adultery from the same motive that we find in *Elioxe*, and in the *lai Le Fresne*, by her wicked mother-in-law, and is exposed with her children in a forest. An ape makes off with one child; the other is stolen by a lion. The first child, Florent, is rescued by a knight and grows up in Paris as the slave of a butcher, Clement. Florent is utterly impractical in petty things, to the disgust of Clement, but he defeats a Saracen sultan who besieges Paris and marries the sultan's pretty daughter. Octavian, the second son, has been reared by the lion and when he is at last recovered by his mother the lion remains with them. They are protected by the King of Jerusalem. Octavian leads out the armies of Jerusalem against the Saracens and rescues the King of France, his own father, the Emperor of Rome, and his brother, Florent. The family is finally united. The author of this *Octavian* may well have used *Floövant*, and possibly he knew the *Yvain*.

The *Jourdains de Blaivies* was discussed for convenience under the twelfth-century epics, but it rightfully belongs in the early years of the thirteenth century. Similarly, the *Aiol et Mirabel* and the *Elie de Saint-*

*Gilles* have already been treated, although their extant form is that of the thirteenth century. *Parise la Duchesse* (3,107 alexandrines in assonance) continues the *geste de Nanteuil* and belongs to the first quarter of the century. Parise, the sister of Gui de Nanteuil, marries Raymond of Saint-Gilles. The felonious family of Guenelon accuses her wrongfully of having slain her husband's brother. She is exiled; a son Hue, is born to her and then stolen. The boy is raised at the court of Hungary and later finds his mother in Cologne. He honors her and begins war against his fickle father. All is at last discovered, the traitors are slain, and Hue marries the Princess of Hungary. This is a rather banal plot. The poet utilized details from *Aye d'Avignon, Ogier li Danois*, and the lost version of *Berthe aus grans piés*.

A long Picard *chanson de geste* of the middle of the thirteenth century is *Auberi le Bourguignon* (27,000 odd decasyllables), whose authors made considerable use of *Garin le Loherenc*, of *Huon de Bordeaux*, and of *Aiol*. The character of Auberi is first mentioned in the twelfth-century *Charroi de Nîmes* (vs. 319). In the first division of *Auberi* the hero has many love adventures with the assistance of his faithful Gasselin; in the second part Auberi is armed knight and fights in Bavaria and in Flanders. Auberi finally marries the Princess of Flanders and Gasselin weds the daughter of Orri of Bavaria, thereby becoming the future father of Naimes of Bavaria. This lengthy poem is not uninteresting.

The vast Lotharingian cycle was continued in the thirteenth century by *Hervis de Mes* (12,000 odd decasyllables in assonance), *Anseïs fils de Girbert*, and the *Yon*. Hervis is the father of Garin. Tierri, the father of Hervis, is a bourgeois and Provost of Metz. He wished his son to show financial wisdom, but, as was the case with Pheidippides of Aristophanes' *Clouds*, the mother's noble blood will show: Hervis persists in largesses. He buys Beatrice of Hungary for fifteen thousand marks, not knowing who her father is, and thus brings down upon himself the wrath of his own father. Hervis and his wife, Beatrice, are forced to undergo privations till her royal birth becomes known and then Tierri is reconciled with his son. But an old king of Spain wishes to steal Beatrice, the beautiful, and he threatens war. Floire, the brother of Beatrice, carries her away; Hervis recovers her, and finally everyone is reconciled; the old Spanish king promises to become a monk.

The *Rei Waldef* (22,000 verses odd) is an Anglo-Norman epic (*ca.* 1200) which is still unpublished (Carl Sachs, *Beiträge*, Berlin, 1850, 50 ff.). The tale was current in England, and there was a version in Middle-English, now lost. King Bede, the father of Waldef, has a wicked seneschal, Frode. This Frode has persecuted the king's sister and on the king's death the life of Waldef is threatened. Waldef is saved by his cousin Florenz, son of the persecuted lady. In the second division of the epic Saracens carry away Waldef's two sons. After many vicissitudes Waldef is burned in a fire at Rochester. His two sons have been reared by the emperor of Germany. In a Latin prose version of the fifteenth century, by Johannes Bramis, there is a conclusion which is lacking to the French poem. The sons return to England and avenge their father. This Latin version was based upon both the Anglo-Norman and the English.

## EDITIONS

Bertrand de Bar-sur-Aube, *Aymeri de Narbonne*, ed. L. Demaison (Paris: *SATF*, 1887, 2 vols.); *Girard de Vienne*, ed. F. G. Yeandle (New York: Columbia Univ. Press, 1930).—*Les Narbonnais*, ed. H. Suchier (Paris: *SATF*, 1898, 2 vols.).—*Bataille Loquifer I*, ed. J. Runeberg (Helsingfors, 1913); extracts by Le Roux de Lincy in *Le livre des légendes* (Paris, 1836), p. 246ff.— On the still unpublished *Moniage Rainouart* consult Max Lipke's *Ueber d. Moniage Rainouart* (Halle, 1904).—The *Enfances Guillaume*, ed. Patrice Henry (Paris: *SATF*, 1935); also ed. J. L. Perrier (New York: *IFS*, 1934).— Adenet li Rois, *Beuves de Commarchis*, ed. A. Scheler (Brussels, 1874). I have in preparation a new edition of the *Berte aus grans piés*. It has been edited by Scheler (Brussels, 1874).—*Galiens li restorés*, ed. Stengel (Marburg, 1890).—*Doön de Mayence*, ed. M. F. Guessard (Paris: *APF*, 1859).—*Gaufrey*, ed. M.-F. Guessard (Paris: *APF*, 1859).—*Macaire*, ed. M.-F. Guessard (Paris: *APF*, 1866); ed. A. Mussafia (Vienna, 1864).—*Gaydon*, ed. M.-F. Guessard-S. Luce (Paris: *APF*, 1862).—*Gui de Bourgogne, Otinel, et Floövant*, ed. M.-F. Guessard-Michelant (Paris: *APF*, 1859).—*Anseïs de Cartage*, ed. J. Alton (Tübingen, 1892).—*Orson de Beauvais*, ed. G. Paris (Paris: *SATF*, 1899).—Herbert le duc de Dammartin, *Folque de Candie*, ed. O. Schultz-Gora (Halle: *GrL*, 1909-1915):—*Jean de Lanson* is still unpublished.—*Parise la duchesse*, ed. Guessard-Larchey (Paris: *APF*, 1860).—*Hervis de Metz*, ed. E. Stengel (Halle: *GrL*, 1903).—*Auberi le Bourguignon*, extracts by A. Tobler in *Mitteilungen aus afr. Handschriften* (Leipzig, 1870, vol. I.).—There are no editions of *Garin de Monglane*, the *Enfances Garin*, and the *Simon de Pouille*.—Johannes Bramis, *Historia regis Waldef*, ed. R. Imelmann (Bonn, 1912).—*Yon*, ed. Simon R. Mitchneck (New York: *IFS* 1935).

# CHAPTER XXIX

## THE ADVENTURE ROMANCE; ROMANCES OF THE ROUND TABLE; *LAIS* AND *NOUVELLES*

Charles V. Langlois, *La Vie en France au moyen âge* . . . *d'après des romans mondains du temps* (Paris: Hachette, 1926).
*Histoire littéraire de la France*, vols. XXII, XXX, XXXI, and XXVIII.
G. Cohen, *Le Roman en France au* XIIIᵉ *siècle* (Paris, n. d.).
On the Arthurian romances consult Bruce *(op. cit.)* and the other references cited at the head of Chapter XVI.

As with the *chansons de geste,* it is extremely difficult to distinguish between a work composed in the late twelfth century and another that belongs to the early thirteenth. Our systems of chronology are based largely upon internal evidence. Some scholars would place several of the romances treated in this chapter in the twelfth century, and *vice versa.* The thirteenth-century romances are generally discussed under three groups:

1. Adventure romances
2. Round Table romances
   a. biographical
   b. episodical
3. Romances of the Holy Grail

A term which began to enjoy great favor at this time was *nouvelle.* Professor Jenkins has traced the semantics of this word from Latin *nova* or *novella,* meaning at first 'speech showing originality,' to the concept of a tale that is 'repeatable, available for public or private entertainment' (*PMLA* XLII, xliii-lii). Suffice it to say that the thirteenth-century *nouvelle* was considerably shorter than the romance and the term was practically synonymous with *lai.* The Celtic *lai* of the twelfth century had lost most of its Celtic content, and, in the thirteenth century, it was rather a slavish imitation of the form used by Marie de France; sometimes it was a mere *fabliau.* In the present chapter we shall make no division between romance, *nouvelle,* and *lai,* except for those *lais* which are obvious imitations of Marie; these we shall place at the end.

The student should note that many of the thirteenth-century romances and *nouvelles* occur in one manuscript only, an indication that they were not widespread and not as popular as so many of their twelfth-century predecessors. The thirteenth-century adventure romance is often nothing but the elaboration of a single folk theme. Chrétien de Troyes was a constant source for all thirteenth-century romance writers; they recognized in him a master whom they could not equal. They drew from him, and from other predecessors, a great many stock motifs such as the lady and the squire of low degree, the unknown knight, the beauty contest with a sparrow hawk as a prize, the lady furnishing arms to her aspirant, the disappointed lover wandering in madness, the noble youth possessed of all good qualifications who comes to court to be dubbed a knight, the two sisters, etc. Consult on this subject J. R. Reinhard, *The Old French Romance of Amadas et Ydoine* (Durham: Duke Univ. Press, 1927).

We know the names of several writers of romance of the thirteenth century. Chief among them was Jehan Renart. He signed his name to the *Lai de l'ombre;* in addition, Paul Meyer, Mussafia, Gaston Paris, F. M. Warren, and G. Charlier have proved that he wrote the *Escoufle* and the *Guillaume de Dôle.* Lucien Foulet assigns to him, with some reason, the *Galeran de Bretagne.* Charles Langlois has gone still further and ventured to suggest that he is the Renart de Dampmartin from whom we have two *tensons* (*op. cit. supra*, pp. 341-357). If the assumption of Langlois is correct we shall be disappointed in the thought of our Jehan Renart as a bibulous, impoverished wanderer; it is not what we should expect in so accomplished a narrator of *fine amour.* The *Escoufle* (9,102 verses, 8-syllable) was dedicated to Count Baldwin, later Baldwin VI of Constantinople, between 1195 and 1202. The story begins with the departure of Count Richard de Montivilliers for the Holy Land. He is received with respect by everyone along the route; on his return he is urged by the Emperor of Rome to remain in Italy for a while. On the same day that the Empress of Rome has a daughter named Aelis, the Countess of Genoa bears Richard a son, Guillaume. The two children are later betrothed. Richard de Montivilliers dies and the Emperor breaks the betrothal. The two children elope. While in Lorraine a buzzard *(escoufle)* carries off Aelis' purse; Guillaume rides in pursuit, thus becoming separated from Aelis. Now there follow many weary wanderings of both boy and girl, and many disappointments. They are at length reunited at Saint-Gilles. They marry and hold their fief in Montivilliers for three years, when the Emperor dies and they return to rule at Rome. The sources of this romance are not apparent, unless the poet was inspired by passages in the book of Job on the transitory nature of human happiness. It was the chance theft of the buzzard that brought such sorrow to Guillaume and Aelis. Of course the theft of a ring or a purse by a bird is a very old motif, found in many places. Whether Renart derived this from some oral theme or from a written source we cannot say. The romance is preserved in a single MS, Arsenal 6565.

The *Guillaume de Dôle* (5,841 verses, 8-syllable) was called by its poet *Li Romanz de la rose*. It was Claude Fauchet who suggested it be renamed *Guillaume de Dôle*, to distinguish it from the great *Romance of the Rose*.[1] This *Guillaume de Dôle* was written between 1210 and 1214 and dedicated to Milon de Châtillon-Nanteuil; it is preserved in a single MS (Vat. Regina 1725), which once belonged to Claude Fauchet. The theme is a familiar folktale (Mt. 882, *FFC, 74*) of the wager between two men on the chastity of the wife of one of them. The other tries in vain to seduce the virtuous wife, and when he has failed he resorts to trickery. An unfaithful attendant furnishes him with a token or with information, or with both, by which he can convince the husband that his wife is no longer faithful. The husband loses all, but he is eventually undeceived and appeals his case to his overlord. In the romance in question the seducer learns of a birthmark, the shape and color of a rose, which the lady has upon her body. There are many other literary versions of this folktale. In Shakespeare's *Cymbeline* it is a mole that becomes known to the seducer, in the *Decameron* it is a mole with a tuft of golden hairs, in one of the *Miracle Nostre Dame,* of Gautier de Coincy, a servant gives the man a ring and a purse; in the sixteenth-century *Eufemia* of Lope de Rueda the seducer learns of a mole with a tuft of three silver hairs. Three other Old French forms of the theme will be given below. These versions and others are discussed by G. Paris in *Rom* XXXII, 481-551. The *Guillaume de Dôle* was the earliest romance to introduce the practice of including miscellaneous refrains by famous contemporary poets. This usage soon became popular.

Between 1217 and 1221 Jehan Renart finished his *Lai de l'ombre* (962 verses, 8-syllable). This poem is an exquisite masterpiece. The most courteous of knights visits the most courteous of ladies and they sit by a well. In vain does the knight sue for the lady's love and slip upon her finger a ring, by a trick. He removes the ring at her insistent demand and gallantly bestows it upon her shadow in the well. So impressed is the lady with this bit of charming wit that she yields and grants the knight her love.[2]

The *Galeran de Bretagne* (8,000 verses, 8-syllable) we shall accept as the work of Jehan Renart, although the MS reads *Renaut* as the au-

[1] *Origine des dignitez et des magistrats de France* (Paris, 1600), p. 28.

[2] L.-A. Vigneras assigns later dates in the thirteenth century to the *Escoufle, Guillaume de Dôle,* and *Lai de l'ombre.* We cannot accept these (see V. F. Koenig in *MPhil* XXXII, 343-52).

thor's name. E. Hoepffner (*Rom* LVI, 212-135) doubts this identity;[3] he gives as sources for the romance Marie's *Le Fresne, Floire et Blanche-flor*, and some version of the *Boeve de Haumtone*. The *Thèbes* and *Troie* romances were also used. This romance is, in reality, a detailed version of Marie's *Le Fresne;* Foulet dates it around 1225. Two knights marry; the wife of the one has twins and the other wife utters a slander, charging that no woman can have twin children save through two men. This remark is paid for when the accuser herself gives birth to twin daughters. In desperation and remorse she has one baby abandoned in the yard of a nunnery. The child is rescued and adopted by the abbess. While still a child she grows fond of the boy Galeran. Later she quarrels with the abbess and disappears. The young lord, her lover, becomes affianced to her sister. After the wedding, Le Fresne, the unfortunate girl, is recognized by her mother. The wedding is broken and Le Fresne marries her lover. This tale is widespread in literature, though we are not certain of its folk origin. There is only one MS, B.N.fr. 24042, discovered by A. Boucherie in 1877. The young knight, the hero, is given much more attention here than was the case in the *lai* by Marie de France.

Gerbert de Montreuil, author of a continuation of Chrétien's *Perceval* and of a *serventois* entitled *De Groignet et de Petit,* was also the author of the *Roman de la violette* (6,654 verses, 8-syllable). The *Roman de la violette* was dedicated to the Comtesse de Ponthieu (1221-1251), and may have been composed shortly after 1224. The story is the same as that of the *Guillaume de Dôle,* though Gerbert may have chosen his theme independently. The birthmark here is like a violet, just as in the other it resembled a rose. Two more romances make use of this theme. They are the *Comte de Poitiers* (1,718 verses) and the prose *Roi Flore et la belle Jeanne.* The interrelation of these with either the *Violette* or the *Guillaume de Dôle* is impossible to establish. In the *Comte de Poitiers* there is some imitation of the *chanson de geste* style, but I cannot see that this is sufficient for arguing that it was written before the influence of Chrétien became strong.[4] I should place both the *Comte de Poitiers* and the above mentioned prose romance in the first quarter of the thirteenth century. In the *Comte de Poitiers,* Girart de Poitiers makes his wager at the court of Pepin. His adversary secures the countess's wedding ring and a lock of hair from the unfaithful attendant. After the reconciliation of husband and wife, the story is carried further. Gui, their son, goes to Rome and aids in the rescue of Nero, who has been captured by the sultan of Bagdad. The prose ro-

[3] See also Hoepffner's remarks in *Rom* LXII, 196-231, and Mlle Rita Lejeune-Dehousse's *L'œuvre de Jean Renart* (Paris: Droz, 1935).
[4] Gaston Paris used to date this 1180-1200.

mance is decidedly less courtly in its tone. Flore, King of Alsace, has married a widow, Jeanne, after two previous wives gave him no heir. She becomes the mother of Florie, future Queen of Hungary, and of Florens, future Emperor of Constantinople. The chastity testing motif then follows. This romance was doubtless written in the vicinity of Tournai (*Rom* XXXII, 481-551).

Another prose romance, also from Hainaut, is the *Fille du Comte de Pontieu,* preserved in MS.B.N.fr. 25462. This may have been written for Marie, daughter of Guillaume de Pontieu, who married Simon de Dammartin in 1208. She died in 1251. The narrative relates how the daughter of the Comte de Pontieu and her husband go together on a pilgrimage to Compostella. They are accosted by robbers and the wife is violated before the eyes of her bound husband. When the robbers depart she tries unsuccessfully to kill her spouse. He completes the pilgrimage and takes his wife home, with frigid courtesy, and reports what has happened to her father, the Comte de Pontieu. The father casts her adrift on the sea. She is rescued, sold to the Sultan of Aumarie, becomes his wife, and bears him a boy and a girl. The husband and father repent; they go on pilgrimage to the Holy Land. On their return they are carried captive to Aumarie where they are released by the efforts of the sultana, their wife and daughter, respectively, who escapes with them, bringing also her son. The daughter eventually becomes the mother of the great Saladin. The question is often asked whether the daughter of the Comte de Pontieu tried to kill her husband because of shame at her disgrace or because she was afraid he would punish her. There is a fifteenth-century version of this *nouvelle.* A. H. Krappe has indicated some Eastern sources (*ZfrPh* XLIX, 544-9).

A poet named Sarrasin was author of the *Roman de Ham* or *du Hem,* as Albert Henry prefers (*Rom* LXII, 386-91). This was composed after 1278, perhaps in the vicinity of Hem-Monacu, on the Somme. The romance is preserved in a single MS, B.N.fr. 1588. A *Roman de Silence* (6,500 verses) was the work of Heldri de Cornualle. Jakemon Sakesep, or more probably Jacques Bretiaus, wrote the celebrated *Châtelain de Coucy* (last quarter of thirteenth century), in which he gives a treatment of the Eaten Heart Legend, which *should* be a folktale although it has not been found in those countries where the folktales are classified. The theme recurs in the Provencal life of Guilhem de Cabestaing, in the *Decameron* (IV, 9) in a German version by Konrad von Würzburg, and in ten other literary versions in various languages. The core of the tale is the killing of the wife's lover by the jealous husband and the serving of the lover's heart as a dish for the woman. On this tale consult Matzke in *MLN* XXVI, 1-8; see also

*Rom* XVII, 456. Jacques placed his setting about 1190 and chose for his protagonist the lyric poet Gui, Count of Coucy (1186-1203) whose lyrics were doubtless familiar to Jacques. If this Jacques is Jacques Bretiaus, or Bretel, as G. Hecq first pointed out, then he is also the author of the *Tournoi de Chauvency* (1285), and he served Count Henry of Salm (Alsace). This Jacques Bretiaus may have been related to Jehan Bretel, the lyric poet. There are two MSS, B.N.fr. 15098 and nouv.acq. 7514.

An interesting character was Philippe de Rémi, sire de Beaumanoir (*ca.* 1250-1298) who served in various important capacities: as seneschal of Poitou and of Saintonge, as bailiff of Touraine and of Senlis. He was an able jurist, composing the famous *Coutumes de Beauvaisis* which is of epoch-making importance for the study of French common law. He wrote minor poems in a gallant style, such as his *Salu d'amours, Conte d'amours, Conte de jole largece,* his two *Fatraisies,* the *Lai d'amours, Ave Maria,* and *Salut à refrains.* His best claim to fame rests upon his two romances, the *Manekine* and *Jehan et Blonde* (or *Blonde d'Oxford*); they were both composed between 1270 and 1280. The *Manekine* (8,590 verses, 8-syllable) is based upon a folktale (Mt. 706 Ia, IIIa, *FFC,* 74) which is first found in the twelfth century *Vita Offae primi;* it occurs also in Chaucer's Man-of-Law's tale and Chaucer drew it, in turn, from Trivet's *Anglo-Norman Chronicle.* A princess leaves her father's kingdom, either to avoid incest or to marry. She becomes lost and wanders about, finally wedding a king in a distant land. While her husband is away hunting she gives birth to a child. Her wicked mother-in-law, or someone else, writes to the father that his wife has given birth to a beast. The king writes back that nothing is to be done till his return; the wicked one changes the letter to read that the mother must be abandoned on the sea, or in a forest. After further wanderings and misadventures the pair are eventually reunited.

A more interesting tale from our modern point of view is the *Jehan et Blonde* (6,062 verses, 8-syllable). It is the story of a young Frenchman, Jehan de Dampmartin, who goes to England to seek his fortune; he takes service with the Count of Oxford. The author furnishes us with a charming and familiar picture of French and English relations in the thirteenth century. Jehan falls in love with his employer's daughter, who is promised to the Count of Gloucester. He must go back to France because of his father's death; but he returns to England and elopes with the girl. The Count of Oxford is reconciled.

H. Bordier (*Philippe de Rémi . . . poète national du Beauvaisis,* Paris, 1869-1873) and A. Salmon (in his edition of the *Coutumes de Beauvaisis,* Paris, 1900) have demonstrated that Philippe visited England and they infer that some of the episodes in *Jehan et Blonde* were biographical. The *Manekine* shows intimate knowledge of eastern Scotland and of the route from London to Dundee. The main theme of *Jehan et Blonde* bears resemblance to the *Horn* and to three *exempla* in the *Gesta Romanorum*. Both of Philippe's romances are found in only one MS, B.N.fr., 1588. Similar to the *Manekine* is Jehan Maillart's *Comtesse d'Anjou* (1316).

There are a number of anonymous romances of the adventure type. About the middle of the century a poet from the south of the Loire, who knew England, wrote *Joufrois* (4,611 verses, 8-syllable). It has been suggested that the character of Joufrois, the protagonist, was in imitation of William IX of Poitiers. The character of Marcabru also occurs in this romance and the mother of Joufrois is given as Aliénor of Poitou. There are a King Henry and Queen Aelis of England who correspond to Henry I of England and his second wife. Joufrois is distinguished in both love and war. His actions are hardly in keeping with a lofty moral tone; he is the Don Juan of the age of Philip Augustus. It is possible that this poem was adapted from a Provençal original. There is only one MS, preserved in the Royal Library at Copenhagen. *Joufrois* is charmingly written.

A comic tale which suggests the Spanish picaresque novel of later centuries is *Wistasse le Moine* (2,305 verses, 8-syllable). The protagonist is a historical character, a pirate who took a prominent part in the wars between Philip Augustus and King John of England for the recovery of Normandy. Wistasse was mostly on the French side but he trafficked also in England and was eventually beheaded as a traitor by Richard, the bastard son of John. The tricks which Wistasse plays upon his suzerain and enemy, Count Renaud of Boulogne, form the main portion of the narrative. It makes amusing reading. The date of composition must lie between 1223 and 1284. The single MS is B.N.fr 7595.

There was a metrical romance, now lost, dealing with the career of Foulques III Fitz-Warin, composed between 1256 and 1264 and based on some genuine facts—the hero's marriage and outlawry. We have a prose rendition of this executed between 1300 and 1314 for Foulques V, and preserved in a single MS, Royal 12. C. XII. of the British Museum.

A long prose romance, *Bérinus,* also survives only in fourteenth-century form, but the discovery of a small fragment of a thirteenth-century original in verse by Morgan Watkin and Antoine Thomas, at Aberystwyth, shows that this is a rehandling. This romance owed its chief inspiration to some form of the *Seven Sages.* It not only reproduces much of the frame story of this collection . . . it also contains certain of the tale motifs, notably that of *Gaza* or *Rhampsinitu*

(Mt. 950, *FFC*, 74), which is in similar form in the Latin *Dolopathos*. An episode known as the *Montagne d'aimant* was traced by Gédéon Huet to a Latin poem which contained an Oriental tale found in part in the Sixth Voyage of Sinbad the Sailor. The author of *Bérinus* knew many of the Old French romances and epics, particularly the *Elie de Saint-Gilles* and the *Girart de Roussillon*. He may have been a native of Burgundy.

*Gautier d'Aupais* (878 verses, 12-syllable in monorhymed *laisses*) is preserved in a single MS, B.N.fr. 837. The hero, Gautier, loses his horse and clothing while gambling. His father maltreats him as a result and causes him to leave home to wander about France. He enters service as a watchman and falls in love with his employer's daughter. When he declares his love and his identity he is accepted, after due investigation. Everyone is reconciled. The date of this poem could be anywhere in the thirteenth century. The author used *Amadas et Ydoine*, the epic *Girart de Vienne*, the *Chanson des Saisnes*, the Tristan legend, and the *Troie* romance.

The *Chastelaine de Vergy* (968 verses, 8-syllable) is a masterpiece of courtly love. It was imitated in later periods, notably by Marguerite de Navarre in her *Heptameron* (VII, 10). The theme is very similar to that of *lais Lanval, Graelent,* and *Guingamor*. The Duchess of Burgundy loves a knight but is rebuffed by him. Following the well-known Phaedra folk-motif, she informs her husband that the knight has been a traitor and has sought her love. The Duke, furious, accuses him; the knight does not betray the Duchess but admits that he loves another and could not therefore woo his liege lord's wife. The Duke, amused, verifies the knight's love affair with the Duke's niece, the Lady of Vergy. The Lady of Vergy had told her lover that their happiness depended upon absolute secrecy. The Duchess, when informed of the affair by her husband, makes a public reference to it. The Lady of Vergy dies and the knight kills himself. The Duke slays his gossiping wife and becomes a Templar. It is quite probable that this is a *nouvelle à clef*. The Lady of Vergy would be Laure de Lorraine who married Guillaume de Vergy between 1259 and 1267; in this case her uncle, the Duke of Burgundy, was Hugh IV; the Duchess of Burgundy was Beatrice of Champagne, wife of Duke Hugh. The dénouement where the Lady of Vergy and others die was, of course, fictitious. The earliest of the ten MSS that include this delightful nouvelle is dated 1288, which established a *terminus ad quem* for the composition. It would have been annoying for Guillaume de Vergy if this tale had circulated during his lifetime; as he died in 1271 it is reasonable to assume that the poem was produced during the years 1271-1288. A number of ivories, since the fourteenth century, are carved with motifs from the *Chastelaine de Vergy*.

*Richart le biau* (5,452 verses, 8-syllable) has two divisions: the old Greek literary theme of an illegitimate child exposed and brought up by a stranger, but who later seeks out his parents and unites them—a suggestion of Marie de France's *Milon;* and the theme of the thankful corpse which is found, in its simplest form, in the Book of Tobit , chap. 12, and in Cicero's *de Divinatione,* I, 27 (G. H. Gerould, *The Grateful Dead,* F L Soc: London, 1907). The poet names himself as a Mestre Requis (vs. 7). Very similar in style to *Richart le biau* is *Blancandrin et Orgueilleuse d'amour* (6,138 verses), perhaps by the same poet. The hero, Blancandrin, is reared in solitude, as was the case with the famous Perceval. He learns about knights and arms through pictures. He steals away with his father's arms to seek adventures. He snatches a kiss from the unsuspecting Orgueilleuse and is hated by her. This aversion is overcome by prowess and a clever manipulation of jealousy.

*Sone de Nansai* (21,321 verses), of the second half of the thirteenth century, is the longest of the adventure romances; it is preserved in a single MS, Turin, 1626, which was damaged by fire in 1904. The author, a Brabantine, made a slavish use of the romances of Chrétien de Troyes. Nansai may be the town of Nambsheim, near Neuf-Brisach. Many adventures in the poem are laid in England, Scotland, Ireland, and Norway, not to mention Alsace and Lorraine. The last two regions the author certainly knew first hand; Nyrop (*Rom* XXXV, 555-69) believed that the poet was also familiar with Norway. The prologue of the poem connects it with the Swan cycle. The peculiar name of *Sone* is the German name *Sueno* which the hero attests as being German, when questioned by the Count of Vaudemont. Sone is in love with Ide de Doncheri, who refuses him; chagrined, he visits the "stingy' Scots and then the "gluttonous" Norwegians. He defends Norway successfully against the Irish and the Scots. When he departs, Odee, the Norwegian princess who loves him, sails with him. They have adventures in Ireland before landing once again in Norway. Again Sone sails away and returns to Nansai. Ide, who loves him after all, has heard of Odee; she flees from Sone in jealousy. The Countess of Champagne seeks to reconcile the lovers, but in vain. Odee is sent for; the King and Queen of France decide that Sone should marry Odee. He does so and is crowned King of Norway. Later he becomes Holy Roman Emperor. He has four sons—one by the Queen of Ireland, during his previous wanderings. Sone and Odee die on the same day. It is of interest that this romance includes references to the Grail cycle. Prior to his defense of Norway against the Scots, Sone hears the story of Joseph of Arimathea, apropos of the Monastery of Galoche. This monastery is the Grail castle. The abbot tells him how Joseph of Arimathea drove out the pagans from Norway, and married a converted pagan princess. But God did not approve of this union and so blighted Joseph that he became crippled—the Fisher King. He was healed before he and his son Adam passed away. The abbot shows Sone the Grail, a relic of the True Cross, and the bleeding lance. Later Sone returns to Galoche to be crowned king of Norway.

In England the theme of *Horn and Rimenhild* was joined with that of *Amadas et Ydoine,* creating the Anglo-Norman *Gui de Warewic* romance (12,926 octosyllables). The poet may have been a monk of Oseney (Warwickshire), who wrote between 1232 and 1242 to glorify the families of Warwick and Wallingford. It is obvious that the hero Gui is supposedly an ancestor of Wigod of Wallingford, cup-bearer of Edward the Confessor. The young Gui, in order to win the love of his lord's proud daughter, Felice, proves his prowess at the German emperor's court, also at Alexandria and at Constantinople. He returns to England, slays a dragon, and wins the girl. He leaves on his wedding night for a pilgrimage to the Holy Land. When he returns he lives as a beggar in his own house, unknown to his wife. He is persuaded to fight the terrible Colebrant and then retires to a hermitage. The remainder of the poem is devoted to his son. Note the influence of Chrétien's *Guillaume d'Angleterre,* of the *Life of Saint Alexis,* and of the *Moniage Guillaume.*

Adenet, *roi des menestrels* at the court of Gui de Dampierre, whom we have mentioned apropos of the *chansons de geste,* composed an extraordinary romance called *Cléomadès* (18,688 verses, 8-syllables) between 1274 and 1282. Moorish princes seek the hand of the King of Spain's daughter, each presenting marvellous gifts. The hateful magician, Crompart, offers a wooden horse that can fly. Cléomadès, the Spanish king's son, jumps upon it to try it out and impatiently flies before he knows the mechanism for bringing the wooden beast down to earth. He lands in Tuscany and promptly woos the beautiful Clarmondine (Mt. 314 IVa, Vc, *FFC,* 74). He takes her back to Spain, but Crompart seeks revenge for ill-treatment and runs away with the lady. Cléomadès scours the world for her; he is eventually successful in his search and they return to Spain to be married (Mt. 400 Va, VI, *FFC,* 74; Mt. 400 *FFC* 78, 81). As in Renart's *Guillaume de Dôle,* Adenet has inserted lyrics by other poets into his text. It is not improbable that this romance had a Spanish-Arabic source. Blanche of Castille, daughter of Louis IX, could have furnished one to Adenet, of whom she was the patron. This romance was composed in orderly fashion, worthy of its distinguished author.

Among the romances of the Round Table, or Arthur's court, we shall begin with the so-called biographical, those that introduce a new hero and frequently recount his youth and initiation to arms.

Raoul de Houdenc was the author of *Meraugis de Portlesguez* (5,938 verses, 8-syllable). He composed this poem in the Francian dialect shortly after 1200. It is easy to observe that his main inspiration came from Chrétien de Troyes. This Raoul was a native of a town about thirty miles due west of Paris which is interesting to-day because of its twelfth-century *donjon,* or castle. Raoul was certainly a cleric; it is possible that he made use of some Celtic material (*Rom* XXIV, 325-38; *ibid.,* XXV, 267, 269, 283). In *Meraugis de Portlesguez* two friends, Meraugis and Gorvains Caduz, quarrel over a lady, Lidoine of Cavalon. The question of which shall be preferred is decided at Arthur's court; the decision goes to Meraugis. The hero and Lidoine set out in quest of Gawain, who is a captive of the Lady of the Isle. Meraugis contrives Gawain's escape but he loses sight of Lidoine. He wanders about in madness. He enters an enchanted garden—*jardin des caroles*—where he must dance continuously with pretty maidens until another knight takes his place. Eventually Meraugis and Lidoine find themselves together in the same castle, which is then besieged by Gorvains. Meraugis aids in the castle's defence; the siege is finally raised. Gorvains and Meraugis fight it out at Arthur's court and the latter is victorious. Meraugis marries Lidoine and he and Gorvains become friends again. The construction of the romance is admirable. Everything, including the time sequence, is worked out with accurate detail. The treatment of love and its proper code is so skillfully done that scholars cannot believe Raoul was also responsible for the more crude *Vengeance de Raguidel,* of which more anon.

The *Gliglois* (2,942 octosyllables), by a Picard poet who was probably not a professional, belongs to the early thirteenth century and was preserved in a single fifteenth century MS: Turin fr. L. LV 33. This MS, since destroyed by fire, was examined by the late Wendelin Foerster who made a copy of the *Gliglois.* The Harvard University Library purchased this with other papers in 1920. The hero Gliglois is a German youth possessed of many fine qualities, although he is not noble. He becomes a squire to Gawain. The lady Beauté appears and she is loved by both master and man. A tourney is held, but Gliglois is left behind. Although pretending to be haughty the lady Beauté sees that Gliglois gets arms and he, of course, distinguishes himself at the tourney. He weds Beauté. The romance is well written, smooth, and unified; it is built on stock themes from Chrétien, from *Amadas et Ydoine* and from *Le Bel Inconnu.*

The *Yder* (6,769 verses, with beginning lost) also dates from the first quarter of the thirteenth century. The name of the hero, Yder, is found in the twelfth-century *De antiquitate Glastoniensis ecclesiae* of William of Malmesbury, but this may be a later interpolation. On the other hand, it is quite possible that the name *Yder* is derived from the character Edeyrn of the Welsh *Geraint, son of Erbin.* It is not impossible that there existed a version of the romance in the late twelfth century. The poet wrote in the language of western Normandy and Francian, mixed. There is only one MS, EE 426 of Cambridge University. Yder is angry at Arthur because the King preferred to chastise a rebel baron rather than aid a lady in distress. Yder receives his knighthood from other hands and helps the rebel against Arthur. He is beaten and eventually joins the Round Table group. Arthur becomes jealous of Yder and Guenevere; he tries to destroy Yder. All ends well when Yder marries Queen Guenloie, freeing the King from his jealous suspicions. The poet of this romance knew Ovid very well. He is emphatic about the superiority of *fine amour* over the asceticism of religion. It is possible that Glastonbury used this romance in its advertising scheme.

*Fergus et Galiene* (6,984 verses) was written in the Francian dialect, about 1216. An unusual feature is the location of the action in Scotland. The poet betrays an intimate knowledge of that country; he names himself (vs. 6,980) *Guillaumes li clers* and he may have written this romance for a Scotch nobleman, Alan of Galloway (d. 1223), who succeeded to his estates in 1200. Chrétien's romances, particularly the *Perceval,* furnished much material. The plot offers but little originality. It begins with the Great Fool theme—Fergus in his ignorance seeks knighthood at Arthur's court. He goes forth to combat the Black Knight of the Black Mountain. Galiene of Lidel, the niece of his host for a night, offers herself to him. He accepts her love on condition that he shall not possess her till his quest has been accomplished. When he returns from his adventure she has disappeared. He wanders about in search. Incognito, he eventually champions her. Finally Fergus and Galiene are wedded before King Arthur at Roxburgh. It is more than probable that Soumilloit, the peasant father of Fergus, was reminiscent of Chief Somarled of Argyle, and that the hero, Fergus, had as his prototype Prince Fergus of Galloway (see Margaret Schlauch in *PMLA* XLIV, 360-376). These two historical characters flourished in the twelfth century; Alan of Galloway was a great-grandson of Fergus.

*Durmart le Gallois* (15,998 verses) is preserved in a single MS of

Berne, Switzerland. This romance can be dated in the second quarter of the thirteenth century. There are five well-defined episodes in the poem: (1) Durmart, the son of Jozefat, has a love affair with his tutor's pretty wife; it comes to naught; (2) he seeks the Queen of Ireland for his love and meets her at a sparrow-hawk contest without knowing who she is; (3) he rescues Queen Guenevere from Brun of Morois; (4) he wars against Nogant, his rival for the Queen of Ireland's hand, and eventually marries the lady; (5) the couple journey to Rome where Durmart delivers the Eternal City from the pagans. The material in this romance is well handled; further, it is not unlikely that the poet used Celtic themes. He knew Chrétien's works and the Wauchier continuation of the *Perceval*. The moral tone is unusually high.

The *Chevalier as deus espées,* or *Meriadeuc,* has come down to us in only one MS (B.N.fr. 12603). It has 12,353 lines in octosyllables; the dialect is Francian with a Picard admixture, and the date must have been about 1250. Chrétien was a frequent source as well as *Le Bel Inconnu* and *Durmart le Gallois.* Meriadeuc, the son of Bleheri *(sic),* is a squire to Gawain. The Lady of Caradigan undertakes the adventure of the Waste Chapel in which she obtains a marvellous sword that she cannot untie. She repairs to Arthur's court and asks that she may have as husband the man who can untie it. She has been told that only that man can remove it who is possessed of the same beauty and excellence as its original owner. Meriadeuc, whose name is unknown even to his master, unfastens the sword from the lady. Kay dubs him the "Knight with the Two Swords"—his own and the one just acquired. To the surprise of all, the young squire immediately departs. He experiences many adventures, in some of which Gawain also participates. The romance ends with the wedding of Meriadeuc and the Lady of Caradigan.

*Claris et Laris* (30,369 verses, 8-syllable) is a long and tedious composition; it also was written in the Francian standard speech, with some Picard influence. The date of composition has been set at or near 1268. The author was familiar with the prose *Lancelot* and with nearly every other romance that existed then. Claris is the son of a French duke, and Laris is the son of the German king. Their adventures are too complicated to be retold with any profit here.

In the episodical romances of the Round Table (those that narrate a single adventure of some well-known hero) Gawain is nearly always the champion. As we have seen, he served as sub-hero in many of the biographical poems. It would be interesting to know why Gawain achieved such popularity over all the knights of Arthur's court.

Raoul de Houdenc is given credit for the *Vengeance de Raguidel* (6,182 verses, 8-syllable), though this is inferior in time sequence and sentiment to his *Meraugis de Portlesguez*. Some scholars attribute this *Vengeance* to two poets rather than to one. It is a Gawain adventure. Gawain also figures in the *Mule sanz frain* (1,136 verses) of Paien de Maisières (preserved in a single MS; 354 of the Stadtbibliothek at Berne). Its date should be placed early in the thirteenth century. A maiden appears at court with a mule without a bridle. She asks for a champion who will aid her in recovering the bridle. Kay is the first to go with her, but he turns back. Gawain undertakes the quest and after many terrors he and the girl reach a revolving castle. They enter. There is a Mutual Beheading contest between Gawain and a shaggy peasant. The peasant allows Gawain to keep his own head after a test of courage. The lady of the castle is the maiden's sister, and she gives them the bridle. The inhabitants of the castle are now free of the lions which used to cause terror, for Gawain has slain them all. The champion returns with the lady and receives many kisses from her in recompense.

Still another Gawain adventure is the *Chevalier à l'espée* (1,206 verses) which is found in the same MS as the above. The dialect is Francian, and the poem belongs to the first decade of the century. It shows knowledge of the *Vengeance Raguidel*. The plot is a tale, supposedly of folk origin, which is commonly referred to as the Imperious Host, but I can find no trace of this theme in the classified folktale indices. The *Merveilles de Rigomer* (17,271 verses with ending gone) is the work of a poet named Jehan, a native of Cambrai or of Tournai. It belongs in the second quarter of the thirteenth century; there is only one MS extant (626 of the Musée Condé). Lancelot seeks an adventure at Rigomer, the castle of Dionise. He is kept captive. Other knights go to his rescue; Gawain is successful. There is an additional adventure at the close.

The *Humbaut* (3,618 verses with ending gone) is entertaining enough but it forms rather an incongruous mixture. Gawain goes to deliver Arthur's summons to a distant king who does not recognize Arthur as overlord; Humbaut accompanies him. They stop at a castle where an Imperious Host bids Gawain kiss his daughter; Gawain kisses her four times and is nearly blinded as punishment. By his persuasive tongue Humbaut saves Gawain from trouble on several occasions. They sail to the distant kingdom. The king's city is guarded by a hideous peasant who makes a Mutual Beheading offer. Gawain wins by holding back the peasant's body, preventing it from seizing its head; the peasant dies. The message of defiance is delivered. The two knights return and rescue Gawain's sister who has been stolen by Gorvain Codrus, a knight errant to whom Gawain had entrusted her. This romance is preserved only in a MS of the Musée Condé at Chantilly which contains several other romances as well.

We find preserved in three MSS, B.N.fr. 2168 and 1433 and the above MS of the Musée Condé, *Li Atres perillox* or 'The Perilous Churchyard.' This was written in the middle of the thirteenth century by two poets, of whom the first may have been a Norman. (See Brian Woledge, *L'Atre périlleux, Etudes sur les manuscrits, etc.,* Paris: Droz, 1930). There are 6,667 lines. Brugger has suggested that the lost *Perceval* of Guiot was a source; this cannot be proved. Characters are drawn from *Meraugis,* the *Vengeance de Raguidel,* and *Durmart.* Escanor de la Montagne abducts a damsel from Arthur's court. Gawain does not set out immediately to recover her, for fear of Arthur's displeasure. Kay is unhorsed by Escanor. Gawain, while in pursuit, spends the night in a churchyard. A girl appears to him; Gawain saves her from her ravisher, a devil, by cutting off the devil's head. Using advice given him by the girl, Gawain attacks Escanor at the proper time and kills him. It appears that the abducted lady was an accomplice of Escanor; theirs was a trick to provoke combat between Gawain and Escanor at a time when Escanor would be strongest. Gawain and his two rescued damsels return to Cardueil. Gawain goes on another quest, this time for a sparrow-hawk; he has adventures with Espinogre, Raguidel, Cordrovain, Tristan-qui-ne-rit, and Li Orgellox Faé. These adventures are all due to an illusion created by Li Orgellox Faé, to the effect that he had slain and dismembered Gawain. All go to Arthur's court and the vanquished knights marry their *amies.* There is an *Aitre Perilleus* in the *Perlesvaus.* A. H. Krappe argues that the fight with the devil in the cemetery is derived from a tale current in the Mediterranean region, which, in turn, goes back to an Indian tale of a combat with a *raksha* (*Rom* LVIII, 260-4).

Perhaps as a sequel to *Li Atres perillox,* Gerard of Amiens wrote *Escanor.* This lengthy romance (25,936 verses with several lacunae) was begun around 1280 for Eleanor of Castile, queen of Edward the First of England. The two main episodes are the love affair of Kay and Andrivete of Northumberland and the enmity of Gawain and Escanor. These episodes are covered by an intolerable prolixity. This is the only romance where Kay, the sharp-tongued, appears as a creditable knight. Dinadan, borrowed from the prose *Tristan,* voices comments on women and chivalry which anticipate the spirit of the coming age when these things will not be held in so great esteem. Another lengthy romance, of some twenty thousand lines, by this Gerard of Amiens is the *Méliacin* or *Chevalier del fûst.* The subject is the same as that of

Adenet's *Cléomadès,* but it is probable that the two romances were independent of each other. This is, of course, a non-Arthurian subject. An imitation of Marie de France's *Bisclavret* is *Melion* (598 verses), a *lai* of the first half of the thirteenth century. The scene is shifted to Arthur's court and the wicked wife changes her husband into a wolf with a magic ring. In *Tyolet* (704 verses) there is a combination of the motif of Perceval's childhood—child brought up in forest away from arms—the motif of the Pied Piper of Hamlin, and the motif of the False Claimant. It is filled with reminiscences from the works of Marie. The *Lai dou lecheor* (124 verses) is of an obscene nature. Its author was doubtless poking fun at the *genre.* In the *Lai dou Trot* (303 verses) a young knight rides forth towards the woods to hear the nightingale. He sees first a group of forty maidens in summer dress; next he sees another forty riding along smoothly, with their lovers. These are followed by some hundred girls in wretched attire who are forced to *trot* in miserable fashion, on spavined beasts. Last there are some hundred men suffering the same afflictions. The young knight asks the cause of this of one of the poor girls. He is told that the two happy groups are ladies and men who enjoyed love during their lifetime; the others are those who had naught to do with love. The knight learned his lesson; he advises the ladies of his own entourage. The *Lai de Nabaret* (48 vv.) has for its subject the fondness of a lady for dress. Her husband sends relatives to remonstrate. Her response is that he must first cut off his moustaches and let his beard grow, then she will yield. From the *Disciplina clericalis* was derived the pleasing *Lai de l'oiselet* (390 verses) which has a lyric content. A rich peasant buys a noble estate and thinks to capture a beautiful singing bird which frequents his garden. The peasant wishes either to sell it or keep in in a cage. The bird is caught but freed when it promises to divulge three thoughts of wisdom: (1) do not weep for that which you never had! (2) do not believe everything one tells you; (3) do not throw away what you have. The bird flies away and never returns.

The last third of the thirteenth century saw many adaptations into prose of earlier verse romances. The *Tristan,* the *Troie,* and many others were remade in this way. Often we have made mention of such prose versions while discussing the metrical forms. The *Lai du conseil* (860 vss.) stresses the value of eloquence in winning a lady.

## EDITIONS

Jean Renart, *Escoufle,* ed. H. Micheland-Paul Meyer (*SATF,* 1894); *Guillaume de Dôle,* ed. G. Servois (Paris: *SATF,* 1893); ed. Rita Lejeune (Paris: Droz, 1936).—*Le Lai de l'ombre,* ed. Joseph Bédier (Paris: *SATF,*

1913); *Galeran de Bretagne*, ed. L. Foulet (Paris: *Cfmâ*, 1925).—Gerbert de Montreuil, *Roman de la violette*, ed. D. L. Buffum (Paris: *SATF*, 1928).— Gerard de Nevers' prose version of the *Violette* has been edited by L. F. H. Lowe (Princeton: *EM*, 1928).—*Comte de Poitiers*, ed. Fr. Michel (Paris, 1831).—*La Fille du comte de Pontieu*, ed. Cl. Brunel (Paris: *Cfmâ*, 1926).— *Le roman de la comtesse de Pontieu*, ed. Cl. Brunel (Paris: *SATF*, 1922).— Philippe de Beaumanoir, *Oeuvres poétiques*, ed. H. Suchier (Paris: *SATF*, 1884-1885, 2 vols.).—*Joufrois*, ed. K. Hofmann-Fr. Muncker (Halle, 1880); ed. W. O. Streng-Renkonen (Turku: Annales Universitatis Aboensis, 1930); Percival B. Fay has in preparation still another edition.—*Wistasse le moine*, ed. W. Foerster-J. Trost (Halle: *BRom*, 1891).—*Fouke Fitz Warin*, ed. Louis Brandin (Paris: *Cfmâ*, 1930).—*Bérinus*, ed. Robert Bossuat (Paris: *SATF*, 1933, 2 vols.).—*Gautier d'Aupais*, ed. E. Faral (Paris: *Cfmâ*, 1919).—*Chastelain de Coucy*, ed. Crapelet (Paris, 1829).—*Chastelaine de Vergy*, ed. G. Raynaud-L. Foulet (3rd ed.; Paris: *Cfmâ*, 1922).—*Richart le Biau*, ed. W. Foerster (Halle, 1874).—*Blancandrin et l'Orgueilleuse d'amour*, ed. H. Michelant (Paris, 1867).—*Sone de Nansai*, ed. Goldschmidt (Tübingen: *LV*, 1899).—A. Henry is editing the *Roman du Hem*.—*Gui de Warewic*, ed. A. Ewert (Paris: *Cfmâ*, 1933).—Adenet li Rois, *Cléomadès*, ed. A. van Hasselt (Brussels, 1866).—Raoul von Houdenc, *Sämtliche Werke*, ed. M. Friedwagner (Halle: Niemeyer, 1897-1909, 2 vols.).—*Gliglois*, ed. C. H. Livingston (Cambridge, 1931).—*Der altfranzösische Yderroman*, ed. H. Gelzer (Halle: *GrL*, 1913).—*Fergus et Galiene*, ed. E. Martin (Halle, 1872).—*Durmart le Gallois*, ed. Stengel (Tübingen, *LV*, 1873).—*Li Chevaliers as deus espées*, ed. W. Foerster (Halle: Niemeyer, 1877).—*Claris et Laris*, ed. Alton (Tübingen: *LV*, 1884).—*La Mule sanz frein*, ed. R. T. Hill (Baltimore, 1911).— *Chevalier à l'espée*, ed. E. C. Armstrong (Baltimore, 1900).—*Merveilles de Rigomer*, ed. W. Foerster (Halle: *GrL*, 1908-1915, 2 vols.).—*Hunbaut*, ed. W. Foerster (Halle: *GrL*, 1914).—*Li Atres perillox*, ed. B. Woledge (Paris: *Cfmâ*, 1936); also ed. Schiemer in Herrig's *Archiv*, XLII, 135-212.—*Escanor*, ed. H. Michelant (Tübingen: *LV*, 1886).—Girardin d'Amiens, *Méliacin*, extracts by E. Stengel in *ZfrPh* X, 460, 615).—*The Lays of Désiré, Graelent, and Melion*, ed. E. M. Grimes (New York: *IFS*, 1928).—The *Tyolet* and the *Lecheor* were published by Gaston Paris in *Rom* VIII, 29-72.—*Lay du Trot*, ed. E. M. Grimes in *RRev* XXVI, 313-21.—The *Nabaret* is published by Michel in his *Charlemagne* (1836), p. 90.—The *Nouvelles françaises en prose du XII<sup>e</sup> siècle*, ed. L. Moland-C.d'Héricault (Paris, 1856) contains, among other prose *nouvelles*, the *Roi Flore et la belle Jehane*.—*Le Lai de l'oiselet*, ed. Raymond Weeks in *Medieval Studies in Honor of Gertrude Schoepperle Loomis* (Columbia Univ. Press, 1927), pp. 341-353.

# CHAPTER XXX

## THE GRAIL ROMANCES AND THE VULGATE CYCLE

Jessie L.Weston, *The Legend of Sir Perceval* (London: Grimm Library, 1906-09, 2 vols.

Maurice Wilmotte, *Le poème du Graal et ses auteurs* (Paris: Droz, 1930); rev. by F. Lot in *Rom* LVII, 117-36.

See also references for Chapter XVI.

Some time after 1174, and before 1181, Chrétien de Troyes composed a portion of his *Perceval* or *Chevalier del Graal.* This is his most famous poem. Gerbert de Montreuil, one of those who wrote a continuation, is our authority that Chrétien died before he could complete the work:

> Ce nous dist Crestiens de Troie
> Qui de Percheval commencha,
> Mais la mors qui l'adevancha
> Ne li laissa pas traire affin (vss. 6984-6987).

Chrétien himself assures us that he got the material from a book in the possession of his patron Philippe d'Alsace:

> Ce est li contes del Graal
> Dont li cuens li baille le livre;
> S'orroiz comant il s'en delivre (vss. 66-68)

What was that book? The story of the portion generally ascribed to Chrétien is as follows:

Perceval, the son of a widowed lady, goes out to hunt in the Waste Forest. He has always lived in isolation with his mother and does not know what to make of a troop of knights which suddenly passes by. An amusing conversation ensues in which he inquires of the knights concerning themselves and their various weapons and pieces of armor. They are knights of Arthur's court. The boy returns to his mother and announces that he, too, will go to Arthur and become a knight. Now it happens that his father and brothers have all fallen in combat and his mother has gone to live in the Forest to avoid such a fate for him. She swoons at his suggestion, but eventually grants him leave to depart. She admonishes him to serve the ladies, to ask the name of any chance companion, to keep company with worthy men only, and to pray whenever he comes upon a church. He soon sees a lady asleep in a tent; he snatches a kiss and a ring without wakening her. At Arthur's court he is taken for a fool, but he slays the Red Knight who has gone off with Arthur's cup, and takes the Red Knight's armor. Perceval travels on, vowing to return to Arthur's court some day to wreak vengeance upon Kay, because the latter had struck a maiden who prophesied Perceval's future greatness. Perceval reaches the castle of an old knight named Gornemant of Gohorz. He dwells there for a time and Gornemant gives him instruction in arms and knightly behavior; he counsels him to avoid asking questions and to cease quoting his mother's instructions at every occasion. (This was bad advice, as we shall see.) Perceval sets out again and after a day's journey arrives at the castle of Gornemant's niece, who is named Blanchefleur. He overcomes her enemy, King Clamadeus, and Clamadeus' seneschal in individual combat, and sends them both to Arthur's court as prisoners. His relations with Blanchefleur remain chaste. He desires to see his mother again and journeys on. Now there follows the principal episode of the romance, the scene in the Grail castle. Perceval comes to a river and perceives two fishermen in a boat. One of them directs him for a night's lodging to a castle nearby. Perceval finds it with difficulty; he enters, disarms, and sees an old man, who turns out to be his fisherman guide, reclining on a couch which is placed near a central fireplace in a large square hall. Four hundred men could sit around the fire. The hall is supported in the center by curiously wrought columns of bronze. A squire enters with a sword on which is written that it will break only on one occasion, known to the maker of it. The Fisher King gives it to Perceval who is adjudged worthy. Then there suddenly enters a queer procession: a squire with a bleeding lance, from the head of which blood drips upon his hand; two other squires, each with a ten-branched candlestick and with them a maiden holding a "graal" in her hand. This grail, or graal, shines so brightly that it is to the candles as the sun is to the stars. Last of all there comes a damsel bearing a silver plate. The procession passes between the fire and the king's couch and enters another chamber. Perceval learns later from the hermit that an old man in that room is fed by the grail. At supper the grail returns with each course. Perceval would willingly have asked the meaning of all this, but he remembers Gornemant's injunction to ask no questions; he decides to put off all inquiries till the next day. On the following day the castle is deserted. Perceval rides forth and meets a maiden with a headless knight in her lap. She explains how the Grail King, wounded through both thighs by a lance, takes his solace in fishing. She reproves him for having asked no questions, by which the Fisher King could have been made whole. She tells him that his mother has died of grief at his departure and that she herself is his cousin. He fights another knight, the lover of the lady from whom he had stolen a kiss and a ring as his first adventure. This knight, too, is dispatched to Arthur's court. Arthur with his knights sets out to seek Perceval. They come upon him when he is deep in reflection; Kay is rude and receives a broken arm and a broken leg for his pains. Perceval follows Gawain before King Arthur. A hideous damsel appears and after upbraiding Perceval for his failure to question concerning the Grail she mentions two pressing adventures which are immediately undertaken by Gawain and Gifles. Perceval vows to continue in quest of the Grail and not to rest till he has asked the necessary questions. Chrétien relates at this point some irrelevant adventures of Gawain. (It is probable that these adventures were inserted to indicate a considerable lapse in time.) He returns to Perceval after that knight has wandered for five years, forgetting God. Perceval goes for confession to a holy hermit whom he discovers to be his uncle. The uncle tells him that it was because of his mother's death that he (Perceval) was in sin and could not ask the Grail questions. He gives him absolution. The remainder of the poem, up to where Chrétien is generally supposed to have broken off (line 10,601 in Potvin edition) is devoted to Gawain.

It was Potvin who, in his edition of *Perceval* (p. 47), pointed out that in the MS 794 of Paris the text is broken at vs. 10,601 with the rubric *Explicit Perceval le viel*. Likewise in the MS Berne no. 354 the text ends at that point with *Explicit li romans de Perceval*. There are, however, sixteen other MSS which do not have any such indication. With this evidence in mind, M. Wilmotte refuses to agree with the common belief of present-day scholars that Chrétien laid down his pen at vs. 10,601; he asserts that Chrétien was not stopped by death until he had composed as far as line 33,755 of the Potvin edition (allowing for a few minor interpolations by anonymous poets). P. A. Becker is still more radical. He holds that the first 9,234 verses of the *Grail* (in the recent Hilka edition) were the work of three poets, Guiot de Provins, Chrétien de Troyes, and possibly Robert de Boron: the three divisions being verses 1-3,430, 3,431-6,198, 6,199-9,234. He will not say definitely whether Chrétien wrote the first or second division (*ZfrPh* LV, 385-445). This is a very extreme view which must be rejected for the time being. Wilmotte discards completely those continuators whom scholars generally call Wauchier de Denain and the pseudo-Wauchier. Wauchier is named in verse 33,755:

> Wauchier de D. qui l'estoire
> Nos a mis avant en memoire

but the nine MSS which possess this passage vary considerably in the exact form of the name: *Wauchier, Gaucier, Gautier* and *Denet, Dons, Doullens, Dourdain, Dordans.* It was Paul Meyer who first identified this Wauchier with the Wauchier de Denain who made a translation of the *Vitae Patrum* for the Marquis de Namur (*Rom* XXXII, 583-86 and *HLF*, XXXIII, 290). However, a careful examination of the narrative covered in verses 10,602-33,755 shows unequal ability in the narrator, as well as varying conceptions of the Grail Castle, etc. This has led scholars to consider verses 10,602-21,916 of the Potvin edition as the work of an unknown poet whom they conveniently call pseudo-Wauchier, and verses 21,917-33,755 as the contribution of the historical Wauchier. (F. Lot in *Rom, LI*, 398, n. 2; and others). It is quite probable that the exact divisioning of all this material needs revision; it is very possible that Chrétien did not stop at verse 10,601; but I do not believe that M. Wilmotte has taken sufficiently into account the unequal content of verses 1-33,755), most of which he would assign to Chrétien. It is possible that the master poet did not always write with equal enthusiasm, particularly during the latter part of his career; it is also possible that his conceptions of various aspects of his poem could have altered; but it is difficult to believe that Chrétien could have contributed the mediocre lines which we attribute to the historical Wauchier. M. Wilmotte has based his conclusions more upon MS readings than upon textual criticism. Having introduced the reservations made by M. Wilmotte and P. A. Becker, we shall retain the divisions commonly accepted, for the sake of convenient reference.

In the narrative which is generally ascribed to Chrétien, and which we have summarized above, the reader will observe three principal elements: the theme known in folklore as the Great Fool motif (Mt. 1539, 1542, etc., *FFC, 74*), the Arthurian setting, and the Grail theme. The first two are understandable but the third is one of the most perplexing problems of medieval literature. If the book of Philippe d'Alsace existed, and this is probable, it must have furnished the Grail theme. So much material is constantly being written by modern scholars upon various aspects of the Grail problem, that any compilation of knowledge on the subject such as the present chapter is in constant need of revision. There are three major theories by which different scholars explain the sources of the curious Grail procession:

(1) The Theory of Christian Origin. (Bruce, *Evolution of Arthurian Romance*, I, 219-268; Henzel, *Denkschriften* of Vienna Academy, *Philos.-Hist. Klasse*, XL, 1891; M. Wilmotte (*op. cit. supra*); Eugène Anitchkof, *Joachim de Flore*, Rome, 1931). According to this explanation, the bleeding lance, the Grail cup, and the silver platter are all employed in

the Byzantine version of the Mass. The Fisher King would be Christ; the mysterious "double" of the Fisher King, the old man in the room, would be the Holy Ghost. Indeed, Chrétien does say (*Perceval* vss. 6,384-5) that the Fisher King was nourished by "une seule oiste," or Host, served in the Grail. (Anitchkof asserts that the old Gallican ritual of the Mass was similar to the Byzantine.) The book given to Chrétien by Philippe d'Alsace was an account of the Relic of the Holy Blood, perhaps telling how a knight won the precious Relic, through his virtues. From the late twelfth-century statement by Hélinant (ed. B. Tissier, *Bibliotheca Patrum Cisterciensium*, Bonnefont, vol. VII) Wilmotte is disposed to believe that this account circulated in both Latin and French. Anitchkof sees a certain amount of Manichaeanism or Montanism in this lost book of the Holy Grail. Against this last consult Mme. Lot-Borodine in *Rom* LVI, 526-557; LVII, 147-205.

(2) The Theory of Celtic Origin (Nutt, *Studies on the Legend of the Holy Grail*, London, 1888; also his *Popular Studies in Mythology, Romance, and Folk-lore*, London, 1902; A. C. L. Brown, *PMLA*, XXV, 1-59). The symbols in the Grail procession are the "shining talismans of the Tuatha Dé Danann"; namely, the Stone of Destiny, the Cauldron of the Dagda, the Spear and Sword of Lug; or possibly the Grail is the cauldron of regeneration of Bran. The talismans of the Tuatha Dé Danann were formerly known only through Keating's *History of Ireland*, but they have since been confirmed in much earlier texts (*ZfcPh* XVIII, 73-89; *Rev. Celt.*, XII, 56-58). A. G. Van Hamel (*Rev. Celt.*, XLVII, 340-382) has recently called attention to the Irish *Altromíl Tighi dá Medar* as preserving elements of the primitive Celtic Grail: rise of a simple youth in two stages, fairy castle, feeding vessel, miraculous fish, high Christian ideals, Siege Perilous. See also R. S. Loomis in *Spec* VIII (1933), 415-31, and in *Rom* LIX, 557-64 (influence from Irish *imrama*).

(3) The Ritual Theory (Simrock; Nitze in *PMLA* XXIV, 365-418); J. L. Weston, *op. cit.*, and *The Quest of the Holy Grail* (London, 1913), *From Ritual to Romance* (Cambridge, 1920); R. S. Loomis in *Celtic Myth and Arthurian Romance* (New York, 1927).[1] Nitze believed that the Demeter cult at Eleusis passing into some Celtic vegetation cult was the ultimate source of the Grail theme. The Fisher King is the guide between the two worlds, the Grail knight is the initiate, the old man "double" is the life god Adonis or Osiris. The Grail is the κίστη containing the divine food; the lance is a symbol of light. Miss

---

[1] Theories (2) and (3) are often held simultaneously by scholars who believe that the Celtic source went back ultimately to a ritual cult.

Weston traced the Grail mysteries to the primitive Vegetation myth or cult of Adonis. The maimed Fisher King is the slain Adonis; the Grail and the lance are phallic symbols. A suggestion recently made orally by A. C. L. Brown at a Modern Language meeting, is that the *Yvain* and the *Perceval* are elaborations of the same source material and motifs. This is difficult to believe. Of course, if Wilmotte is right in saying that Chrétien wrote as far as verse 33,755 of the *Perceval*, then the Christian explanation must be the correct one. Wilmotte also puts forth the claim that later poets who dealt with the legend had Chrétien's source at hand. Hélinant, whom we have already cited, was not so fortunate: "Hanc historiam latine scriptam invenire non potui; sed tantum gallice scripta habetur a quibusdam proceribus. . . ." I incline towards the Celtic explanation, although I admit that the immediate source of Chrétien may have been suffused with some Christian elements. The odd appearance of the Grail hall, the maidens carrying the talismans . . . these factors do not fit well into a purely Christian interpretation. Further, in the Byzantine ritual the lance which is used, in miniature, to divide the Holy Eucharist, is not thought of as bleeding. Was this lance knife used in the Gallican ritual?

Who was the Kiot, or Guiot referred to by Wolfram von Eschenbach as the immediate source for his German *Parzival?* What was the relation between Guiot and Chrétien? Wolfram mentions Kiot six times; the most significant passage is:

> Kiot ist ein Provenzal,
> der dise aventiur von Parzival
> heidensch geschriben sach.
> Swaz er en franzoys da von gesprach
> bin ich niht der witze laz,
> das sage ich tiuschen furbaz (vs. 12,474 ff.).

This seems to mean that the *Perceval* or *Roman du Graal* was originally a heathen tale and that Guiot, a Provençal, put it into French! Wolfram says that Chrétien will anger Guiot if he does not retell the tale correctly. K. Wackernagel (*Altfranzösiche Lieder und Leiche,* Basel, 1846, p. 191) was the first to identify Guiot de Provence with Guiot de Provins, the author of the satirical *Bible,* the *Armeure du chevalier,* and of five surviving lyric poems. This Guiot de Provins went to the Holy Land with Henry of Champagne in 1179-80, served the second count Henry of Champagne in 1190-1197, and became a monk shortly after that date. Still another Guiot is mentioned in a thirteenth-century miracle poem which lists among prominent writers a Guiot "qui traita de cele demoisele Qui sen pere enfante pucele" (Gröber, *Grundriss,* I, 430, n. 2). Apparently Wolfram's source had Angevine sympathies since

Wolfram identifies the hero of the Grail quest with the Angevine dynasty. In this connection M. Wilmotte refuses to admit that Wolfram's Guiot was Guiot de Provins. He believes that this first Grail poem, by an otherwise unknown Guiot, was compiled in 1179, that Chrétien obtained possession of this source also and that Chrétien began his version before May 14, 1181, the date of the Pact of Gisors. Wilmotte says that this Guiot was a Provençal who owed allegiance to the Angevine kings of England and that this accounts for the interest in that dynasty. Of course, we may propose as alternative that Guiot, Wolfram's source, drew from Chrétien's poem.

P. A. Becker proposes that Robert de Boron had written a version of his *Joseph d'Arimathie* at an early date which was Chrétien's original source and suggestion. After Chrétien had worked upon his poem, aided by Guiot de Provins, Robert de Boron revamped his *Joseph* into the form which has survived and also composed his *Merlin*.

We have mentioned the lines attributed generally to the pseudo-Wauchier and to Wauchier de Denain. The pseudo-Wauchier portion is very well told. Perceval returns to the Grail castle where the Grail is brought in again and mysteriously fills the tables with food. Land around the castle is described as a waste. Next follows the *Livre de Caradoc* section where the Mutual Beheading motif, the Faithless Mother folktale, and the Chastity testing theme are interpolated very entertainingly. The Chastity test theme demonstrates that Caradoc alone of Arthur's knights has a chaste wife. Most scholars agree that this *Livre de Caradoc* had independent existence as a romance before it was inserted here.

In the Wauchier division, which follows, the Quest motif is not treated very seriously. There are further adventures by Perceval. Gerbert de Montreuil was the next continuator who added some 17,000 verses to the narrative, around 1220. The last continuator, Manessier, did not know the Gerbert continuation. He began at verse 33,755, as Gerbert had done, and finished the Quest to his satisfaction in 10,445 lines. It is a very unlikely assumption that Manessier knew Chrétien's own solution of the mystery. Manessier drew from the prose romances and from certain *chansons de geste* as well as upon his imagination. The Fisher King received his wound in the legs from the sword with which his brother was killed. The murderer is Partinal. Perceval slays the murderer and the Fisher King, who chances to be his uncle, is healed. Perceval returns to Arthur's court. The Grail King dies and Perceval departs with the Grail into the wilderness, as a hermit. He dies after ten years and the precious Grail relics are never seen again. They must have mounted to heaven.

Between 1191 and 1201 a knight named Robert of Boron, from east central France, served Gautier de Montbéliard. He communicated to Gautier a poem which is next in importance after Chrétien's; we call it the *Roman de l'estoire dou Graal*, or simply the *Joseph d'Arimathie*. The intention of this romance was to give the early history of the Grail, for Robert definitely establishes its identity with the cup of the Last Supper and the cup in which the blood of the Lord was received after His removal from the Cross. There is no conclusive evidence that Robert knew Chrétien's sources or concept of the Grail although Wilmotte asserts that he did. It is generally assumed that Robert, of his own accord, meditated upon the unfinished *Perceval* and undertook a personal interpretation. The *Joseph d'Arimathie* begins with a résumé of the Bible and an account of Christ's descent into hell. Then we hear of Joseph of Arimathea, a soldier of Pilate. He was granted the body of Christ and, as he washed it, he caught the freshly flowing blood into the chalice which had been used at the Last Supper. After the Resurrection the angry Jews imprisoned Joseph who had removed Christ from the Cross, intending to starve him to death. Joseph was miraculously kept alive without food for forty years; Christ appeared to him bringing the Holy Cup, or Grail, and gave him instructions, thereby instituting the Mass, or Memorial Sacrifice. Joseph was freed by Emperor Vespasian. He wandered about with the Grail, accompanied by his sister and her husband, Hebron or Bron, with certain other followers. Misfortune fell upon them all, because of certain sinners among them. These sinners were sifted out by having all the followers of the Grail pass before the sacred vessel. One of the men, Petrus, spoke explaining the Grail and its powers. Hebron and his wife had twelve sons, among them Alein. Alein was commanded by heaven to lead his brothers westward. Joseph transmitted the holy vessel to Hebron, who henceforth should be called Bron, the Fisher King. Bron went west (to Britain?); Alein's son shall someday succeed him.

This poem is 3,514 lines in length in eight-syllable rhymed couplets. The dialect is a current mixture of Francian and Picard. The chief sources were the Bible, the aprocryphal *Evangelium Nicodemi (Gesta Pilati), a chanson de geste* on the destruction of Jerusalem by Vespasian, and some edifying treatise on the origins of the Mass, such as the *Gemma animae* of Honorius of Augsburg. The name *Hebron* occurs in the Bible (Numbers 3:19) as one of the sons of Kohath who guarded the sacred Ark. There can be little doubt, as Nitze has proved (*Schoepperle-Loomis Med. St.*, pp. 135-145), that Robert of Boron intentionally confused this keeper of the Ark's name with the hero of Celtic tradition, Bran the Blessed, who voyaged among the Isles in search of Paradise and who possessed a cauldron of regeneration. Presumably this Celtic Bran is also two persons combined. Gautier de Montbéliard was associated with Flemings on the Fourth Crusade, in 1201. In that event it is probable that he had connections with Flanders during his earlier career. Did Robert of Boron receive his first urge to treat the Grail story from Flanders, as Chrétien received his from Philippe d'Alsace, Count of Flanders? The assumption is an interesting one and full of possibilities.

Robert wrote a second poem, a *Merlin*, intended to connect the early history of the Grail with Arthur's court. It was based very largely upon Geoffrey of Monmouth or upon Wace's *Brut*. It ended with the crowning of Arthur. Only 502 lines of this *Merlin* have been preserved. Both the *Joseph* and the *Merlin* of Robert of Boron were turned into prose almost immediately. These prose versions were infinitely more popular than the verse and they have survived. A prose Perceval story, commonly called the *Didot-Perceval*, continues Robert's *Merlin*. It is a question whether some other author wrote this with the intention of completing a trilogy or whether it, too, was a prose rendering of two poems, now lost, by Robert. The second supposition is more likely.

By 601 there was an ecclesiastical settlement at Glastonbury, in Somersetshire, about twelve miles from the coast. When the waters were high this site used to be almost entirely surrounded by salt marshes so as to form an island. The Abbey grew in fame from the eighth century on. (Consult Clark Slover in *Spec* XI, 129-32.) Apparently the abbots of the community were anxious to call public attention to the fact that they were the source of Christianity in Britain. William of Malmesbury wrote his *De antiquitate Glastonensis ecclesiae* (1129-35) during his residence at Glastonbury, in which he showed a supposed connection between the Abbey and St. Patrick. But a master stroke, worthy of our best modern "advertising engineers," was the discovery of the bodies of Arthur and Guenevere and their reinterment in the Lady Chapel in 1191. After the murder of Thomas Becket in 1170 Henry II of England was none too pleased with the pretensions and growing power of the See of Canterbury. It is entirely possible that the monks came to his support in 1184-88 with the claim that they had discovered Arthur and his queen. But alas, it was Richard I who was present at the translation of the bodies in 1191. Giraldus Cambrensis in his *De principis instructione* (1193-96) was the first to give an account of the ceremony. (See Nitze in *Spec* IX, 355-61).

In keeping with this advertising activity of the community at Glastonbury was the composition of the *Perlesvaus,* somewhere between 1191 and 1250—but probably not long after 1191, (Nitze in *MPhil* XVII, 151-

66; 605-18, and in *SPhil* XV, 7-13). The tombs of Arthur and Guenevere are mentioned in a colophon to this prose romance. The narrative may be divided into eleven branches or chapters. In Branch I Arthur visits Saint Austin's chapel for the recovery of his prowess and his honor. A young page, Cahu, the son of Yvain, precedes him there in a dream, and is slain in reality, as in his dream. Miss Marjorie Williamson associates this episode with the Irish *Voyage of Maelduin* and the *Navigatio Sancti Brendani* (*MPhil* XXX, 5-11). After this visit Arthur is forced to fight a black knight with a flaming lance. This is supposed by Anitchkof to be a reference to Manichaeanism (*op. cit.,* p. 312). Arthur learns of the lineage of Perceval, or Perlesvaus, who had failed to accomplish the Grail Quest through not asking questions. This Perlesvaus is the son of Alain or Julain, who, in turn, was the son of Gais or Glais (not Bron). The Fisher King and the wicked King of Chastel Mortel are Perlesvaus' uncles. In Branches II-VI there is told Gawain's search for the Grail. He fails to ask the necessary questions when distracted by three drops of blood on a tablecloth. Lancelot now tries the search. He visits the king of the Waste City with whom he makes a mutual beheading wager. Nitze traces this motif back ultimately to a vegetation myth (*MPhil* XXXIII, 351-66). Branch VII introduces Perlesvaus in person. In Branch VIII Lancelot fails in the quest because of the sin of his love for Guenevere. There are further adventures of Perlesvaus: he is urged to rescue the Grail Castle from the King of Chastel Mortel who has usurped it since the death of the Fisher King. In Branch IX Perlesvaus liberates the Grail, Guenevere dies in grief at the death of her son Loholt, and Brien des Isles (who is drawn from the real Brian of Wallingford)[2] foments sedition with the aid of Keu (or Kay). There is a Three Day Tournament in which Gauvain must *faire au noauz,* as Lancelot did in Chrétien's *Lancelot.*

In Branch X Arthur makes a pilgrimage to the Grail Castle and learns the Sacrifice of the Mass in the five manners. He visits Guenevere's tomb at Avalon, or Glastonbury. Brian des Isles seeks to ruin Lancelot. Finally in Branch XI Perlesvaus clears up all complications, visits the Grail Castle for the last time, and sails away for ever. Note that there are three Grail quests in this romance.

The author suppresses most of the references to adultery and love and seeks to stress the "militant service of Christianity" and the New Testament as opposed to the Old. He claimed to have translated his narrative from the Latin original of a Josephus. Josephus Flavius, the historian, was considered a Christian priest in the Middle Ages, and we know that his work was owned and appreciated at Glastonbury. He was chosen as a fictitious source in order to lend as much credence as

[2] J. L. Weston in *Rom* LI, 362 and *MPhil*, XXII, 403.

possible to the Perlesvaus story. The real sources of the romance were Chrétien de Troyes and Robert of Boron.[3] The Christian solution of the Grail is very evident in the *Perlesvaus*, as in the work of Robert of Boron. The name Perlesvaus, for Perceval, is explained as equivalent to Par-lui-fez. The second volume of the edition prepared by W. A. Nitze and the late T. A. Jenkins will contain an exhaustive treatment of the sources of this material.[4] There are two extant redactions; we have been discussing the older.

We now come to the famous Vulgate prose romances, sometimes called the pseudo-Walter Mapes cycle. This group became the standard Arthurian reference for future readers; it was the *vulgate*, or common, general reference. Some of the MSS claim that Walter Mapes (d. 1210) wrote the entire cycle. Scarcely anyone today believes this; we doubt whether one medieval man could have written such a compilation, occupying seven volumes in the modern Sommer edition. This group of prose romances begins with the prose *Lancelot*, a work which, in its surviving form, is two and a half times as long as Dickens' *Pickwick Papers*. This *Lancelot* was first constructed in the last decade of the twelfth century and is based upon Chrétien's *Lancelot* and upon another biographical source, now lost. Anitchkof sees Manichaean or Montanist doctrine here also (*Archiv Rom* XIII, 519-38). It told of Lancelot's birth, of his education by the Lady of the Lake, of his early experiences at Arthur's court, of his love for Guenevere, and of his friendship for Galehout until the latter's death. In the early thirteenth century other writers inserted additional episodes, from other romances or to suit their fancy: among these are the *enserrement* of Merlin, the episode of the False Guenevere, the Wars of Claudas, the characters Bohort and Lionel, and the adventures of Hector. In this expanded form we commonly speak of the *Lancelot* as in three divisions: the *Galehout*, the *Charette*, and the *Agravain*. The *Agravain*, which is later, was perhaps the work of the same compiler who wrote the *Mort Artu*. It was this *Lancelot* that Paolo and Francesca were reading when they yielded to their fatal kiss (Dante, *Inferno*, V, vs. 128). Ferdinand Lot insists that the entire *Lancelot* was by one writer. Jesse L. Weston opposed this vigorously.

In the first years of the thirteenth century an unknown Cistercian monk composed a prose *Queste del Saint Graal*, showing a knowledge of the *Perlesvaus*, of Robert of Boron, and of the great *Lancelot*. He introduced, however, one tremendous innovation. Perceval was not pure enough to accomplish the Quest of the Grail. This writer introduced another character, the spotless Galahad, son of Lancelot. The Land of Galaad was the last stop of the Hebrews before they entered

[3] Nitze in *MPhil* I, 1-11.                    [4] This has since appeared (1937).

the Promised Land. The use of this name by the author of the *Queste* was prophetic (Anitchkof in *Rom* LIII, 388-391). This Cistercian was a mystic. With him, as Gilson has said (*Rom* LI, 321-347), "La quête du saint Graal est la recherche des secrets de Dieu, inconnus sans la grace, et inexprimables pour qui les a connus, c'est-à-dire la recherche de l'extase." There is no profane interest in this *Queste;* all is bent towards the implied goal, the pursuit of ecstasy through grace.

By 1205 another prose romance, the *Mort Artu,* was added to the preceding two. This was to become a prime source for the fifteenth century *Morte d'Arthur* of Malory. The *Mort Artu* was based upon the two earlier prose romances, and upon Chrétien's *Perceval* and *Lancelot.* Between 1205 and 1216 a fourth prose romance, the *Grand Saint Graal,* or *Estoire del Saint Graal,* was written. This retold the material in the prose version of Robert of Boron's *Joseph.* It was followed (*ca.* 1230) by the last of the Vulgate series, the *Estoire de Merlin* which included and continued the prose *Merlin* from Robert of Boron's poem.

In 1886 Gaston Paris indicated the existence of another cycle group of prose Arthurian romance, an abridgement of the material in the Vulgate group. All the MSS refer to these as the work of Robert of Boron, which is, of course, absurd. We call this group the pseudo-Robert of Boron cycle. Only fragments of the French originals have survived. The chief originality of this material is a closer association with the Tristan theme and much variation in treating the later adventures of Merlin. This second cycle had an *Estoire del Saint Graal,* a version of Robert Boron's *Merlin,* a Merlin continuation, a *Queste del Saint Graal,* and a *Mort Artu.* The Merlin continuation is in a MS of the Huth collection (Brit. M., Add. 38117), so we refer to it as the *Huth-Merlin.* A fragment of the *Mort Artu* of this cycle is in a MS of the Bibliothèque Nationale (fr. 340). A still later addition to the pseudo-Robert of Boron cycle was the *Brait de Merlin,* or 'Cry of Merlin,' which survives only in the Spanish *Baladro.* Indeed, it is through the Spanish and Portuguese *Demandas,* or 'Quests,' that we derive most of our knowledge of this cycle.

The reader will find an accompanying diagram intended to show the Vulgate prose romances in their proper setting. It would have been impractical to attempt the indication of every source. The crossing of lines would have become too complicated. We have marked the main relationships and shown how the Tristan legend and the Lancelot material were eventually bound up with the Grail. The *Palamedes,* a prose romance composed before 1240 (when it is mentioned by Frederick II), has two parts: the *Meliadus de Leonnoys* and the *Guiron le courtois* which were considered separate romances in the sixteenth century. In the first division, Palamedes, the son of Esclabor, a Babylonian, has

# GRAIL ROMANCES AND VULGATE CYCLE

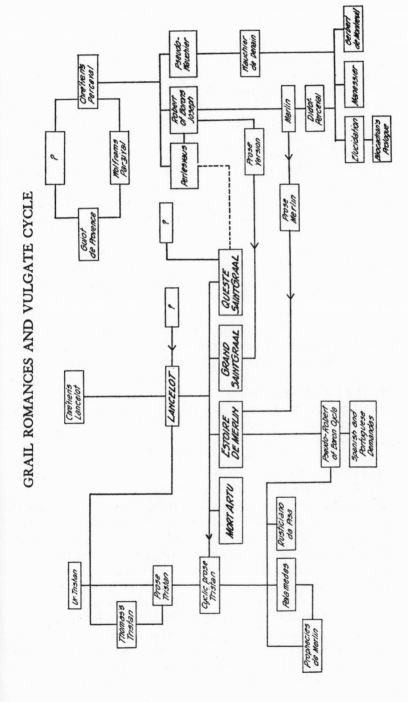

a very minor rôle; he has virtually no rôle at all in the second. It is odd that the romance should have been known by his name. The hero of the first part is Meliadus, the father of Tristan. Eventually Meliadus carries off the Queen of Scotland and would have been worsted by the opposition, including Arthur, if he had not been saved by Guiron le Courtois. The second division now begins. Guiron was related on his mother's side to the Grail family; by his father to Chlovis, King of the Franks. His friend, Danain of Maloaut, leaves his wife under the protection of Guiron. Guiron protects her virtue in spite of the greatest temptations and difficulties. Danain, not so loyal, later attempts to carry off Guiron's lady love. Guiron rescues her and dismisses his false friend unharmed. Danain finally requites such good treatment by saving both Guiron and the lady, whose name is Bloie. The romance of *Palamedes* was a great favorite in Italy—particularly with Boiardo and with Luigi Alamanni.

The *Compilation* of Rusticiano da Pisa was very unoriginal. He adapted it from a book belonging to Edward I of England—probably the cyclic prose *Tristan* itself. Edward was in Palestine from May, 1271, till August, 1272. Rusticiano says that he saw the book while Edward was on a crusade. The adaptation must have been made in 1272-1274. This Rusticiano is the same individual who took down from dictation the travels of Marco Polo while the latter was a fellow captive at Genoa in 1298. The thirteenth-century *Prophecies de Merlin* has no connection with the prophecies inserted by Geoffroi of Monmouth into his *Historia,* in the first half of the twelfth century. Written after 1272, this new list of prophecies was the propaganda of a Venetian Guelph. The sources used by the Venetian were the *Palamedes,* the cyclic prose *Tristan,* and the Vulgate cycle. The cyclic *Tristan* to which we have been constantly referring was an expansion of the earlier prose form, containing much additional material. For the Grail theme in the prose *Tristan* consult P. H. Coronedi in *Arch Rom* XV, 83-98.

It remains to say a few words about the *Elucidation* and *Bliocadran's Prologue.* Two MSS of Chrétien's *Perceval* (the Mons and Brit. Mus. 36614) have a preface of 1,282 lines, of which the first 484 are termed the *Elucidation* and the final portion (vss. 485-1,282) is called *Bliocadran's Prologue.* It is possible that the second portion is all that remains of a lost romance which gives the history of Perceval's father, who is here called Bliocadran. In verses 12 ff. of the *Elucidation,* a Maistre Blihis is cited as authority; he can only be the Bleheris mentioned in pseudo-Wauchier vs. 19,434, whom we have referred to before. This double preface in its existing form was composed late in the thirteenth century.

The etymology of *Graal,* or 'Grail,' is not definitely known. Robert of Boron places in the mouth of Petrus, a character in the *Joseph d'Arimathie,* the explanation *Graal < graer* to please. This is fantastic. More likely is the derivation from *cratalis* < Greek κρατήρ cup (Nitze in *MPhil* XIII, 681-4).

## EDITIONS

Chrétien de Troyes, *Li Contes del Graal,* ed. A. Hilka-Baist (Halle: Niemeyer, 1932); ed. C. Potvin [including the work of all continuators except Gerbert de Montreuil] (Mons: Soc. Biblioph. Belg., 1866, 6 vols.). Robert de Boron, *Estoire dou Graal* [including the *Merlin* fragment], ed. W. A. Nitze (Paris: Cfmâ, 1927).—*Didot Perceval,* ed. Jesse L. Weston in her *Legend of Sir Perceval* (London, 1909), II, 9-112. A. Pauphilet is preparing a new edition.—*Le Haut Livre du Graal, Perlesvaus,* ed. W. A. Nitze-T. A. Jenkins (Univ. Chicago Press, 1932, vol. I only; the second volume is in press).—Gerbert de Montreuil, *Continuation du Perceval,* ed. Mary Williams (Paris: Cfmâ, 1922-1925, 2 vols.).—*Vulgate Version of the Arthurian Romances,* ed. H. Oskar Sommer (Washington: Carnegie Institute, 1909-1916, 8 vols.); *Queste del Saint Graal,* ed. A. Pauphilet (Paris: Cfmâ, 1923); *Mort Artu,* ed. J. D. Bruce (Halle: Niemeyer, 1910). *Merlin* [containing the Huth-Merlin and the prose version of Robert of Boron's poem], ed. G. Paris-J. Ulrich (Paris: *SATF,* 1886, 2 vols.).—Consult also Brugger's "Studien zur Merlinsage" in *ZfrSL,* vols. XXIX, XXX, XXXI, XXXIII, XXXIV, XXXV. He publishes some texts.—For the prose *Tristans,* the *Palamedes,* and the compilation by Rusticiano da Pisa, consult E. Löseth in *Le Roman en prose de Tristan, le roman de Palamède et la compilation de Rusticien de Pise* (Paris: BEcHE, 1891).—*Les Prophécies de Merlin,* ed. L. A. Paton (New York, MLA Monograph, 1927).—*The Elucidation, a Prologue to the Conte del Graal,* ed. A. W. Thompson (New York: *IFS,* 1931).

# CHAPTER XXXI

## THE *ROMANCE OF THE ROSE:* ITS PREDECESSORS AND IMITATORS

E. Faral, "*Le Roman de la Rose* et la pensée française au XIIIᵉ siècle," in *Rev. Deux Mondes,* Sept. 1926 (430-57).
Ernest Langlois, *Sources et Origines du Roman de la Rose* (Paris and Lille, 1891).
H. O. Taylor, *The Mediaeval Mind* (4th ed.; Macmillan, 1925).
G. Paris in *HLF* XXIX, 455-525 [on the minor *Arts of love*].

Three currents, flowing through the ages from remote antiquity, united in the thirteenth century to form a great masterpiece, the *Roman de la Rose* of Guillaume de Lorris (4,058 verses). These currents were: dream literature, allegory, and the conception of love as an art. Jehan de Meun undertook to continue the nearly completed work of Guillaume, but he altered the style and tone, and his continuation had different predecessors. We shall begin with a consideration of the predecessors of Guillaume de Lorris.

Dreams always fascinate men when they cannot explain them. In the floating unreality of dreams or visions, sages of antiquity believed that they were nearer to Divinity, Wisdom, Prophecy and other occult matters which eluded them in conscious, normal life. The Bible is filled with the significance of dreams: the story of Joseph, Jacob's ladder, the Apocalypse, or Book of Revelations. Macrobius in his *Saturnalia* classified dreams into five types: *sommium, visio, oraculum, insomnium,* and *phantasma,* or *visum,* of which the first three alone had prophetic value. The vision of Philosophy which Boethius saw in his prison cell *(De Consolatione philosophiae)* is an example of the development of the dream motif in Latin literature. Medieval Irish literature is filled with *fisi,* or visions, where the saint sees Hell, Purgatory, Heaven, or all three. These Irish visions were certainly inspired by another Apocalypse, the *Apocalypse Saint Paul,* an apocryphal work in which the angel Michael lifts up Saint Paul and shows him the miseries of earth, the City of Christ, Hell, and lastly, Paradise with all the Old Testament fathers. (There are fifty-one sections.) The *Visio Tnugdali,* or *Tundali,* is a twelfth-century Latin version of such a descent into hell. We also have a Latin *contentio* in which the poet witnesses in a vision his body and soul in active debate. Such a dream debate became a regular convention in vernacular literature. In the early thirteenth-century, Raoul de Houdenc,

# ALLEGORY

whom we have noted as a writer of Arthurian romances, composed his *Songe d'Enfer* and *Songe de Paradis.* (The second of these is often attributed to an imitator and not to Raoul himself.)

Allegory as a device is extremely ancient; it is particularly pleasing to the Eastern or Oriental mind. Teaching in parables is common in the New Testament. Jewish exegesis has always made extensive use of allegory, which may be defined as "exposition by a sense other than literal." In Alexandria, where one sought to unite Christianity and Platonism, allegory was essential to attain *gnosis.* Philo the Jew, whose influence was so immense on the early Church fathers, employed it, and made a gift of it to Origen, who firmly fixed the Christian Bible exegesis. Saint Augustine and Saint Jerome continued allegory as one of the four ways of interpreting scripture by a multiplicity of senses (*Spec* IV, 282-290). The *Psychomachia,* a battle of the Vices and the Virtues, by Prudentius (348-*ca.* 410), is a masterpiece. Its influence during the entire Middle Ages was constant. We must not forget the *Nuptials of Philology* (410-427), of Martianus Capella where Philology marries Mercury, and her bridesmaids are the seven Liberal Arts. This is in mixed prose and verse. With such models it is no wonder that allegory was scarcely ever absent from the later medieval mind. As the *Rationale divinorum officiorum* of Gulielmus Durandus explains, in the second half of the thirteenth century, the Mass and entire Church liturgy had a complicated allegorical significance.

The crowning work of allegory in the twelfth century was the *Anticlaudianus* of Alanus de Insulis, or Alain de Lille, composed in the 1180's. The *Hymns* of Adam of Saint Victor, which preceded the *Anticlaudianus,* were masterpieces of symbolism, but the work of Alain de Lille reached a height in religious and philosophic allegory that was to be surpassed only by the *Divina Commedia* of Dante. Alain (d. 1202) was probably a Fleming who taught at Paris. There is a legend concerning him, that he became so shocked at his own daring in attempting to explain the Trinity in a single lecture, that he withdrew into a Cistercian abbey as sheep-herder. According to another tale, he entered Clairvaux under Saint Bernard. He was called, in his day, *Doctor universalis.* He was the author of a *Liber in distinctionibus dictionum theologicalium,* a *Liber de planctu naturae* (inspired by Boethius), some *theologicae,* and a book of *sententiae,* in addition to his *Anticlaudianus.* To summarize the contents of this last: Nature does the best she can on Earth; but she must call upon her heavenly sisters, Concord, Plenty, Favor, Youth, Laughter, Shame, Modesty, Honesty, Reason, Dignity, Prudence, Piety, Faith, Virtue, and Nobility, if she would accomplish a perfect task. Nature and her sisters resolve to make Man a mirror of their powers. Reason and Prudence are sent to God in a chariot prepared by Wisdom, where, with the help of Theology, they obtain a human soul for Man. He is made and endowed by all with gifts. Alecto and her evil vices are enraged and prepare for battle against the creating Virtues; the Vices are defeated. Love reigns in place of Discord.

We have not begun to enumerate all the allegorical figures which Alain introduced into his poem. The same Raoul de Houdenc who wrote the dream of Hell, and possibly that of Paradise, was also the author of a distinctive allegorical work, the *Roman des eles* (583 verses) or 'Romance of the Wings'. Chivalry, a dove, has two wings, Generosity *(Largece)* and Courtliness *(Courtoisie)*. These wings are made of wondrous feathers, among them love, in the form of a rose, of wine, and of the endless sea. Huon de Méri composed, in 1234, a *Tournoiement Antechrist* which was a battle of the Vices and the Virtues. It has 3,544 verses in the familiar octosyllabic meter. Be it noted that the allegory thus far employed was all on a religious or philosophic basis, with the exception of the chivalric poem of Raoul de Houdenc. Another allegory of chivalry was the *Ordene de chevalerie* (506 verses). The anonymous poet narrates how Hue de Tabarie, a prisoner of Saladin, is asked to tell of the ceremonial used in making a Christian knight. Hue lists the stages, with symbolical meaning: care of hair, bath, bed, white linen, underclothes, vermilion robe, hose of brown *saie,* small white girdle, spurs, sword, white *coiffe,* and *colée.* The duties of a knight, according to Hue, are: good judgment, no treason, respect for women, abstinence, and the hearing of Mass daily. Saladin is so charmed that he releases Hue with presents. This *Ordene* was put into an abridged prose form, also in the thirteenth century.

There is the *Songe du Castel,* of the late thirteenth century, in which Man is likened to a Castle. He stands siege from the seven Deadly Sins and is at length overcome by Death. The World looks on without interfering. Miss Roberta D. Cornelius publishes this in *PMLA* XLVI, 321-332. This is quite similar to the *Chasteau d'Amour* of Bishop Grosseteste, written in or near 1230, where the Virgin is the Castle offering refuge to Man.

The study of Eros, the god of love, and of his commands was a favorite theme since Ovid. Boethius contributed to it, under Platonic inspiration, and we have observed how the Provençal troubadours and the Countess Marie de Champagne elaborated the theme into a system of courtly love, with Cupid as a feudal lord who was accessible only to the upper classes. Andreas Capellanus, Marie's chaplain, gave this doctrine permanent and tangible form in his famous *De arte honeste amandi,* composed between 1174 and 1186. In the thirteenth century, Ovid and Andreas Capellanus were the joint inspiration of polite society. A certain Jacques d'Amiens adapted Ovid's *Ars amandi* into French with the title *Ovide de art en roumant* (2,384 octosyllables), and in 1290 Drouart la Vache put into French Andreas' work as the *Livre d'amours* (more than 7,500 octosyllables). This was often attributed wrongly to Gautier, the individual to whom it was dedicated. Jacques d'Amiens, whose adaptation also belongs to the close of the century, substituted for Ovid's Roman and pagan allusions more up-to-date examples. The Beguines are his ideal women. We have already referred to the *Bestiaire d'amours* of Richart de Fournival; we must mention, also by him, a *Poissanche d'amours* and a *Consaus d'amours,* both in prose. In the latter Richart professes to answer a letter from his sister in which she requests advice on *amer par amours.* He replies that "amours en general n'est autre cose fors que ardeurs de pensée qui gouverne le volenté du cuer," and he then defines the conditions of spiritual and of temporal love, with learned quotations and observations of experience. The *Poissanche* is in dialogue form between Richart and a pupil, the subject being "par coi ne de coi ne comment corages de femme est par force de nature esmeus en amour."

The *Clef d'amors* (3,426 octosyllables), by an anonymous poet of western Normandy, enjoyed immense popularity. Because of a riddle which it contains (vs. 3,413 ff.) this treatise is usually dated in the year 1280. The poet renovates Ovid in the style approved by Jacques d'Amiens, but he adds certain dialogues of the type employed by Andreas. The god of love appears to him in a dream and bids him write down the rules of love. There are references to certain *fabliaux,* moralizing passages, and an occasional disapproval of womankind. The poet is a vigorous writer with some roughness and obscurity of style. He names himself and his lady in an acrostic (vs. 3,377 ff.), but this has not been successfully interpreted. As further specimens of this type of literature we must mention the fragmentary translation of the *Ars amandi* made by Mestre Elie (1,308 octosyllables surviving) in the first half of the thirteenth century; also the *Lai d'Amors* of a clerc Girart, with 518 verses, and the *Set ars d'amours* of André Fabre. Such arts of love continued to flourish in the fourteenth century, which is not our province here. We shall do no more than mention the names of such fourteenth-century writers on love as Mahius de Poiriers, Raymont Adam, Baudouin de Condé, and the poet of the *Ovide moralisé.* Guillaume de Lorris wrote earlier than most of the treatises on love which we have just listed, but his work had much the same purpose, combined, as we have remarked, with a skillful use of the dream motif and of allegory.

Guillaume de Lorris began his *Romance of the Rose* sometime between 1225 and 1237. This date is based upon a statement by Jean de Meun. We know that Jean wrote his continuation, in part at least, before 1277. He says that Guillaume died forty years before and it is assumed that Guillaume died before he could complete his poem. Jean de Meun adds further that he himself was born at approximately the time Guillaume died and we believe he had sufficient basis for his statements. Guillaume's chief source may have been actual experience. We infer that he met a young girl who treated him pleasantly (with *Bel Accueil*). He was carried away with desire and made advances, which caused her innate sense of modesty *(Dangier)* to drive him away. He saw his folly and entertained with her a more moderate friendship, for a while, until her parents became alarmed and removed her from his sight. At the same time there can be little doubt that Guillaume intended to write a treatise on instruction in love. In verses 2,087-2,765 the God of Love gives a dissertation on his "commands," the ills to be endured, and the good things accruing from love. The poet's main sources were, aside from such experience, Chrétien's *Cligés,* Ovid's *Ars amandi* and *Metamorphoses,* and Andreas Capellanus. The late F. M. Warren once suggested as a source the *Hysmene and Hysmenias* of the Byzantine Eustathius Macrembolites (*PMLA* XXXI, 232-46). This is far from likely. M. Aroux, as long ago as 1854, and now M. Anitchkof, have held the theory that Guillaume was an Albigensian because of certain dialogue. This theory goes too far. The town of Lorris lies between Orléans and Montargis, so Guillaume was an Orléanais; he may have frequented Paris. Whether he was of noble or humble parentage we cannot say.

The plot of this first part of the *Romance of the Rose* (4,058 verses, 8-syllable) is quite simple. Five years before, when the poet was but twenty, he had a dream. It seemed to him that he rose early and took a stroll beside a river, broader but shallower than the Seine. He came upon a garden with a wall and no visible gate. Painted on the wall were representations of Hatred, Wickedness, Lowness *(Vilenie),* Covetousness, Avarice, Envy, Sadness, Age, Hypocrisy, and Poverty. The garden beyond the wall looked so charming that the poet resolved to enter. He was admitted, after searching for a gate, by Idleness, the "love" of Amusement. It was Amusement, or *Deduit,* who had constructed this garden of exotic plants and trees. Guillaume was led to a spot where he found Amusement with another lady named Gladness, Lady Generosity with a knight of the lineage of Arthur, and Nobility, Courtesy, and Youth, each with a partner. The God of Love was also there. Guillaume inspected the gardens; he saw the spot where Narcissus had died. In a rose garden he was much impressed by the beauty of a bud. Alas! the God of Love had followed him: Guillaume was pierced by five of Love's arrows. The poet gave in at once and was possessed and instructed in his behavior by Love. Fair Welcome *(Bel*

*Accueil),* a youth, advanced and invited the poor lover to approach the roses. When the latter suggested that he would like the precious bud, Modesty, or Womanly Resistance *(Dangier),* advanced and drove him away. He sought the counsels of Friend. On Friend's advice the poet-lover sought pardon of *Dangier,* once more obtained the company of Fair Welcome, and approached the Rose with care. He was allowed to give it a chaste kiss, but Slander was active and noised this kiss about to Resistance and Jealousy. Jealousy resolved to shut the Rose within a strong wall. Resistance, Shame, Fear, and Slander were appointed guardians of the gates. Guillaume was overcome by grief, for Fair Welcome was enclosed within the stronghold, and he could no longer approach the Rose. Thus terminates the portion of the *Romance of the Rose* by Guillaume de Lorris. In two of the three hundred odd MSS there is a conclusion of eighty lines of inferior workmanship, by some anonymous poet, which narrates how Pity, Beauty, Fair Welcome, Loyalty, Soft-Glance, and Simplicity stole forth when Jealousy was asleep and presented the Rose to the poet. After a night of joy the Rose was returned to its prison, the lover promised fidelity and woke up.

A few poets show direct influence from the first portion of the *Romance of the Rose* and apparently did not know the second part by Jean de Meun. The *Fablel dou Dieu d'amors* was formerly considered a source, but Ernest Langlois in his edition of the *Romance of the Rose* (I, 5) takes the stand that the influence flowed the other way. The beginning of the *Voie de Paradis* of Rutebeuf (composed after 1261) shows influence from vss. 45-83 of Guillaume de Lorris; possibly there is a similar trace in a song by Thibaut de Champagne. An unknown Messire Thibaut was the author of the *Roman de la Poire* (3,027 verses). Professor F. M. Warren wished to make this also a source, but I am more inclined with Langlois to accept it as a poem dependent upon Guillaume de Lorris. This *Roman de la Poire,* composed between 1237 and 1270, is a remarkable composition. Its author was a man of the upper classes who understood arms and who was at the same time a well-read scholar, citing Plato by name, the contents of Ovid's *Metamorphoses,* and other classical references. He also knew such characters in popular literature as Cligés and Fenice, Tristan and Yseult, Guenelon, Alexander, and Pyramus and Thisbé. The poem is apparently the first in France to conceal names in acrostics (vss. 837-1424, 2413-2604, 2793-2951). After the fashion which was inaugurated in the *Guillaume de Dôle,* Thibaut has inserted into his text twelve independent love lyrics. The content of the poem is flattery of Thibaut's lady, who lives in Paris, and comment on his own feelings and upon love in general. There are some Picard forms in the rhyme.

Jean Clopinel was born at Meun-sur-Loire. By court record we know that he died before November, 1305. His house on the rue Saint-Jacques was regarded as a landmark till after the middle of the sixteenth century when it was demolished. As Jean, in his continuation of the verses of Guillaume, mentions the death of Manfred (1266) and does not refer to Charles of Anjou, King of Sicily, as King of Jerusalem (1277), we may conclude that his famous continuation was composed between 1266 and 1277; it was probably begun before 1268, the year Charles of Anjou ascended the throne of Sicily. Jean Clopinel was also the author of numerous translations: of the *De re militari* of Vegetius, of the *Marvels of Ireland* of Giraldus Cambrensis, of the *Letters* of Abelard and Eloise, of a treatise by an English monk Aelred, and of the *De consolatione philosophiae* of Boethius. Other original works were: the *Testament* (2,175 verses, 12-syllable) written between 1291-1295, and possibly the *Codicile* (eleven strophes of eight verses each). Many other compositions, of the fourteenth and fifteenth centuries, have been erroneously assigned to him, from time to time. Seven of these have been published under his name, so they will bear listing: *Le Pèlerinage, La Forest de tristesse, La Destruction et le ravissement d'Hélène, Le Dodechedron de fortune, Le Miroir d'alchymie, La Complainte de nature à l'alchymiste errant, La Response de l'alchymiste à nature.* Jean de Meun's version of the *Marvels of Ireland* is lost. The translation from Boethius has not been positively identified. Langlois believes it is a certain prose translation of the *Consolatio* which is preserved in four MSS (*Rom* XLII, 331-69); Paul Meyer and Gaston Paris identified it with another similar translation which is extant in seventeen MSS (*Rom* II, 271). See also F. Nagel in *ZfrPh* XV, 1-23.

We now proceed to a summary of Jean de Meun's continuation of the *Romance of the Rose*. The lover prepared for death when he saw that the Rose was denied him. Reason flew down from her tower and in a very licentious speech offered consolation, showing him how fatal it was to remain in the service of the God of Love (vs. 7,223). The poet turned to Friend who also gave encouragement, but of a different sort. Sweet-Thought and Sweet-Speech now returned to the lover, but not Sweet-Glance. The lover walked towards the path of Much-Giving but Riches refused him entry. The unhappy poet went for a stroll in the garden, where he was reproached by the God of Love for his long conversation with Reason. The poet made confession and was given pardon for his momentary weakness. Love gathered his forces for an attack upon the prison of the Rose and proceeded to harangue them. False-Appearance gave trouble for a moment as Love did not wish to admit him into the army; he was deemed indispensable with his "foxiness" *(Renardie)*. False-Appearance and Constraint-Abstinence succeed in getting the lover into the fortress by guile. When Guillaume sought to pick the Rose he was repulsed and evicted again. Venus was sent for. The priest, Genius, was sent by Nature who complained of the refusal of man to follow her laws. The army thus encouraged attacked; it was successful and Fair Welcome granted the Rose to the lover (vs. 22046). And thus the poem ended: "It was day and I awoke."

This brief abstract of the portion of the romance composed by Jean de Meun does no justice to the vast amount of mythology, classical lore, and medieval science which Jean introduced, particularly in the speeches of Reason and Nature. He is hard upon women and the mendicant orders—Dominicans and Franciscans. He also denies the Divine Right of kings and declares that kings are but servitors of the people. Jean was obviously a libertine, but his metaphysics and his theology seem thoroughly orthodox. To seek for the sources of Jean de Meun among the ancients would be a complicated task, for he knew and cited them all—all that were used in his day. Aristotle, Plato (*Timaeus*), Vergil, Ovid, Horace, Juvenal, even Lucretius, all contribute to his learning. The four chief sources were the *De planctu naturae* of Alain de Lille, the *De consolatione philosophiae* of Boethius, Ovid, and the writings of Guillaume de Saint-Amour. Jean knew of the scientific work of Geber and Roger Bacon; he had considerable interest in alchemy. Jean de Meun has been called the "Voltaire of the Middle Ages." Nearly three hundred MSS of the completed *Romance of the Rose* are still in existence, which, with liberal allowance for those disappeared, speak well for its popularity. Since 1290 there existed a rehandling of the material by a Picard priest, Gui de Mori, which could not compete in popularity with the original.

The continuation by Jean de Meun aroused a large number of imitators but most of these were in the fourteenth, fifteenth, and sixteenth centuries. The *Dit de la panthère d'amors,* of Nicole de Margival, was written after 1290, for that was the year in which Drouart la Vache died, leaving unfinished his *Traité d'amour,* his adaptation of Andreas Capellanus. Nicole de Margival most certainly used Drouart's translation. He also utilized the *Bestiaire d'amour* of Richart de Fournival, but the first suggestion of the *Panthère* was owed to the *Romance of the Rose.* The poem has 2,665 octosyllables. The poet fell asleep one night at Soissons; he was carried away by birds (in his dream, of course), and laid down in a forest, where he saw beasts of marvellous beauty, among them a lovely panther who was cared for by all, save the Dragon. This panther had a delicious breath. The God of Love appeared as the beasts disappeared. The poet admitted his servitude, received instructions, and departed on horseback in quest of the delicious panther. He finally came upon the panther in a ditch at the bottom of a valley, surrounded by a hedge. The God of Love explained

the sense of all this. The Dragon was Envy. The poet cleared all ob-
stacles and arrived before the panther. He was dumb and could say
nothing. He noticed that he was torn and wounded. Love took the
poet with him, where he was visited by Venus. After much discussion,
the poet was advised to appeal to fickle Fortune for favor in his love.
Fortune was eventually appeased and the poet viewed once more his
beloved panther. Nicole de Margival, the poet, ended by telling us
that the allegory of this poem was all too true, save for the happy ending. This *Panthère d'amors* contains a number of inserted lyrics by other
poets. Nicole de Margival was also the author of a brief poem of two
hundred and sixteen verses entitled *Les Trois mors et les trois vis*.
This theme was by no means original with him.

## EDITIONS

Raoul de Houdenc, *Songe d'Enfer, Songe de Paradis,* and *Roman des
Eles de Prouesse,* ed. Scheler in his *Trouvères belges,* nouv. série (Louvain,
1879).—The *Anticlaudianus* of Alain de l'Isle is in Migne, *P.L.,* vol. CCX,
and in Wright's *Satirical Latin Poems of the XIIth and XIIIth Centuries*
(London, 1877), vol. II.—Huon de Méri, *Li Tornoiemenz Antecrit,* ed. G.
Wimmer (Marburg, 1888).—*Ordene de chevalerie,* ed. R. T. House (Chicago,
1918).—Robert Grosseteste, *Chasteau d'Amours,* ed. J. Murray (Paris,
1918).—Jacques d'Amiens, *L'Art d'amors und Li Remèdes d'amors,* ed. G.
Körting (Leipzig, 1868).—*Drouart la Vache, traducteur d'André le Chapelain,*
ed. R. Bossuat (Paris, 1926). W. M. McLeod has prepared an edition of the
*Poissanche* and the *Consaus d'amours* of Richart de Fournival, as a doctoral
dissertation at the University of North Carolina. The second of these has
been printed in *SPhil* XXXII (1935), 1-21.—*La Clef d'amors,* ed. A. Doutre-
pont (Halle: *BN,* 1890).—Maistre Elie, *Oeuvres,* ed. Kühne-Stengel (Marburg, 1896).—*Le Roman de la Rose,* ed. Ernest Langlois (Paris: *SATF,* 1914-
1924, 5 vols.). The portion by Guillaume de Lorris, ed. R. W. Linker,
(Chapel Hill, 1937).—*Li Fablel dou Dieu d'amors,* ed. Charles Oulmont in *Les
Débats du Clerc et du Chevalier dans la Litt. Poét. du m.-â* (Paris: Champion,
1911). Messire Thibaut, *Li Romanz de la Poire,* ed. F. Stehlich (Halle: Niemeyer, 1881).—The minor poems which have been attributed to Jean de Meun
are published by Méon in his edition of the *Roman de la Rose* (Paris, 1814),
vol. IV.—Jean de Meun, *Art de chevalerie,* ed. U. Robert (Paris: *SATF,*
1897).—Jean Priorat, *Li Abrejance de l'ordre de chevalerie* (Paris: *SATF,*
1897). This is a versification of Jean de Meun's prose.—Nicole de Margival,
*La Panthère d'amors,* ed. H. A. Todd (Paris: *SATF,* 1883).—*Les Trois mors
et les trois vis,* ed. Montaiglon in *L'Alphabet de la mort de Hans Holbein*
(1856); *Les Cinq poèmes des Trois mors et les trois vis,* ed. S. Glixelli (Paris,
1914).

# CHAPTER XXXII

## LYRIC VERSE IN THE THIRTEENTH CENTURY

Consult the same general references as in Chapter XIX; also,
Gröber, *Grundriss*, vol. II, pt. 1.
L. Clédat, *Rutebeuf* (2nd ed.; Paris: Hachette, 1909).
H. P. Dyggve in *NeuphMitteil* XXX, 177-214; XXXI, 1-62.

Lyric poetry in the thirteenth century is ordinarily classified in two
groups: from 1200 to 1230 and from 1230 to 1280. During the first
period, conditions were similar to those of the late twelfth century.
Patrons were still plentiful and bourgeois movements were not yet
prominent. Perhaps it was owing to the reforms of Saint Louis, perhaps to the wearing out of the chivalrous ideal, that the second half
of the twelfth century saw the passing away of many great feudal
houses; activity shifted away from Champagne and the Ile-de-France. Picardy and the Walloon territory became the center of wealth and com-
mercial activity. In this second period *puis,* or bourgeois contests of
poetry, were established in many of the wealthy towns, in Arras,
Valenciennes, Douai, Lille, and Tournai. The courtly poetry which
had been wont to charm the ears of lords and ladies of delicate feelings and refinement became a game that the people could enjoy.
There was a notable rise of interest in the *jeux partis* and in
other *genres* which were more amusing than expressive of feeling. The
*chanson,* or love song, continued in popularity but became more conventional. The transition towards the fourteenth century, with its in-
terminable, long-winded verse, was under way.

In the thirteenth century, the *chanson,* the *serventois,* the *pastourelle,*
and the *jeu parti* continued in high favor, but other types with fixed
form also appeared. The *motet* and the *conduit* were sung by two
or three voices, usually in *deschant* with the melody carried by a *tenor*
(or intermediate voice). The *balade, virelai, estampie,* and *rondeau*
were fixed with regard to refrains and stanzaïc structure; then there
were the *grant chant* and the *complainte.* All of these showed a trend
towards artificiality. The *chansons* regularly ended with *envois* towards some special patron. An innovation, which causes no surprise, is
the lyric with religious theme, most often a prayer or greeting to the
Blessed Virgin. Gautier de Coincy, the author of a collection of Virgin
miracles, was one of the earliest, if not the very first poet who gave expression to his lyric vein in this pious manner. The others are anonymous. (Consult A. Långfors in *Rom* LIII, 474-538).

We shall now proceed to list the more important poets of this century. A nearly complete list can be found in Gröber, *op. cit.*

Guillaume de Ferrières, the Vidame de Chartres, took part in the Fourth Crusade and, presumably as Grandmaster of the Templars, died at Damietta in 1219. One of his lyrics was inserted into the *Guillaume de Dôle* romance, which would speak for his popularity. It is a pity that we do not have more than a half dozen of his poems preserved. Richart de Semilli was famous for his *pastourelles.* Three lyrics are preserved to us from Gilles des Vieux-Maisons. Auboin de Sézanne (d. 1221-1229) was a Champenois who wrote for the Countess Marie of Brie. Other poets of the first period in the thirteenth century were Hue II of Lusignan, Count of the Marche (1208-1249), Maurice de Craon, Renaud de Sableuil, Thibaut de Blaison, Audefroi le Bastart, and Richart de Fournival. We possess twenty of Richart's lyrics, mostly *chansons* of allegorical content. One poem is a *jeu parti.*

Thibaut IV (1201-1253) was Count of Champagne (1214) and King of Navarre (1234). He was a grandson of Henry the Liberal, of Champagne, patron of Chrétien de Troyes, and through his mother he was related to Sancho VII, King of Navarre. Defamers in his own day accused him of poisoning Louis VIII of France, and later authorities assume that he was guilty of a very intimate liaison with Queen Blanche of Castille, the mother of Louis IX of France. It is certain that both of these accusations had no foundation. Thibaut joined the coalition against Blanche, on the death of Louis VIII, and he deserted it very readily, which drew upon him the hatred of his fellow plotters. Thibaut made a Crusade voyage to the Holy Land (1239) but returned when he realized the hopelessness of the situation. He was a restless character. Constantly moving back and forth between Rheims, Blois, and Pampelune (in Navarre) he encouraged tourneys, endowed abbeys and colleges, served as patron to men of letters, and indulged in many private wars. He was an active man though somewhat of a dilettante. There are preserved to-day sixty-nine lyrics which are certainly his, and ten others which are more doubtful in their authorship. Dante attributed a lyric to Thibaut (*De vulgari eloquentia,* II, chap. VI, 5) which belonged to Gace Brulé. Eight of Thibaut's lyrics are *jeux partis;* there are two *pastourelles* and one *serventois;* the remainder are *chansons* and Crusade poems.

Another poet of high degree was Pierre Mauclerc, *conte de Bretagne* (1192-?-1250). He held the title of Count of Brittany only during the minority of his son (1217-1237). After that period he was Pierre de Braine, *chevalier.* By courtesy he was often referred to as the Count of Brittany. Some authorities believe it is his son who was the poet.

Another noble troubadour was Jehan de Brienne, King of Jerusalem, and Emperor-regent of Constantinople from 1231-1237. A very picturesque character was Colin Muset, a native of Lorraine. He was a travelling jongleur whose chief patrons were the Count of Vaudemont, the Lord of Vignory, and "la bone duchesse," whoever she may have been. There is a chance that he can be identified with the so-called anonymous *trouvère de Choiseul,* a poet from whom we have two pieces, who frequented what is to-day the arrondissement of Chaumont (Haute-Marne). Aside from these two poems of uncertain ascription we possess thirteen lyrics by Colin Muset. Muset flourished around 1234 and possibly was in the service of Thibaut de Champagne and of Jehan de Joinville, biographer of Saint-Louis. His lyrics are very personal, betraying their author's Epicurean instincts.

It has been difficult to distinguish between Guiot de Dijon and Jocelin de Dijon. We have sixteen lyrics by Guiot and three by Jocelin.

After 1230, Arras became a great center for the poets. Almost one half of the quantity of lyric verse preserved (previous to the fourteenth century) was the work of poets from that district. Charles d'Anjou, fourth son of Louis VIII and the younger brother of Saint Louis, was a patron of some of them; also Robert II, Count of Artois. The majority of these northern poets were probably staid burghers for whom poetry was an avocation.

Jehan Bretel (d. 1272) was a most productive lyricist and for years was leader of the poetic circle at Arras: he was one of the hereditary *sergens* of the river Saint-Vaast. He was a specialist in *jeux partis;* we have a large number of these preserved (ninety pieces). Our information on his death and many other useful particulars on the *pui* at Arras are found in the *Register* of the *Confrérie des jongleurs et bourgeois d'Arras* (B.N. fr. 8541).

Adam le Bossu, or Adam de le Halle, or Adam d'Arras, as he is variously called, was born in the middle of the thirteenth century. He left school in order to marry a young girl, named Marie; after several years of wedded life they decided to separate for a time so that he might go to Paris to finish his studies. This departure was to have taken place in 1275 or 1276. We have his comedy, the *Jeu de la feuillée,* and a *Congé,* or departure poem, written on the eve of Adam's departure. Whether he actually left at the time we do not know. The Count of Artois took Adam to Italy with him in 1282 and it is probable that Adam died there in 1288. He was a musician as well as a poet. There remains of his poetry two dramatic *jeux* (*Jeu de la feuillée* and *Jeu de Robin et Marion*), his *Congé,* and various *motets, chansons, rondeaux,* and *jeux partis;* also a *dit d'amours,* several strophes on death, and the first nineteen laisses of a *chanson de geste* on the Roi de Sezile.

From 1250 to 1280 there flourished a poet of most independent and, shall we say, quarrelsome nature, who is none the less great. His name was Rutebeuf and he was a native of Champagne, domiciled at Paris. He married for the second time on January 2, 1261. We know a great deal about his likes and dislikes but most of the events in his life will ever remain an enigma. He had a particular antipathy toward the mendicant orders, the Dominicans and the Franciscans. The Dominicans were allowed to established chairs of theology within the University of Paris and their teaching was becoming popular. The Franciscans also were attracting crowds of worshippers to their churches. The secular clergy, both at the University and in the parish churches, were disgusted at this rapidly growing popularity of the monastic orders. There was a keen struggle within the University (1250-1257) led by the secular cleric and rector, Guillaume de Saint-Amour (d. 1272). This Guillaume was finally dismissed by papal order, together with three other regents or professors. Rutebeuf sympathized heartily with Guillaume's stand and sought to defend him. In some of his poems Rutebeuf went farther and attacked the secular clergy also for avarice and vanity. He excepted the students, or clerics in minor orders, who were studying at the universities, and for whom he showed genuine sympathy. Rutebeuf was an opponent of the King's Crusades; he deplored the preference many people had for their bodies rather than for their souls. On the whole, Rutebeuf was a poet and thinker of considerable talent; but he could not have been a pleasant neighbor. His extreme bitterness and his personal style of writing have caused some to compare him with François Villon and call him the Villon of the thirteenth century. The Italian Brunetto Latini may have had him in mind when he wrote in his *Livre dou tresor*, "Le rire, le jeu, voilà la vie du jongleur, qui se moque de lui-même, de sa femme, de ses enfants, de tout le monde." He had a number of patrons, among them the Count of Poitiers (d. 1270), brother of Saint Louis. He owed much inspiration to the first part of the *Roman de la Rose* (by Guillaume de Lorris), and there can be no doubt that he himself influenced the second part (by Jean de Meun). He had a close familiarity with most of the *chansons de geste* and romances which preceded him. Was he the model for Jean de Meun's character of *Faux-Semblant*, or False Appearance?

A list of Rutebeuf's writings must be a long one. He was so well-known and appreciated that his work was not allowed to become anonymous or to fall into obscurity. We know the following: *Chanson des ordres, Chanson de Pouille, Chanson de Nostre-Dame, Ave Maria, Dit de Nostre-Dame, Dit des propriétés de Nostre-Dame* (or *Neuf joies Nostre Dame*), *Complainte d'Anseau de l'Isle-Adam, Complainte au comte de Nevers, Complainte au roi de Navarre, Complainte du comte de Poitiers, Ordres de Paris, Dit des Beguines, Vie du monde* (or *Complainte Sainte Eglise*), *Dit de la mensonge* (or *Bataille des vices contre les vertus*), *Dit des cordeliers, Dit des Jacobins, Pharisian* (or *Hypocrisie*), *Dit de l'Université de Paris, Discorde de l'Université de Paris, Discorde de l'Université et des Jacobins, Dit de Maistre Guillaume de Saint-Amour, Complainte de Maistre Guillaume de Saint-Amour, Plaies du monde, Dit des règles, Complainte de Jofroi de Sergines, Complainte de Constantinople, Complainte d'outre mer,. Dit de Pouille, Disputoizon du Croisé et du Décroisé, Dispute de Charlot et du Barbier, Dit de la voie de Tunes, Dit de la pauvreté de Rustebeuf, Nouvelle complainte d'outre-mer, Dit des Ribauds de Grève, Renard le Bestourné, Voie de Paradis, Estat du monde, Mariage de Rustebeuf, La Griesche d'esté, La Griesche d'yver, Paiz de Rustebeuf, Mort de Rustebeuf,* and the *Complainte de Rustebeuf.*

This is a list of the works of Rutebeuf which can be called lyric. Note that there are no love poems. Satires, Crusade poems, and laments occupied his tastes and attention. For the sake of completeness we shall list here his non-lyric works, although they are also given elsewhere. They are: (dramatic) *Dit de l'herberie,* the *Miracle de Théophile;* (lives) *Vie d'Elizabel, Vie de Marie l'Egyptienne; (fabliaux) Vengeance de Charlot le Juif,*[1] *Dit du frère Denyse, Pet au vilain, Testament de l'âne,* the *Sacristain et la femme du chevalier,* and the *Dame qui fist trois tors entor le mostier.*

It would be a long task to list all the poets whom we find recorded in the second half of the thirteenth century. Baude Fastoul, Gilles and Guillaume le Vinier, Adam de Givenchy, Gilbert de Berneville, Perrin d'Angicourt, Cardon de Croisilles, Simon d'Autie, and a poetess, Oede de la Corroierie, are a few of the best. We might mention also Jehan Erart, Thomas Erier, Colart le Bouteillier, Carasaus, Jehan de Dampierre, and Jacques de Cysoing. These men belonged in the north, at Arras, Lille, and Brabant. With the exception of Rutebeuf only minor poets flourished in Champagne and the Ile-de-France in this later period. We mention a few of these: Jehan Moniot de Paris, Gavaron Grazelle, the Moine de Saint-Denis, Gautier de Bregy, and Oudard de Lacegni.

When the thirteenth-century poet sang of love he was no longer aware of any distinction between an Ovidian type and a courtly love. This distinction of the twelfth century had become dulled and the two concepts had merged into one. The thirteenth-century lyricist might sing to a married or unmarried woman; in any case he exalted and lauded her to the skies. He would talk of code and secrecy, and of service, in the best manner of Andreas Capellanus, but this was now

[1] Also entitled, *De Charlot le Juif qui chia en la pel dou lièvre.*

artificial and contained no echo of the earlier conditions which had brought about courtly love.

In the Latin lyric verse of the twelfth century a particular favorite was the debate, (Walther, *Das Streitgedicht in der lat. Lit. des MA*, München, 1920). We have, preserved, such debates between Water and Wine, Wine and Beer, Lazarus and Dives, Winter and Summer, Ganymede and Helena, Acis and Polyphemus, World and the Poet, Body and Soul, the carnal and the spiritual Man, Justice and Mercy, Man and Death, Fortune and Philosophy, between two maidens on the value of a cleric's love as opposed to the love of a knight *(Phyllis and Flora)*, between the King of France and the King of England, the poor man and the wealthy, the poor scholar and the priest, the impotent husband and his wife who seeks divorce, and between Death and the Rich Man. A tri-debate was written, between a Christian, a Jew, and a Saracen, on the value of their religions. There was also a dialogue between a Jew and a blind Christian. It is only reasonable to observe similar themes finding favor in the vernacular of the thirteenth century. In the second half of the thirteenth century a clerk named Clopin(?) wrote a *Disputoison de la sinagogue et de sainte eglise* (36 four-lined monorhymed strophes in alex.). There is a *Desbat entre un juif et un chrestien* (in alex.) in MS B.N. fr. 19,152. There is a *Dit du cors* (16 strophes) and a *De cors et d'ame* (85 strophes of four lines each); the latter was adapted directly from the Latin *Visio Philiberti*, after 1280. A *Desputoison du vin et de l'iave* (570 octosyllables) and a *Bataille de karesme et de charnage* (586 octosyllables) both date from the last quarter of the century. The *Estrif de l'iver et de l'esté* (177 octosyllables) was composed in England. There is a *Dit du denier et de la brebis* (270 octosyllables) on the relative value of sheep and money, also belonging to the end of the century. Such debates occasionally took an obscene turn. The discussion between two maidens on the cleric and the knight as lovers found considerable favor in the vernacular. It is the theme of the *Jugement d'Amours* (424 octosyllables) as well as of certain other poems which we call *Hueline et Aiglantine, Blancheflour et Florence*, and *Melior et Ydoine*. The girl who defends the cleric is the winner. (Compare the judgment on this by Andreas Capellanus). For the debate between Wine and Water consult J. H. Hanford in *PMLA* XXVIII, 315-67.

We must mention certain Judaeo-French poems of a lyric content. The Jews in Europe, during the Middle Ages, wrote Hebrew as well as the language of their country of residence. They combined the two somewhat by writing French, Spanish, Italian, etc., in Hebrew characters. This was particularly the case when they added glosses in Romance to explain the more difficult words of their Hebrew texts. The

reader will readily see the value which these Romance words, in Hebrew spelling, have for the study of pronunciation. Four elegies, a
marriage poem, and two hymns survive, composed in this Judaeo-
French, in the last quarter of the thirteenth century. In 1288, thirteen
Jews were burned by the Inquisition and this was an occasion for Jacob
ben Juda of Lorraine to voice a lament. The poet names over the vic-
tims and ends with the exclamation: "Est finie la version. Que Dieu
nous sauve du peuple violant!" This elegy is in monorhymed quatrains.
The Hebrew original from which it was adapted, also by Juda who
there names himself, is likewise extant. This Judaeo-French poem is
commonly known as the *Elégie de Troyes*. Louis Brandin (D. S. Blond-
heim in *Rom* LII, 17-36) discovered three other elegies of a liturgical
nature which are less sorrowful. Although he dated these in the early
fourteenth century it is quite possible that they were written shortly before the year 1300. Next we have a macaronic marriage song which il-
lustrates the opposite emotion, joy. This marriage song is preserved in
the Mahzor Vitry MS of the Jewish Theological Seminary of New York.
It is dated in the second half of the thirteenth century because of its
dialect. Professor A. Marx believes it originated in the East. Heinz
Pflaum has recently published two newly discovered hymns, preserved
in a MS at the University of Heidelberg, 362ª n. 28 XII, Hebraic (*Rom*
LIX, 389-422).

On Judaeo-Romance in general the student should consult the late
D. S. Blonheim in his *Poèmes judéo-français du moyen âge* (Paris:
Champion, 1927), and in the *Revue des études juives* II, 199 ff.

## EDITIONS

For the various poets consult the bibliographies of G. Raynaud and of A.
Jeanroy. We add a few outstanding and readily accessible editions. *Thibaut
de Champagne*, ed. A. Wallensköld (Paris: *SATF*, 1925).—Colin Muset,
*Chansons*, ed. Joseph Bédier-Jean Beck (Paris: *Cfmâ*, 1912).—Guiot de Dijon
et Jocelin de Dijon, *Chansons*, ed. E. Nissen (Paris: *Cfmâ*, 1929).—Adan de
le Hale, le Bochu d'Arras, *Canchons und Partures*, ed. Rudolf Berger (Halle:
*BRom*, 1900).—Rutebeuf, *Gedichte*, ed. Adolf Kressner (Wolffenbüttel, 1885);
ed. A. Jubinal (rev. ed.; Paris: Delahaye, 1874, 3 vols.).—Audefroi le Bastard,
*Lieder und Romanzen*, ed. Arthur Cullman (Halle: Niemeyer, 1914).—
Raoul von Soissons, *Lieder*, ed. E. Winkler (Halle: Niemeyer, 1914).—Richart
de Semilli, *Gedichte*, ed. G. Steffens (Halle: Niemeyer, 1902).—Gilbert de
Berneville, *Gedichte*, ed. H. Waitz (Halle: Niemeyer, 1899).—*Chansons
satiriques et bachiques*, ed. A. Jeanroy-A Långfors (Paris: *Cfmâ*, 1921).—
*Recueil général des jeux-partis*, ed. A. Långfors with A. Jeanroy and L.
Brandin (Paris: *SATF*, 1926).—*Rondeaux, Virelais, und Balladen, etc.*, ed.
F. Gennrich (Halle: *GrL*, 1921-1929, 2 vols.).—*Motette*, ed. A. Stimming
(Halle: *GrL*, 1906).—*Le Chansonnier d'Arras, reproduction en phototypie*, ed.

A. Jeanroy (Paris: *SATF*, 1925).—The *Débat de la Vierge et de la croix* (ed. A. Långfors in *Rom* XLIII, 21-27) belongs probably to the fourteenth century. —Michault Taillevent, *Débat du cœur et de l'œil*, ed. T. Wright in *Latin Poems Attributed to Walter Mapes* (London, 1841). This collection by Wright also contains the *Desputoison du vin et de l'iave* (p. 299) and a *Débat du cors* (p. 321).—Jubinal in his *Mystères inédites* (1837) publishes the *Disputoison de la sinagogue et de sainte Eglise* (p. 404).—*La Bataille de Caresme et de Charnage*, ed. G. Lozinski (Paris: *BEcHE*, 1933).—The *Dit du denier et de la brebis* has been printed by Jubinal in his *Nouveau recueil*, etc., II, 264.—Stengel in *ZfrPh*, VIII, 74 ff. has printed another *Débat du cors et de l'ame.—Le Jugement d'Amours*, ed. Julius Schmidt (Borna-Leipzig: Noske, 1913); *Les Débats du Clerc et du Chevalier dans la Litt. Poét. du m. â*, ed. Charles Oulmont (Paris: Champion, 1911).—H. Pflaum, *Die religiöse Disputation in der europäischen Dichtung des M. A.* (Florence, 1935).

# CHAPTER XXXIII

## THE THIRTEENTH-CENTURY *FABLIAUX*

Joseph Bédier, *Les Fabliaux*, 4th ed., Paris: Champion, 1925.
C. H. Livingston in *RRev* XV, 1-67.
Lutz Mackensen, ed. *Handwörterbuch des deutschen Märchens* (Riga, 1933—).

The origins of the *fabliau*, and its definition, have been discussed in chapter XX. It remains here to give some statistics concerning its growth and spread in the thirteenth century. One hundred and forty-two have survived from this period of which thirty-two seem to have taken form in Picardy, fourteen in the Ile-de-France, nine in Normandy, five in England, three in the Orléanais, two in Champagne, and one each in the Nivernais and Syria. The remaining seventy-five have but little evidence bearing upon the dialect or geographic location, though it is probable that many belonged in Flanders and Picardy.

In keeping with the literary traditions of the early Middle Ages, few of the composers of these boisterous tales made known their names. We have had occasion to mention elsewhere that it was not till after 1300 that the author was visible behind his work. The reason must be sought in the peculiar status of the poet or entertainer. In the twelfth and thirteenth centuries he was a transient, he wandered the country-side, retailing his wares, seeking only to amuse his host for the night or the first passer-by. He was welcomed everywhere. In the Middle French period, the fourteenth and fifteenth centuries, the poet was usually a household retainer of some powerful noble, or of the king. It was to his interest to sign his work. His own personality was more in the public eye than were his verses. That we have the names of some men of letters in the earlier period, and that names are sometimes lacking in the later centuries, was due to occasional interchange of these conditions. Where advertising is profitable the ambitious man does not neglect it. It is interesting to note that such public figures as Rutebeuf, Huon le Roi de Cambrai, and Adenés le Roi, did not forget to sign their contributions in the thirteenth century; but the fifteenth-century *Maistre Pathelin* was unsigned.

Charlot the Jew, Jehan de Journi, Jehan de Boves, Colin, Hauvis, Hersent, and Jetrus were *fabliau* writers whose names but not their work have survived. We follow with a complete list of the known authors of surviving thirteenth-century *fabliaux:*

1. Bernier, late thirteenth century, author of *La Housse partie*.
2. Colin Malet, author of one of the most ignoble of all *fabliaux*, *Jouglet*.
3. Durand, author of *Les Trois bossus* (Mt. 1536B, FFC, 74).
4. Enguerrand d'Oisi, who composed, in illiterate and careless fashion, the *Meunier d'Arleux*.
5. Eustache d'Amiens, author of the *Boucher d'Abbeville*.
6. A certain Garin, or Guerin (these names may denote more than one person), who wrote *La Grue, Le Chevalier qui faisait parler les muets, Berengier, La Dame qui fist son mari entendant qu'il sonjoit*.
7. Gautier le Leu (called Gautier le Long, or simply Gautier; see Livingston, *op. cit.*) who wrote *Du sot chevalier, Del fol vilain, De deus vilains* (Mt. 1363*A, FFC, 90), *De Dieu et dou pescour, Connebert, Le Prestre teint, La Veuve* (Mt. 1510, FFC, 74), and *Li Valez qui d'aise a malaise se met*.
8. Cortebarbe, who wrote *Les Trois aveugles de Compiègne*.
9. Guillaume, who composed a version of the *Male Honte*.
10. Guillaume le Clerc of Normandy, whom we have already noticed as the author of moral poems, miracles, and of a bestiary, who composed the *fabliau Du Prestre et d'Alison* (Mt. 403, III, IV, FFC, 74; 403 FFC, 78, 81).
11. Haiseau of Normandy who wrote *L'anneau qui fist grandir les viz, Les trois dames qui troverent l'anel au conte, Les quatre prestres*, and *Le prestre et le mouton* (this last is the shortest *fabliau* known).
12. Henri d'Andeli, author of the *Lai d'Aristote* (Mt. 1501, FFC, 74).
13. Huon le Roi de Cambrai, who wrote the *Vairs Palefrois*, the *Male Honte*, and probably the *Estormi* (same motif as no. 3, but preachers, not hunchbacks) and *Sire Hain et dame Anieuse*.
14. Jean Bedel, perhaps the Jean Bodel already discussed, in which case his *fabliaux* could be attributed to the close of the twelfth century, author of *Deux chevaux, Morteruel*, the *Vilain de Bailluel, Gombert et les deux clercs* (Mt. 1363, FFC, 74), *Brunain la vache au vrestre* (Mt. 1735, FFC, 74, 81), *Le leu que l'oue deçut*, the *Deus envieus cuivers*, and *Barat et Haimet*.
15. Jehan le Chapelain, a Norman knight, who composed the *Dit du soucretain*.
16. Jehan le Galois d'Aubepierre, a Champenois, who was the author of the *Pleine bourse de sens*.
17. Le Maire du Hamiel, author of the fragmentary *Dan Loussiet*.
18. Milon d'Amiens, who wrote *Le prêtre et le chevalier*.
19. Philippe de Beaumanoir, author of *La fole largece*.
20. Rutebeuf, whose complete work has been given in the previous chapter, who composed *Charlot le Juif, Frère Denyse, Le pet au vilain, La dame qui fist trois tors entor le mostier*, the *Testament de l'âne*, and the *Sacristain et la femme du chevalier*.

The majority of the *fabliaux* are anonymous. We shall mention here a few of the best. The Widow of Ephesus theme, which is omnipresent in the world's literature, occurs not only in the Old French version of the *Seven Sages,* but also in two independent forms: *La dame qui se fist f . . . sur le tombeau de son mari* and the *Veuve* of Gautier le Leu. The folk motif is classified as Mt. 1510, *FFC,* 74. Other anonymous *fabliaux* are *Estula, Le dit des perdrix* (Mt. 1381, *FFC,* 74, 78, 81), *Le pescheur de Pont-sur-Seine, Les quatre souhaits de Saint-Martin* (Mt. 750A, *FFC,* 74; 750, *FFC,* 78, 81), *Li vilains qui conquist Paradis, Le cuvier, Le pré tondu* (Mt. 1423, *FFC,* 74), *L'enfant de neige* (Mt. 1362, *FFC,* 74) *Le prestre qui abevete* (Mt. 1243, *FFC,* 74), *Constant du Hamel* (Mt. 1730, *FFC,* 74, 78, 81), *Des tresces* (Mt. 1417, *FFC,* 74), *Le convoiteux et l'envieux* (Mt. 1331, *FFC,* 74), *Le pouailler* (Mt. 1419 A, *FFC,* 74), *Lai de l'épervier* (Mt. 1419 D, *FFC,* 74), and *Auberee.*

*Auberee* tells a well-known legend found in the Eastern versions of the romance of the *Seven Sages;* it is there called *Pallium.* The *Lai d'Aristote* was immensely popular. It narrates how an Indian lady, loved by Alexander, punished Aristotle for advising her lover against her. She succeeded in infatuating the great philosopher himself. As a favor of love he allowed her to saddle him and ride about the garden, after she had placed Alexander in an observing position. When Alexander jested with the old philosopher on his vulnerability, Aristotle replied that the lady was all the more dangerous when she could make a fool of *him.* This *fabliau* has been the subject of many church carvings at Rouen, Caen, Gaillon, and elsewhere. Both Adam de le Halle and Jehan Bretel refer to it. The *Fole largece* and the *Vairs palefrois* are the only surviving *fabliaux* which appear to have been written for the upper classes. The others are persistently bourgeois in tone and spirit. *Li vilains mire* is an ancestor of Molière's *Le médecin malgré lui.*

*Li muniers et li deus cler,* extant in two variant versions, contains folk motifs (Mt. 1363, *FFC,* 74), which were elaborated also by Chaucer in his Reeve's tale, by Boccaccio (IX, 6), and elsewhere—even in Ireland (*ZfcPh,* II, 156-9).

As a rule there is not much variation in theme among the *fabliaux.* The village priest comes in for much criticism, because the true essence of comedy is ridiculous dignity and the priest, by virtue of his office, had dignity. Other common materials for humor were the natural functions, the fickleness of women and their ability to turn any man into a fool, the cheating of rogues, the helplessness of the blind, and plays upon words. The *Male Honte* is the best of the word-play fabliaux: the title means either the "bag of Honte" or "Evil Shame." One should bear in mind that the great majority of the *fabliaux* were written in Picardy, Flanders, and Hainaut, the regions which we have described as important industrial centers in the thirteenth century. Tales of this sort delighted the bourgeois even more than the noble, and the bourgeois centers encouraged their circulation.

There are five MSS which are *fabliau* collections: *B.N.fr.837* (62 *fabliaux*), *Berne 354* (41 *f.*), Berlin, *Hamilton, 257* (30 *f.*), *B.N.fr.1593* (24 *f.*), *B.N.fr. 19152* (26 *f.*).[1] Twenty-seven other MSS each contain a few of the tales. Only ten of the *fabliaux* cannot be dated in the thirteenth century; apparently the age of Saint Louis and his sons offered ideal conditions for the spread of this class of literature.

Recently, in a MS of the municipal library in Lyons, a new *fabliau* has been discovered by L.-F. Flutre, which we will call *Dans Garins et dame Odierne* (*Rom* LXII, 1-16). It has very little value and is mostly a diatribe against the peasants by a member of the clerical class. We have included this in our statistics on the *genre*.

## EDITIONS

*Fabliaux et contes des poètes français des XI, XII, XIII, XIV, et XV siècles*, ed. E. Barbazan et M. Méon (Paris, 1808).—*Recueil général et complet des fabliaux des XIIIe et XIVe siècles*, ed. A. de Montaiglon et G. Raynaud (Paris, 1872-1890). This reference is the best.—Achille Jubinal, *Nouveau recueil de contes, dits, fabliaux et autres pièces inédites des XIIIe, XIVe, et XVe siècles* (Paris: Pannier, 1839-1842).—*Choix de fabliaux mis en vers*, ed. Barthélemy Imbert (Paris: Prault, 1788). This is of very little value.—C. H. Livingston has edited the newly discovered *fabliaux* of Gautier le Leu in *RRev* XV, 1-67. He is working upon a complete edition of the *Dits et fabliaux* of Gautier le Leu. *Sechs altfranzösische Fablels*, ed. G. Rohlfs (Halle: *SrT*, 1925).—*Das altfranzösische Fablel du Vilain Mire*, ed. C. Zepperling (Halle: Niemeyer, 1912).—Huon le Roi de Cambrai, *Le Vair palefroi*, ed. A. Långfors (3rd ed.; Paris, *Cfmâ*, 1927). This also includes the *Male Honte* by Huon and the version of the same by Guillaume.—Bartsch in his *Chrestomathie de l'ancien français* (12th ed.; Leipzig, 1920) publishes the *Fabliau des perdrix* and the *Housse partie* of Bernier.—*Auberee*, ed. G. Ebeling (Halle: Niemeyer, 1895).—The *Estula* is reproduced entire in Paget Toynbee's *Specimens of Old French* (Oxford, 1892).

[1] This last has been reproduced beautifully by E. Faral, *Le manuscrit 19152 du fonds français de la Bibliothèque nationale* (Paris: Droz, 1934). MS *fr. 837* was reproduced by H. Omont (Paris, 1932).

# CHAPTER XXXIV

## THE DECAY OF THE EPIC AND THE ROMANCE IN THE FOURTEENTH CENTURY

*Histoire littéraire de la France,* vols. XXV-XXXVI. Gröber, Gustav and Hofer, Stephan, *Geschichte der mittelfranzösischen Literatur* (Berlin: De Gruyter, 1933).

Social conditions and resulting literature are not the same in the so-called Middle French Period (fourteenth and fifteenth centuries) as they were during the exuberance of the twelfth-century enlightenment. The sublime philosophies of Saint Bonaventure and of Saint Thomas Aquinas gave way *unofficially* to nominalism or materialism. The feudal system, which had made it possible for a host of small nobles to hold court throughout the extent of France, was weakening; the smaller noble was spending more and more of his time as a retainer in the court of king or duke, and minstrels did not find it so easy to secure a maecenas. The country was impoverished by the Hundred Years' War between France and England (1336-1457), which brought thousands of *routiers,* or pillagers, as a plague upon the fields of France. Travel became less and less safe. Men of letters secured court favor if they wished to continue writing, and remained in one service where they could grind out verses to fit state occasions. We may say that the prevailing literary *genres* in this Middle French Period were satire, chronicle, brisk *contes* of the Italian style, religious drama and farce, played by burghers within walled towns, and lyric verse of a formal, artificial type, such as *ballades, rondeaux, chants royaux,* and *dits.* I think of Old French literature as rural—a literature composed among the open fields and along the highways. Even though such a concept is not entirely accurate, the Frenchman of the twelfth and early thirteenth centuries spent much of his life outside of town walls. The middle period Frenchman, herded into towns and cities for protection, learned the joys of satire and of matching wits, and at the same time favored plague and lack of sanitation.

But the *chanson de geste* and the romance, which are predominantly Old French literary types, did not die at once. There was no Christian muezzin who, on midnight, Tuesday, March 24th, 1299, sighted the star Arcturus with his astrolabe and, verifying its midnight height in the heavens, cried out, "The Old French period is ended and the Middle French now begins!" The verse romance and epic hung on, more or less as they were in the preceding century, until after 1350, when they passed definitely into popular prose chapbooks of a much altered character, which were destined to influence such later writers as the Italians Boiardo and Ariosto, and Rabelais and the French *conteurs*. It is the continuance of the verse *chanson de geste* and of the romance in prose and verse into the first part of the fourteenth century which now concerns us.

Among the *chansons de geste*, the *Entree d'Espagne* (15,805 mixed alexandrines and decasyllables) and the *Prise de Pampelune* (6,113 verses preserved) tell about the "set anz toz pleins" which Charlemagne and his army spent in Spain before the events of the *Chanson de Roland*. The *Entree* is concerned with the first five years and the *Pampelune* narrates the events of the remaining two. Gaston Paris (*Histoire poétique de Charlemagne*, p. 176) thought that both of these poems were the work of Nicolà di Padua or di Verona. Gautier (*Epopées françaises*, III, 411) believed that the *Pampelune* (*ca.* 1343) was written by a Lombard unknown to us, and that the *Entree en Espagne* was merely reworked by Nicolà. The opinion given by Gaston Paris is usually cited as the correct one.

The *Entree* is preserved in only one MS, *no. 21* of the Library of Saint Mark's in Venice. There are three main divisions of the poem: the victory of Roland over the Saracen Ferragus, the taking of Naples by Roland and the Twelve Peers without Charlemagne's consent, and the exile of Roland in Persia. This work which belongs to the opening years of the fourteenth century is decidedly disproportioned; even the versification is mixed rather bizarrely. The *Prise de Pampelune* is superior. It, too, is preserved in a single MS, *no. 5* of the Library of Saint Mark's. Charlemagne and his army capture Pampeluna, held by Malceris and Isoré. Malceris refuses to be baptized unless he is made a peer of France. He escapes and prepares to harry Charlemagne's advance. Altumagor and Malceris attack Charlemagne before Stoille; they are defeated, thanks to Roland, and Altumagor turns Christian. Next is the story of the hanging of Basan and Basile, thanks to the treachery of Guenelon. Guron goes as a messenger to Marsilies. He carries off the pagan's crown, after winning a combat, but he is fatally waylaid, thanks again to Guenelon. The Christians in revenge capture Toetelle and Cordres, and are besieging Astorga when the poem breaks off. The beginning and end of this *chanson* are missing.

In the *Charlemagne* (23, 320 vss. in twenty-line strophes) by Girart d'Amiens, written for Charles de Valois early in the century, we find a decadent, arid piece of work. The action is so complicated that it does not lend itself to a résumé. Gautier remarked concerning it (*op. cit.*, II, 423): "l'on ne peut lire sans colère une aussi irritante et intolérable rapsodie." *Hue Capet* (6,361 alexandrines) has considerable merit. Following the popular etymology, also known to Dante, that *Capet* was related to *capler* "to hack," Hue is depicted as the son of a butcher's daughter. He travels through Brabant and Friesland in the character of a Don Juan, distinguishing himself at tourneys. Ten of his bastard sons, of unusual courage, gather around him. On the death of Louis they go to Paris and defend the widowed queen, against Savari. Hue becomes Duke of Orleans, then marries the queen, Marie, and becomes King of France. He continues to fight Savari's brother, Fedry, and the Saracens. He dies after a reign of nine years. The *Lion de Bourges* narrates the adventures of its protagonist, bearing that name. It follows the *Huon de Bordeaux.* It contains the motif of the Grateful Dead.

There are two crusade epics of the fourteenth century which merit considerable attention. These are the *Baudouin de Sebourc* (30,000 verses) and the *Bastart de Bouillon* (6,554 verses). The *Baudouin de Sebourc* (after 1316), may be called a comico-heroic poem. It centers all sorts of adventures around Baldwin the Third, King of Jerusalem. Some of these must have been inspired by *Hue Capet*—or it is possible to say that the influence ran the other way. The *Baudouin de Sebourc* is judged by many critics, including Gaston Paris (*Poésie du m. â.,* II, 192), as the outstanding work of the fourteenth century. The *Bastart de Bouillon* is inferior. It continues the adventures of Baudouin; the Bastard is a secondary figure. It has been suggested that both these fourteenth-century crusade poems were by the same author. Granted the difference in interest and treatment, I should doubt this, although the *Bastart* was certainly intended as an immediate continuation of the other *chanson.*

Another *chanson de geste* which offers but little amusement to the reader is *Ciperis de Vignevaux* (7,995 verses preserved), written after the middle of the century. Krappe says it belongs to the period 1396-1415. (See A. H. Krappe and A. Steiner in *MLN* L, 343-46; XLIX, 255-60; 559-61.). The poem is preserved in only one MS and the beginning is lost. Ciperis, the illegitimate son of Philippe, King of Hungary, and of Clarisse, marries Orable, daughter of King Dagobert. Seventeen sons are born of this marriage, all dubbed knights by Dagobert. In a series of monotonous battles, imitated from earlier *chansons de geste,* Ciperis succeeds in winning brides and lands for his sons. One of the sons, Guillaume, becomes King of England. There is the episode of Dagobert's son whose education had been entrusted to Ciperis, and who was poisoned. After Dagobert's death, Ciperis holds the throne of France for which he has to dispute with Dagobert's brother, Louis. The name *Ciperis* is a distortion of Chilperic.

Earlier than *Ciperis* is the *Theseus de Cologne* (around 15,700 alexandrines) where Theseus, the son of a relative of Dagobert and of

Florides of Cologne, is exiled, goes to Rome, and wins the love of the Roman emperor's daughter. The Emperor of Constantinople besieges Rome and forces the princess to marry him. Theseus becomes Emperor of Rome. The poem continues with the story of Gadifer, and is also concerned with the fate of Gadifer's wife, who is finally recovered by her sons in Jerusalem.

*Charles le Chauve* (some 15,000 verses preserved) is also extant in a single MS. Upon the death of Clothaire, France is left without a king. An angel tells them to wait for Melsiau of Hungary, who has been appointed by God. This Melsiau is eventually crowned and known as Charles the Bald. His son, Philippe, is falsely accused by traitors, exiled, and finally made King of Hungary, after marrying the Hungarian princess, Doraine. Philippe goes on an expedition to Jerusalem. A son, born in his absence, is abandoned by traitors, is found by a nobleman, and is christened Dieudonné. This Dieudonné is now the hero of the *chanson*. He marries Supplante, obtains magic gifts from the fairy Gloriana, saves his mother, becomes the father of Dagobert and of an illegitimate son, Corsabrin, and finally expiates his sins as a hermit, accompanied by Supplante. They are murdered by thieves and both are carried to heaven.

*Florent et Octavian* (around 18,000 verses) contains enough plot for a score or more of *chansons de geste,* if properly developed. The main portion is a reworking of the thirteenth-century *Octavian.* This poem belongs to the first decade of the fourteenth century; some scholars date it as early as the late thirteenth century. Florimonde, suspected of being unfaithful, is exiled by her husband, Emperor Octavian, along with her newly born twins. One of the children is stolen by a monkey while the mother sleeps; the other is borne off by a lion. The mother rescues the child from the lion and carries it to Jerusalem, followed by the interested lion. Years pass. The first son, stolen by the monkey, is now called Florent and becomes a butcher at Dagobert's court. He conquers the pagan, Fernagu, and is knighted by Dagobert. He wins the love of the Saracen princess Marsebille. Later he and his father, Octavian, are taken prisoner together and carried off by Saracens who flee before Saint Denis and Saint Maurice, sent by God. The young Octavian, who is the son reared in Jerusalem, comes to Rome, learns of his father's plight, rescues father and brother, and eventually reconciles the Emperor and his mother. The poem continues with the loves of young Octavian, Margalie, and Esclarmonde.

*Florence de Rome* (6,410 alexandrines) has survived in a form written after 1312, in addition to an older version of the thirteenth century (1200–1230). There is another extant form, of 4,562 verses, but this is of still later date. There are two divisions to the Florence: the war against Gausire of Constantinople and the adventures of Florence after she is abducted by Milon. Florence, daughter of Emperor Otto of Rome, is refused in marriage to old Emperor Gausire of Constantinople. He gathers his armed forces and sails for Italy to enforce his wooing. Esmeré and Milon are the two sons of King Philippe of Hungary. Since the death of their father tney have been resting with the King of Slavonia. They hear of the approaching conflict and set out for Rome. Esmeré is virtuous and Milon is wicked. After several treacheries by Milon, Esmeré eventually wins the princess Florence and becomes the Emperor of Constantinople in Gausire's place. Just before Esmeré's triumphal return, Milon succeeds in stealing Florence. The unhappy princess is protected by a magic brooch or necklace which preserves her chastity against all odds. This brooch or *noche* is referred to in the thirteenth-century *Roman de la Violette*, and in the L redaction of the *Roman d'Alexandre* (dated *ca.* 1280), which enables us to postulate with certainty a lost early form of the *Florence de Rome*. (See Armstrong's article in *Mélanges Jeanroy*, pp. 131-140). Milon, since he cannot possess Florence, hangs her up by the hair and goes to serve Guillaume de Dôle. Here continue the misfortunes of Florence. A would-be possessor has her accused of murder; she is sold as a slave; eventually she enters the nunnery of Beau-Repaire. There her reputation as a faith-healer grows so strong that she is visited by all her would be-ravishers, including Milon, who now seek cures for all their ills. Esmeré also comes to be healed of a wound. Not knowing who she is, the evil men confess their ill-treatment of her. She cures them by her prayers. She makes herself known to Esmeré and returns with him to his empire, where she becomes the mother of a son. The *Crescentia* folktale (Mt. 712 *FFC*, 74) is the base for the entire story. The *Crescentia* is so called from its version in the German *Kaiserchronik* (*ca.* 1150). Perhaps this tale was a variant of a certain miracle of the Virgin which occurs in thirty-eight texts. There is some influence on the French romance from the actual life of Saint Elizabeth of Hungary (d. 1231).

In the *Reine Sibille*, a fragment of 202 vv. preserved in a single MS, we have a reworking of the same theme as that of the thirteenth-century *Macaire*. Krappe has discovered another episode of this mutilated *Reine Sibille*, which is preserved in Norse (*Rom* LVI, 585-8). Gröber dates this poem into the thirteenth century; there is no valid reason for assuming that it is older than the fourteenth-century MS in which it occurs. This fragment was a source for the *Tristan de Nanteuil* (24,000 alexandrines, with ending lost), a *chanson* which Paulin Paris (*HLF*, XXVI, 268-269) characterized as "le dernier écho de la chanson de geste française." The thirteenth-century *Gui de Nanteuil* closed with the wedding of Gui and the beautiful Eglentine of Gascogne. In the *Tristan de Nanteuil,* the unknown poet begins his story with the flight of Gui and his wife before a Saracen invasion. The wife is captured and carried off to Babylon; little Tristan, their son, is preserved by a siren who feeds him with her milk thus causing him to grow to monstrous size. A hind drinks of this same milk on one occasion and is thereby altered into a giant, savage beast. Tristan lives for a time in savage state with this monstrous hind. His father Gui has a son by Honoree of Rochebrune. This son, named Doon le Bastart, meets Tristan and becomes his constant companion, aiding in civilizing him. As yet they do not know their relation. Tristan has a son by Blanchandine, the daughter of Galafre of Armenia. This same Blanchandine, after Tristan's marriage to her, is changed into a man by an angel to avoid complications with Clarinde. This Clarinde and Blanchandin (as the individual is now called) are the parents of Saint Gilles of Provence. The involved series of circumstances which precede and follow all this are too complicated for résumé here, but these details will suffice to show the presence of the Eustachius motif, and of the sex-changing episode. A. H. Krappe indicates a connection between the details of this *Tristan de Nanteuil* and India. (*Rom* LXI, 55-71). The anonymous poet of this work knew many of the older epics, including the *Reine Sibille, Huon de Bordeaux,* and all the *chansons* of the Nanteuil and Saint-Gilles cycles.

It is the custom to refer to *Le Combat des trente,* which narrates a mortal pitched battle between thirty Frenchmen and thirty knights, mostly Bretons, fighting on the English side, as the last of the epics. This fight actually took place in 1351.

The *Pharsale* is based upon Lucan's *Pharsalia* and the *Faits des Romains.* Its author was Nicolà di Verona who composed the *Prise de Pampelune.*

In closing the question of the fourteenth-century epic, let us add that we have very short fragments of a *Hernant de Beuland* and of a *Renier de Gennes.* New versions were made of the *Huon de Bordeaux,* of the *Girart de Roussillon,* and of the individual poems of the Crusade cycle.

Among the fourteenth-century romances it is the Alexander legend which holds chief place. The *Vœux du paon* is the first and most influential of these, having been composed by Jacques de Longuyon between 1310 and 1316. There are some eight thousand lines. This work is well written, offering a pleasing alternation of battle scenes and courtship in a well varied manner. The lovers thus portrayed are not moved by great passions, but they are pleasing. Jacques de Longuyon was the first to introduce the figure of the Nine Worthies, Joshua, David, Judas Macchabaeus, Hector, Alexander, Julius Caesar, Arthur, Charlemagne, and Godfrey of Bouillon, into literature. Throughout his work we find an excellent portrait of contemporary social life in the France—not the Greece!—which Longuyon knew. Alexander is on his way to Tarsus and he promises aid to Cassamus against Clarvus, brother of King Porus. While Alexander is consulting his oracles, Cassamus, with his nephews, Gadifer and Betis, give battle without him. Cassamus and his forces are victorious but they are ambushed by four sons of Clarvus. Porus is taken prisoner and kills a peacock which is served at table. As the peacock is passed around each knight and each lady make a special vow to do some deed of valor or courtesy. The prisoners are exchanged. There is a great battle the next day when Alexander arrives, each champion seeking to fulfill his vow. Porus is again made prisoner and he joins forces with Alexander. There is a wedding of five couples. The poet laments Alexander's approaching death.

The *Restor du paon* (2,660 alexandrines) is by Jean Brisebarre and was written before 1338, the date of one of the MSS. In the prologue, Brisebarre retells roughly the previous Alexander material, particularly his immediate predecessor's poem, the *Vœux du paon*. One of the ladies, Edea, had made a vow to substitute for the slain peacock another made of gold and precious stones. When this is done Edea gives a discourse on the symbolism of each part. There is also the story of Emenidus and how he came to be a peer of Alexander's. Alexander marries Rosenes (Roxane). The *Parfaict du paon* (3,900 alexandrines) continues the material still further. It was written by Jean de la Motte, in 1340, for Simon de Lille. Alexander, on his way to Babylon, fights with Melidus, brother of Clarvus. Three of his generals are taken prisoner and led before Melidus, where the latter's daughters fall in love with them. Alexander asks for a truce and takes part in a poetic competition in the presence of the four daughters. He is thrilled by his newly discovered skill. The struggle is renewed and Alexander is decisively victorious. One of the daughters of Melidus commits suicide, in accordance with a vow; the others marry peers of Alexander's court. The *Vœux du Hairon* (440 verses) and the *Vœux de l'épervier* (562 verses) belong to this group.

A vast prose compilation, *Perceforest,* was also written with the *Vœux du paon* as a starting point. This unwieldy prose narrative is preserved complete in one MS, in the Arsenal library, but it was printed twice in the sixteenth century; there is also an Italian translation. It has not been published since the sixteenth century and it may be conservatively stated that scarcely anyone, except Antoine Thomas, has read it complete during the past two centuries. The purpose of this prose romance was to join Alexander heroes with themes of the Holy Grail.

One episode, called by Gaston Paris the *Conte de la rose* was published by him in *Rom* XXIII, 78-116. *Hue Capet,* a *chanson de geste* already discussed, was also profoundly influenced by the *Vœux du paon*.

In 1316, Jean Maillart, an official in the royal chancellory, composed for Pierre de Chambli the *Comtesse d'Anjou* (around 8,000 verses), another version of the tale found in *La Manekine* of Philippe de Beaumanoir, and in Chaucer's Man-of-Law's tale. The *Comtesse d'Anjou* has been suggested as Chaucer's source; on the other hand Chaucer may have drawn this narrative from the *Chronicle* of Nicholas Trivet (before 1334). The daughter of the Count of Anjou is the heroine; after leaving home because of her father's incestuous intentions, she weds the Count of Bourges. The Countess of Chartres, aunt of the husband, is the villainess who persecutes the poor girl. The aunt meets her end at the stake when the wedded pair are reunited. *Eledus et Serene* (7,314 verses) is preserved in *B.N.* nouv. acq. 1943. The story is mentioned as early as the *Breviari d'amor* (1288) of Matfrei Ermengaud; so there was an earlier version belonging to the thirteenth century. The girl Serene is disputed for by both Eledus and Maugrier, the former finally winning her. It is possible that this is reminiscent of the triangular affair between the historical Placidia of Rome, Constantine, and the Goth Athaulf. Consult Suchier in *ZfrPh* XXI, 112-127. The *Dit des annelets* is a short tale which rehandles the theme of the thirteenth-century *Fille du comte de Pontieu*. The wife is not ravished by robbers but is caught in wilful adultery while on a pilgrimage to Compostella. She is cut adrift at Wissant; her gold ring is cast into the sea, and iron rings are embedded into her finger. The ring is returned to the husband in the body of a fish. He repents and finally recovers his wife. The iron rings miraculously drop off.

The great chronicler, Jean Froissart (1338-1404), wrote the romance *Meliado* (30,771 extant verses) somewhere around 1380. Although the existence of this poem was known from several references, it was not brought to light till 1891 (in four fragments). It may be called an Arthurian romance, although its content is so involved that it has been likened to the species of romance which drove Don Quixote out of his head. Hermondine, daughter of the King of Scotland, is annoyed by a knight, Camel, who desires to marry her. He is a victim of somnambulism, which renders him highly undesirable. Hermondine is aided by her friend, Floree de Maugries, in drawing up her plans. Hermondine decides to announce that she will wed the knight who, after five years of adventures, will be deemed the best knight at an election in King Arthur's court. The hero of the romance is Meliador, son of Duke Patris of Cornwall. Needless to say, it is he who finally marries Hermondine.

There are several other weddings. It is a decided fault in this tale that Froissart has overdeveloped some of the minor characters.

A Minorite friar, perhaps a native of Poitou (see *Rom* XLI, 390-400), compiled for Jeanne, Queen of Philip the Fair, a vast work (72,000 octosyllables) called the *Ovide moralisé*. There are fourteen extant MSS (*HLF* XXIX, 502). All the fables in Ovid's *Metamorphoses* are retold and then followed by one or more allegorical explanations. Often these explanations introduce contradictory conclusions, but this did not disturb the compiler. The good friar himself was responsible for most of this interpretation, but he was not the author of all the fable adaptations. We find, for instance, the story of *Philomena* adapted by Crestiens li Gois who may, or may not, be the same as Chrétien de Troyes. There are also some historical interpretations offered for the fables, and these are based slightly on fact. The date of composition may be earlier than 1305.

The *Roman de Renart* is not, properly speaking, a romance, but its continuation in the fourteenth century must not be forgotten here. Beside the early branches there were in the thirteenth century such additions as the *Couronnement de Renart* (before 1270) and *Renart le novel* (1285), which tend towards satire. In the fourteenth century we have *Renart le contrefait* (before 1342) written by some good bourgeois with an antipathy towards rapacious clerics and nobility. There are two versions; the second, composed between 1328 and 1342, is much the better work. It has 41,150 lines as opposed to 32,000 in the earlier version. Probably both texts are by the same poet. This *Renart le contrefait* is greatly dependent upon the *Roman de la Rose*. There are eight branches in the second version and six in the first. In the lion's court it is decided that the poor shall be oppressed. Renart goes to Rome to confess; refused absolution, he satirizes Rome and the trades he might follow. There is a version of the folktale in which the wolf is made to descend into the well to take Renart's place. Percehaie, Renart's son, is killed in a hen yard, despite his father's many "conseils de moralité." The wolf brings suit against the fox for the debauching of his wife. In court the king asks Renart many questions on Charlemagne, the emperors, the popes, ethnology, and the four ancient realms, and then dismisses the case. Renart is tossed about by the stag and the bear; he laments. He goes to the buzzard for absolution. There is a prologue on man's ingratitude towards God. Renart shows the cat that man suffers for his mistakes. There follows a conversation on women. Renart endeavors to trap the birds by preaching obedience and patience. The wolf pursues Renart and it is there that the second version of *Renart le contrefait* ends. In the last branch there is also the story of Samson and

Delilah, which shows the perils of love, and the tale of the famished tigress who died of hunger rather than eat lawyers, monks, usurers, landlords, etc. (Any other prey was vastly in the minority.)

Another satire, based also upon the *Roman de la Rose,* was *Fauvel* (3,280 rhymed couplets) completed in 1310 by Gervais du Bus. Fauvel, a horse, is analogous to Renart in evil deeds. This satire is directed against the Church prelates and the mendicant orders.

## EDITIONS

Probably because of their length and their small artistic value, the *chansons de geste* and romances of the fourteenth century have received little attention from editors.—*La Prise de Pampelune,* ed. A. Mussafia (Vienna, 1864).—*Entree d'Espagne,* ed. A. Thomas (Paris: *SATF,* 1913, 2 vols.).—*Baudouin de Sebourc,* ed. Bocca (1877).—*Bastard de Bouillon,* ed. A. Scheler (Valenciennes, 1841, 2 vols.). There is a brief extract in the Bartsch *Chrestomathie,* no. 82.—The *Ciperis de Vignevaux* and the *Theseus de Cologne* have not been published; but on the *Ciperis* consult V. Machovich's dissertation in vol. VII of the *Bibl. de l'Institut français à l'Université de Budapest* (1928).—*Hugues Capet,* ed. La Grange (Paris: *APF,* 1864).—*Charles le Chauve,* and *Florent et Octavian,* still remain in MS form only.—*Florence De Rome,* ed. A Wallensköld (Paris: *SATF,* 1909).—An edition of the *Tristan de Nanteuil* has been announced.—Professor Paul Högberg of Upsala has announced critical editions of the *Vœux du paon* and of the *Restor du paon,* which I have not seen as yet. Les *Vœux du paon,* ed. R. L. Graeme Ritchie in *The Buik of Alexander* (Edinburgh and London: *Scot. Text Soc.,* 1921-1929), 4 vols. The *Restor du paon* can be found, in brief extract, in the *Otia Marseiana,* III, 27-44, ed. C. Bonnier. The *Vœux du hairon* have been published by T. Wright in his *Political Songs, etc.,* I.—Aside from fragments by Gaston Paris (*Rom* XXIII, 78-116) and Karl Bartsch (*Chrestomathie de l'ancien français,* no. 98) the *Perceforest* can be best consulted in the early printed edition by Galiot du Pré (Paris, 1528, 6 vols.) or in that of Gilles Gourmont (Paris, 1531-2, 6 vols.). Jean Maillart, *La Contesse d'Anjou,* ed. Schumacher-E. Zubke (Greifswald 1920).—*Eledus et Serene,* ed. J. R. Reinhard (Univ. Texas Press, 1923).—Jean Froissart, *Méliador,* (ed. A. Longnon (Paris: *SATF,* 1895, 2 vols.).—*Ovide moralisé,* ed. C. De Boer-Martin G. De Boer-Jeanette Van 'T Sant (Amsterdam: Akademie van Wetenschappen, 1929), vols. I, II, III.—*Renart le contrefait,* ed. G. Raynaud-H. Lemaître (Paris: Champion, 1914, 2 vols.).—Gervais du Bus, *Fauvel,* ed. A. Långfors (Paris: *SATF,* 1914-1919, 1 vol.).—*Le combat des trente,* ed. H. R. Brush in *MPhil* IX and X.

# SUPPLEMENT (1962)

Introduction.—*p. 4.* Research in Old French literature is still concerned with folk origins and individual authorship; but now there are other points of view. Modern criticism encourages study of the creative process in the mind of the poet: archetypal and apperceptive background, his reaction to conflicting pressures and ideas. This has been stimulated by the *Europäische Literatur und lateinisches Mittelalter* (Bern, 1948) of Ernst R. Curtius. There is an English translation of this: Willard R. Trask, tr., *European Literature and the Latin Middle Ages* (New York, 1953). Some mediaevalists have carried this methodology almost to the point of psychoanalysis. Most important for this is Helmut Hatzfeld's "Esthetic Criticism applied to Medieval Romance Literature", *Romance Philology,* II (1948), 305-27. This sort of study is so closely related to the literary style of the individual authors that we should mention also Professor Hatzfeld's *Bibliografía crítica de la Nueva Estilística aplicada a las literaturas románicas* (Madrid: Gredos, 1955). This was published first in English (Studies in Comparative Literature, University of North Carolina Press); another revision, in the French language, will appear shortly in France.[1] Furthermore, symbolism, both Christian and non-Christian, is being stressed. Still another methodology is possible in mediaeval literature. This is deduction made from a careful analysis of all the surrounding factors of a given work, or of an author whom we may know. Thus Mme Rita Lejeune of the University of Liège is the leader of a group which, since 1949, has concentrated on an historical approach to the *chansons de geste.*

*P. 9.* All Old French verse was sung, so that knowledge of mediaeval musical forms is essential for understanding of versification. The *virelai, rondeau, ballade,* and *rotrouenge* became well established musical forms and their meter set patterns for the poets. Examples can be found conveniently in Archibald T. Davison and Willi Appel, *Historical Anthology of Music,* vol. I (Harvard Press, 1947). The *chansons de geste* and other narrative forms were performed to a single line of music which was repeated over and over. There may have been an additional musical line introduced to attract special attention from the audience. Possibly a refrain line also was sung to such a variant tune, with auditors participating. Mediaeval musicians often performed with a percussion accompaniment: the beat of a finger drum, a taborine, a bell, or clapping of the hands.

*P. 14.* There is now a splendid bibliographical guide to French literature previous to 1500. This is Robert Bossuat, *Manuel bibliographique de la littérature française au moyen-âge* (Paris: Bibliothèque Elzévirienne. Nouv. Série. Etudes et documents, 1951). This has two supplements "avec le concours de Jacques Monfrin". One is for the period 1949-53 (Paris, 1956); the other is for 1954-60 (Paris, 1961). There is another bibliography: *A Critical Bibliography of French Literature,* Volume I (The Mediaeval

[1] Helmut Hatzfeld et Yves Le Hir, *Essai de bibliographie critique de stylistique française et romane.*

Period), edited by Urban T. Holmes, Jr., 2nd ed. (Syracuse University Press, 1952). This gives a selection of titles with critical comment. By the close of 1962 the Modern Language Association of America will publish *A Review of Research in Medieval Literature*. This too will be a selective bibliography with comment; it will cover other mediaeval fields as well as French. In view of these bibliographies there is no need for a thorough revision of bibliography in this present supplement. We will list a few new titles only which offer most necessary material.

The ZfrPh bibliography now goes as far as 1955. The HLF reaches vol. XXXIX in 1962. An indispensable reference for the control of current periodical material is Otto Klapp, *Bibliographie d'histoire littéraire française* (Frankfurt am Main, 1960—). Vol. I of this contains the years 1956-58; Vol. II is for 1959-60. The *Catalogue général . . . de la Bibliothèque Nationale* is now as far as *Thiry*. The current Arthurian bibliography is handled in the *Bulletin bibliographique de la Société Internationale Arthurienne*, I (1949)—. The last volume of *The Year's Work in Modern Language Studies* which has come to our attention is XXI (1959). Another publication is the *Bulletin bibliographique de la Société Rencesvals* (1958—) which is concerned with *chansons de geste*. Of the utmost importance for folk themes is the Stith Thompson, *Motif-index of folk-literature;* a classification of narrative elements in folktales, *ballads, myths, mediaeval romances, exempla, fabliaux, jest-books and local legends*. Revised and enlarged edition (Bloomington, Indiana, 1955-58), 6 vols. As can be seen from the subtitle this now contains plot themes from mediaeval literature.

Raphael Levy, *Chronologie approximative de la littérature française du moyen-âge* ZfrPh Beiheft 98 (1957).

Paul Zumthor, *Histoire littéraire de la France médiévale* (Paris, 1954).

*P. 16.* Another outstanding reference for Latin mediaeval literature is F. J. E. Raby, *A History of Secular Latin Poetry in the Middle Ages,* 2 vols. (Oxford, 1934).

Chapter I.—p. 24. Guy de Poerck in *Romanica Gandensia,* IV (Gent, 1955), 31-66, has a fine new transcription of the *Jonas fragment*. This sermon was probably delivered at Saint-Amand in the period 938-50, during a pagan Norman occupation of the area.

Chapter II.—p. 30. According to P. Aebischer in the ZfrPh LXXIII (1957) it is doubtful that the Hague fragment was a schoolboy exercise. In that case it would hardly have been engrossed on parchment. It could date from the late tenth century. It was perhaps an attempt to make a poem more intelligible by putting it into prose.

Chapter III.—p. 33. Marshall Clagett, Gaines Post, Robert Reynolds, eds., *Twelfth-century Europe and the Foundations of Modern Society* (Madison, Wisconsin, 1961); U. T. Holmes in Spec. XXVI (1951), 644:

"The Idea of a Twelfth-Century Renaissance".

Chapter V.—*p. 50.* Grace Frank, *The Medieval French Drama* (Oxford, 1954); Arnold Williams, *The Drama of Medieval England* (East Lansing, Michigan, 1961). Some idea of the Roman theater must have been known to the mediaeval scholar from Book 18 of Isidor of Seville's *Etymologiae.*

Chapter VI.—*p. 59.* Florence McCulloch, *Mediaeval Latin and French Bestiaries* (Chapel Hill, 1960).

Chapter VII.—*pp. 71 ff.* Ferdinand Lot's articles on the origins of the epic have been published together by Robert Bossuat: *Etudes sur les légendes épiques françaises* (Paris, 1958). During the past dozen years some notable studies have appeared, mostly inspired by M. Lot: Maurice Delbouille, *Sur la genèse de la chanson de Roland* (Bruxelles, 1954), Dámaso Alonso, *La Primitiva Epica francesa a la luz de una Nota Emilianse* (Madrid, 1954), Jean Rychner, *La chanson de geste, essai sur l'art épique des jongleurs* (Geneva and Lille, 1955), Martín de Riquer, *Les chansons de geste françaises,* 2e ed. (Paris, 1957). The first edition of this book by Martín de Riquer was published in 1952, in Spanish. In his new edition, completely reworked, he has been able to take account of the other books which we have just mentioned. He gives the best over-all picture of what is believed today about the *chansons de geste.* We resume this. Not long after the campaigns of Charlemagne and Charles the Bald there came into existence short narratives: ballads, and perhaps some short epics, celebrating the events. They were not written down. Each reciter carried an outline in mind and expanded on this at will, making use of epic formulae. Local legends, family traditions, chronicles, biographies, and perhaps some kinds of Latin epic verse of the Carolingian type, served as sources. (A. Burger has insisted on the Latin predecessors; such a source could be the *Geste Francor* which is frequently mentioned in the Oxford *Roland*). The early existence of the *Roland* theme is attested by baptismal names *Oliverius* and *Rodlandus,* presumably given to brothers as early as 999-1031. See Rita Lejeune in *Annales de l'Institut de Phil. et d'Hist. Orientales et Slaves,* X (1950), 371-401. After 1000 there probably came into existence a longer, more elaborate version of the *Roland* narrative—what might be called the epic type of poem as we now define it. Delbouille is probably correct in saying that Christian military activity in Spain created this. The new slogan, as we imagine it, was: "If Charlemagne could do it in 778, we can do it again—now". Dámaso Alonso has found a note in a Spanish MS of the third quarter of the eleventh century where it is evident the scribe knew something about Roland different from our surviving Oxford poem. For some reason the *Roland* was recorded in writing, *as we know it,* towards the close of the eleventh century. Perhaps the reason for this was the First Crusade. This version was that of Turoldus.

Chapter VIII.—Rychner has been inclined to make an exception for the *Roland* among the early epics, suggesting a very superior creating poet. Stephen G. Nichols, Jr. in his *Formulaic Diction and Thematic Composition in the Chanson de Roland* (Chapel Hill, 1961) insists that oral circulation passing from minstrel to minstrel does not preclude creative genius. Rychner, basing much of his remarks on the comparison with epic poetry of the South Slavs (to which Martín de Riquer adds the Spanish *romances*) stresses the oral formulaic diction of the Old French epics. Nichols applies this specifically to the *Roland*. The non-rigid *laisse* was a great aid to improvisation. The oral poet made use of formulaic expressions, of certain archetypal ideas, and of formulaic units in his narrative.

The *ensenhamen* of Guiraut de Cabreira (1150-68) mentions certain *chansons de geste: Aigar et Maurin, Aiol et Mirabel, Amis et Amiles, Anseïs de Cartage, Aye d'Avignon, Beuve de Hantone, Daurel et Beton, Elie de Saint-Gilles, Girart de Rossilhó, Gormont et Isembart, Mainet, Ogier, Raoul de Cambrai, Roncevaux,* and the *Chanson des Saisnes.* He mentions in addition, characters from the William cycle and from the Lotharingian epics. See Martín de Riquer, pp. 332-51.

The *Pèlerinage de Charlemagne* remains an enigma. I do not insist upon my suggestion in *Symposium* I, 75-81, except that I believe definitely the poem was a parody. Certainly there is little evidence of its being a relic poem composed at Saint-Denis. Jules Horrent in *Le pèlerinage de Charlemagne, essai d'explication littéraire* (Paris, 1961) brings together all the bibliography. He thinks the poet of the existing version told the tale much as Pulci would have done: the poem is comic not satirical. Like the *Roland* it is the work of a *conscience individuelle.*

There is a new edition of the V⁴ version of the *Roland:* Giuliano Gasca Queirazza, S. J. *La Chanson de Roland nel testo assonanzato franco-italiano* (Torino, 1952).

Chapter IX.—p. 93. Jan de Vries, "La chanson de Gormont et Isembart" in Rom XXXX (1959), 34-62; Pierre Le Gentil, "Girard de Roussillon" in Rom LXXVIII (1957), 328-89, 463-510; Pierre Le Gentil, "Ogier le danois" in Rom LXXVIII (1957), 199-233.

Chapter X.—*p. 101.* Jean Frappier, *Les chansons du cycle de Guillaume d'Orange* (Paris, 1955).

Chapter XI.—*p. 122.* Josephine E. Vallerie, ed. *Garin le Loherenc* (New York, 1947); Pauline Taylor, ed. *Gerbert de Mez* (Louvain and Lille, 1953); H. J. Green, *Anseys de Mes,* (Paris, 1939).

Chapter XIII.—*p. 134.* In the *Roman de Flamenca* (vv. 617 ff) there is a list of *contes* and romances, some of which are lost to us. There were *contes* of Orpheus, Hero and Leander, Eracles. There were Biblical *contes* of Golias, Samson, Macchabees.

Chapter XVI.—*p. 157 ff.* There continues to be much written on the Arthurian material, particularly upon the Grail theme (see Chapter XXX), with little agreement. There are three basic approaches: that of the *Celtisants* (which is the view presented in our text), the Christian and Judaeo-Christian (now held by this author), and what might be called psychological interpretation. In this last it is held that conflict between certain ideals within the poet's mind produced the allegory. The outstanding reference at present is Roger Sherman Loomis, *Artnurian Literature in the Middle Ages: A Collaborative History* (Oxford, 1959). In this volume of 564 pages many scholars have covered nearly all aspects of the Arthurian field. It is unfortunate that no German scholars are represented. Our own position is stated very briefly in a review of this Loomis volume in Spec XXXVI (1961), 144-49. We admit that the romances drew upon Celtic themes, but not so much as the *Celtisants* insist. It is our contention that Chrétien's romances, from the very first, were put together with some allegory in mind, not as a hodgepodge of stray Celtic motifs. In the case of the *Conte del Graal* (see Chapter XXX) this allegory, for us, has a definite Christian and allegorical meaning. The *Lancelot* we think of as an effort on the part of a perfect knight to rescue a lady (Guenevere) from Extravagant Vanity. This romance, like the *Conte del Graal,* is a Quest. The *Erec* and the *Yvain* are episodical; but surely there also subtle meaning is intended. In the *Yvain* the episodes of the *vavassor* with his castle and his daughter, at the entrance to the forest of the Magic Fountain, must have had *sens* other than a random one. The Grateful Lion we consider a Byzantine tale, brought from the East. For the individual Celtic motifs which were used we prefer Welsh sources—including the "Estre-gallois", the Celts who lived in what is now Cumberlandshire and Westmorelandshire. Others still believe that continental Brittany was the origin.

In Urban T. Holmes, Jr. and Sister M. Amelia Klenke, O.P., *Chrétien, Troyes, and the Grail* (Chapel Hill, N. C., 1959) we have attempted a study of the city of Troyes and a possible identification of Chrétien. We have printed there a most important document, called to our attention by John Benton, which proves that Marie, daughter of Eleanor and Louis of France, married Henry of Champagne in 1159—not 1164. There has been a tendency in recent years to date all of Chrétien's romances within the decade 1170-80, because of a proposed dating of the *Erec* after 1169. The year 1159 for the marriage of Marie de Champagne makes it very probable that the *Erec* and the *Lancelot* were earlier than that.

The name *Chrétien* was not a common one in Champagne in the second half of the twelfth century, as many have been stating without proof. See John F. Benton "The Court of Champagne as a Literary Center" in Spec XXXVI (1961), 551-91. This makes it possible that a certain Chrétien de Saint-Loup (in Troyes) and Chrétien, chaplain of Saint-Maclou of Bar-sur-Aube (twenty-five miles from Troyes)—mentioned in documents —were the same. A Chrétien, doubtless Chrétien de Saint-Maclou, had a brother Girart de Bar (*Obituaires, Recueil des historiens de la France,* p. 260E). This Girart de Bar was, in turn, a canon of the cathedral at Troyes (in document classified as Aube G 3331). Chrétien the poet signs himself *de Troyes* only in the *Erec;* elsewhere he is signed as *Crestiens* only. In the surviving *Philomena,* which some of us ascribe to the great poet, the ascription is to *Crestiens li Gois.* The latest document signed by Chrétiens de Saint-Maclou is from 1190 (in B.N. nouv. acq. lat. 110, a cartulary of Saint-Maclou). Chrétien died while writing his *Conte del Graal* which would, consequently, be as late as this, if our identification is correct. We know nothing of the racial origin of Chrétien de Troyes, nor that of Chrétien de Saint-Maclou. We should remind the reader, however, that Troyes was a center for Jewish culture and education; it had a large Jewish population including many converts. There are elements in the *Conte del Graal* which can be best explained by reference to some knowledge of Jewish motifs.

*P. 172.* The late Fr. Alex. J. Denomy, C.S.B. emphasized the conflict between the rationalizing in the first two books of the *De arte honeste amandi* and the theological position assumed in the third. He concluded that Courtly Love was owed, in content at least, to Avicenna (d. 1037). See *Mediaeval Studies* (Toronto). VI-VIII (1944-46). There is a dualistic viewpoint in the surging of the soul, eager for union with a being superior to it. D. W. Robertson and others have been emphasizing that this Courtly Love did not exist as an actual behavioral practice—that it was merely a literary convention. One cannot say with finality that some individuals did not practise it, attempting to reconcile sensuality with asceticism—but we feel sure that for most people of the time this kind of love was merely a convention.

Chapter XVII.—p. 180. Bartina H. Wind, ed., Thomas, *les fragments du Roman de Tristan* (Geneva and Paris, 1960); Alberto del Monte, *Tristano* (Napoli, n. d.).

Chapter XIX.—*p. 195.* Discussion over the origins of lyric verse received new impetus when in 1948 Samuel M. Stern published his "Les vers finaux en espagnol dans les muwassahas hispano-hebraïques", *Al Andalus,* XIII, 299-346. There have been recovered fifty muwassaha poems in Hebrew, written by Spanish Jews. These have the final division of the poem (kharja) in Mozarabic Spanish. The earliest of these can be dated ca. 1042. The muwassaha is a Spanish-Arabic type of verse invented in 888-912 (which was adopted also by Hebrew poets) in which the poet begins his composition with a two-rhymed couplet or quatrain existing already in vulgar Arabic or Romance. He prefixes to this a poem structure in Arabic or

Hebrew, resulting in these rhymes A B BBB A B CCC A B (the three line verse with A B refrain can continue with rhymes DDD etc.). Note that the A B refrain in Hebrew or Arabic has the same rhymes as the final kharja in Romance. Those kharjas which survive are feminine laments over a lover. The lament of the *mal mariee* (*cantar de amigo*) type is basic, then, in popular poetry—and therefore in the May dances—probably from a very distant past. In a capitulary of 789 Charlemagne forbade the making of *winileodos* 'friend songs' by abbesses and nuns. To judge by the versification scheme of the muwassaha these popular laments were in virelai or rondeau form—assuming that the kharja refrain plus its original Romance stanzas had the same structure as the complete muwassaha. Did such popular poetry spread to France from the Spanish—or was it indigenous in France and other lands, as well as in Spain? Certainly the meter represented a wide-spread melody type. This we cannot answer. We prefer to assume that such dance poetry was indigenous in France as well as in Andalusia and Galicia. Certainly it seems to have existed independently in those two areas, separated from each other. See Klaus Heger, *Die bisher veröffentlichte Hargas und ihre Deutungen,* ZfrPh Beiheft 101; Pierre Le Gentil, *Le virelai et le villancico. Le problème des origines arabes* (Paris, 1954); Rodolfo A. Borello, *Jaryas andalusies* (Buenos Aires, 1959).

While a popular verse must have a single poet in its beginning, subsequent adapters could alter at will. When a popular verse is finally taken up by a learned poet it becomes more fixed. Those kharjas which we have were all given a learned form by the poets who composed the finished muwassahas. A. R. Nykl in his *Hispano-Arabic Poetry* (Baltimore, 1946, privately printed) wrote before the discovery of the kharjas. He argued for Arabic influence on French and Provencal coming from the zejel. Nykl gave a careful biography of William of Poitiers, the earliest known troubadour. This William was in the Holy Land in 1102-03, for eighteen months, where he could easily have learned something of Arabic love lyrics through an interpreter. Nykl believed that William, and Marcabrun, obtained translations of such songs whose melodies they liked. Marcabrun was imitated directly by Peire d'Alvernhe. Bernart de Ventadorn shows also additional material from Ovid, as well as this Platonic philosophy of love transmitted from the Arabic.

P. 196. A few *rotrouenges* are extant.

P. 198. The theme of the love poetry is the lover who is a coward before his lady, only bold in spite of himself. Roger Dragonetti in *Romanica Gandensia,* VII, (1959).

Chapter XXII.—p. 211. Robert Bossuat, *Le Roman de Renard* (Paris: Hatier, 1957). A full treatment of this subject will soon be published by Dr. Flinn of Toronto.

Chapter XXIV.—p. 236. V. F. König is reëditing *Les miracles de Nostre Dame* of Gautier de Coincy. Two volumes have already appeared: I (Geneva, 1955), II (Geneva, 1961).

Chapter XXV.—p. 240. The *Secré de secrez* of Jofroi de Watreford has 2,383 lines. There was not a co-author named Copale.

*P. 241. La petite philosophie,* ed. W. H. Trethewey (Oxford, 1939) is a verse adaptation of the *Imago mundi.* This has 2,920 lines.

Chapter XXVI.—*p. 246.* The *Resurrecion* was probably composed in the late twelfth century. A second MS (Br. Mus. add. 45103) is now available. It has 522 verses; the Paris MS has only 371.

Chapter XXVIII.—*p. 259.* Carla Cremonesi, ed. *Enfances Renier* (Milan, 1957). This long poem is not uninteresting, despite its length of 20,068 verses.

Chapter XXIX.—p. 269. Carla Cremonesi, *Jean Renart* (Milan, n. d.) thinks that *Galeran de Bretagne* was an early work by Jean Renart. Jean's heroines are bold and self-possessed.

Chapter XXX.—p. 284. See references given for Chapter XVI; also Sister M. Amelia Klenke, O.P. in PMLA LXX (1955), 223-43, in SPhil LIII (1956), 1-21. Sister Amelia, and the present author, believe that Arthur was thought to be of the type of Christ, an Eternal High Priest. This is reflected in twelfth-century art as well as in literature. The Synagogue-Church motif was a burning problem in Champagne in the last quarter of the twelfth century; Chrétien's *Conte del Graal* was an allegory representing its solution. This poem is honey-combed with Biblical and liturgical parallels and allusions; the spiritual ascent of Perceval is beautifully conceived and developed. The Gawain adventures are in contrast to those of Perceval: Gawain was a perfect knight but not endowed with Grace. For other explanations of the Grail theme see E. Köhler in ZfrPh LXXV (1959), 523-40; Stefan Hofer in RFor LXVII (1955), 36-54; David C. Fowler, *Prowess and Charity* (Seattle, 1959); Helen Adolf, *Visio Pacis* (Pennsylvania State Univ., 1960). The present author and Sister Amelia are supported in their belief (that the Grail was a sacred Christian vessel carried in triumphant procession) by Mario Roques in Rom LXXVI (1955), 1-27.

Chapter XXXI.—p. 301. Charles Dahlberg, "Macrobius and the Unity of the Roman de la Rose" in SPhil LVIII (1961), 573-82; Alan M. F. Gunn, *The Mirror of Love* (Lubbock, Texas, 1952); C. S. Lewis, *The Allegory of Love* (London, 1936). Although C. S. Lewis thought otherwise, it is beginning to be conceded that there is unity of development between the work of Guillaume de Lorris and that of Jean de Meun. The best definition of Allegory is that of St. Augustine: "a trope or figure in which one thing is said and another meant".

Chapter XXXII.—p. 309. Edmond Faral et Julia Bastin, *Oeuvres com-*

*plètes de Rutebeuf,* 2 vols. (Paris, 1959-60); Edmond Faral in Rom LXX
(1948), 257-69. E. B. Ham has in press a study of Rutebeuf's relations with
Louis IX which includes a fuller interpretation of the *Renart betourné.*

Chapter XXXIII.—p. 317. Per Nykrog. *Les fabliaux* (Copenhagen, 1957).

# INDEX

(Names and titles in the bibliography sections have not been listed, with rare exceptions.)